A collaborative project assembled by scholars who have played crucial roles in the recent explosion of Twain criticism, *The Cambridge Companion to Mark Twain* offers new and thought-provoking essays on an author of enduring preeminence in the American canon. Accessible enough to interest both experienced specialists and students new to Twain criticism, the essays examine Twain from a wide variety of critical perspectives and include timely reflections by major critics on the hotly debated dynamics of race and slavery perceptible throughout his writing.

The volume includes a chronology of Twain's life and a list of suggestions for further reading, to provide the student or general reader with sources for background as well as additional information.

THE CAMBRIDGE
COMPANION TO
MARK TWAIN

Cambridge Companions to Literature

The Cambridge Companion to Faulkner
edited by Philip Weinstein

The Cambridge Companion to Hemingway
edited by Scott Donaldson

The Cambridge Companion to Wharton
edited by Millicent Bell

The Cambridge Companion to American Realism and Naturalism
edited by Don Pizer

The Cambridge Companion to Twain
edited by Forrest G. Robinson

The Cambridge Companion to Thoreau
edited by Joel Myerson

The Cambridge Companion to Whitman
edited by Ezra Greenspan

The Cambridge Companion to Eliot
edited by A. David Moody

The Cambridge Companion to Joyce
edited by Derek Attridge

The Cambridge Companion to Ibsen
edited by James McFarlane

The Cambridge Companion to Beckett
edited by John Pilling

The Cambridge Companion to Brecht
edited by Peter Thomson and Glendyr Sacks

The Cambridge Companion to British Romanticism
edited by Stuart Curran

The Cambridge Companion to English Poetry, Donne to Marvell
edited by Thomas N. Corns

The Cambridge Companion to Shakespeare Studies
edited by Stanley Wells

Continued on page following Index

THE CAMBRIDGE
COMPANION TO
MARK TWAIN

EDITED BY
FORREST G. ROBINSON

University of California, Santa Cruz

CAMBRIDGE
UNIVERSITY PRESS

Published by the Press Syndicate of the University of Cambridge
The Pitt Building, Trumpington Street, Cambridge CB2 1RP
40 West 20th Street, New York, NY 10011-4211, USA
10 Stamford Road, Oakleigh, Melbourne 3166, Australia

First published 1995

Library of Congress Cataloging-in-Publication Data
The Cambridge companion to Mark Twain / edited by Forrest G. Robinson.
p.   cm. – (Cambridge companions to literature)
Includes bibliographical references (p.   ) and index.
ISBN 0-521-44036-X. – ISBN 0-521-44593-0 (pbk.)
1. Twain, Mark, 1835–1910 – Criticism and interpretation.
I. Robinson, Forrest G. (Forrest Glen), 1940– .   II. Series.
PS1338.C36   1995
818'.409 – dc20   94-24658
                                                                    CIP

A catalog record for this book is available from the British Library.

ISBN 0-521-44036-X Hardback
ISBN 0-521-44593-0 Paperback

Transferred to digital printing 2003

FOR EMMA-CHAN

CONTENTS

CONTRIBUTORS

STANLEY BRODWIN is Professor of English at Hofstra University. He has published articles on nineteenth-century American authors primarily, but especially on Mark Twain and his theological imagination. He is co-editor, with Amritjit Singh and William S. Shiver, of *The Harlem Renaissance: Reevaluations* (Garland Publishers, 1989); co-editor, with Michael D'Innocenzo, and contributor to *William Cullen Bryant and His America* (AMS Press, 1983); and editor of *The Old and New World Romanticism of Washington Irving* (Greenwood Press, 1986).

LOUIS J. BUDD is James B. Duke Professor Emeritus of English at Duke University. His books include *Mark Twain: Social Philosopher* (Indiana University Press, 1962) and *Our Mark Twain: The Making of His Public Personality* (University of Pennsylvania Press, 1983); his edited books include *New Essays on "Adventures of Huckleberry Finn"* (Cambridge University Press, 1985).

EVAN CARTON is Professor of English at the University of Texas at Austin. He is the author of *The Rhetoric of American Romance* (Johns Hopkins University Press, 1985) and *The Marble Faun: Hawthorne's Transformations* (Twayne Publishers, 1992). He has co-authored, with Gerald Graff, a forthcoming volume, *Criticism Since 1940*, in the new Cambridge History of American Literature and is writing a book on contemporary American literature, politics, and pedagogy.

SHELLEY FISHER FISHKIN is Professor of American Studies at the University of Texas at Austin. She is the author of *Was Huck Black? Mark Twain and African-American Voices* (Oxford University Press, 1993) and *From Fact to Fiction: Journalism and Imaginative Writing in America* (Johns Hopkins University Press, 1985; Oxford University Press, 1988). She is co-editor, with Elaine Hedges, of *Listening to Silences: New Essays in Feminist Criticism* (Oxford University Press, 1994) and Executive Director of the Charlotte Perkins Gilman Society. Current projects include serving as editor of the forthcoming multivolume set *The Oxford Mark Twain*.

SUSAN GILLMAN is Associate Professor of Literature at the University of California, Santa Cruz. She is the author of *Dark Twins: Imposture and Identity in Mark Twain's America* (University of Chicago Press, 1989) and co-editor, with Forrest G. Robinson, of *Mark Twain's "Pudd'nhead Wilson": Race, Conflict, and Culture* (Duke University Press, 1990). She is currently working on a book entitled *The American Race Melodramas, 1877–1915*.

MYRA JEHLEN is Board of Governors Professor of Literature at Rutgers University. Among her writings are *The Literature of Colonization* in the new Cambridge Literary History of the United States and *American Incarnation: The Individual, the Nation and the Continent* (Harvard University Press, 1986). She is also editor, most recently, of *Melville* in the series New Century Views.

ERIC LOTT teaches American Studies at the University of Virginia. He is the author of *Love and Theft: Blackface Minstrelsy and the American Working Class* (Oxford University Press, 1993), and his work on the racial politics of culture has appeared in *American Quarterly, Representations,* the *Village Voice,* and the *Nation.*

FORREST G. ROBINSON is Professor of American Studies at the University of California, Santa Cruz. His books include *The Shape of Things Known: Sidney's Apology in Its Philosophical Tradition* (Harvard University Press, 1972), *In Bad Faith: The Dynamics of Deception in Mark Twain's America* (Harvard University Press, 1986), *Love's Story Told: A Life of Henry A. Murray* (Harvard University Press, 1992), and *Having It Both Ways: Self-Subversion in Western Popular Classics* (New Mexico University Press, 1993).

JOHN CARLOS ROWE teaches the literatures and cultures of the United States and contemporary critical theories at the University of California, Irvine, where he is also the Director of the Critical Theory Institute. He is the author of *Henry Adams and Henry James* (Cornell University Press, 1976), *Through the Custom House* (Johns Hopkins University Press, 1982), and *The Theoretical Dimensions of Henry James* (University of Wisconsin Press, 1984). He has co-edited, with Rick Berg, *The Vietnam War and American Culture* (Columbia University Press, 1991).

NEIL SCHMITZ is Professor of English at the State University of New York, Buffalo. He is the author of *Of Huck and Alice: Humorous Writing in*

American Literature (University of Minnesota Press, 1983). Recent essays on Abraham Lincoln, Black Hawk, and Gertrude Stein have appeared in the *Arizona Quarterly, American Literary History,* and *American Literature.* He is completing a book on Civil War writing.

DAVID LIONEL SMITH is Professor of English and Chair of Afro-American Studies at Williams College. He has published articles on literary theory, the black arts movement, Southern literature, and Mark Twain. He is co-editor, with Jack Salzman and Cornel West, of *The Encyclopedia of African-American Culture and History,* forthcoming from Macmillan, and he is completing *Racial Writing, Black and White,* a study of how American writers have constructed accounts of racial identity.

PREFACE

In the 1939 Metro-Goldwyn-Mayer production of *Huckleberry Finn*, starring Mickey Rooney in the title role, much is made of the fact that Jim
(played by Rex Ingram) conceals from Huck that pap is dead. When Jim
asks what he would do in the event of his father's death, Huck replies that
he would return to St. Petersburg and that he would take the runaway slave
back with him. Jim's worst fears are thus confirmed. The white boy's sole
motive for fleeing downriver is fear of his father. Jim is acceptable as a
companion, but Huck is hardly an abolitionist and would dutifully restore
the slave to Miss Watson were the way clear to his doing so. Later, when Jim
at last tells the truth about pap, Huck calls him an ungrateful "thing" and
runs away in anger. Though we are finally brought around to the obligatory
happy ending, this old movie nonetheless brings us closer to tragedy than
any of the more recent popular productions of the story.

It took the critics almost thirty years to catch up with Mickey Rooney.
The prevailing view of *Huckleberry Finn* until the mid-1960s cast the boy-
hero as a figure of "instinctive humanity" who without hesitation joins Jim
in his "quest for freedom."[1] James M. Cox, in *Mark Twain: The Fate of
Humor* (1966), was the first to challenge consensus, arguing that "a quest is
a positive journey, implying an effort, a struggle to reach a goal. But Huck is
escaping. His journey is primarily a negation, a flight *from* tyranny, not a
flight toward freedom." Huck "is certainly not a rebel," Cox adds. "The
role of Abolitionist is not comfortable nor comforting to him and in turning
over to Tom Sawyer the entire unpleasant business of freeing Jim, Huck is
surely not acting out of but remarkably *in* character."[2]

Cox's sharp break with critical tradition gave rise to a major overhaul
of accepted opinion on America's favorite novel. The image of Huck has
been transformed. He is more uncertain and troubled, more divided against
himself, than he used to be. Jim has also become more complex. We are
readier now than in the past to glimpse a mingled array of feelings and
motives behind the mask of the docile slave that he presents to the world.

Jim has fears and desires that he does not share with anyone, not even Huck
– who scorns abolitionists, plays dirty tricks, and wavers terribly when
the chips are down. Such major interpretive shifts have in turn drawn attention to the dynamics of audience response. How is it that we have over-
looked so much for so long? How has it served our cultural and ideological
agendas to settle for such partial and incomplete readings? Other, related
questions have arisen in tandem with those that attach directly to *Huckleberry Finn*. We are now more than ever alert to Mark Twain's attitudes
toward women, and to the female characters in his work. His later writings,
concerned as they are with major social and political issues, and fascinating
as studies in the thematics of form, are also very much with us in this lively –
if also rather sobering – reassessment of our leading author and national
icon.

The Cambridge Companion to Mark Twain faithfully mirrors the trajectory of recent developments in the field. This is true in good part because
most of the scholars represented in the volume have had a role in the
formation of the broad new critical consensus. I was also guided in my
selection of topics by an ambition to provide responsible coverage of the
subjects currently of most interest to students of Mark Twain. Several essays
address aspects of race and slavery in his work. Others deal directly with
women, religion, humor, and class. The travel writing, strategies of performance, and Mark Twain's enduring popularity are also discussed. In all, we
have approached our materials with a wide-ranging audience of specialists
and nonspecialists in mind. I have urged the contributors to proceed with
freshness and originality as their leading objectives. Throughout it has been
our goal to be lively and thought-provoking, not merely comprehensive or
somehow standard.

As editor, I have been the happy beneficiary of no little support and
cooperation. The contributors – a stellar company of scholars – were
generous in consenting to undertake this work, very able in its commission,
and unfailingly tolerant of my appeals for brevity, clarity, and what Mark
Twain must have referred to somewhere as promptitude. I am grateful to
Eric Sundquist for asking me to serve as editor and for his valuable coun-
sel along the way. Julie Greenblatt and T. Susan Chang, humanities editors
at Cambridge University Press, have been superb colleagues, patient with
my inexperience, and always ready with advice and good humor. Finally,
I count as chief among my blessings a large, loving family. Special thanks
as always to Colleen, Grace, Renate, Emma (to whom the book is dedicated), and Marie for their unflagging support of my many and curious
enterprises.

NOTES

1   Leo Marx, "Mr. Eliot, Mr. Trilling, and *Huckleberry Finn*," in *Huck Finn Among the Critics*, ed. M. Thomas Inge (Washington: USIA, 1984), p. 115. The essay first appeared in the *American Scholar* 22 (1953): 423–40.
2   James M. Cox, *Mark Twain: The Fate of Humor* (Princeton, N.J.: Princeton University Press, 1966), pp. 172–3.

1835, Nov. 30	Samuel Langhorne Clemens, sixth child of John Marshall Clemens and Jane Lampton Clemens, born in Florida, Missouri.
1839	Clemens family moves to Hannibal, Missouri.
1847	Father dies.
1848	Works as printer's apprentice on the *Missouri Courier.*
1849	Finishes education.
1851	Serves as journeyman printer and journalist on brother Orion's *Hannibal Journal.*
1852	"The Dandy Frightening the Squatter" appears in the Boston comic weekly, the *Carpet-Bag.*
1853–6	Leaves Hannibal and works as a printer in St. Louis, New York, Philadelphia, Keokuk (Iowa), and Cincinnati. Serves as a correspondent for brother Orion's *Muscatine* (Iowa) *Journal* and other local newspapers.
1857	Becomes an apprentice ("cub") Mississippi River steamboat pilot under Horace Bixby.
1859	Receives pilot's licence; is steadily employed on the Mississippi until the outbreak of the Civil War.
1861	Serves briefly in a volunteer Confederate battalion; leaves for Nevada with brother Orion; seeks fortune in mining.
1862–5	Works as a reporter and humorous writer for the *Virginia City Territorial Enterprise,* the *San Francisco Daily Morning Call,* the *Golden Era,* the *Californian,* and other newspapers in Nevada and California. Adopts pseudonym "Mark Twain." "Jim Smiley and His Jumping Frog" is published.
1866	Serves as a correspondent for the *Sacramento Daily Union* in Hawaiian Islands; begins career as lecturer;

contracts as correspondent for the *Alta California* and leaves for New York.

1867   *The Celebrated Jumping Frog of Calaveras County, and Other Sketches* is published. Works as a correspondent for the *Alta California* in Europe and the Holy Land.

1868   In Washington, D.C., serves as secretary to Senator William Stewart of Nevada and correspondent for several newspapers; in California as lecturer, journalist, and travel writer.

1869   *The Innocents Abroad* is a great commercial success. Commences friendship with William Dean Howells.

1870   Marries Olivia Langdon. Becomes part owner and associate editor of the *Buffalo Express*. Son Langdon is born.

1871   Moves to Hartford, Connecticut; goes on extended lecture tour.

1872   Daughter Olivia Susan (Susy) is born. Langdon dies. *Roughing It* secures his reputation as America's leading humorist. Makes first visit to England.

1873   *The Gilded Age* (co-authored with Charles Dudley Warner) is published. Travels with family in Europe.

1874   Daughter Clara is born. Mansion in Hartford is completed.

1875   "Old Times on the Mississippi," a series of seven articles, appears in the *Atlantic Monthly*.

1876   *The Adventures of Tom Sawyer* is published.

1878–9   Travels with family in Europe.

1880   Daughter Jean is born. *A Tramp Abroad* is published.

1881   *The Prince and the Pauper* is published.

1882   Travels on the Mississippi.

1883   *Life on the Mississippi* is published.

1884–5   Goes on lecture tour with George W. Cable. *Adventures of Huckleberry Finn* is published.

1889   *A Connecticut Yankee in King Arthur's Court* is published.

1891   Leaves Hartford for a decade (spent mostly in Europe).

1892   *The American Claimant* is published.

1894   *The Tragedy of Pudd'nhead Wilson* is published. Failure of Paige typesetting machine results in bankruptcy.

1895–6	Goes on world lecture tour
1896	Daughter Susy dies. *Personal Recollections of Joan of Arc* and *Tom Sawyer, Detective* are published.
1897	*Following the Equator* is published.
1898	Begins work on *The Mysterious Stranger.*
1899	"The Man That Corrupted Hadleyburg" is published.
1900	Returns to the United States; settles in New York City; publicly opposes imperialism.
1901	Receives honorary degree from Yale. "To the Person Sitting in Darkness" is published.
1904	Wife Olivia Langdon Clemens dies.
1906	*What Is Man?* is privately printed.
1907	Receives honorary degree from Oxford. *Christian Science* is published.
1909	Daughter Jean dies.
1910, Apr. 21	Dies in Redding, Connecticut.
1916	*The Mysterious Stranger* is published.

THE CAMBRIDGE
COMPANION TO
MARK TWAIN

I

LOUIS J. BUDD

Mark Twain as an American Icon

That Mark Twain parades on as a prominent American icon is obvious – visually, audibly, and palpably. The fact is validated by the most dynamic force in the United States – the profit-driven economy. To reassure customers who worry that "this country is running out of natural gas," a corporation prints a full-page ad depicting a bushy-haired, white-suited, cigar-smoking Twain under the heading "The reports of my demise are greatly exaggerated."[1] To highlight the case against reregulation, the Association of American Railroads disseminates a photograph of a solemn Twain, holding a book rather than a cigar but again in basic whites, under his maxim "Loyalty to petrified opinion never yet broke a chain or freed a human soul." In a newspaper ad, a bank ("We frown on get-rich-quick schemes, but we are not opposed to helping people make money") features his "I'm opposed to millionaires, but it would be dangerous to offer me the position"; the experts in subliminalism at its ad agency reinforced this with a Huck Finnish boy fishing. But a cemetery, selling "dignity and simplicity in a setting of great natural beauty" through a full-page spread in the *Los Angeles Times*, understandably prefers a close-up of a solemn, elderly Twain along with his epitaph for Susy Clemens.

Of course, he also serves in more hedonistic venues. Stretching a thin link, a bureau of tourism croons, "Experience Mark Twain's Hawaii." Elliott's Amazing Fruit Drinks prints his maxims inside the bottle caps. (In 1991 "The Popular and the Private: 100 Years since Twain [Moved out of Hartford]," mounted at the Mark Twain House, displayed an extreme variety of such knicknacks.) Yet since even Twainians doubt that many people will buy those fruit drinks for the maxims, they suspect a fellow enthusiast in the bottler and other local entrepreneurs. Surely the Tom Sawyer Painters of Durham, North Carolina, were pleasing themselves as much as they were hoping to attract business. Some enthusiasts grow emulative. The Asheville, North Carolina, Cleaners and Dyers' ad depicts a Twain frowning and holding a turkey drumstick, his white suit soiled; its headings, "Grime

Marches On" and "Gravy Twain," lead into "Though Mark Twain was fond of fowl, he liked his suits snow-white. We'd have drycleaned those foul stains." Twain surpassed most professional humorists in patience with amateurs. He would, as they assume, have felt no offense to his dignity.

Fully committed to the rising sun of publicity, he tolerated – for decades, gratis – commercial uses of his face and either of his names. However, though a futurologist before that craft was organized, he would boggle today at the weedlike spread – thicker in relevant locales but liable to spring up anywhere – of banks, hotels, golf courses, and other enterprises that billboard him or his most famous characters. A motel in Oregon that keys its rooms to specific authors has a Mark Twain suite; the luxurious *Delta Queen,* which stops at Hannibal, often promises a Twain expert for its excursionists. Clearly, the go-getters believe that he triggers a positive response; while riverboats like Marietta, Ohio's *Becky Thatcher,* with H. B. Finn's Restaurant & Temperance Tavern aboard, are inevitable, *Mark Twain's Sure-Fire Programmed Guide to Backgrounds in American Literature* (1977), with a comic drawing of its mentor on practically every page, cuts a barely plausible path. By now no Twainian is surprised when turning a corner or page to find still another marker of his popularity.

Or apparent popularity. It is snatched up as a weapon in the always hotter battle for a piece of the public's attention and so gets reinforced. Television commentators doing "color" segments for the National League playoffs in 1990 noticed the *Huckleberry Finn,* a riverboat at Cincinnati; one result was a *Newsday* story, "Twist of Twain Spices Series," that featured his interest in baseball. The author of a book on self-publishing gets reporters to repeat his grabber: "What do Mark Twain, George Bernard Shaw, Edgar Allan Poe, and [his own name] have in common?" Regularly, the detective-story pulps dangle such titles as *Huckleberry Fiend* (Mysterious Press, 1975) and *The Mark Twain Murders* (Dell, 1989). No niche is too small now, but neither is any too large, too commercially valuable for its experts to bet on his appeal. An inquisitive Mark Twain complicated the final segment of the 1991–2 season of *Star Trek*; indeed, he was made a bridging character who would figure in the first segment in the fall.

In strictly terrestrial culture, Twain functions as commonly shared knowledge. Characters in the "Pogo" comic strip quarrel about attributing a quotation ("Well, ever'body talks 'bout the weather but nob'dy does nothin' 'bout it – as the feller says") to Mister Twain as against Mister Clemens; when Mole hears that friends thought him dead, he chuckles, "As another great humorist once remarked: That remark is a great exasperation," and starts another squabble. Twain and his books enter into not just "Peanuts,"

"Calvin and Hobbes," and "Shoe" but into nonwhimsical strips. Apparently, anybody feeding the mass media serves him up whenever possible; cartoonists, whether for the *New Yorker* or the debased *New York Evening Post,* eke out any Twain-related idea that's salable.

He also gets conscripted for serious campaigns. For its "Earth Day '90" issue *Newsweek*'s cover announced, over a Grant Wood–Thomas Hart Benton–like tableau with Tom and Huck rafting: "Life on the Mississippi: Huck's River Faces All of the Nation's Environmental Problems." The dean of the Duke University School of Law, engaging in the debate over the sociopolitical rationale of his profession, drew a parallel between the self-discipline it both needs and inculcates and Twain's training to pilot a steamboat.[2] Reprinted in several venues, the speech stirred hot responses that boiled over into the newspapers. While the basic issue is important, Twain enhanced its color and verve. Beyond his utility for merchandising and gimmickry, he has become a profitable subject for news himself, just as he did in his lifetime. Though the local press likes controversies about censorship, the moves to strike *Adventures of Huckleberry Finn* from the reading assigned in a secondary school get registered nationally.[3] Actually, it is the best-publicized rather than the most frequent target. When the long-missing two-fifths of the holograph manuscript turned up in 1991, that rated print, radio, and television coverage. Academics who have written about Twain learn to expect telephone calls from journalists.

Such viability more than three-quarters of a century after Twain's death can result only from a multimedia process, so insistent that he occasionally graces a television commercial without an identity check. The first film biography (1944) still gets rerun, though the inventory of glossier versions, mostly shaped for the PBS market, has outclassed – authenticity aside – *The Adventures of Mark Twain* starring Frederic March.[4] More gratefully yet, PBS welcomes versions of Twain's works. Beyond the expected Tom and Huck classics, a diverse anthology of other books and short pieces has accumulated. Meanwhile, Hollywood keeps trying to encapsulate the magic of *Huckleberry Finn* while doing better with *The Prince and the Pauper,* though not with *A Connecticut Yankee in King Arthur's Court.* Twainians regularly hear, because the mainline media care, that another filmed biography or dramatization is projected. For those able (or forced) to settle for audio, a lineup of cassettes continues to expand. For those with deluxe taste and income, the Broadway musical "Big River" (1985) adapted *Huckleberry Finn* lavishly.

When the comic book was flourishing, Tom Sawyer dominated his first one in 1942. Before then, a daily strip, "Tom Sawyer and Huckleberry

Finn," had lasted, with pauses, almost twenty years since 1918.[5] Once the Classic Comics series started, Twain's books – five, eventually – were pre-destined choices, and they have marched into competing series. As long as print forms survive, Twain will get more space than any other American author – in weekly and monthly magazines, in Sunday supplements, and indeed in the dailies if a reporter or columnist sees a topical angle. Editors of specialized or in-house journals also hook on to him whenever possible; for instance, in *Aramco World* magazine (May–June 1986), "Never the Twain . . ." retraced his (and Herman Melville's) travels in the Middle East. He would have conceded resignedly that another chance for punning on his pen name was too handy to pass up.

In that article's full-page illustration, two barefoot boys on a raft are dwarfed by a bust of the white-color-coded Twain – another drop in the stream of his likenesses that makes him instantly recognizable. He himself started it up early and helped to keep it thickening. Around 1851 – at the age of sixteen – he posed for a daguerreotype and two years later for a tintype. A conservative estimate puts the eventual reservoir of photographs at 650.[6] Their emotional ambience varies so richly that any enterprise can find an appropriate print and, because Twain obligingly posed in any town or country he visited, a relatively fresh one. Furthermore, in 1859 he sat for a journeyman painter; by the 1890s top portraitists were courting him. In 1884 his first bust was cast in bronze, and posthumous ones still follow, as do other sculptures, meant usually for public spaces. In 1985 President Ronald Reagan welcomed him into the White House collection. For ephemeral but widely seen images, newspaper and magazine editors commission drawings that stylize, ordinarily, an elderly Twain.

All of these images encourage the demand for Twain impersonators, who were quick to join the rise of one-person acts during the 1950s. Hal Holbrook soared into the lead so capably that most of the other living Twains actually imitate him, insisting on the white suit, long cigar, and pitched drawl. They have multiplied locally until no census is feasible and no estimate firm. The crucial point is that they draw audiences. Holbrook can dictate stiff terms because the buyers of his records and cassettes and the fans of his television special want to experience him directly. Since Twain's platform magic included an effect of spontaneity, his impersonators need not fear obsolescence through robots that hawk some message or else co-anchor, with Benjamin Franklin, the panorama of U.S. history at EPCOT Center of Walt Disney World.[7] No other author or politician – and no entertainer except, currently, Elvis Presley – comes near to matching the swarm of Twain clones.

Though Disney spun his empires out of a genius for gauging salability, the markers were obvious here. Ever since the American tourist developed a gusto for bric-a-brac beyond postcards, Twain items have proliferated. T-shirts and coffee mugs so abound as to bore some collectors, who stick to pricey ceramics like the Royal Doulton "original" or elaborate dolls of his child characters. Solemn scholars feel no sacrilege in buying Mark Twain napkins (with or without a maxim) or a necktie or a tote bag or cookbooks or even the Tom Sawyer videogame. After all, he invented and promoted Mark Twain's Self-Pasting Scrapbook (in several models at a range of prices) and, during his years of finest artistic creativity, put much effort into a board game, guiding it through manufacture.

Eponymous bookstores and good-reading festivals at a public library can count on devotees of the sequenced sentence. Besides mainline works, his varied sketches or parts of books, once past copyright, get produced in showily illustrated pamphlets; booklets of his epigrams and wittiest passages float about. Every few years a new coffee-table volume challenges the six or so out there. The dogged general reader buys remodelings of his career such as Nigey Lennon's *The Sagebrush Bohemian: Mark Twain in California* (1990). More and more, Twain strolls into fiction, as in Darryl Brock's *If I Never Get Back* (1990), and he dominated David Carkeet's *I Been There Before* (1985). Satisfyingly, all three of these books stand on much correct, even arcane, detail – proving both that Twain scholarship has an impact beyond the campus and that journalists feel compelled to explore beyond the clichés retailed about most authors. The several biographies for juveniles also honor reasonable accuracy, and the May 1984 issue – "The World of Mark Twain" – of *Cobblestone, the History Magazine for Young People* depends on solid research. Garlanded with photographs throughout, its cover favors the post-1907 Twain with an Oxford University gown over that stereotyping suit and therefore foreshadows the future shape of his image.

The paradigmatic photograph or drawing of an aged Twain has many dimensions, however; its props vary and it carries a penumbra of knowledge, usually, about his career. He is more complicated than the modern celebrity who becomes famous mostly for being famous; yet structuring him into the kind of hero that Joseph Campbell extols also becomes reductive. The Twain icon is a gallery itself of not only images but personalities; intricacy is the simple key here. To a unique degree Twain enshrines different, even differing, values for a span – now a cable-spread – of audiences, eluding the critic's unitary rationale and the scholar's certainty. Elderly movie fans remember the *frisson* raised by "the man of a thousand faces"; but Twain raises pleasant awe for his shape shifting.

Many admirers prefer, maybe react to, just one face. Which is the most popular cannot be established by computer-boosted statistics; fervency of choice counts too. But Twain charms millions as the magic flutist of nostalgia for childhood in a simpler, nicer time. Most full-page displays of his snowy head devote a corner to two boys on a raft; surely he is still reminiscing about them. The *Dictionary of Cultural Literacy* grants an entry only to *The Adventures of Tom Sawyer* among his books.[8] Its two sentences on the author slot him as "famous for his settings along the Mississippi River." This alerts us to recognize that illustrators take care to suggest an obviously wide, long river, which adds depth to the rafting and appeals to the American passion for movement and, subliminally, evokes the mythic qualities of water, cool running water. Dan Hoffman's poem "Mark Twain, 1909," which sketches Twain's sitting for still another photograph ("his hair an aureole" above the "Palm Beach white" suit), comes itself to focus on "always rivers" and the raft that "bears us onward, onward, back to our threatened paradise."[9] John Barth elevates that raft into one of the four greatest images created by world literature.

The haze of nostalgia is thinned by humor. Having typed Tom as a "wily and adventurous boy," the *Dictionary of Cultural Literacy* rounds off: "In one famous episode" he "tricks his friends into whitewashing a fence for him by pretending it is a great privilege and making them pay to take over the job." That is *the* most famous episode, easily outclassing the scenes in the schoolroom, graveyard, or cave. Though the novel glosses it pompously, illustrators spread on the humor very broadly; adult readers also enjoy its implicit cynicism about what fools we mortals be. Only academic rigorists can discuss Twain for long without breaking into a smile – as he would have done himself at any detailed proof that humor weaves inseparably through his writings, character, and body language. For Max Eastman, "He did not [at his best] as an author 'undertake' to be humorous. He asks no similar undertaking of the reader. He *was* humorous. He could not see, or think, or argue, or remember, or exist, for very long, in other terms."[10] The public likewise thinks of him as doing what came naturally.

A specialized genre of Twain's humor, the pithy sayings that he started highlighting in the 1890s, pops up in every medium from Holbrook's monologue to paperweights. Vice-president Dan Quayle tried to finesse a blunder by appealing to his "I don't give a damn for a man that can spell a word only one way" – redacted also as "You should never trust a man who has only one way to spell a word." Researchers who couldn't find the ur-text were not surprised since Twain's image benefits from the magnet or flypaper effect: the retailer/reteller of a witticism may attribute it to him for greater panache. He gets authorship for grousing that "a banker is a fellow who lends you his umbrella when the sun is shining and wants it back the minute it begins to rain." That bit wins him an international smile,[11] though it baffles scholars who expect both to get requests for pinpointing a source and to fail half of the time. To the regret solely of the purist, because Twain wrote and spoke prodigally for about fifty years they can seldom demagnetize absolutely.

In fact (or despite it), the public likes to improve its favorite maxims. In 1897, busy working in bed, Twain scrawled a reassuring note to a reporter: rumor had confused him with a cousin named Clemens and "the report of my illness grew out of his illness, the report of my death was an exaggeration." That note quickly evolved into "the report of my death is greatly exaggerated" – or close variants – available today in every medium including posters. A British edition of his short bits is entitled *Greatly Exaggerated* (1988). Familiarity has brought careless or self-conscious changes. Early in 1992 the "ABC Evening News" had Boris Yeltsin declaring, "The reports of my demise are somewhat exaggerated." In the strip "Steve Roper" (January 16, 1993) an awesome tough gloats, "Let me misquote Mark Twain, old boy! Reports of my demise are *highly* exaggerated." With little effect, purists have disclaimed for him the well-known "Everybody talks (or complains) about the weather but nobody does anything about it." (Justin Kaplan hedges with "Attributed" for the latest edition of Bartlett's *Familiar Quotations*.) Unfortunately, the staged Twains, stringing together quotable sentences, can stretch toward preachiness.

Maxims typically involve some degree of amusement at not just their pithiness but also their wry universalizing. Though Twain's darkest side ("Pity is for the living, envy is for the dead") appeals mostly to pessimists, a large audience appreciates him not so much for funny one-liners (". . . cauliflower is nothing but cabbage with a college education") but for word-bytes of wisdom from an elderly sage who, solemn toward the point of melancholy in posed photographs, suffered an overdose of late tragedies. It enjoys better yet his cynicisms that are not dangerously corrosive: "Be good and you will be lonesome" has earned many a chuckle since Twain put it to work on the frontispiece of *Following the Equator* (1897). With proper credit it has entered *A Dictionary of American Proverbs* (1992). Still, the cracker-barrel philosopher – observant, seasoned, obliquely irreverent – was allowed to be positive at heart. Librarians know that Twain gets laughs for " 'Classic.' A book which people praise and don't read," but their guild has absorbed enough faith in him and his appeal to produce a large poster harrumphing, "The man who does not read good books has no advantage over the man who can't read them" – another "attributed" maxim.[12]

A cross section of Twain's public would show an attitudinal tower of Babel. One layer, which can't find the nearest library, relishes the off-color maxims ("Chastity – it can be carried too far") or the once-bannable guffawings such as "[Date, 1601.] Conversation as It Was by the Social Fireside, in the Time of the Tudors." For men more than women he is the raunchy individualist, incorrigible from childhood to the grave, a Tom-Huck who never gave in fully to anybody's discipline. In spite of the documented facts, they need to believe that young Sam ran away from home – as the narrator yarns in *Life on the Mississippi*. They would agree with a review of *Roughing It* declaring that his humor is "evidently the natural outgrowth of the unsettled, adventurous, wild life he has led." That the old Clemens smoked heavily, poured his bourbon often, and shone at stag festivities they remember approvingly. American males like, furthermore, to make individualism central to the national character. *The Innocents Abroad* (1869), the book most firmly identified with Twain until his death, had already added the chord of cocky, surging Americanism that other cohorts have also chosen to hear always more distinctly. Crucially, though he could parade as "God's Fool" to get out of a self-inflicted bind, its narrator is New World shrewd, not Henry Jamesian innocent. Likewise, without the coaching of critics, admirers sense Twain's reassurance that behind his blunders as a tenderfoot out West looms a real-life person who has learned skepticism without petrifying into cautiousness.

A more accepting Twain continues to dazzle as a globe-trotter who lived our Tom Sawyerish fantasies, who followed the river out into all the seas, as bold as Ulysses; the sights and experiences of *Following the Equator* still impress most Westerners as exotic. Yet he warms other or even the same hearts as a husband and father who never strayed emotionally from his Penelope and three daughters. Their house in Hartford, Connecticut, attracts feature writers and – gorgeous visually – photographers for tableaus of a family Thanksgiving or Christmas. Luckily, as recent biographers analyze Olivia Langdon Clemens they find intelligence and toughness beneath the quiet warmth. Without undermining the domestic idyll, her personality adds counterpoint and resonance.

Tirelessly concerned and often livid about politics, Twain has narrower publics who prize images as diverse as those of the rambunctious traveler and the devoted husbànd. Soviet critics praised him as a worthy pre-Marxist because his commitment to romantic democracy burned so fiercely. The New Left could find material for mimeographed handouts, include him in

Revolutionary Quotations from the Thoughts of Uncle Sam (1969), and support "The War Prayer" as a protest against U.S. actions in Vietnam. His anti-imperialism rated a national reprise on the April 1992 cover of the *Atlantic Monthly*. But shape shifter on the hustings also, Twain passes as an exemplar of attitudes the rank-and-file Republican cherishes: faith in technology, entrepreneurship, and risk taking that will lead the self-made individual to riches. Curiously, the Left and the Right honor some of the same maxims, finding, for instance, either a cold-eyed rejection of the power structure or a playful attempt to make it function still better. ("Fleas can be taught nearly everything that a congressman can"; "It could probably be shown by facts and figures that there is no distinctly native criminal class except Congress.") Both Left and Right, along with the middle, probably like *The Political Tales and Truth of Mark Twain* (from the Classic Wisdom Collection, New World Library, 1992).

Lately, another image of Twain has grown vivid, and his outings on *Star Trek* will intensify it; enthusiasts of science fiction proclaim him a founding father. The accumulating praise for the time warp of *A Connecticut Yankee in King Arthur's Court* rose into a critical mass. While Philip José Farmer's *The Fabulous Riverboat* (1971) still honored Twain just as a kindred personality, by 1992 the editor of *Fantasy & Science Fiction,* after puffing the longest story in its July number for centering on him as a character, elaborated on his innovative novel and added: "Much of Twain's short fiction are tall tales with fantastic elements, and some use ghosts, angels, and other supernatural beings to make a point. He wrote mysteries and stories which, if written today, would be considered science fiction." In *Asimov's Science Fiction,* Norman Spinrad, well known in that field, enthusiastically revisited Twain's success in manipulating time travel "for such thoroughly modern science fictional purposes."[13] Cynics could suspect here a borrowing of his prestige to make the passage to literary respectability that he once navigated, but Twain himself suggests an indestructible sci-fi substance that acquires, with a rapidity that would have baffled Charles Darwin, the most contemporary shapes.

The torrent of images evokes Twain's anecdote about the drunk who, having staggered up his stairs, sighs, "God help the poor sailors out at sea on such a night as this." Nevertheless, several centers give it firm channels as well as intellectual depth. The Mark Twain Home Foundation presents a meticulously restored building; though no superhighway as yet feeds Hannibal, well over a hundred thousand visitors pay up annually besides those who merely want to photograph the white fence, the river with its big island, or the cave. National candidates – Jimmy Carter, George Wallace, the Clinton–Gore buscapade – target Hannibal for an appropriately pointed speech; writers for the Sunday supplements come steadily, as do latter-day authors of travel books. Michael Pearson's *Imagined Places: Journeys into Literary America* (1991) made it one of his six main stops in order to revisit "our Homer of boyhood." (He mentions that a restaurant in Manchester, Vermont, serves up a Huck Finn Mississippi Mud Drink – a mixture of Southern Comfort, Kahlua, and ice cream.) The flow of visitors will increase because fresh energy is pouring into the Mark Twain Birthplace Museum at nearby Florida and into the associated Research Foundation, which has restarted the *Twainian* newsletter. The Hannibal cadre's *Fence Painter* reached Volume 14 in 1994.

The house administered by the Mark Twain Memorial in Hartford is unforgettably arresting both inside and out. Most of its more than fifty thousand annual visitors feel awed by its luxuries and its relics of a closely knit domesticity, though journalists tend to follow a jocular vein that reaches back to the mid-1870s, when Twain often still posed as a "phunny phellow." The spread in the October 1992 *Yankee* is flagged with, "Huck Finn Wouldn't Have Come Near It: Mark Twain's 'cuckoo clock' of a house . . . is chock-full of what you don't expect to find"; a critic from the *New York Times* (July 20, 1993) less gapingly interpreted the house as a mirror of Twain's quirkiness. Such a slant obviously comes from, plays to, deeply held impressions that will soften as the Mark Twain House continues its program of lectures, symposia, local outreach, and institutes for teachers. While the Becky Thatcher Book & Gift Shop fills the need of many tourists to buy proof-of-visit to Hannibal, the House's own shop carries a tonier quality of items. Just beyond, Harriet Beecher Stowe's house adds contrast, anecdotes, and mainstream history to the neighborhood.

A latecomer, the Elmira College Center for Mark Twain Studies at Quarry Farm, controls the house, grounds, and "study" where Twain did much of his writing as his family relaxed during the summers. While the Center obliges the ten thousand annual visitors to that study, it moves toward an academic spin with a mounting archive, resident scholars, publications, and visiting lecturers; it arranged three-day conferences in 1989 and 1993. Of course, it encourages the biographical "musical drama" in a dome seating three thousand that started in the summer of 1987. All in all, Elmira, first home of his wife, conjures up a more normally paced Twain, climbing "damp from the breakfast table" to his study or inventing lawn games for his daughters. Inevitably, through the private enterprise of bars and gift shops, Virginia City, Nevada, markets him at his wildest and wooliest.[14] The rebuilt cabin on Jackass Hill in California gets listed in tourist guides, and Calaveras County attracts reporters for the most profitable of the frog-jumping contests. The Mark Twain Project perched in the library of the University of California at Berkeley attracts tourists without inviting them. Desire to touch Twain physically as best possible has persisted, encouraging in the 1970s a losing battle to preserve the house on Fifth Avenue in Manhattan where he lived for three and a half years.

That Twain has generated more commentary than any other American author probably seeps into general awareness. Academic biographers and critics have split into, roughly, loyalist and skeptical camps. The skeptical or quizzical camp, furthermore, puts more weight on his pessimism, making his humor less vital than his cultural typicalities, often regrettable; increasingly it darkens the image refracted through the mass media. Still, both camps and the nonaligned have, since 1986, widened the Mark Twain Circle of America into more than four hundred members with their newsletter, titled what else but the *Circular.* They all watch the Mark Twain Project for totally authoritative, lapidary editions of his books and sketches, unpublished manuscripts, notebooks, and letters; these volumes help validate the impression that Twain has conquered high culture and is deservedly taught in courses devoted to "masters" of world as well as American literature. Since Thomas A. Tenney occupied the editorship of the *Mark Twain Journal* in 1983, it has favored research and the principle that any relevant details are important. The browser who encounters the almost nine hundred pages of *The Mark Twain Encyclopedia* (1993), unleavened by photographs, has to infer that same principle.

Consumers of the mass media saw it reinforced during the summer of 1992 when not just the *Chronicle of Higher Education* but major dailies and then *Newsweek* paid close mind to a book yet to come out, *Was Huck Black? Mark Twain and African American Voices.* For example, the *Kansas City Star* discussed it on the first page of a section of its Sunday edition, with a drawing of Huck and Jim on their raft and a heading about "politically correct?"; Clarence Page's commentary occupied an entire syndicated column. The crux was the promised exoneration after those demanding the banning of *Huckleberry Finn* during the past several decades charged that this avatar – author or book – of the best American qualities is racist in attitude or else in effect. To argue that Twain showed far keener empathy with blacks than did his enveloping society does not satisfy those who want to keep him a culture hero. So attractive is his aura that few of those who reject the novel as offensive have attacked him more broadly. Minimally, the rest can enjoy one of his other faces.

More fluid than a mosaic, Twain's image shimmers like endless MTV. The most diligent observers cannot claim full coverage; what they find depends on how and where they watch; plain serendipity matters – for instance, they may come across something in a newspaper bought at an airport between flights. Regional base matters likewise; no bibliography will lead to a dry cleaner's blurb in Asheville, North Carolina; in fact, ProQuest does not include ads in its fine-screen indexing of eight major newspapers. That Twain's image dances out there incessantly is undebatable, but under tight focus it blurs, shifts, and splits like a superameba. No literary geneticist will chart all its chromosomes; no cultural anthropologist will achieve a thick description that convinces most peers; no culture critic can harmonize all the impressions, often emotional and subconscious rather than cerebral.

These caveats apply far more forcefully to judging how Twain appears to foreigners as a native icon. That he does figure prominently is clear. His works steadily issue in at least seventy-two languages of fifty-five countries.[15] In the most intriguing case, Soviet critics wrote copiously about him. While Americans welcomed such a tribute to their taste, they puzzled over his appeal to malign radicals, who, furthermore, accused them of suppressing his harshest social criticisms.[16] A questionnaire establishes Twain's appeal among college students in nine countries; "six countries like Samuel Clemens the most" out of a list of ten American authors, and the other three pick him second.[17] For the Occasional Newsletter of the Elmira College Center a guide counted up to thirty-five nationalities at the photogenic study, with Germans as the "most populous and interested foreign visitors, outside of the Canadians." This self-selected sample often asked whether Twain was "racist," though in the summer of 1991 the "focus shifted to the ownership" of the rediscovered manuscript of *Huckleberry Finn.* The guide added her own domesticating stroke to the image by playing up "his love of cats and his fanatical devotion to his pets." Twain's worldwide appeal is so provable as to defy the bite of his maxim "Faith is believing what you know ain't so." But only a multinational team could gather the facts in depth, and they would still need friends who pointed out, for instance, the October 1985 issue of *The Rising Generation,* in which Twain is the "special feature" of the essays in Japanese.

The origins of Twain iconography are easier to sketch, partly because the mass media had not yet accumulated such multifarious, invasive energy and because, even so, some materials are now buried in effect when not in fact. Yet the basic caveats still apply; the most dogged screening for evidence to support theory needs help nevertheless from serendipity and diligent friends. More crucially, the content of American uniqueness not only changed steadily during Twain's career, especially after 1900, but differed substantially from that of the late twentieth century all along.[18] Though Twain's sense of national identity was firm from the start, then was honed for *The Innocents Abroad,* and sharpened by restless travel later, he didn't hold an insistent pitch until the late 1890s, when he jotted (presumably thinking of himself): "Are you an American? No, I am not *an* American. I am *the* American."[19] Significantly, he was living in Europe, doubtless meeting much comment on his native qualities or hearing it at secondhand; to a mutual friend who had introduced him in Paris, Ivan Turgenev exclaimed: "Now, there is a real American – the first American who has had the kindness to conform to my idea of what an American ought to be. He has the flavor of the soil. Your other friends . . . might as well be Europeans."[20] From Twain's first book onward, British reviewers analyzed his native flavors more closely than did the American guardians of culture, who registered such an approach ambivalently. Much of the time, Twain himself hoped to merge into the great (that is, Western) humanistic tradition through patient and imposingly substantial reading.

Analyses of popularity likewise involve highly debatable judgments. The word implies a warmer respect than notoriety, which Twain welcomed into the 1870s; "icon" implies a margin of solemn reverence, even devotion. With surprisingly few dips, the graph of Twain's fame, however ambiguous, rises firmly throughout his career.[21] But no graph can pinpoint when or why he was transformed from a professional humorist into an American hero both comic and serious, both scapegrace and role model, or the year or event when the heroic, serious side became revered. The base point is fixable, anyway. Following up on the wildfire success of his yarn, pirated by newspapers across the country, he cobbled together *The Celebrated Jumping Frog of Calaveras County and Other Sketches* (1867), which elicited more than twenty reviews. Mostly positive, they focused on a raucous, bold "Western" brand of humor even when grudging. Old-style literary historians argue that critics, anxious to heal sectional hatreds, promoted the West because it had taken little part in the Civil War. However, a surprising number of reviewers wondered if a sui generis talent had not surfaced.

Almost every newspaper of consequence reviewed *The Innocents Abroad* while Twain was attracting notoriety as well as popularity through a brash approach to lecturing. Promoted vigorously, the book, in addition to projecting a self-consciously proud American, not just Westerner, made the comic persona Mark Twain famous among the literate. Also publishing helter-skelter in newspapers and magazines, Twain often presented himself – that is, a fluctuating persona – within his texts.[22] Brassy and prescient enough to appreciate the multiplier factor of publicity about well-done publicity, he was pleased when newspaper wits joked about his posturing. More calculatingly, like his near contemporary P. T. Barnum he perceived that the public could enjoy self-advertisement as a species of performance. *Roughing It* (1872) enriched his image of Westerner, as original as "go-ahead" Davy Crockett while smoother socially and better informed. However, *Tom Sawyer,* besides the melodramatic plot, comedy, and soft quaintness, displayed an explicitly contrasting Twain, capable of starchy prose and middle-class attitudes toward money and criminals. Meanwhile, his persona had now and then rejoined the literary comedians who chased after any paying bit for the newspapers. Yet those newspapers soon carried summaries of his effective, perhaps eloquent speech at some worthwhile occasion like a reunion of veterans. He was emerging as astonishingly versatile, tireless, prodigal with his talents, willing to take long chances, and apt to droll provocatively on any subject.

Since the interview as a genre was still inching toward respectability during the 1870s, comparison of bulk is tricky. Nevertheless, the amount and, better yet, the implicit respect of the stories greeting his return in 1879 from a European tour rate as quantum jumps. Reviews of *A Tramp Abroad* consciously dealt with a substantial author, a humorist by trade but a sturdy bourgeois on his family side. *The Prince and the Pauper* (1881) raised mild praise for its unexpected, scholarly side and a relieved acclaim for Twain's ability to express "finer" sentiments and show reverence for the morally deserving, kings included. Besides confirming Twain's many-faceted creativity, *Life on the Mississippi* was accepted as coming from an affluent man of affairs who had outgrown the naïveté though not the enthusiasm of the cub pilot. Hardly anybody cares much now about the last two-fifths of the book, but it did establish a thoughtful observer of social and economic trends. More and more, reviewers and reporters treated Twain as a famous personality, continuously gaining prestige while always liable to revert to the irrepressible humorist who first attracted notice.

The volume and the quality of the well-wishing for Twain's fiftieth birthday demand a reversal of perspective. Before 1885 it is more enlightening to focus on how, deliberately or instinctively, he presented himself while interacting, of course, with the press. But the dignity now offered along with the first tinge of awe was greater than his strategies could claim credit for and must have surprised him. His image had taken on its own dynamic or, more simply, had been preempted by mass opinion, which would adapt it to culturally determined needs. At the time, *Huckleberry Finn,* more specifically, could claim little of the credit; few reviews were glowing, while the various associated quarrels at best balanced out in the newspapers.

The joint lecture tour with George Washington Cable deserved far greater credit because the tour's reception, overall, was enthusiastic and, furthermore, Twain won most of the inevitable comparisons. When he was not on the move, Hartford, identified by then as home base, was adding the Northeast to his network of regional identities. Stepping forward as a Mugwump in 1884, if perhaps winning no more devotees than it lost him, thickened his reputation for activist citizenship. Luckily timed success as the publisher of Ulysses S. Grant's memoirs led to stories about not just his talent for business but his mounting wealth. When interviewers joked with him, hoping for a memorable bolt of humor, they showed no doubt as to who ranked higher. Though Twain could still plunge into clowning, it had an air of earned self-indulgence no longer evocative of Barnum's crass theatricality. Twain seemed no longer on the make as a phunny phellow either. His speeches, openhandedly gratis, graced a ceremonial affair appropriately while the audience wondered how much humor would erupt this time.

In November 1885 friends and admirers concertedly sent birthday greetings and even poems – by a leading British man of letters and, far more consequentially, by venerable Oliver Wendell Holmes; lesser luminaries cooperated for an issue of the *New York Critic* that feted his "semicentennial." Twain had arrived in two senses. He was eminent and affectionately respected. His image had also arrived at, essentially, the rounded, filled-in personality that would change only through the process of normal aging (his hair was still reddish), life's pounding, and accreting honors. In 1878 Richard Harding Davis had assured his father, "I am going to write a story that will raise my name to fame above that of Mark Twain, Max Adler, Danbury news man and Joakin Miller."[23] By 1885 a fourteen-year-old boy would have realized that such a list committed a misalliance. When Duke's Cigarettes glued a 1½- by 3-inch "biography" of Twain to its packages, it was hoping to improve its respectability more than to suggest kinship.[24]

Twain's prestige soon rose faster than before. Some rumors made him absolutely rich; reporters gave glimpses of a businessman, dressed upscale, who had the creative energy but not the time for literary work. When he managed to finish *A Connecticut Yankee,* the results were reassuring. His comic gift still effervesced; twisting the tail of the British lion, along with egalitarian sermons, revalidated his grass-roots democracy; his hero throbbed with clear-the-road enterprise that would empower technology. The unexpected news in 1891 that the Clemenses would temporarily move abroad to cut expenses was regrettable except for persons prone to *schadenfreude,* who kept quiet. Nobody sensible hinted that Twain had pushed his luck too far or that his family was deserting the United States. In 1893 a milling company thought it shrewd to market a Mark Twain flour.

As the news about his solvency darkened, people understood that he was fighting hard to pull through, that his output as author had speeded up to earn royalties, forgivably more vital to him at present than artistry. Editorial opinion blamed his formal bankruptcy in 1894 on the "panic" or economic downdraft, and he justified that sympathy by announcing a "world" tour of lecturing to pay off his publishing firm's debts, which were legally avoidable. Along the first American leg from Cleveland to the Northwest, his manager's diary recorded surprise at the outpourings of sympathy with steady prompting from the press. Stories wired from Australia, New Zealand, India, and South Africa celebrated, besides the foreign acclaim of his integrity as businessman, his triumphs at charming exotic audiences into appreciating his country's humor while he was, some journalists intimated, running on empty physically. By the sweat of his aging brow he had earned the domestic closure frustrated by the sudden death of a daughter. Yet the buoyant American had evidently held on to enough idealism, to the uplifting worship in *Personal Recollections of Joan of Arc* (1896), which filled out his balancing act between the hype of the subscription-book trade and the genteelist's crusade for an ennobling, high-culture literature.[25]

Though the Clemenses wanted to mourn reclusively, he could not pass unnoticed. As the latest technology made it easy for newspapers to print the many photographs available, strangers initiated contact on the street. His image, maintaining its dynamic, supported *Following the Equator* as a feat of will that, fighting off grief, had achieved another entertaining book, short of rollicking comedy, however, also because readers knew too much to enjoy him as a feckless bumbler. When, from Vienna, journalists described his rounds of salons and soirées, the extroverted citizen now of the world began scintillating again, all the more deservedly after the spring of 1898 when creditors were paid off in full, as that world heard immediately. The *Pall Mall Gazette* recorded that a letter had informed the London *Times* "under yesterday's date": "I venture to think that many of your readers will be glad to learn" that Twain "has already discharged the task he set himself"; *St. James's Gazette* predicted a "spontaneous impulse of homage" for such "chivalrous honour in business relations." Back home, even Anglophobes gloated over the transcontinental praise; a survey of magazine articles during 1898 demonstrates that, during his absence, his image had won fresh constituencies there.[26] As its greatest demographic conquest, the *Ladies' Home Journal* carried, with many photographs, "The Anecdotal Mark Twain." Evidently, middle-class matrons or aspirants to the status wanted/needed to learn more about him. Anybody au courant was expected to join in having an opinion about his personality and current knowledge about his family, more visible than ever because a wife and stylish daughter had gone along on that lecture tour, because the oldest, reputedly gifted daughter was conspicuous through death, and because that stylish daughter was studying piano with the best teacher in Vienna, music capital of Europe.

Even so, Twain's homecoming in 1900 startled Americans with their own fervor. Reporters from all New York City dailies and wire services met him at dockside, and he cooperated enthusiastically. Claiming to vibrate with health and optimism, he blew the patriotic bugle. Because he mixed in a protest against imperialism that included the United States and launched frontal attacks in the months ahead, its flag bearers went so far as to charge treason. But most of those avid for empire excused his trademark individuality or simply could not bear to disown him. S. S. McClure, monitoring the common pulse, offered to charter a special train for him to resurvey his home continent and do a series of articles; his lecture manager guaranteed $10,000 for ten performances; the dining room of a hotel could burst into applause when he strolled in. Social historians feel called to probe beyond the self-feeding of mass psychology or the too obvious possibility that Twain deserved such adulation because of his genius for humor and his unique spirit. His contemporaries idolized success and especially his exciting path toward and use of it while, in the crunch, behaving ethically. But no capitalist, not Andrew Carnegie, inspired a litany that climaxed: "More than a humorist, his writings, especially the later books, abound in wisdom, shrewd ideas of human nature, sympathy and enthusiasm. He is a man of striking personality, rare conversational powers, and in manner, kindly and democratic."[27] Several recent biographers might counter with Twain's anecdote about how the Reverend Thomas K. Beecher deflated a shamelessly overblown elegy. But snickers, doubts, or grumbles over the adoring consensus were rare in 1900.

Riding a comet more than guiding it, Twain kept his charms and virtues visible, including his exemplary devotion as husband. For many they had grown more important than his writing, though after the House of Harper rounded up all the rights to his books in 1903 the collected editions testified that he rated as an enduring author. Except for a suitable period of mourning after his wife's death, he reigned as a prince if not the king of the banquet culture, still more supremely at ease, as relaxed as we all yearn to be. His hair turned whiter, bushy like a natural crown, some thought. The lavish banquet for his seventieth birthday swamped any anxiety he had left about the fickleness of mass love; regally, he allowed instantly popular photographs of himself in bed.[28] By December 1906 he screwed up the nerve to flaunt his white suit in winter – only on occasion, actually – and instantly added a quasi-saintly glow to his image. On vital or alluring questions, he obliged requests for statements to the press, which expected a mind-catching opinion; reporters understood that interviews were a boon to be treated gratefully, as were sessions for a photograph. Partly by coincidence, Twain's doings, judgments, state of health, and face appeared in some New York City daily on most days of April 1906.

As far as outsiders knew, he was happily active while not senile or careless about the main chance. In 1907 his business agent registered trademarks for Mark Twain Whisky and Mark Twain Smoking Tobacco, and a Mark Twain Company filed its charter the next year. But the spotlight stayed on his vibrancy. *Harper's Weekly* (April 7, 1906), having asked, "Who among us has the most fun nowadays?" went on: "We guess Uncle Mark Twain has a fair amount of daily sport. He is a very kind man, and finds many opportunities nowadays to do public services of a benevolent sort to great advantage. The papers, as we write, say he is going to preside at a meeting for the benefit of the blind. He does such things often, and makes very good speeches and on all occasions when he speaks at all." While this tribute meant to imply no faults, another editorial centered on his dynamism as a home-grown moral philosopher whose "sound breezy Americanism is a corrective to all sorts of snobbery." It itemized learnedly: "Mark Twain in his 'last and best of life for which the first was made' seems to be advancing rapidly to a position which makes a kind of joint Aristides, Solon, and Themistocles of the American metropolis – an Aristides for justness and boldness as well as incessancy of opinion, a Solon for wisdom and cogency, and a Themistocles for the democracy of his views and the popularity of his person."[29] He kept certifying such praise with speeches for reform candidates or a pamphlet excoriating atrocities in the Belgian Congo. The elegant honor of a Litt. D. from Oxford University surprised his devotees less than it delighted them as totally deserved.

What template fits Twain's iconography? Who can codify the illusions of the public – of the publics, really? How much credit belongs to his self-proclaimed "talent for posturing" precisely when the print media needed subjects for their human-interest marketing?[30] A psychohistorian can argue that Twain appealed to the Victorianized male's wish for greater freedom of manners. Some literary critics have adapted cultural anthropology, particularly its paradigm of the Trickster figure, but while Twain could until his death soar into a madcap routine, his era had far more complexities than a localized, preliterate society. In its own constantly restated terms he exemplified, beyond self-made (and remade) success, an Emersonian flowering hardened by strenuous risk taking and grace under pressure. Finally, thrusting Twain into the crossfire of multiculturalism, any detailed analysis must account for his image as the archetypal American. A current-events weekly asked eminent persons to pick the ten books most characteristic of the native spirit and experience. By that criterion a foreign-born professor of philosophy at Harvard listed *A Tramp Abroad* (though "certainly not his best book"); Owen Wister and Brander Matthews listed *Huckleberry Finn,* while Hamlin Garland preferred both *Roughing It* and *Life on the Mississippi* as "deeply typical of Western New World humor"; a professor of belles lettres at the University of Virginia also preferred *Roughing It* "without deprecating the full Americanism of the boys' prime favorite," *Huckleberry Finn;* Grace King as Southerner coupled the works of Twain and Joel Chandler Harris as the most native of all while again singling out *Roughing It.*[31] Of course, Twain dominated the mention of living writers, helped by a varied oeuvre that exemplified the multiplicity of his appeal.

Twain's death in 1910 made the top news story of the day, with a lesser peak at the funeral. While the elegies were lightened by anecdotes and informal poses, they keyed on the loss of a national treasure – a motif especially attractive for the editorial-page cartoonists. Crucially, though Thomas Edison shot a jerky ninety-second film in 1909, Twain's icon would have to carry on without his voice and charismatic touch. His official biographer rushed out with a multivolume hagiography. However, immortality does not come easy on this spinning earth. In Twain's era, a "life and letters" followed soon after the death of authors and politicians with any fame. For instance, influential Annie A. Fields quickly enshrined Charles Dudley Warner, also propped up with a fifteen-volume set of his writings, but only literary historians remember him beyond his ties with Twain. So there were broad currents helping Albert Bigelow Paine, who, while insisting that Twain had loved people of all ranks and tastes, aimed his biographies and editions at middle-class buyers.

Van Wyck Brooks ended the near hiatus of World War I with *The Ordeal of Mark Twain,* an indictment of New England philistinism and of Twain as its most lamentable but willing victim that pleased intellectuals who resented the official complacency of the 1920s. As Thomas A. Tenney's *Reference Guide* shows, interest in Twain nevertheless kept rising, on average, driven primarily by fans of the boy-centered novels. Marketing a board game, "Adventures of Tom Sawyer and Huck Finn," looked worthwhile to somebody. Higher up the ladder of seriousness, Cream of Wheat banked on "Tom Sawyer's secret – how mothers are using it today," the heading of a full-page plan for luring children "to do things," that is, to enjoy productive work like whitewashing a fence. Some advertising agency – the modern providence that, to update Twain, "don't fire no blank cartridges" – had sensed a sizable target audience. Little of the credit belongs to Cyril Clemens, an eccentric third cousin, twice removed, who, having taken over the International Mark Twain Society, administered it by mail, awarding grand titles and imaginary offices to eminent persons at home and abroad. Confirming Twain's ongoing prestige, an astoundingly distinguished cadre accepted, or at least did not demand having their names struck from the society's letterhead. In 1936 he financed the *Mark Twain Quarterly* (later *Journal*), which served up grandiosity, irrelevance, and a few worthwhile essays by others. He rode a rising tide. From whatever reasons, the number of Twain entries jumped from ten in Bartlett's *Familiar Quotations* (1914) – his first appearance – to thirty-nine in the next edition (1937).

After warning shots, Bernard DeVoto had made literary news in 1932 with a prolonged assault on Brooks that, passionately and eloquently, extolled Twain's indigenous, democratic humor. Their skirmish is still replayed, though it never penetrated beyond the top level of general readers and the few academics specializing near the subject. Twain as yet had low visibility for departments of English. In 1935 a *Mark Twain Zephyr* started steaming between St. Louis and Burlington, Iowa, but just two universities substantially recognized the centennial of Twain's birth. The Great Depression impeded such outlays, though it ultimately helped Twain by encouraging the vogue for literary Americana, for going back to origins (or roots, we now say).

However, nonacademic Hannibal and a Mark Twain Centennial Commission based in Manhattan kept a hundred candles burning throughout 1935. In January, President Franklin Delano Roosevelt activated by wire a lighthouse above Hannibal; and after galas such as a mass fence painting, a huge banquet there honored the thirtieth of November. With the steady help of the *New York Times,* Nicholas Murray Butler, chair of the commission, directed efforts toward establishing a national model for programs at primary and secondary schools and toward the proclaiming of a Mark Twain Day by governors of the states (thirty-three would cooperate). With his usual impishness, Mayor Fiorello La Guardia addressed a "small army" of boys organized to parade with floats, but the topper was a banquet broadcast nationally from the Waldorf-Astoria Hotel.

The centennial also raised consciousness that had later results. In 1939 the Mark Twain Society of Chicago inaugurated the *Twainian,* mimeographed but rich in contents. Broader, demotic currents were also quickening. Press agentry for Will Rogers had long proclaimed his kinship with Twain, who benefited in turn as that folksy oracle had flourished. Campbell soups had thought it profitable to devote most of a full-page ad in the *Saturday Evening Post* (September 15, 1934) to a white-suited Twain contemplating a huge tomato. Commissioned by Heritage Press in 1935 to illustrate the Tom–Huck novels, Norman Rockwell gauged mass taste beautifully again; his technicolor tableau of whitewashing the fence will reappear past our times. Meanwhile, the Mark Twain Museum, built by the Works Progress Administration, opened in Hannibal. Aiming at upscale tourists, the menu of the Willard Hotel in Washington, D.C., featured a photograph proving that Mark Twain slept here. Old Taylor Straight Bourbon Whiskey picked *Fortune* magazine for its portrait of the stag-group raconteur (who might be encoring his anecdote about the unmarried woman who excused her baby as so tiny). Morally, the Twains may never meet. The centennial had included publishing *The Family Mark Twain,* and the belief that he stayed a virgin until marriage at age thirty-four persists. Complicating such polarities, at the 1993 Elmira conference a biographer suggested that Twain had homosexual liaisons during his Western years; journalists followed up avidly but, so far, gut responses have varied too much for a neat polling.

After World War II, dominating voices announced that the American Century had begun. Former enemies as well as allies tended to agree; along with neutral countries they wanted to learn about the United States in depth. For its literature Twain was invitingly appropriate, and *Huckleberry Finn* his most winning book. Those choices set up a reciprocating process with his image; despite formalist critics, readers want to hear and see more and finally to mythologize an author whose writings they like. On campuses the new courses in American literature needed – as the trend went – paperback texts. Introductions by Lionel Trilling (1948) and T. S. Eliot (1950) put a surprisingly sophisticated, much-imitated spin on what was towering into Twain's masterpiece, but more influential were the simple facts that it rated a spot in any plausible syllabus and that instructors explicated it solemnly. By the thirteenth edition of *Familiar Quotations* (1955), the entries for Twain had tripled.[32] More than coincidentally, the Hartford group that had saved Twain's house from being torn down in 1929 began an active program in 1955 to restore its original splendor.

Two essays are especially indicative. Delivered at three universities and then to *Harper's Magazine,* a culture critic's "What's 'American' about America?" answered its title with a list of a dozen artifacts "not likely to have been produced elsewhere." He included *Leaves of Grass* and Twain's "writing" and, when elaborating, cited *Huckleberry Finn* as "perhaps . . .

the greatest book written on this continent."[33] More eminent academically, Henry Nash Smith, already influential through his saints-on-the-raft lead-in for a teaching edition (1958), spelled out, for a Voice of America series, the qualities that make Huck archetypal.[34] Americans could feel a little better about themselves as his descendants and totally so if they tolerated – open-minded like Huck – his "moral improvisation" and "antinomian attitude toward established authorities." They also could only feel good about his creator.

Outside academia the substantially different *Tom Sawyer* remains almost as evocative. From on the spot, Russell Baker began: "All over the world, wherever men can read, everyone knows Hannibal. Everyone has lived here for a precious moment and there are few men who do not revisit it still in search of forgotten tranquility and lost dreams"[35] – dreams – he conflates – of the "glory of boyhood in Tom Sawyer and Huckleberry Finn." His emphasis on boyhood and men can be defended against the charge of sexism by the contention that males have always made the heart – whether stout or nostalgic – of Twain's audience. Beyond gender, Baker tied the dream of lost glory to the "saddened perspective" of his "middle age." Soon Justin Kaplan, with his multiawarded *Mr. Clemens and Mark Twain* (1966), probed deep beneath sadness into a tortured, increasingly disoriented pathology. But many more readers saw the hearty series of ads for Old Crow bourbon such as the one in *Time* magazine (October 5, 1962). Accurate in having Rudyard Kipling come to pay homage in 1889, it anachronistically featured an elderly Twain that post–World War II psyches presumably demand, whether as the strong grandfather they lost or never had or as embodied proof that they need not go meekly, much less soberly, into the dark.

Since the 1960s the image industry has grown exponentially; Colonel Sellers would gloat that "there's millions in it" just from Twain. Though the country's two hundredth birthday dwarfed the centennial for *Tom Sawyer*, *Huckleberry Finn*'s brought news stories, lectures, conferences, books, and bibliographies of articles and books. Before then, the broader dynamic had become so evident that in 1981 a symposium at the University of Alabama examined, gratefully, the "mythologizing" of Twain. In 1982 Quarry Farm passed on to Elmira College, which founded another center supported, as in Hannibal and Hartford, by business and civic groups. Throughout the expansive 1980s Twain's viability increased at every demographic level in every channel, even as a "collectible."[36] It is gratifying that the "scramble for Twainiana," "the extraordinary demand," does include his books. Attuned observers can foresee, however, another Twain riding the flow toward pure images without the printed word.

The New Critics helped to make "icon" fashionable. While holding on to its connotations of reverence due, they made it denote a rich subject for explicators that has achieved inward-directed autonomy. Icon also still implies a solid tangibility, a visual marker, a portable semiotic sign. Since it has moved into computerese, its future is as bright as Twain's.

As an academic icon, Twain towers firmly. Nobody goggles to see that a Mark Twain/American Studies seminar will meet for a month in Chile. Likewise, his institutional base deepens. Having completed a true restoration of the boyhood home, his Hannibal enclave is planning a state-of-the-art museum, scheduled to open on Memorial Day weekend in 1995; the Mark Twain Memorial, having reached excellence in refurnishing and refurbishing the Hartford house, is nevertheless gearing up for self-improvement; the Elmira Center has lately reclaimed another building at Quarry Farm. Even without such support, Twain would stay prominent because of *Huckleberry Finn*. If it regularly comes under fire for racism, its rescuers – many of them nonacademics – rush in. The *Presbyterian Survey* (January–February 1993) draws a healing lesson from it: "The sin of racism is buried deep within us. Only the grace and power of God can erase it." That crux aside, scholars and critics are pondering the reunited manuscript and will report in detail, doubtless disagreeing enthusiastically. Nor will the Disney *Adventures of Huck Finn* (1993) discourage other filmmakers from trying to catch the novel's magic.

Twain's visibility in workaday society rolls on likewise because he is exploited as a come-on. When a wire service picked up an analysis of William Bennett's "pessimism" from the *Chicago Tribune,* it added a photograph of Twain because the columnist had dragged in the fact that "among the many things he railed against was the insanity plea." The background story (*Kansas City Star,* July 18, 1993) on the historic flooding opened, "Trying to control the Mississippi River, Mark Twain wrote, was about as smart as trying to bully a comet onto a new course"; its next paragraph was a relevant passage, quite serious, from *Life on the Mississippi.* On that same Sunday, George Will's column, on the way to his main argument, remarked that the Mississippi "runs through America's imagination. On it Huck Finn found freedom by floating away from Aunt Sally and other chafing facets of civilization." The novel has become cultural currency, passed almost casually with small mistakes in making change.

Headed "The Voice of America," an extended essay in the *New Yorker* (June 14, 1993), after stressing that Twain both shared and spoke for the consensus of his era, updates him completely: he "was a nineteenth-century figure – the hardest thing to remember when you are caught up in reading him. He seems so close in time that you wouldn't be surprised to look up from the book and see him talking to Larry King on television. But he can seem so familiar only because the America we like best sounds like him, not because he sounds like it." To be sure, the "we" is easier to flourish than to flesh out, and what we "like best" is still less easily itemized. Many Americans prefer, ironically, Twain the iconoclast. Or, more vaguely, they prefer the unpredictable, blithely willful personality and settle for a *Huckleberry Finn* that signifies episodically, abandoning any master plan whenever humor beckons. The rank-and-file Twainian doesn't feel obliged to choose between experts, who should respond more sensitively to "popular reception and understanding. Whether the general public has 'got Twain right' is finally beside the point. Because Mark Twain is an American institution, the public will always have a say in how he is to be understood. Scholars or critics who remain indifferent to popular belief about the man or his work will have missed much that is significant in their subject."[37] That is perfect advice when "belief" includes the auditory, visual, and almost indefinable paths of images that make Twain into, as well as a lively institution, a major American icon.

NOTES

1 Ephemera are not documented unless they are especially significant or unusual. An editorial ("Great Leaps Forward") in the *Washington Post,* February 20, 1990, characterizes the Jumping Frog Jubilee in Calaveras County as a "tribute to the particular genius and enthusiasm with which this country often manages to keep its literary treasures alive by converting them into pure boosterism. . . . Mark Twain, foremost student of American hustle, would love it."

2 Paul Carrington, "Of Law and the River," *Journal of Legal Education* 34 (1984): 222–8.

3 Nat Hentoff, *Free Speech for Me – But Not for Thee* (New York: Harper-Collins, 1992), begins with "The Right to Read a Book with 'Niggers' in It" (chap. 1).

4 Wesley Britton's "Media Interpretations of Mark Twain's Life and Works" is gratifyingly detailed; in *The Mark Twain Encyclopedia,* ed. J. R. LeMaster and James D. Wilson (New York: Garland, 1993).

5 The authoritative source is M. Thomas Inge, "Comics," in ibid.

6 Nick Karanovich, "Photographs," in ibid.

7 Jane Kuenz, "It's a Small World After All: Disney and the Pleasures of Identification," *South Atlantic Quarterly* 92 (Winter 1993): 63–88, analyzes EPCOT with more sophistication than is needed here. Eccentrics and indigents may not know that the Magic Kingdom at Disney World includes "Tom Sawyer's Island" and "Aunt Polly's Landing."

8 *The Dictionary of Cultural Literacy,* ed. E. D. Hirsch, Jr., Joseph F. Kett, and

James Trefil (Boston: Houghton Mifflin, 1988), p. 136. Some critics will be sorry to read that *Huckleberry Finn* is simply "a sequel to Tom Sawyer; Huck Finn is Tom's best friend."

9 *New Yorker,* October 29, 1984, p. 48.

10 Max Eastman, *Enjoyment of Laughter* (New York: Simon & Schuster, 1936), p. 302.

11 See Olgierd Budrewicz, *Orzel na Gwiazdzistym Sztandarze* (Warsaw: Wydawnictwo Interpress, 1975), p. 240.

12 For this item as well as the classic "greatly exaggerated," see Ralph Keyes, *"Nice Guys Finish Seventh": False Phrases, Spurious Sayings, and Familiar Misquotations* (New York: Harper-Collins, 1992), pp. 109–11. Keyes entitles the relevant chapter "The Twain Syndrome." The poster I cite is dated 1986. Lately, several different constituencies have used, while improving upon, Twain's (attributed) "I never let my schooling interfere with my education."

13 Norman Spinrad, "On Books," *Asimov's Science Fiction* 16 (November 1992): 312–15.

14 Fred Setterberg, *The Roads Taken: Travels Through America's Literary Landscapes* (Athens: University of Georgia Press, 1993), p. 84, gives a candid description of the privately owned Mark Twain Museum there.

15 *Mark Twain International: A Bibliography and Interpretation of His Worldwide Popularity,* ed. and comp. Robert M. Rodney (Westport, Conn.: Greenwood, 1982), p. xxii. This volume abounds with impressive details. Of course, some "countries" have come or gone in recent years.

16 The most interesting, though brief and polemical, document is Charles Neider's *Mark Twain and the Russians: An Exchange of Views* (New York: Hill & Wang, 1960).

17 Bruce Daniels, "Everybody Loves Abraham, Martin, John – and Paul and Meryl: International Views of American Culture," *American Studies International* 30 (October 1992): 76–7.

18 Since the idea of distinctive American qualities was central then as now, we cannot ignore it even though no one who has read Sacvan Bercovitch's *The Rites of Assent: Transformations in the Symbolic Construction of America* (New York: Routledge, 1993) can particularize with blithe certainty.

19 Quoted from his notebooks in John Lauber, *The Inventions of Mark Twain* (New York: Hill & Wang, 1990), p. 287.

20 H. H. Boyesen, "The Plague of Jocularity," *North American Review* 161 (1895): 532. Boyesen, born and educated in Norway, was of course sensitive to Twain's nationality himself.

21 In *Our Mark Twain: The Making of His Public Personality* (Philadelphia: University of Pennsylvania Press, 1983) I have tried to follow in detail the course of Twain's reputation during his lifetime. Alan Gribben's highly insightful essay, "Autobiography as Property," in *The Mythologizing of Mark Twain,* ed. Sara deSaussure Davis and Philip D. Beidler (University, Ala.: University of Alabama Press, 1984), pp. 39–55, conducts an analysis similar to mine.

22 Jeffrey Steinbrink, *Getting to Be Mark Twain* (Berkeley: University of California Press, 1991), convincingly analyzes both Twain's self-images and responses to them from 1867 to 1871.

23 Quoted in Arthur Lubow, *The Reporter Who Would Be King: A Biography of Richard Harding Davis* (New York: Scribner's, 1992), p. 27.

24 Such items were especially ephemeral. This marketer of tobacco used Twain in other forms also, including a "trade card" with his visage and a "view of tramping abroad"; Bella C. Landauer, "Literary Allusions in American Advertising," *New-York Historical Society Quarterly* 31 (1947): 148–59.

25 Many critics, starting with Van Wyck Brooks and continuing on past Henry Nash Smith – who explores the matter the most sensitively of all without hauteur – have seen tragedy or unfulfillment in Twain's tension between low and high culture as the gap widened quickly after the Civil War. Though Michael Denning does not conclude that Twain always mastered that tension, he finds substantial successes and creative stimulus for Twain within it; see *Mechanic Accents: Dime Novels and Working-Class Culture in America* (London: Verso, 1987), pp. 208–11.

26 Such a survey is made easy and thorough by Thomas A. Tenney's *Mark Twain: A Reference Guide* (Boston: G. K. Hall, 1977).

27 Matthew Irving Lans, Introduction to a reprinting of *English as She Is Taught* (Boston: Mutual Book Co., 1900).

28 I develop this phenomenon in greater detail in "Mark Twain: Still in Bed but Wide-Awake," *Amerikastudien* 30 (Spring 1985): 177–85.

29 Quoted in Clara Clemens, *My Father Mark Twain* (New York: Harper, 1931), pp. 261–2.

30 Greg M. Zacharias, "Henry Rogers, Public Relations, and the Recovery of Mark Twain's 'Character,'" *Mark Twain Journal* 31 (Spring 1993): 2–17, speculates that agents for the Standard Oil Co. and H. H. Rogers, Twain's new crony, revitalized his celebrity as a moral hero, which – Zacharias contends – had dimmed badly in the preceding years.

31 *Outlook* 72 (December 6, 1902): 776–88.

32 Naming the Twain section as one of the three that he "thoroughly revised," Justin Kaplan reduced it from 119 to 82 entries for the sixteenth edition (1992). However, any Twain quotation that is faintly familiar does still appear in Kaplan.

33 Essay reprinted in John A. Kouwenhoven, *The Beer Can by the Highway* (Garden City, N.Y.: Doubleday, 1961), esp. pp. 42, 62.

34 In *The American Novel,* ed. Wallace Stegner (New York: Basic Books, 1965), pp. 61–72.

35 "Observer," *New York Times,* August 26, 1963.

36 The situation has only intensified since John C. Gerber wrote "Collecting the Works of Mark Twain," in *The Mythologizing of Mark Twain,* ed. Davis and Beidler, pp. 3–14.

37 Tom Quirk, "Huckleberry Finn's Heirs," in *Coming to Grips with "Huckleberry Finn": Essays on a Book, a Boy, and a Man* (Columbia: University of Missouri Press, 1993), p. 107. I admire greatly the extended passage, pp. 107–12.

2

FORREST G. ROBINSON

The Innocent at Large: Mark Twain's Travel Writing

Mark Twain was far and away the most successful travel writer of his time. *The Innocents Abroad,* published in 1869, sold 67,000 copies in its first twelve months in print, reached about 100,000 a year later, and established its author as the nation's premier humorist. *Roughing It,* which appeared in 1872, was a triumph of only slightly less gaudy proportions.[1] His reputation firmly established, Mark Twain enjoyed continued success with "Old Times on the Mississippi" (1875), *A Tramp Abroad* (1880), *Life on the Mississippi* (1883), and *Following the Equator* (1897).

Travel writing well suited the humorist, Richard Bridgman observes, because it freed him "to use his special literary gifts . . . short bursts of pointed observations, anecdotes, episodes, and tales. He could examine the diversity of the world without worrying overmuch about such matters as consistency or transitions." Thanks to "the sequence of the journey itself," the narratives have "at least a simulacrum of coherence." Otherwise they are notably weak in structure. This defect, Bridgman goes on, is the outward manifestation of Mark Twain's groping, usually unresolved meditations on "a world whose ostensible order remained tantalizingly elusive for him." Still, the humorist's digressions can be "importantly revealing" as a guide to "the hidden transactions that the intuition conducts with the "unconscious." It is here, then, in their "psychological patterns" and "brilliant associative sequences" that the deeper interest and meaning of the travel narratives are to be found. Thus, Mark Twain's treatment of an obscure letter from Horace Greeley, a sketch of the Jungfrau, and a fruit called the dorian are plausibly construed as manifestations of the writer's unconscious.[2]

Taking Bridgman's work as my point of departure, I want to propose that within the flow of Mark Twain's associations we can glimpse a pattern, a rough kind of index to the topics that gripped his moral imagination. The stunning variety of human life, as it passes before the traveler's eye, is a constant spur to reflections on the relative success or failure of American "civilization." Thoughts of home are sometimes accompanied by troubling personal memories, most often from childhood. More generally, it is the brevity and uncertainty of life, the universality of cruelty and suffering, and the absence of acceptable explanations for the human lot that impress the traveler. Such grave topics come unsolicited and generally without warning into consciousness. They are endured as tolerances for pain and ambiguity permit, and then dismissed – sometimes with solemnity, sometimes with a jest – from sight and mind. The result is a fitful train of usually brief associations, often intensely focused, loose – even obscure – in their linkages, frequently humorous in tone, but just as frequently geared in their abrupt shifts to the promptings of anger, pain, guilt, and pity. This vigorous, abruptly changeable pattern was not, I think, a generally conscious rhetorical strategy. Rather, it was Mark Twain's way of having it both ways with a world he could neither completely accept nor completely ignore.

At the root of the humorist's discontent lay the knowledge that all mortal things are false. The word "fraud" was forever on his tongue. From his earliest travels to his last tour of the globe, he was impressed most of all with the apparently universal impulse to deceive and the perversely answering impulse to be deceived. Humans balk at the meager fare the world sets before them, yield to the more satisfying prospects present to imagination, suffer the collapse of those happy illusions, and then, no more than half-knowingly, commence the cycle all over again. Meditation in this vein brought Mark Twain to a position not unlike the one advanced by Peter L. Berger and Thomas Luckmann in their classic treatise, *The Social Construction of Reality*. The book contends – as its title clearly suggests – "that reality is socially constructed."[3] The everyday world of assumptions and values and conventions that we take for granted, and that we regard as "natural," is in fact a fabrication, a gradually evolving construction that we inherit from our cultural forbears, inhabit generally without deep misgivings during our lifetime, and hand along in due course to our successors. Social reality, so understood, is a fiction that passes in most company for fact; and happily so, for bereft of our world constructions, say Berger and Luckmann, we would fall prey to anomic terror. "*All* social reality is precarious," they insist. "*All* societies are constructions in the face of chaos."[4]

At the end of *The Mysterious Stranger*, August Feldner learns that "*nothing* exists; all is a dream. God – man – the world, – the sun, the moon, the wilderness of stars: a dream, all a dream."[5] A type of solipsism, this bleak view nonetheless clearly implies that all reality is a human construction, albeit by a society of one. There is a less extreme brand of constructionism on display in *The Innocents Abroad*, when Mark Twain pauses to reflect on the numerous "clean, spacious, comfortable 'grottoes'" that one comes across in the Holy Land and that tourists are encouraged to regard as actual sites of major events in the life of Christ. "It is an imposture – this grotto stuff," he declares; but we should be grateful nonetheless for "the happy rascality" that produced

> these bogus grottoes in the rock; for it is infinitely more satisfactory to look at a grotto where people have faithfully believed for centuries that the Virgin once lived, than to have to imagine a dwelling-place for her somewhere, anywhere, nowhere, loose and at large all over this town of Nazareth. There is too large a scope of country. The imagination cannot work. There is no one particular spot to chain your eye, rivet your interest, and make you think. . . . The old monks are wise. They know how to drive a stake through a pleasant tradition that will hold it to its place forever.[6]

Though perfectly "bogus," the grottoes give faith a foundation to build upon. Religious belief so construed is at once necessary for our individual and social sense of well-being and necessarily the product of illusory human constructions. We acquiesce in fond fabrications, it is suggested, rather than consciously confront the diminished reality the world holds out to us.

Travel fueled Mark Twain's humor because it gave him a window on the manifold deceit and self-deception at large in human social life. It is ironic, of course, that his emergent analysis of the mortal resort to comforting fictions should apply in turn to the "method" of his humorous travel writing. Yet that irony was not entirely lost on him. "Lying is universal," he insists in his essay "On the Decay of the Art of Lying"; "we *all* do it; we all *must* do it" (20: 367). Artful simulation is the key to genuine humor, as he analyzes it in "How to Tell a Story." "Truth is stranger than fiction," he declares in *Following the Equator* – with a knowing glance at his own pretensions to objectivity – "but it is because Fiction is obliged to stick to possibilities; Truth isn't" (5: 155). Thus, the exposure of deceit and self-deception finds its way back to the fitful false starts and distortions, the breakdowns and evasions, of the travel writing itself. Viewed in this light, the travel narratives are a record of Mark Twain's approach over time to a reckoning with his entanglement in the fabricated web of reality.

In the Preface to *The Innocents Abroad* (1869), Mark Twain represents his book as a corrective to the misleading accounts of Europe and the Holy Land written by previous travelers. "I think I have seen with impartial eyes," he boasts, "and I am sure I have written . . . honestly" (1: xxxvii). Yet his narrative is notable for its failure to arrive at a fixed, objective perspective on his experiences abroad. Nothing in the world that he encounters, and nothing in his response to that world, is at all stable or predictable. This is so because the traveler is everywhere confronted with fraudulence. – in merchandise, artifacts, religious relics, and historical sites – and because he is also ready, and even willing, to be taken in by the seductive fakery in his path. The romance of the Old World, especially as it is represented in popular literature and legend, is at times brought down to size, though just as often it paralyzes common sense and triumphs over a reasonable skepticism. Mark Twain is impatient with inflated travel writing, but indulges himself at intervals in the very style he deplores. He is critical of other tourists for their blind surrender to romantic impressions, yet cannot conceal the fact that historical melodramas, not to mention popular travel books, have influenced his own expectations and responses. The record of his visit to Venice well illustrates the general run of things. As he catches sight of the "great city, with its towers and domes and steeples drowsing in a golden mist of sunset," his rhetoric registers the rapid elevation of his mood. But it drops just as abruptly as the landscape comes more clearly into focus. The Venice of his imagination "is departed, and with her crumbling grandeur of wharves and palaces about her she sits among her stagnant lagoons, forlorn and beggared, forgotten of the world" (1: 277–8).

And so it goes. Sharply opposed impressions of the city flash in and out of the traveler's consciousness, and as they do so he is prompted to reflect on the power of perspective in the shaping of our realities. "In the glare of day, there is little poetry about Venice," he writes,

> but under the charitable moon her stained palaces are white again, their battered sculptures are hidden in shadows, and the old city seems crowned once more with the grandeur that was hers five hundred years ago. . . . In the treacherous sunlight we see Venice decayed, forlorn, poverty-stricken, and commerceless – forgotten and utterly insignificant. But in the moonlight, her fourteen centuries of greatness fling their glories about her, and once more is she the princeliest among the nations of the earth. (1: 283–4)

This is no brief for realism. The sunlight is "treacherous," and for that as misleading as "the charitable moon." The "real" Venice is no longer centrally at issue here; rather, it is the mind's power to inhabit antipodal constructions of the same place that holds the traveler's attention.

A heightened awareness of the mind's shaping movements is, of course, an essential step along the way toward the constructionist position. Recognizing as he does that his expectations of Europe and the Holy Land are largely defined by novels, guides, and travel books, the traveler is brought "inevitably," as James M. Cox argues, to the questions "What *is* the true self?" and "Where *is* the genuine emotion as opposed to the spurious?" The answer resides in the characteristic humor of *The Innocents Abroad*, which issues in good part from ridicule by simulation, the conscious "putting on" of foolish attitudes. "Impersonation," Cox insists, is the humorist's "chief art of exposure" – an art carried to such extremes that "burlesque imitation and genuine emotion seem to dissolve into each other." Indeed, we may find ourselves persuaded "that Mark Twain is trapped in his own impersonation," that he has been "gradually forced to yield his identity to a mask." Cox does not in fact believe that the humorist is overtaken by his impersonations. Rather, his shifting postures are adopted on purpose to bring the alert reader to a proper skepticism about the world. "In *The Innocents Abroad*," Cox concludes, "the ultimate truth turns out to be the burlesque spirit of negation impersonating 'genuine' emotion."[7]

Still, there are moments in *The Innocents Abroad* when readers may detect something more deeply felt, something really "personal," pushing past the managed surface of the text. There is little evident simulation, for example, in the angry description of the American tourist who so slavishly imitates European ways that he makes "of himself a thing that is neither male nor female, neither fish, flesh, nor fowl – a poor, miserable, hermaphrodite Frenchman!" (1: 301). Something of the same thing comes across in a curiously inconsistent impersonation of an Italian traveler, liberally endowed "with modern Roman sloth, modern Roman superstition, and modern Roman boundlessness of ignorance," who goes on at length about the awesome superiority of the American way of life. But then, in midparagraph, his attention turns to New World affluence, and awe abruptly gives way to anger. "There is really not much use in being rich, there. Not much use as far as the other world is concerned, but much, very much use, as concerns this; because there, if a man be rich, he is very greatly honored, and can become a legislator, a governor, a general, a senator, no matter how ignorant an ass he is – just as in our beloved Italy the nobles hold all the great places, even though sometimes they are born noble idiots" (1: 339–41). Suddenly the humorous Italian mask grows strained, and beneath its attenuated surface we glimpse the very American face of Mark Twain, disillusioned observer of postbellum venality and future co-author of *The Gilded Age*. The passage, which continues in this vein, dramatizes quite without ironic detachment the painful erosion of national pride. Such extreme and apparently unguarded shifts in tone, here and elsewhere in *The Innocents Abroad*, betray a marked ambivalence about America and a conspicuous incapacity to sustain a tone of humorous impersonation when that subject arises.

Mark Twain's mood is equally brittle at points in his narrative where the romantic contemplation of the Old World leads, quite without warning, to painful perspectives on his personal past. Picturesque Venice forms a threshold in memory to "an overflowed Arkansas town," complete with "a dirty high-water mark on the houses, and with the streets full of mud and rubbish" (1: 283). An effusion on Lake Como leads, for obvious reasons, to a proud comparison with Lake Tahoe, which in turn becomes, by some rather more mysterious associative process, a diatribe on "the Fenimore Cooper Indians" (1: 264). Most upsetting of all, perhaps, the Milan Duomo, which seems to promise a feast of aesthetic pleasures – "Howsoever you look at the great cathedral, it is noble, it is beautiful!" – contains the sculptured figure of a man without skin, "a hideous thing, and yet there was a fascination about it somewhere. I am very sorry I saw it, because I shall always see it, now. I shall dream of it, sometimes. I shall dream that it is resting with its corded arms on the bed's head and looking down on me with its dead eyes." Slowly, obsessively, Mark Twain turns the terrible, strangely familiar specter in his mind, realizing at last that he has seen it and dreamed of it before. "It is hard," he acknowledges wearily, "to forget repulsive things." It is impossible, apparently, to forget that as a boy he once hid at night in his father's law office, only to find himself in close quarters with a corpse. "That man had been stabbed near the office that afternoon, and they carried him in there to doctor him, but he only lived an hour. I have slept in the same room with him often, since then – in my dreams" (1: 226–31).

There are intervals in *The Innocents Abroad,* then, when the veil of impersonation falls abruptly away, revealing strong, vexed feelings coiled up behind the ironic mask. At such moments, we are witness to a mind not so much cool as volatile, not so much detached as deeply divided. Little wonder that Mark Twain gives great emphasis in his narrative to the pleasures of remote perspectives on experience – to moonlit vistas, dreamless sleep, and the amelioration wrought by time on memory. Against this backdrop, his penchant for impersonation may be viewed as a leading manifestation of his effort to "distance" himself from the painful freaks of consciousness brought on by the experience of travel. Detachment for him, as I have elsewhere argued in much greater detail, was not so much an achieved state as an elusive condition of repose, yearned for amid much mental tumult, but never enjoyed for long.[8]

The reality of the Old World in *The Innocents Abroad* is a collaborative construction with foundations deep in romance. The returning pilgrims "will tell of Palestine," Mark Twain predicts, "not as it appeared to *them,* but as it appeared to [the travel authors] Thompson and Robinson and Grimes" (2: 272). If fatigue has somewhat darkened their impressions, no matter, time will work its magic, and the journey "will be an enchanted memory a year hence – a memory which money could not buy from us" (2: 363). The reality of the American West in *Roughing It* (1872) is a similarly collaborative construction, but grounded this time in the lure of opulent wealth. In both narratives the mind feeds on images that win assent even as they betray their lack of real substance. And in both narratives the mind's willing acquiescence in the world's manifold deceit emerges as a leading focus for reflection. But in *Roughing It* the personal stakes in the play of illusion are higher, the bitterness of the inevitable fall is greater, and the dismay at the spectacle of human contradiction is deeper.

As Henry Nash Smith long ago pointed out, the "voice" of the tenderfoot narrator in *Roughing It* is from the very outset mingled with that of "the veteran," who takes a sardonic view of his callow youth. The contrast between the two voices implies a "judgment upon the tenderfoot's innocence and a corresponding claim for the superior maturity and sophistication of the old-timer" and "is the consequence of precisely that journey which the book will describe."[9] Primed as he is to believe that easy riches await him on the mining frontier, the tenderfoot's journey illustrates in bold relief the play of deceit and self-deception in human experience. The characteristic humor of *Roughing It* turns on the sudden, often painful deflation of wildly exaggerated expectations. Like many others in California and Nevada at the time, the narrator is infected with what historian Gilman M. Ostrander describes as "the Comstock fever," a "vision of a whole mountain of gold and silver [which] overwhelmed the senses of thousands of investors and brought them to financial ruin." Here was a potently seductive construction of reality, utterly at odds with the objective evidence, yet so appealing to the victim's self-interest as to subdue his common sense entirely.[10]

The traveler is not far along toward Eldorado before he encounters a famous desperado named Slade – a man at once gentle and savage, heroic and degraded, fearless and craven, whose example illustrates that appearances cannot be trusted and that human behavior "is a conundrum worth investigating" (7: 98). Slade's example is an apt prologue to the narrative that follows, in which Mark Twain comes face to face with a world literally formed out of misleading illusions. Politics, he learns, is a front for venality and gross self-interest. The legal system, rife with hidden ignorance and corruption, is an obstacle to justice. The police, though ostensibly the servants of justice, are in his eyes "the dust-licking pimps and slaves of the scum" (8: 135). A crooked assayer is forced out of business not because he is dishonest, but because his success stirs the envy of his equally deceitful competitors. And American missionaries are pious hypocrites, though they are no more subject to Mark Twain's ridicule than their victims, the Hawaiians. It is simply a case of moral idiots in the hands of moral idiots.

More crucially, in discovering that the world is throughout deceptive the narrator also learns, to his deep chagrin, that he is himself quite easily taken in. Indeed, there is a neat but devastating symmetry to the situation. The world is replete with deceivers; but the deceivers are also pitifully self-deceived. This is, of course, the lesson writ large in the experience of the mining frontier, where the rumor of a bonanza opened the way to every variety of fraud and folly. "The most certain way of deceiving was to tell the truth," wrote Eliot Lord, a contemporary witness, "for the exact opposite would then be commonly believed."[11] Prolonged exposure to such ubiquitous deception could, one imagines, foster a kind of healthy skepticism – something on the order of the sophistication, maturity, knowledge, and wisdom that Smith has in mind. As Mark Twain represents it, however, the revelation of the world's manifold illusions issues in cynicism and in a gathering contempt for both self and others.

This is hardly to deny that *Roughing It* is liberally laced with intervals of youthful ebullience and outrageous humor – moments that contrast sharply with the developing pessimism I have described. The result is a narrative pattern of flow and reflux, of rapidly alternating emotional currents. This radical swing between opposed states, a leading symptom of the mining frontier "boom pathology," is conspicuous in the mingled voice of the narrator. Yet even as it forms a comic counterpoint to the crumbling moral fabric that the tenderfoot perceives and reacts to, the humor of *Roughing It* takes its rise from the discovery of hollowness, pointlessness, collapsed illusions, willful deception, hapless self-deception, and defeat. This is increasingly the case in the later sections of the book, when the comedy forms a kind of epicycle to a progressively more dominant downward curve into disillusionment. Rooted in the perception of shifting surfaces and unreliable appearances, and registering formally in the narrator's distinctive tone, this evolving pattern binds the parts of *Roughing It,* scattered as they are geographically, into a tentative but discernible unity.

I am strongly inclined, then, to replace Smith's mature veteran with an increasingly bitter cynic. There is little of wisdom or sophistication in the narrator's declaration that he will "go about of an afternoon . . . and pick up two or three pailfuls of shining slugs and nuggets of gold and silver on the hillside" (7: 16). The irony that cuts through the simulated innocence is bitter for the simple reason that it is freighted with self-contempt. The same sentiment is much more dramatically evident in a familiar episode involving a coyote, "a long, slim, sick and sorry-looking skeleton, with a gray wolf-skin stretched over it, a tolerably bushy tail that forever sags down with a despairing expression of forsakenness and misery, a furtive and evil eye, and a long, sharp face, with slightly lifted lip and exposed teeth." For all of his apparent destitution, the despicable coyote has a way of asserting himself. When pursued by an ambitious and overconfident dog, he contrives to prolong the chase until the frustrated pursuer is far from his wagon. Only then does the coyote exercise his real speed, leaving his victim "solitary and alone in the midst of a vast solitude!" The humiliated dog "jogs along back to his train, and takes up a humble position under the hindmost wagon, and feels unspeakably mean, and looks ashamed, and hangs his tail at half-mast for a week" (7: 48–51).

Smith argues quite persuasively that "this anecdote summarizes Mark Twain's imaginative interpretation of the Far West. It involves a tenderfoot with a higher opinion of himself than he can make good in the frontier environment; a veteran who looks disreputable (and is disreputable, by town-bred standards) but is nevertheless in secure command of the situation; and the process by which the tenderfoot gains knowledge, quite fresh and new knowledge, at the cost of humiliation to himself."[12] While this is certainly a seminal episode and while inflated self-esteem clearly figures in the tenderfoot's downfall, it is a strain on the evidence to confer wisdom, knowledge, maturity, and sophistication on the coyote, or to describe him, as Mr. Smith does at another point, as "a triumphant and heroic figure, endowed with supernatural powers."[13] The coyote is disreputable not simply by town standards, but by *any* standard. He is an odious fraud who evens his score with Fate by seducing innocent fools into the humiliating exposure of their folly. Nor does the dog acquire wisdom and knowledge from his painful experience. He acquires precisely what the coyote wants him to acquire: a powerful insight into the cruel consequences of trusting appearances and a shattering revelation of his own vanity and capacity for self-deception. The dog is not educated or initiated; he is utterly crushed.

By Smith's calculus, the net psychological result of the dog's experience should be reflected in the wisdom and maturity of the voice that presides over the incident. But in fact the narrator admires the coyote's gratuitous cruelty only slightly less than he relishes the shattering humiliation of the dog. "If you start a swift-footed dog after" the coyote, he says, "you will enjoy it ever so much – especially if it is a dog that has a good opinion of himself" (7: 49). Quite true, the speaker here is an insider and an old-timer;

just as certainly, this is a voice that bespeaks an experience in the Far West not at all unlike the dog's. But it is emphatically not a wise voice, or a mature voice. That the narrator is familiar with crushing humiliation is no less evident than the fact that he takes positive pleasure in seeing it inflicted on others. Indeed, as a result of his rough initiation into the ways of the mining frontier, he has become, with the coyote, a dedicated and extremely accomplished practical joker.

Practical jokes are not funny; nor are they intended to be. They are intended to hurt, to expose and humiliate. While we must deplore the malice of the practical joker, we must also pity him, for his joke will succeed only if he is capable of putting himself, at least imaginatively, in the place of his intended victim. Indeed, it is probably fair to assume that most practical jokers have in fact experienced the hurt and humiliating exposure they inflict on others, for the hurt and humiliation explain what is otherwise extraordinary – the malicious impulse that prompts the contriving and the execution of the joke. By extension, it is difficult to conceive of a successful practical joke born, as it were, *ab ovo*. Rather, one practical joke is the child of an earlier practical joke, and that of another, and so on in a sequence suggesting that a practical joke, however trivial in itself, is the manifestation of a sustained, repeating, and possibly accelerating historical cycle. Where the joking started is a conundrum worth investigating. In *Roughing It* the joke starts in the first paragraph and goes on for hundreds of pages. The victims, numerous and scattered as they are, form an aggregate that points back to an innocence-shattering practical joke from which the narrator never recovered, and through myriad repetitions to a kind of ur–practical joke that has deeply penetrated the culture of the mining frontier.

This is to say that the form of *Roughing It* – its narrative voice, its disconnected anecdotal rhythm, and its characteristic humor – is a principal bearer of its meaning. William Dean Howells was particularly astute in observing that his friend's exaggerations and ironies were ideal rhetorical devices for describing the Far West. "All existence there," he wrote, "must have looked like an extravagant joke, the humor of which was only deepened by its nether-side of tragedy."[14]

Life on the Mississippi (1883) is the most haunted of Mark Twain's travel books. It confirms in an especially emphatic way our notion that the confusion brought on by travel is manifest both in the content of his writing and in its form. The record of his return to the Mississippi in 1882, the narrative is a patchwork of anecdotes and recollections, featuring eruptions of painful personal memory and seemingly random reflections on the horrors of the

Civil War and the cruelty of the human lot. The world is false, life is brief, and there are no explanations. True, the narrative includes passages of humor and several extended meditations on the beauty and serenity of the great river, but these serve as intervals of relief from the book's dominant gravity of tone.

The conspicuous exception to this general characterization appears in the first third of *Life on the Mississippi,* chapters 4–17, which were originally published in 1875 as a series of seven sketches – entitled "Old Times on the Mississippi" – for the *Atlantic Monthly.* When Mark Twain got down to making a travel book out of his experiences on the river in 1882, he simply incorporated the sketches wholesale into the beginning of his narrative. The "Old Times" chapters are a warmly nostalgic account of the humorist's boyhood initiation into the elite fraternity of Mississippi riverboat pilots. Like the tenderfoot in *Roughing It,* the "cub" pilot comes to his new experience with a head full of romantic illusions that make him vulnerable to all manner of falls. Unlike his predecessor, however, the young narrator in "Old Times" learns from his mistakes and rapidly rises to the maturity and sophistication expected of him in his high calling. His education proceeds through a series of practical jokes designed to reveal to him the danger of trusting illusions – those he harbors about himself and those the river sets in his way. But he looks back with gratitude upon his mentors, those veteran pilots who "wisely" trained him "by various strategic tricks to look danger in the face a little more calmly. A favorite way of theirs," he recalls, was "to play a friendly swindle upon the candidate" (9: 115).

The element of deception is most perilous and irreducible in the Mississippi itself, for its face is inherently unreliable – "eluding and ungraspable" (9: 75), in Mark Twain's words. Thus, the cub's education reaches its completion only when he learns to penetrate to the truth beneath the river's misleading surface. As a result of his having "mastered the language" of the Mississippi, however, he finds that "all the grace, the beauty, [and] the poetry, had gone out of the majestic river!" (9: 83). But his professions of regret are belied by numerous subsequent reveries on the river's beauty and by the sentiments that attach to his grand achievement. "I loved the profession far better than any I have followed since," he declares, "and I took a measureless pride in it" (9: 119). The sense of mastery over an elusive but finally manageable reality is the key to the genial tone of "Old Times." The tenderfoot endures a number of falls, but his innocence and suffering are retrospective simulations, controlled and thereby neutralized in the genial good humor that comes with success and maturity.

"Old Times" surveys the past from a relatively remote vantage; it unfolds as a formally integrated, highly self-conscious construction of a past held comfortably at arm's length. The rest of *Life on the Mississippi* is also about the past, even the same past, but it is composed of memories much more recently formed, or re-formed, during the return journey to the river. The freshness and relative proximity of the impressions make all the difference in the quality of the narrative. Where "Old Times" is unified and coherent, *Life* is fragmentary, episodic, without clear focus, utterly erratic in tone, padded with seemingly irrelevant "filler," and a mine field of unconscious eruptions and fretful evasions.[15] It is as though Mark Twain's worst nightmares, many of them held safely at bay in the earlier narrative, rose to within striking distance of his consciousness, and therefore of his equanimity, during the return journey to the river.

The contrast in tone is nowhere more graphically evident than at that point in *Life on the Mississippi* where the "Old Times" chapters give way to the more recently completed narrative. The transition from old to new turns on an account of the 1858 sinking of the steamboat *Pennsylvania*, a fiery accident that took the life of Henry Clemens, the writer's younger brother. I have elsewhere analyzed Mark Twain's lifelong remorse over Henry's death, with detailed attention to its recurrent appearance in his writings.[16] Suffice it here to say that the memory's resurfacing in *Life on the Mississippi* precipitates a general transformation of tone most strikingly manifest in the figure of Brown, a pilot who appears first in "Old Times" as a garrulous but utterly harmless old fool. When he reappears in the *Pennsylvania* episode, Brown has become a vicious tyrant who makes life on board the steamboat intolerable for both the Clemens brothers. Linked as he is with Henry's death, the offending pilot makes a convenient target for Mark Twain's repressed self-reproach, which surfaces in a broadside of righteous wrath. "I often wanted to kill Brown, but this would not answer," he recalls. "However, I could *imagine* myself killing Brown. . . . I threw business aside for pleasure, and killed Brown. I killed Brown every night for months" (9: 162–3).

This initial resurgence of conflicted, explosive emotion sets the tone for much that follows in *Life on the Mississippi*. Quite suddenly, and for no apparent reason, the narrator's consciousness is overtaken by memories of long-forgotten horrors and catastrophes. For example, a rapturous description of a Mississippi sunrise – "one of the fairest and softest pictures imaginable" – is followed, without transition, by the memory of a man who, in attempting to save his wife's life, inadvertently crushes her skull (9: 242–3). The prolonged agony of the Civil War is everywhere present to mind, most painfully at Vicksburg; there is a pervasive sense of moral disorder, best exemplified perhaps in the tormented story of Karl Ritter; and the history of the South unfolds as a chronicle of fraud and mass self-deception. The pattern grows especially pronounced as Mark Twain's attention turns to Hannibal and to memories of his childhood. Standing on a hill overlooking the sleeping village, he is struck by an intimation that his nostalgic feelings for the place may themselves be vulnerable to sudden, jarring transformations. As James M. Cox has observed, the memories that surface when he descends from the hill, like the earlier memories of Henry, are "essentially guilt fantasies cast in the form of nostalgic recollections and boyhood adventures."[17] These go on at great length and conclude – predictably – in the recollection of a guilt-laden encounter with his long dead brother.

In the course of enduring the perverse play of his memory, Mark Twain makes numerous retreats to alternative, much less troubled states of mind. In the immediate sequel to his account of the bloody Darnell–Watson feud, for example, he is drawn to the great river, with its "majestic, unchanging sameness of serenity, repose, tranquility, lethargy, vacancy, – symbol of eternity, realization of the heaven pictured by priest and prophet, and longed for by the good and thoughtless!" (9: 213). The Mississippi appears to him in a similar guise toward the end of his narrative, where "it is," he finds, "as tranquil and reposeful as dreamland, and has nothing this-worldly about it – nothing to hang a fret or a worry upon" (9: 432). Leaving the South is also a source of relief, for it bears him away from reminders of that personal and regional past that so unsettles him. "From St. Louis northward," he reports, "there are all the enlivening signs of the presence of active, energetic, intelligent, prosperous, practical nineteenth-century populations. The people don't dream; they work. The happy result is manifest all around in the substantial outside aspect of things, and the suggestions of wholesome life and comfort that everywhere appear" (9: 421). Enough, then, of surrender to the treacherous currents of mind and memory. Dwell instead with the "substantial outside aspect of things"; or, alternatively, take refuge in the oblivion, the total "vacancy" of mind, represented by the Mississippi.

The shifting content and tone of *Life on the Mississippi* are thus geared in a significant way to the emergence and dispersal of discordancies in the mind of the narrator. This is hardly a self-conscious phenomenon. Indeed, that the pattern is undetected and therefore largely uncontrolled helps to account for the harried, rather fretful mood that so often overtakes the narrative. Still, in ways reminiscent of the earlier travel writings, Mark Twain does at points pause to reflect on the vagaries of consciousness. "The happenings and the impressions" of childhood "are burned into my memory," he acknowledges, but "the study of them entertains me as much now as they themselves distressed me then" (9: 415–16). The pain of youthful remorse has been replaced, he insists, by the detached scrutiny of the curious mental processes which produced that earlier suffering. Clearly cognate with such reflections are his periodic resorts in *Life on the Mississippi* to a variety of incognitos and to the dawning recognition that identity is a fiction, a negotiable construction subject to change. In relating how he "confiscated" the pseudonym "Mark Twain" from Isaiah Sellers, for example, the narrator pledges, with knowing irony, that the name will serve as the "sign and symbol and warrant that whatever is found in its company may be gambled on as being the petrified truth" (9: 371). He arrives at a similar position on the construction of emotions, which are, he observes, "among the toughest things in the world to manufacture out of whole cloth; it is easier to manufacture seven facts than one emotion" (9: 214). We feel what we are taught to feel, just as we see what we are taught to see. A fine oil painting "representing Stonewall Jackson's last interview with General Lee," he wryly declares, "means nothing without its label. And one label will fit it as well as another" (9: 332).

The constructedness of more broadly based social realities is also brought home to the Mississippi traveler. In his chapter "The House Beautiful," for example, he reflects humorously on the random ugliness and clutter that somehow pass with genteel Southerners for elegance in interior design. The irrationality of Southern attitudes toward cremation and embalming is also an index to the simultaneous authority and cynical exploitation of outmoded fictions. "It's human nature – human nature in grief. It don't reason, you see. . . . All it wants is physical immortality for [the] deceased, and they're willing to pay for it" (9: 326). Most crucially, Mark Twain is struck with the cultural currency among Southerners of Sir Walter Scott's novels. The South stood to gain immeasurably, he insists, by the example of the French Revolution and Napoleon, with their "great and permanent services to liberty, humanity, and progress." But

> then comes Sir Walter Scott with his enchantments, and by his single might checks this wave of progress, and even turns it back; sets the world in love with dreams and phantoms; with decayed and swinish forms of religion; with decayed and degraded systems of government; with the sillinesses and emptinesses, sham grandeurs, sham gauds, and sham chivalries of a brainless and worthless long-vanished society. He did measureless harm; more real and lasting harm, perhaps, than any other individual that ever wrote. (9: 347)

The plausibility of Mark Twain's argument aside, his angry critique of "the Sir Walter disease" is testimony to a close, conscious awareness of the power of fictions to define vital aspects of social experience. Scott's Romantic medievalism, however bogus and misplaced it may have been, gave life in the South to a culture of rank and caste and honor and purity that was ultimately responsible, Mark Twain insists, for the Civil War. All of this is irresistibly clear to the traveler, who returns to find that the world which once seemed so "natural" to him now appears a perverse, profoundly tragic fabrication.

From the critical point of view adopted here, A Tramp Abroad (1880) is the least interesting of the travel books. It includes the usual grousing about the fakery that tourists must endure, but the complaints never rise to a more general view of the human condition. Literary posturing and absurd artistic conventions come up for their share of abuse, but the humorous commentary does not open on constructionist perspectives. Identity – its varieties and their negotiation – is never significantly an issue. There are occasional flashes from the past, painful memory traces that rise momentarily toward the surface of consciousness. The mockery of French duelists triggers a brief, glancing recollection of the narrator's craven retreat, years earlier, from a showdown in Virginia City (3: 70).[18] His equally humorous rendering of a boyhood dream about Mississippi steamboat "explosions, and conflagrations, and sudden death" (3: 91) betrays the deeper, more troubled preoccupation with poor Henry's undoing on the *Pennsylvania*. And a series of associations involving dentists, doctors, and death leads in turn, as Richard Bridgman has observed, to skeletons, and thence to Jimmy Finn, the Hannibal drunkard who sold his body to the village doctor for the price of a terminal binge (3: 228–33).[19] But, again, such dark episodes, while familiar enough, do not so dominate the narrative as to constitute a major pattern.

There is something fundamentally distracted about A Tramp Abroad. Mark Twain most certainly took the trip that he records in its pages, but we have the strong impression as we read that his mind was frequently elsewhere. It is telling in this regard that his painful flashes of memory are all of episodes that he treats more fully in books written just before or just after this one. Most of the best things in the narrative – "Jim Baker's Bluejay Yarn," "The Man Who Put Up at Gadsby's," the story of Nicodemus Dodge – have no clear connection to the journey itself, and are dragged in to leaven what is otherwise pretty flat going. Mark Twain took no pleasure in the composition of A Tramp Abroad, and at times he despaired of ever completing it. "I have been fighting a life-&-death battle with this infernal book," he complained to William Dean Howells at the beginning of 1880.[20] "I want to make a book which people will *read*," he explained in an earlier letter of his friend, "& I shall make it profitable reading in spots – in spots merely *because* there's not much material for a larger amount."[21] Justin Kaplan reports that when he mislaid one of the two notebooks for the volume, Mark Twain was relieved because the project was "simply impossible" without it. "Down went my heart into my boots," he complained, when the missing notes were found.[22]

The distractedness of *A Tramp Abroad* may be traced to the fact that the book records a journey that stirred very little enthusiasm in Mark Twain. "Formerly I went Abroad as an Innocent," he observes in an unpublished preface, "but this time, fortified with experience and guile, I went Abroad as a Tramp."[23] The traveler disburdened of inflated expectations is no longer prey to painful disenchantment, and thus brings to the narrative of his journey no ambivalent mingling of perspectives and of selves. Mark Twain had no illusions about what to expect on his tour through Germany, France, and Italy. He disliked the trip; he disliked writing about it; and the result, as he glimpsed in a letter to Howells, was the loss of the tension so vital to his earlier travel narratives. "I *hate* travel," he fumed to his friend, "& I *hate* the opera, and I *hate* the Old Masters – in truth I don't ever seem to be in a good enough humor with ANYthing to *satirize* it; no, I want to stand up before it & *curse* it, & foam at the mouth, – or take a club & pound it to rags & pulp."[24]

Mark Twain knew that such strong, uniformly negative sentiments had no place in his book. But he recognized as well that the humorous style of his earlier travel narratives, embodied in the complex persona of the tenderfoot/veteran, was not readily emergent from the materials at hand. In the upshot, his irritation with all that the journey entailed found its antidote in a mood of aimless wandering – "a lazy, delightful, irresponsible high-holiday time on the road," as he puts it.[25] The true charm of travel in this mindless key, Mark Twain assures us in *A Tramp Abroad*, lies not "in the walking, or in the scenery, but in the talking." He goes on to describe a species of conversation whose genial meandering reminds us of nothing quite so much as *A Tramp Abroad* itself. "It is no matter whether one talks wisdom or nonsense, the case is the same, the bulk of the enjoyment lies in the wagging of the gladsome jaw and the flapping of the sympathetic ear" (3: 225–6).

Such talk, on a course going nowhere – or, more precisely, going anywhere *except* toward discord – has a close physical analogue, and its ideal setting, in the aimless drift of a raft on a broad river. "The motion of the raft is the needful motion," Mark Twain observes, in a passage that brings *Huckleberry Finn* immediately to mind. "It is gentle, and gliding, and smooth, and noiseless; it calms down all feverish activities, it soothes to sleep all nervous hurry and impatience; under its restful influence all the troubles and vexations and sorrows that harass the mind vanish away, and existence becomes a dream, a charm, a deep and tranquil ecstasy" (3: 123–4). Such serene, oblivious drifting, like the easy, wandering talk it so much resembles, speaks obliquely of an antipodal state of mind held at bay on the surrounding shores of consciousness.

Like *A Tramp Abroad*, *Following the Equator* was a trial to its author, both in the travel itself and in the writing about it. The record of a global lecture tour undertaken to repay the enormous debts resulting from his bankruptcy in 1894, the enterprise was weighed down with assorted tribulations that culminated at journey's end in the shattering news of his daughter Susy's sudden death. Composition was understandably an ordeal, though Mark Twain emerged confident that he had successfully concealed his true feelings of anguish and fatigue. "This book has not exposed me," he wrote to his benefactor, Henry Huttleston Rogers. "I would rather be hanged, drawn and quartered than write it again. All the heart I had was in Susy's grave and the Webster debts. And so, behold a miracle! – a book which does not give its writer away."[26]

The same claim made of *A Tramp Abroad* would seem plausible enough. But it is striking confirmation of Mark Twain's notorious blindness to the deeper drift of his writing that he so thoroughly misgauged the actual tone and purport of *Following the Equator*. Its humorous interludes notwithstanding, the book is first and foremost a troubled, often angry report on the misery wrought by Western imperialism along the equatorial black belt. The narrator's dark sentiments register most memorably in dozens of brief, sharply ironic observations on human greed, cruelty, self-delusion, and suffering. These barbed generalizations appear everywhere in the text, but most frequently and predictably in the maxims (excerpted from Pudd'nhead Wilson's New Calendar) that appear as epigraphs to each of the book's seventy chapters. Though the gravity of their humor varies, the maxims are most memorable for their mordant commentary, sometimes direct, sometimes oblique, on the painful spectacle that falls open to the traveler's eye. "Pity is for the living," we are told, "envy is for the dead" (5: 189). "Man is the Only Animal that Blushes. Or needs to" (5: 264). And perhaps most tellingly of all: "Everything human is pathetic. The secret source of Humor itself is not joy but sorrow. There is no humor in heaven" (5: 119).[27]

Mark Twain's misconstruction of his last travel book is no more striking perhaps than the revelation of his desire to conceal his deeper feelings. The letter to Rogers on this score is echoed in another to Howells. "I wrote my last travel-book in hell," he admits; "but I let on, the best I could, that it was an excursion through heaven. Some day I will read it, & if its lying cheerfulness fools me, then I shall believe it fooled the reader. How I did loathe that journey around the world! – except the sea-part & India."[28] The characteristic impulse to submerge painful discordancies is one of several elements common to the travel narratives. Another is Mark Twain's imperfect success in his "lying cheerfulness" and the familiar tonal ambivalence – the rapid movement back and forth between opposed emotional states – that results. These and other recurrent elements are notably on display in the traveler's sharply shifting responses to India. In Bombay he is at first wide-eyed with delight at the physical beauty of the people and the brilliant "color, bewitching color, enchanting color." But before long "the land of dreams and romance," with its "soft and gentle race," is painfully transformed. A burly German tourist, irritated at some minor offense, suddenly strikes his Indian servant. "I had not seen the like of this for fifty years," Mark Twain observes. "It carried me back to my boyhood, and flashed upon me the forgotten fact that this was the *usual* way of explaining one's desires to a slave." Running darkly through his memories, which descend in a rush, is a burden of guilt that the emergent, constructionist perspective on the moral ideology of slavery cannot completely dispel. Striking slaves "seemed right and natural" when he was a boy, "I being born to it and unaware that elsewhere there were other methods; but I was also able to remember that those unresented cuffings made me sorry for the victim and ashamed for the punisher." He allows that his father's physical abuse of slaves "proceeded from the custom of the time, not from his nature." But such mitigating appeals to convention give way under the memory of a brutal killing of a slave "for merely doing something awkwardly – as if that were a crime." Custom in this instance is not enough to obscure the face of iniquity. "Nobody in the village approved of that murder, but of course no one said much about it" (6: 25–9).

This furtive, troubled train of thought comes partially to rest in a reflexive turn inward on itself, as Mark Twain dilates on the mystery of his own mental processes. "It is curious," he remarks rather coolly, "the space-annihilating power of thought. For just one second, all that goes to make the *me* in me was in a Missourian village, on the other side of the globe, vividly seeing again these forgotten pictures of fifty years ago, and wholly unconscious of all things but just those; and in the next second I was back in Bombay, and that kneeling native's smitten cheek was not done tingling yet!" It is the speed, the intensity, and above all else the independence of the mind's charged movements that impress him. Both the world and the self, he recognizes, are coextensive with consciousness – with the "space-annihilating" dance of images across the rapt mind's eye. "Back to boyhood – fifty years; back to age again, another fifty; and a flight equal to the circumference of the globe – all in two seconds by the watch!" (6: 29–30).

Such guilty memories, surging upward into consciousness even in the midst of a spectacle of bright, distracting color, have their part in the traveler's retrospective recoil from the nightmare of his journey. For it is not the reader's equanimity alone that prompts the narrator's recourse to "lying cheerfulness"; it is his own as well. The trajectory of Mark Twain's interior journey is telling in this regard. His consciousness moves first from present to past – with an accompanying increase in the human suffering on display, and to a sharper, more precise focusing of personal guilt – and then, as if in retreat from the pain, back to the present. Indeed, his remarks on "the space-annihilating power of thought," for all of their brilliance, are integral to the cooling down, for they remove attention from what is profoundly troubling in the scene to what is merely "curious" in the mechanisms of its projection.

Strategies of moral and emotional withdrawal are obliquely the subject of what immediately follows in the narrative, an apparently unrelated, humorous tribute to the Indian crow. This utterly enigmatic bird, "the hardest lot that wears feathers," is admirable in Mark Twain's eyes because it enjoys complete immunity to guilt. "One can't make a bird like that in a day," he insists. Rather, the Indian crow "has been incarnated more times than Shiva," but always – in "his sublime march toward ultimate perfection" – as a scoundrel of one kind or another. "The strange result, the incredible result, of this patient accumulation of all damnable traits is, that he does not know what care is, he does not know what sorrow is, he does not know what remorse is; his life is one long thundering ecstasy of happiness, and he will go on to his death untroubled, knowing that he will soon turn up again as an author or something, and be even more intolerably capable and comfortable than ever he was before" (6: 30–1). Blithely fanciful as it may appear, the humor of the passage is rooted in the questions about sin, guilt, and the mysteries of consciousness that surface more openly in the foregoing section on slavery. By the darkly humorous logic of the Indian crow's example, sin will disappear from the world only in the mind of those most immersed in it. Happiness, defined negatively as immunity to sorrow and remorse, is the exclusive province of reprobates – writers prominent among them – so familiar with iniquity that it no longer stirs their concern. Here, then, is constructionism taken in fantasy to a pathological extreme, where only the completely fallen enjoy peace.

Mark Twain's esteem for the Indian crow is, of course, a humorous simulation. As his two-second journey from India to Missouri and back again makes clear, he has none of the hardened sinner's indifference to misery and guilt. To the contrary, his humorous reflections evince an array of sentiments, none of them compatible with the achievement of the blissful complacency attributed to the fabulous crow. Most obvious, perhaps, is a weariness of sorrow and remorse for human suffering, especially for the suffering of slaves in America, and most especially for the suffering of the slaves in his personal past. There is also a kind of pride to be glimpsed in the oblique admission that he is not the kind of "author or something" that the crow is likely to become in his next incarnation. Finally, there is the acknowledgment, no less weary or oblique, that his mind's penchant for sudden, morally and emotionally painful associative leaps shows no signs of slackening.

This very striking section aptly illustrates both the strong lines of continuity between *Following the Equator* and the earlier travel books and the subtle differences between them. There is the characteristic drift – along largely unconscious lines of association – into vexing moral questions as they emerge from personal memory and from reflections on the state of the nation. Race and slavery are persistent, troubling intrusions into consciousness. Life is brief; human nature is corrupt; the direction and significance of things are obscure. Social reality and individual identity, in their variety and mutability, are manifest constructions, fictions rooted in self-interest and the need for order. In the midst of much that is familiar, however, *Following the Equator* displays a greater gravity of tone – more attention to the world's woe, with less, and less ebullient, humor – than the earlier travel books, and a tendency on Mark Twain's part to include himself more fully in the joke, or in the trouble, that occupies the focus of his consciousness. Sobered and chastened no doubt by the adversity of his advancing years, the humorist is less prone than in the past to retreat from painful subjects, and more empathetic and compassionate in his responses, than ever before. He is able, for example, to locate and accept the jest in a practical joke at his own expense (5: 256); he is everywhere sensitive to the suffering of the poor and oppressed; and he readily acknowledges that talk, even the best and brightest kind of talk in which he specializes, is a poor substitute for proper action. "To be good is noble," he observes, with an ironic eye to his moralizing maxims; "but to show others how to be good is nobler and no trouble" (5: v).

The mingling of old and new in *Following the Equator* is most conspicuous perhaps in Mark Twain's preoccupation with the widespread fraudulence to be found among the people of the world. Humanity is simply immersed in lies – "The principal difference between a cat and a lie," we read, "is that the cat has only nine lives" (6: 320) – and in all manner of "interested" fictions – "The very ink with which history is written is merely fluid prejudice" (6: 392). Having adopted this harsh view, however, Mark Twain is quick to take a place at the front rank of the frauds. "Truth is stranger than fiction – to some people, but I am measurably familiar with it" (5: 155). "The whole secret" to lying, he insists, with an air of authority, "is in the manner and method of" the telling. "I never could tell a lie that anybody would doubt," he admits, "nor a truth that anybody would believe" (6: 308–10). Deceit has its corollary in varieties of self-deception, most flagrantly and perniciously on display among the Western colonial powers everywhere in evidence along the black belt of the globe. "There are many humorous things in the world," the traveler observes, "among them the white man's notion that he is less savage than the other savages" (5: 216). He cannot restrain an angry thrust at European slave drivers who fail utterly to understand why their activities are not popular with native populations. So pervasive, in fact, is Western deceit and self-deception that its influence is discernible even in matters of dress. "Yes," he insists, "our clothes are a lie, and have been nothing short of that these hundred years. They are insincere, they are the ugly and appropriate outward exposure of an inward sham and a moral decay" (6: 22).

But even as he takes aim at Western hypocrisy, Mark Twain casts a grateful eye on the results of colonialism. India of old was a brutal place; but now, thanks to the British, the country has the benefit of new "factories, schools, hospitals, reforms" (6: 68). Colonization "was the best service that was ever done to the Indians themselves, those wretched heirs of a hundred centuries of pitiless oppression and abuse" (6: 202). "In our day," he concedes, "land-robbery, claim-jumping, is become a European governmental frenzy." But such aggressiveness is a staple of history. "All the territorial possessions of all the political establishments in the earth – including America, of course – consist of pilferings from other people's wash. No tribe, howsoever insignificant, and no nation, howsoever mighty, occupies a foot of land that was not stolen." Nor is "land-robbery" always a bad thing. "All the savage lands in the world," he predicts, "are going to be brought under subjection to the Christian governments of Europe. I am not sorry, but glad. . . . The sooner the seizure is consummated, the better for the savages. The dreary and dragging ages of bloodshed and disorder and oppression will give place to peace and order and the reign of law" (6: 321–4).

Mark Twain's vision of a world in peace under Euro-American domination was more wish than moral certainty. And no amount of wishful thinking could reconcile him to the pious rationalizations of colonial ideology. Still, he acknowledges that such lies are part and parcel of the world, even a peaceful world; they come, much to his chagrin, with the territory. Pretensions to right thinking are a sham, self-interested constructions designed, as often as not unconsciously, to conceal – both from the self and from others – departures from public standards of truth and justice. "There is a Moral Sense," Mark Twain observes, "and there is an Immoral Sense. History shows us that the Moral Sense enables us to perceive morality and how to avoid it, and that the Immoral Sense enables us to perceive immorality and how to enjoy it" (5: 162). Thus, the unacknowledged objective among humans is to have things both ways. This is especially the case, perhaps, when it comes to the dark predator at large in our natures. "The joy of killing!" Mark Twain exclaims, in reflecting on the murderous Indian Thugs; "the joy of seeing killing done – these are the traits of the human race at large. We white people are merely modified Thugs; Thugs fretting under the restraints of a not very thick skin of civilization" (6: 125).

Witness as he is to the variety and fathomless complexity of the human condition – "We dwellers in the world are strangely made," he concedes (5: 323) – the traveler is prompted at intervals to adopt a constructionist perspective. The belief in the superior beauty of white skin, he observes, is a fiction widespread among Europeans and Americans, but difficult to sustain "when it comes into competition with masses of brown and black" (6: 63). He is equally dismissive of the happy illusion that the world was created with human welfare in mind. "Nature makes the locust with an appetite for crops; man would have made him with an appetite for sand" (5: 297). Our individual and collective beliefs do not so much reflect the world as they do our wishful accommodations to it. The contradictions that result – "Dear me! It is a strange world" (6: 210) – begin to make sense to Mark Twain when he reflects that "custom makes incongruous things congruous" (6: 88). "Let me make the superstitions of a nation," he goes on in the same vein, "and I care not who makes its laws or its songs either" (6: 179). The word, he recognizes, is a leading agent in the formation of human social constructions. "Language is a treacherous thing, a most unsure vehicle, and it can seldom arrange descriptive words in such a way that they will not inflate the facts – by help of the reader's imagination, which is always ready to take a hand" (6: 270). As Susan Gillman has very aptly observed, such passages clearly anticipate the constructionist emphasis in Mark Twain's dream tales, which he took up just days after finishing *Following the Equa-*

tor. These narratives spell out with impressive clarity the traveler's insight into the human dependency on fictions of law and custom.[29]

In his darkest moods, which descended with increasing frequency as he grew older, Mark Twain was inclined to want to withdraw altogether from the heartbreaking falsity and hollowness of the world. At such times he craved utter oblivion, the blessed surcease of the mind's commerce in illusions. Relief of this sort overtook him as his ship left the troubling spectacle of India behind. "The world is far, far away; it has ceased to exist for you – seemed a fading dream along in the first days; has dissolved to an unreality now" (6: 313). But during those much longer intervals when the darkness lifted, Mark Twain's view of the world combined contradictory elements to form a kind of radical conservatism. He was radical, of course, in his critique of Euro-American imperialism and in his implied advocacy of reform. This dimension to his thought is frequently on display in *Following the Equator* and in much that followed it. On the conservative side was his belief that fallen human nature is irretrievably mired in illusions. "There are those who scoff at the schoolboy, calling him frivolous and shallow. Yet it was the schoolboy who said, 'Faith is believing in what you know ain't so'" (5: 132). Fictional constructions of reality are in fact so pervasive that there is no doing without them. "Don't part with your illusions," he warns. "When they are gone you may still exist but you have ceased to live" (6: 266).

This being the case, the mantle of wisdom and serenity falls to those who favor constructions of reality that promote stability and otherwise answer their perceived needs. Hindus of all classes resist conversion to Christianity, the traveler observes, largely because their own faith provides them with more numerous and much stronger gods (6: 132–4). Mark Twain is struck by the credulity that people bring to their own curious world constructions and by their incredulity when it comes to those of others. Faith, he finds, is so arbitrary and yet so unbending. This is the way it must be, however, because the alternative to faith is unbearable uncertainty. How else can one explain the behavior of the Indian widow, bent on observing the custom of suttee and apparently proof against pain as the flames engulf her? (6: 144–50). Just so, the force of custom shields the child bride from a painful reckoning with the "irksome restraint" and "weary captivity" that go with Indian marriage (6: 51). Human social constructions define reality as we know it, and even at their most irrational they may serve to advance our interests. It is just this way, Mark Twain recognizes, with American patriotism. "Calling it Fanaticism cannot degrade it; nothing can degrade it. Even though it be a political mistake, and a thousand times a political mistake, that does not affect it; it is honorable – always honorable, always noble – and privileged to hold its head up and look the nations in the face" (5: 336).

It was not, of course, that Mark Twain unequivocally approved of blind patriotism. To the contrary, and as his later assaults on U.S. imperialism would demonstrate, there was much he could not abide in his country's aggressive behavior, and in the righteous rationalizing and self-deception that went with it. But his own disenchantment confirmed for him that faith, without which we have no life, is fragile. In the equatorial world of predators and prey he found confirmation of the belief that humans are everywhere in thrall to fictions of their own devising. He saw as well that the collapse of those fictions, especially those that express and reinforce national pride, was fatal in the relentless struggle for territory and domination. It was not a pretty picture. Real truth and justice and progress had small place in it; false, inflated pride was at a premium. Little wonder that Mark Twain came increasingly to embrace the moral reprieve of determinism and to envy the other animals their lack of the Moral Sense. Little wonder, as well, that he came to view his own life as a pointless but painful dream and that he looked forward so eagerly to its end.

NOTES

1 James D. Hart, *The Popular Book* (Berkeley: University of California Press, 1963), pp. 146–8.
2 Richard Bridgman, *Traveling in Mark Twain* (Berkeley: University of California Press, 1987), pp. 1–4.
3 Peter L. Berger and Thomas Luckmann, *The Social Construction of Reality* (Garden City, N.Y.: Doubleday, 1966), p. 1.
4 Ibid., p. 103.
5 Mark Twain, *The Mysterious Stranger*, ed. William M. Gibson (Berkeley: University of California Press, 1970), p. 404.
6 Mark Twain, *The Innocents Abroad*, in *The Writings of Mark Twain*, the author's National Edition, 25 vols. (New York: Harper Bros., 1907–18), vol. 2, pp. 293–4. Hereafter all references to this edition will be cited parenthetically, by volume and page numbers, in the body of the text.
7 James M. Cox, *Mark Twain: The Fate of Humor* (Princeton, N.J.: Princeton University Press, 1966), pp. 53, 55, 59.
8 See my essay, "Patterns of Consciousness in *The Innocents Abroad*," *American Literature* 58 (1986): 46–63, a section of which is distilled here.
9 Henry Nash Smith, "Mark Twain as an Interpreter of the Far West: The Structure of *Roughing It*," in *The Frontier in Perspective*, ed. Walker D. Wyman and Clifton B. Kroeber (Madison: University of Wisconsin Press, 1965), p. 21. My essay, "Seeing the Elephant: Some Perspectives on Mark Twain's *Roughing It*,"

American Studies 21 (1980): 43–64, contains a more detailed version of the critical argument advanced here.

10   Gilman M. Ostrander, *Nevada: The Great Rotten Borough, 1859–1864* (New York: Knopf, 1966), p. 13.

11   Eliot Lord, *Comstock Mining and Miners* (Washington, D.C.: U.S. Geological Survey, 1883), p. 319.

12   Smith, "Mark Twain as an Interpreter," p. 214.

13   Ibid., p. 213.

14   Howells's remarks appeared in the *Atlantic Monthly*, June 1972, as quoted by Justin Kaplan in *Mr. Clemens and Mark Twain* (New York: Simon & Schuster, 1966), p. 148.

15   On the biographical and literary background of *Life on the Mississippi*, and on its composition, see Horst K. Kruse's very helpful *Mark Twain and "Life on the Mississippi"* (Amherst: University of Massachusetts Press, 1981).

16   See Forrest G. Robinson, "Why I Killed My Brother: An Essay on Mark Twain," *Literature and Psychology* 30 (1980): 168–81.

17   Cox, *Mark Twain: The Fate of Humor*, p. 164.

18   I discuss the episode in "Seeing the Elephant," pp. 60–1.

19   Bridgman, *Traveling in Mark Twain*, pp. 89–90.

20   Twain to Howells, January 8, 1880, in the *Mark Twain–Howells Letters*, 2 vols., ed. Henry Nash Smith and William M. Gibson (Cambridge, Mass.: Harvard University Press, 1960), vol. 1, p. 286. See also vol. 1, p. 290: "That most infernally troublesome book is at last hidden from my sight & mind in the jaws of three steam presses."

21   Twain to Howells, January 30, 1879, in the *Mark Twain–Howells Letters*, vol. 1, p. 250.

22   Kaplan, *Mr. Clemens and Mark Twain*, p. 220.

23   *Mark Twain's Letters to His Publishers*, ed. Hamlin Hill (Berkeley: University of California Press, 1967), p. 109.

24   Twain to Howells, January 30, 1879, in the *Mark Twain–Howells Letters*, vol. 1, pp. 248–9.

25   *Mark Twain's Letters to His Publishers*, p. 109.

26   Twain to Rogers, November 1897, in *Mark Twain's Correspondence with Henry Huttleston Rogers*, ed. Lewis Leary (Berkeley: University of California Press, 1969), p. 309.

27   On the provenance and thematics of the maxims, see William M. Gibson's useful account in *The Art of Mark Twain* (New York: Oxford University Press, 1976), pp. 158–76.

28   Twain to Howells, April 2, 1899, in the *Mark Twain–Howells Letters*, vol. 2, p. 690.

29   Susan Gillman, *Dark Twins: Imposture and Identity in Mark Twain's America* (Chicago: University of Chicago Press, 1989), pp. 134–5. Gillman's discussion of the dream tales (pp. 136–80) provides illuminating parallels to my analysis of the travel books.

3

SHELLEY FISHER FISHKIN

Mark Twain and Women

What roles did women play in Mark Twain's life, and what roles did Twain assign them in his work? Until recently, most critics who have addressed these questions at all have tended to fall into one of two camps: those who felt women were bad for Twain and those who felt Twain was bad for women. Both of these positions have their supporters, yet each is flawed.

The "women were bad for Twain" argument was first voiced by Van Wyck Brooks in his influential 1920 study, *The Ordeal of Mark Twain,* in which he charged women – and Twain's wife, Livy, in particular – with having censored, bowdlerized, and emasculated Twain's work. "From the moment of his marriage," Twain's "artistic integrity," Brooks wrote, was "virtually destroyed." Justin Kaplan, in his 1966 Pulitzer Prize–winning biography, blamed Livy for having forced her bankrupt husband to embark on a grueling schedule of lecturing to pay back his creditors when easier (and, in Livy's view, less ethically spotless) routes had been available to him. Whether they were editing his prose or editing his person, whether they were running up household expenses that forced Twain to write too much or creating moral imperatives that allowed him to write too little, women were "bad for Twain."[1] So the argument went.

Although even early admirers of Twain, like William Dean Howells and Bernard DeVoto, had noted the paucity and thinness of women characters in his work, critics didn't begin to consider this issue in depth until the 1970s and 1980s. During those two decades, what one might call the "Twain was bad for women" argument, articulated by critics including Mary Ellen Goad, Judith Fryer, Joyce Warren, Emmanuel Diel, and Wilma Garcia, put forth the idea that, as Warren put it, "Mark Twain was unable to portray a woman as a person."[2] And while some critics faulted Twain for having failed to grant women fully realized lives in his fiction, others charged him with having exerted a negative influence on the real women in his life. Hamlin Hill claimed that Twain tragically sabotaged the mental and physical health of all of the women in his family; Guy Cardwell accused

Twain of having had a prurient interest in the young girls whose company he sought during his final years.[3] Whether he was casting women in stereo-typical roles in his fiction or forcing them to play self-effacing or self-destructive supporting roles in his life, Twain, so the argument ran, was "bad for women."

While all of these critics raise interesting and important questions about Twain's attitudes toward women, recent scholarship suggests that a more nuanced, complex perspective on the subject is in order. Twain's relation-ships with women, both in his life and in his work, were more complicated – and more interesting.

Let us start by reexamining the "women were bad for Twain" argument. In his autobiography Twain wrote:

> In the beginning of our engagement the proofs of my first book, *The Innocents Abroad*, began to arrive and [Livy] read them with me. She also edited them. She was my faithful, judicious, and painstaking editor from that day forth until within three or four months of her death – a stretch of more than a third of a century.[4]

Brooks was the first to maintain that Livy's genteel Eastern editing and feminine values eviscerated Twain's virile, rough-hewn Western prose and sensibilities and ruined him as an artist. Just as Mrs. Clemens "had no just sense of the distinction between virility and profanity and vulgarity," Brooks complained, she "regarded his natural liking for bold and masculine language, which was one of the outward signs of his latent greatness, merely as a literary equivalent of bad manners, as something that endangered their common prestige in the eyes of conventional opinion."[5]

As Peter Stoneley notes, Brooks's conviction that "Mark Twain's great-ness lay in his partial evasion of women and feminine values" was echoed by Bernard DeVoto's enthusiasm for "the 'enormously male' literary tradition" that valued "an escape from feminine influence." In a similar vein, James Cox observed that "DeVoto, for all his passionate refutations of Brooks, saw [Livy] in equally pejorative terms."[6] Both Brooks and DeVoto implic-itly shared Fred Lewis Pattee's opinion (expressed in *The Feminine Fifties*) that "the worst moments in American history" were the "results of feminine perversion of right-minded masculinity."[7] Others echoed Brooks's and De-Voto's distaste for "feminine" aesthetic judgments; Justin Kaplan, for exam-ple, maintained that Twain's willingness to acquiesce to the effete, refined taste of his daughter Susy helps explain his production of and enthusiasm for such inferior, openly sentimental books as *Joan of Arc* and *The Prince and the Pauper*.[8]

A fresh look at the record, however, combined with a perusal of recent critical studies, yields a rather different set of insights. While Twain's wife and daughters (and other women whose advice Twain sought) may, indeed, have encouraged and approved of some of his lesser works, they were also central to the production of his greatest ones. Women, as it turns out, far from being detrimental to Twain's work, were key to his creative process during his most productive and successful periods as a writer.

We do not know precisely when Twain developed a clear sense of what he wanted to be and what he wanted to do. (There is no moment analogous to, say, Whitman's insight, shortly after publishing his first book, that he enjoyed, more than anything else, "making poems.") But at some point Mark Twain, popular columnist and writer of humorous short sketches, decided he wanted to be a successful, respected author. He may have suspected, quite rightly, that he stood in need of some tutelage if he were to achieve that end – in matters of grammar and taste, certainly, but also when it came to understanding his audience. Put simply, the majority of people who bought books during the last third of the nineteenth century were women; on some level Twain must have sensed that his own very limited experience with women would prove to be a major liability on this front. He looked to Mary Mason Fairbanks, a fellow passenger on the *Quaker City,* for guidance on matters of grammar and taste; soon he would invite his fiancée, Olivia Langdon, to play a similar role. (As we can see from an occasional fiasco like the Whittier Birthday Dinner Speech – where Twain shocked the Boston Brahmins assembled with an inappropriately irreverent and off-color story – Twain had good reason to doubt his own judgment now and then on matters of propriety.) Several critics have argued that the editorial comments these women made were, in fact, trivial and negligible; be that as it may, it does not follow that Twain overvalued their contribution to his work. For in the process, ostensibly, of applying for tutelage in matters of grammar and refinement, Twain established a kitchen cabinet, so to speak, that both fueled his creativity and helped him channel those creative sparks into forms that would appeal to a broad, book-buying public. Livy taught Twain that "the only right thing was to get in my serious meaning always, to treat my audience fairly, to let them really feel the underlying moral that gave body and essence to my jest."[9] One might argue that as a result of this lesson, Twain produced some rather dull and forgettable writing; while that may well be the case, this lesson also informed the achievements for which he is most admired and remembered.

Like most literary men of his day, Twain did his writing against a backdrop of domestic harmony orchestrated by an "angel in the house" (the phrase was Coventry Patmore's, but Twain readily applied it to Livy) who took charge of supervising the performance of domestic chores, and who ensured that pleasing meals appeared on time and that quotidian cares did not intrude to break the Great Man's concentration.[10] But the women in Twain's life did much more than leave him free to do his writing and feed him when he was done.

Twain's sister-in-law, Sue Crane (Livy's adopted older sister), built Twain the famous octagonal study on the hilltop at Quarry Farm, in Elmira, New York; it was there, during summer stays with her and her family, that Twain reached his peak of productivity and creativity. (During the nearly twenty summers Twain spent there between 1871 and 1889, he wrote major portions of *Roughing It, Tom Sawyer, Huckleberry Finn,* and *A Connecticut Yankee.*) At Quarry Farm, Twain would work in his study all day and after the evening meal would share the day's work with a family group that included Livy, Sue Crane, his three daughters, and Mary Ann Cord, the cook. Laura Skandera-Trombley notes, "To this female audience, then, Clemens would read his work. The varied opinions Clemens received constituted his literary wellspring." Citing Alan Gribben on the importance Twain placed on "oral readings before other people, a practice that surely helped develop the flexible narrative voice he strove to reproduce in his fiction," Skandera-Trombley suggests that "this reading before a female audience resulted in more than perfecting Clemens' narrative voice. The women became, in a sense, the text's co-constructors." Throughout his most productive periods, Skandera-Trombley argues, "women in effect functioned collectively as Clemens's personal and creative touchstone." (She goes on to suggest that the waning of Twain's creative talents in his later years – after the death of his daughter Susy and his wife – was related to the absence of the group of women who helped provide access to the "feminine consciousness" that had been so central to Twain's success as a writer.)[11]

Mary Ann Cord nourished Twain with much more than his evening meal. A story she told not only inspired his first contribution to the *Atlantic Monthly* ("A True Story," 1874) but also helped awaken Twain to the narrative power of vernacular speech generally and was an important influence on the book that would become *Huckleberry Finn.*[12] Twain's daughters, whose favorite game required their father to make up spontaneous stories, linking ideas or images that they supplied, provided much more than simple diversion during his nonwriting hours. As Twain notes in his final series of autobiographical dictations, Susy "was both his inspiration for the autobiography itself and his mentor" and had "in fact, influenced his decision to dictate his autobiography as early as 1885."[13] Michael Kiskis has observed that Twain's "dependence upon her descriptions of the family's life [in the biography she wrote of her father] and his memories of her played an important role in the design and process he chose for his dictations."[14]

Twain was widely read in the work of innumerable women writers and often used their books as jumping-off points for his own – and not just in the well-known cases of *The Prince and the Pauper* and *Joan of Arc*. Caroline Rosa Praed's *Australian Life, Black and White* (1885), for example, included chillingly vivid accounts of various episodes of Australian genocide that Twain quoted from extensively in *Following the Equator*.[15] Twain considered Catherine Waite's history of Brigham Young, *The Mormon Prophet and His Harem* (1866) to be "concise, accurate, reliable," and drew on it in *Roughing It;*[16] he found Lady Stuart-Wortley's *Travels in the United States* (1851) instructive as he worked on *Life on the Mississippi*.[17]

It is interesting that two male scholars, Peter Stoneley and Gregg Camfield, have published the most extensive examinations to date of precisely *how* aesthetic strategies associated with women writers shaped Twain's fiction. In *Mark Twain and the Feminine Aesthetic,* Stoneley notes that "rather than investigating the contending aesthetics of masculinity and femininity as interdependent concepts in the context of broader social struggles," critics like Brooks and DeVoto who deplore Twain's links to feminine traditions manifest a "view of the feminine aesthetic" that equates (in Jane Tompkins's words) "popularity with debasement, emotionality with ineffectiveness, religiosity with fakery, domesticity with triviality, and all of these, implicitly, with womanly inferiority."[18] In recent years, critics like Nina Baym, Jane Tompkins, and Cathy Davidson have pushed for a radical revision of our understanding of pre-twentieth-century American women's fiction and the cultural work it endeavored to accomplish. But, as Stoneley astutely notes, "The feminist revision of the issue, which has emphasized the various uses women made of their cultural advantages, has tended to avoid consideration of the male uses of the same aesthetic."[19] Stoneley examines the difficulties Twain had trying to privilege a "masculine" over a "feminine aesthetic" in his work, lending implicit support to Skandera-Trombley's contention that a "feminine consciousness" was an important component of Mark Twain's own mental map. The questions Stoneley raises, combined with Skandera-Trombley's interesting discussion of *Huckleberry Finn* as an androgynous blend of the (feminine) sentimental novel and the (masculine) quest novel,[20] suggest that a "feminine aesthetic" may, indeed, have shaped even Twain's most famous work in indelible ways.

Albert E. Stone commented some thirty years ago on "the twin tendencies toward sentimentality and realism which characterize virtually all of

Twain's fiction." Susan Harris also noted Twain's "frequent recourse to sentimental discourse." Today, scholars are increasingly aware of the ways in which rhetorical and aesthetic approaches commonly associated with fiction by women shaped Twain's work. Of particular note is Gregg Camfield's lucid and insightful essay, "Sentimental Liberalism and the Problem of Race in *Huckleberry Finn*," which argues that "Twain often attacked sentimentalism on utilitarian grounds, but he often endorsed sentimental conventions by using them straight." Noting that critics tend to consider Twain "a 'masculine,' which in their terms is to say antisentimental writer," Camfield observes that Twain's stance toward sentimentalism

> is complicated. The meanings of this complexity have been almost entirely obscured by the modernist response to sentimentality, a response that dismissed the entire intellectual tradition behind American sentimental literature so effectively that only in the last ten or fifteen years have scholars seriously begun to unearth the nineteenth-century intellectual context in which sentimentalism flourished.[21]

Linking Twain's work to the "sentimental rhetoric of the antislavery movement," Camfield charts the ways in which Twain uses sentimentality in *Huckleberry Finn* "to tell the reader to sympathize with the black man's humanity." Huck's battle with his conscience, Camfield maintains, is clearly "based on sentimental ethics, and its development depends on many conventions of sentimental fiction."[22] Here and elsewhere, Camfield makes a persuasive case for the idea that much of the novel's power over the reader is rooted in aesthetic conventions associated with writing by women.

To return to the second half of the "women were bad for Twain" line of reasoning, what are we to make of the implication that Livy inhibited the writing Twain might have done during his later years by setting out such harsh, "ironclad" conditions under which Twain was to repay his debts during his bankruptcy? It is true that Twain might have easily paid off his debts earlier (and had more time to write) had he not abided by Livy's rigid rules. (Some creditors were willing to settle for being paid fifty cents on the dollar, and some friends would have been glad to hold fundraisers for Twain, but Livy insisted that the creditors be paid in full and that Twain earn the money by lecturing.) But her policy, as it turned out, had great merit. As Twain's financial adviser, Henry Huddleston Rogers, put it, "A literary man's reputation is his life; he can afford to be money poor but he cannot afford to be character poor; you must earn the cent per cent and pay it."[23] As Kaplan notes, Twain "had no legal obligation to pay one hundred cents on the dollar, but he began to say publicly that 'honor is a harder master than the law' and he intended to serve it." Louis Budd observes that "even while Rogers was challenging [the creditors] toe to toe, he was advising Twain that his literary and his broader popularity rated as the asset to protect at all costs, that the high road would prove the most profitable in good time."[24] Livy was right: Twain bounced back from bankruptcy with his honor and status healthier than ever before. Whether she was urging Twain to hold to the highest moral standard during his bankruptcy, or whether she was steering him away from a public row with *New York Tribune* editor Whitlaw Reid (Livy made Twain see how weak his case against Reid was), Livy's levelheaded judgment about decisions affecting Twain's career often saved him from potential embarrassment.[25] Her sense of decorum helped Twain preserve his untarnished reputation and keep his future options open; she knew – even when he didn't – what behavior became a national icon.

Now let us reexamine what might be called the "Twain was bad for women" argument, first in connection with the portrayal of women in his work and then as it relates to the women in his life.

As far as Twain's art is concerned, the litany of charges against him on this front is a familiar one: his women characters tend to be severely limited, stereotypical, and flat; all the truly interesting and fully rounded characters – with some key exceptions – are male. Even Twain's most ardent supporters have recognized this failing. Speaking of Twain's portrayal of women, William Dean Howells observed in 1910, "I do not think he succeeds so often with that nature as with the boy-nature or the man-nature, apparently because it does not interest him so much." In a similar vein, Bernard DeVoto bemoaned the fact that "none of Mark Twain's nubile girls, young women, or young matrons are believable: they are all bisque, saccharine, or tears." As Mary Ellen Goad commented in 1971, Twain "was simply unable to create a female character, of whatever age, of whatever time and place, who is other than wooden and unrealistic." Judith Fryer reiterated this idea in 1976, when she charged that "Mark Twain created really no significant women." Or as Joyce Warren observed in 1984, Twain's "novels show us humorous old ladies and silly little girls, but there is no woman of any substance. Even the few young women of marriageable age who do appear are only girls grown tall. For the most part, Twain is simply not interested in the female characters in his works."[26]

Despite the fact that nineteen women were present on the *Quaker City* cruise, and one of them became an extremely close friend of Twain's, Warren notes that "the female passengers are scarcely mentioned" in *The Inno-*

cents Abroad, and women are even less present in Twain's next book, *Roughing It.* Laura Hawkins in *The Gilded Age,* the first female character Twain developed in any depth and one who, temporarily at least, has the potential to become a fully rounded figure, fails to transcend conventional stereotypes, as Susan Harris notes in her illuminating essay on the novel. "Never a literary feminist," Harris writes:

> Twain's portraits of women are persistently cast in one or another stereotypi-cal mode, making them reducible to one or another literary paradigm and consequently controlled as more self-creating characters are not. Not only Laura but all women are other-directed in Twain's work; he could not imagine them other than in relation to men.[27]

"Old ladies and little girls" appear in *Tom Sawyer:* the "little girl" catego-ry is filled out by Becky, an "insipid and rather boring little girl" whose name Twain himself forgets in *Huckleberry Finn,* and by Tom's cousin Mary, who is similarly boring and dull; the "old lady" category is occupied by Aunt Polly, whom Warren finds

> kind and good-hearted, but . . . rather slow-witted. She has all of the character traits of the little girls except that she is no longer pretty. She is an amusing stock figure, whose simplicity and gullibility make her the easy butt of Tom's and Twain's good-natured humor.

Aunt Polly reappears in *Huckleberry Finn,* where she is almost interchange-able with her sister, Aunt Sally. Warren believes that "the other old ladies" in this novel –

> Miss Watson, the Widow Douglas – are vaguely defined civilizers who worry about manners, clothes and religion. The younger female characters in *Huck-leberry Finn* are even less fully developed than the old ladies.

In a similar vein, Warren asserts that

> *The Prince and the Pauper* (1882) and *A Connecticut Yankee in King Arthur's Court* (1889) feature no more memorable female characters than *Tom Sawyer* or *Huckleberry Finn.* Lady Elizabeth and Lady Jane in *The Prince and the Pauper* are only storybook characters, and Sandy in *A Connecticut Yankee* is a shallow simpleton.[28]

(To this list of stereotypical women characters one might add an occasional figure like Morgan le Fay in *A Connecticut Yankee,* who is heartless, evil, and cruel – a departure from the "old ladies" and "little girls" mode, but decidedly "other" and flat, nonetheless.)[29] These characterizations of Twain's women remain, for the most part, unfortunately accurate. But it would be a mistake to equate the limited range of roles Twain accorded women in his work with the idea that women were of limited importance in Twain's mind.

Those women whom Warren refers to as Twain's "vaguely defined civilizers" are, in Twain's view, extremely important in the grand scheme of things – even if he failed to individuate them successfully in his fiction. Even Twain's stereotypical characters deserve a second look, as Susan Harris and Gregg Camfield suggest. Harris, for example, writes that "the women who have been most studied in Twain's fiction are those who function as foils for a young protagonist's adventures." While they may be "sexless and rigidly conventional . . . "

> these women provide the stability out of which Twain's young protagonists emerge. They are the guardians – perhaps even the creators – of moral order among men. . . . The women's most important function is to ask the boys to make the first movement outside their own egos, to adopt another person's viewpoint and to recognize that other people also can experience pain.

Nancy Walker notes, along these lines, that "for all Twain's mockery of middle-class 'respectability,' without the real human virtues represented primarily by the women in *Huck Finn* there would be little opportunity for Huck to grow." Camfield expands on this theme, observing the important role that women in *Huckleberry Finn* play in Huck's moral development. "Twain's vision of Huck's relationship to his father does not paint an attractive vision of a 'masculine' world," Camfield comments. By way of contrast, "listening to Mary Jane echo the widow's morality, and watching that morality in action, and feeling the benefits of it himself, he is converted to sentimental altruism." Camfield probes Twain's manipulation of conventional representations of women in the novel to suggest the "superior morality of sentimental Christianity" over Calvinism. Huck's battle with his conscience – the high point for readers and critics of the novel – is, in Camfield's view, "based on sentimental ethics."[30] While Twain himself may be, at root, ambivalent about the values these women embody, a part of him finds those values appealing enough to make them central to his protagonist's most memorable and dramatic scene.

Stereotypical women characters may be the norm in Twain's opus, but there are occasions when we see him struggling to push beyond the gender conventions that he usually simply accepted. Sometimes they occur as transient episodes in the life of a character who, by the end of the tale, gets sealed safely in a conventional box. As Susan Harris notes, when confronted by the stupidity of a bookstore clerk, Laura Hawkins (in *The Gilded Age*) briefly takes on "the tone and attitude of Twain's debunking personas," sounding, momentarily, like Twain himself; but Twain "felt the necessity of terminating his character's adventures" when they got out of hand.[31] "Twain kills Laura because he could not allow a female trickster to add to the chaos of the male sphere"; an "alienated woman" like Laura, Harris writes, "threatens to destroy [Twain's] cosmic scheme, a scheme in which women's primary function is to provide security for men suffering from self-doubt, to be a refuge from alienation rather than to exhibit it themselves."[32]

Joan, in *Joan of Arc,* had the potential to transform familiar gender conventions dramatically, but her ethereally virginal unreality and the woodenness of Twain's evocation of her character prevent her from coming alive as a believable woman, despite the unconventional plot she inhabits. Indeed, Joan reinscribes conventional gender ideology in fresh ways: while she leaves the traditional "women's sphere" of the home behind, she does so not out of "self-interest" or "personal ambition" but as an act of self-abnegation, fulfilling in a different context women's role of sacrificing herself "for her appointed dependent" – in this case "France (envisioned in this novel as a masculine rather than a feminine entity), at once Joan's wayward father and helpless child."[33] Nonetheless, Christina Zwarg is struck by the "incipient feminism of Mark Twain's project," and Margaret Thompson argues convincingly that "Twain uses Joan's position as a female outlaw to subvert gender stereotypes on both literal and figurative levels." J. D. Stahl sees Joan's character as representing an "implicit critique of male charac-ter," since the "virtues at the core of Clemens's portrayal of Joan . . . [serve] as a measure of the deficiencies of men in general and of the male characters represented in the story in particular." The novel, Stahl believes, represents Twain's "effort to envision the fusion, in one figure, of virtues conven-tionally and selectively assigned to women and men separately in Twain's era. Specifically, Joan as Twain imagined her embodies a fusion of courage and compassion, authority and gentleness."[34]

Roxy in *Pudd'nhead Wilson* is always cited as the great exception in Twain's portrayals of women; she is that rarest of beings in his work: an attractive, passionate, adult woman (although her primary defining trait is that she is a *mother,* her sexual activity having taken place in the past). Twain's rigid gender stereotypes, Warren suggests, applied strictly to *white* womanhood; by virtue of her race, Roxy escaped the strictures Twain nor-mally placed on women. Her pain is real. (Indeed, it prefigures that of Sethe in Toni Morrison's *Beloved* [1988], who decides, as Roxy does early in the novel, that death is preferable to the fate she imagines for her child under slavery.) Physically prepossessing, enterprising, cunning, and genuinely in-teresting and engaging, Roxy demonstrates Twain's ability to conceive of women as something other than prepubescent schoolgirls, matronly old ladies, or demonic sorceresses. Roxy is also more complex than either of the stereotypes most commonly used by white authors to portray women of her race and status, as Carolyn Porter has noted: Roxana "exposes not only the falseness of the Mammy/Jezebel opposition, but also the inadequacy of either 'Mammy' or 'Jezebel' to contain or represent the slave woman." Indeed, as Myra Jehlen has observed, Twain endows Roxy with "a considerable degree of transcendence"; her "sovereignty over the children extends naturally to the story of which she is a sort of author. She achieves the highest status available to a fictional character when she and the narrator are the only ones who know what is going on and can truly identify the participants."[35]

Several other female characters in Twain's shorter works also demonstrate Twain's ability to portray a greater range of women than he is usually given credit for. The former slave "Aunt Rachel," in "A True Story," for example, is a powerful, proud, articulate woman whose emotional depths dwarf those of the genteel narrator – "Misto C" – who introduces her. And in another brief sketch titled "The Judge's Spirited Woman," which appeared, like "A True Story," in *Sketches, New and Old*, Twain portrays with sympathy a Mexican woman who murders her husband's killer in a crowded courtroom when a corrupt jury fails to convict him. As Margaret Thompson has noted, Twain's depiction of the murderess in this piece shows his ability to empathize with a female outlaw figure:

> Her crimes are motivated by the male killer and the failure of the jury system, she is characterized as simultaneously threatening yet physically attractive, she gains popular support from the judge and onlooking audience, and she eventually attains a position of moral authority for having forcefully righted a blatantly unfair verdict.[36]

Twain's interest in the possibility of women characters who break out of familiar molds becomes apparent in many of the experimental pieces that remained unpublished at Twain's death. Twain's Eve and her daughter, Gladys (in the posthumously published "Extract" and "Passage" from "Eve's Autobiography"); the spunky tomboy heroine "Hellfire Hotchkiss" in the fragment by that name; Twain's Scherezade, the "masculine" princess "Fatima," and the "feminine" prince Selim in "The 1002d Arabian Night"; and the cross-dressing Nancy Jackson in "Feud Story and the Girl Who Was Ostensibly a Man" (recently published as "How Nancy Jackson Married Kate Wilson") all attest to an imagination genuinely intrigued by gender-bending, gender-blending alternate realities and open to the possibility of women who break out of stereotypical roles.

While some critics find Eve's devotion to Adam a somewhat cloying reinscription of Victorian ideals of marriage, Eve's sense of self remains independent from her status as Adam's helpmate. She represents, as critics have observed, "Mark Twain's most ambitious attempt to use a feminine first-person narrator."[37] She is curious and creative, and takes genuine pride in her "discoveries." That Twain identifies with her deeply is suggested by the fact that he endows her with a talent that was his own: the ability to spell. (Eve tells us, "Spelling is a gift, too, I am sure of it. . . . I can spell, and so can Abel.")[38] As Twain notes in his foreword to Susy's biography of him, during his school days "good spelling was my one accomplishment."[39]

While Eve has elicited a fair amount of commentary, however, there has been very little comment on her daughter, Gladys, the little sister of Cain and Abel who was accidentally left behind by her older brothers when they were out picking berries in "a new region" someplace very "far away." She is missing for six days, when her brothers are sent to find her. "She had had adventures," Twain writes.

> In the dark, the first night, she fell in the river and was washed down a long distance, she did not know how far, and was finally flung upon a sandbar. After that, she lived with a kangaroo's family, and was hospitably entertained, and there was much sociability. The mama-kangaroo was very sweet and motherly, and would take her babies out of her pocket and go foraging in the hills and dales and fetch home a pocketful of the choicest fruits and nuts; and nearly every night there was company – bears and rabbits and buzzards and chickens and foxes and hyenas and polecats and other creatures – and gay romping and grand times. (EEA 88–9)

Brave, enterprising, able to have "gay romping and grand times" with bears and foxes and hyenas and polecats, Gladys seems almost closer to Maxine Hong Kingston's mythical heroine in the "White Tigers" section of *The Woman Warrior* (1975) than to any of the conventional "molds" into which Twain's women are traditionally cast. She resembles, as well, some of the unconventional heroines in fantasies and fables spun by Charlotte Perkins Gilman, a turn-of-the-century writer who would make the project of breaking out of prescribed gender roles a major concern, both as a critic and an artist.[40] (Gilman, a member of the Beecher family, was a neighbor of the Clemenses during her Hartford childhood, but there is no record of her path having crossed Twain's.) Against the backdrop of women in Twain's published work, Gladys's presence seems rather startling. She commands our interest as testimony to the fact that Twain was, indeed, capable of imagining, if only briefly, a picaresque fantasy centered on a cheerful, sensitive, curious, open-minded young girl.

Twain's smart, tough, capable Rachel – also known as Hellfire Hotchkiss – in the posthumously published "Hellfire Hotchkiss Sequence," is even more unconventional than Gladys. She makes her entrance in the story like this:

> Now arose the ringing sound of flying hoofs, and a trim and fair young girl, bareheaded and riding bareback and astride, went thundering by on a great black horse.[41]

A boy is drowning in an icy river; Rachel rushes to the rescue:

> The girl did not wait for the rest, but rode off up stream, peering across the chasm as she went, the people following her with their eyes, and commenting.
> "She's the only person that had enough presence of mind to come fixed to *do* something in case there was a chance. She's got a life-preserver along."
> (HH 187)

Twain clearly likes his high-spirited heroine: "She had a business head, and practical sense," he tells us, "and it had been believed from the first, by Judge Carpenter and other thoughtful people, that she would be a valuable person when she got tame" (HH 191). Left to raise herself, for the most part, with an invalid mother and a "musing, dreaming," self-absorbed father, Rachel "was stored to the eyelids with energies and enthusiasms" (HH 192). She finds the preoccupations of little girls – dolls, name calling – "a weariness" (HH 193).

> They would not jump from high places; they would not climb high trees; they were afraid of the thunder; and of the water; and of cows; and would take no perilous risks; and had no love of danger for its own sake. She tried to reform them, but it failed. So she went over to the boys.   (HH 193)

The boys would have none of her; "she had to whip two or three" before they agreed to let her join them. Rachel found "in their rough play and tough combats and dangerous enterprises the contentment and joy for which she had long hungered. She took her full share in all their sports and was a happy child" (HH 194). Rachel learns to fish, boat, hunt, trap, break horses, and box. "She had good judgment and coolness in danger, she was spry and active," and she became an honorary member of the local fire department, which "allowed her to scale the roofs of burning houses and help handle the hose; for she liked that sort of employment" (HH 195). Twain clearly enjoyed sketching out her adventures (they go on for a number of pages), but then seems to have been puzzled about what to do with her. Although she learns to be a competent housekeeper as well as horse breaker by the time she is sixteen, a kindly aunt takes her aside for a word of caution: some enemies are spreading nasty gossip about her; she'd be best advised to change her ways. Rachel makes some resolutions, the first of which is "Withdraw from the boys" (HH 200). But just after she has made these resolutions and gone to bed "refreshed and contented by this whole-sale purification" (HH 200), Twain breaks off the story.

The "Hellfire Hotchkiss" story is memorable in part because, unlike the "Fatima" in "The 1002d Arabian Night" or Nancy Jackson in the "Feud Story," Rachel is recognized as a girl but finds conventional gender roles hopelessly confining. In "The 1002d Arabian Night," an evil witch switches the apparent genders of two babies at birth, so that a child who is really born a boy appears to be, and is reared as, a girl ("Fatima") and a child who is really born a girl appears to be, and is reared as, a boy ("Selim"). Here the gender roles are confusing to the townspeople, for Fatima has none of the expected feminine preferences, habits, or virtues and Selim has none of the masculine ones. But since Twain consistently uses the pronoun "he" to refer to Fatima and "she" to refer to Selim, and since he lets the reader (but not the townspeople) in on the secret of their birth, gender expectations are simply inverted rather than challenged. The real challenge to expectations comes from the storyteller, Scherezade, who manages marvelously to break out of the role into which she has been historically cast. She spins out her final story at such extraordinary length that the executioner dies before she finishes, and so does the king. Scherezade outlives them all and has the final word:

> The beautiful Scherezade remained as fresh as in the beginning, and straight-way ordered up another king; and another, and still another; and so continued until all the people were alarmed for the perpetuity of their royal line, its material being by this time very greatly reduced. So all the nation knelt before the beautiful Scherezade and implored her to desist from her desolating narra-tions. But she said no – not until she had sent as many kings to the tomb as the late king had sent poor unoffending Queens, would she stay her hand. . . . She nobly stood to her purpose, until one thousand and ninety-five new tombs had been added to the royal cemetery; then she said her poor slaughtered prede-cessors were avenged and she was satisfied.[42]

What begins as a conventional continuation of *1001 Arabian Nights* thus ends as a triumphant tale of woman's revenge on an abusive despot. Here, as in "Hellfire Hotchkiss," Twain breaks off his story just when it gets truly interesting. For the "continuation" – for a scene where a Rachel can be unabashedly capable and competent without raising eyebrows, and where a Scherezade can rule in peace, one must turn, once again, to Charlotte Perkins Gilman's feminist utopian fantasies (such as *Herland* [1915] or "What Diantha Did" [1909–10]); these tales were not for Twain to write, and he knew it. But the fact that he imagined this much demonstrates that part of him could entertain possibilities that stretched conventional gender expectations to their limits.

In other posthumously published stories Twain experiments with crossdressing figures forced, under various forms of duress, to act as if they were of the opposite sex. Nancy Jackson, for example, in the "Feud Story," is blackmailed by an enemy into spending the rest of her life pretending to be a man. Alice, in "Wapping Alice," for reasons that remain murky, turns out to be a man pretending to be a woman. Twain is clearly confused himself by what Susan Gillman calls the "sexual and epistemological disorder" generated by his tales of transvestism;[43] his often unexplained, surprise endings raise more questions than they answer.

Twain's tantalizingly truncated explorations of these questions during the last twelve years of his life (the time in which he wrote the aforementioned experimental, unpublished pieces) coincided with a change in his attitude toward women's role in society. At the beginning of his career, Twain was appalled by the notion of women's suffrage, and wrote peevish satires trivializing the subject. In 1867, for example, he charged, tongue in cheek, that if women were put in charge of things, the "State printer" and "Supreme court clerks" would be replaced by a "State Crinoline Directress," a "State Hair Oil inspectress," and a "State milliner."[44] Twain's idealized notion of women's proper sphere led him to seriously oppose the idea of granting the vote to women. (He expressed "shock" at the idea of seeing "one of our blessed earthly angels peddling election tickets among a mob of shabby scoundrels she never saw before"; FS 221). But Livy, who was a friend and admirer of feminists and suffragists, including Anna Dickinson and Isabella Hooker, managed to convince Twain that "because women were of finer material than men they should be allowed to vote and correct society's flaws."[45] In the long run, Livy's gentle persuasion proved more effective with Twain than did Anna Dickinson's biting sarcasm. (Twain expressed relief that Livy was cut from a different mold.) Soon Twain was making prosuffrage speeches of his own and giving financial support to the movement.[46] "No civilization can be perfect until exact equality between man and woman is included," he wrote in his notebook.[47] Four months before his death Twain told an interviewer that he supported "any methods" that women chose "to attain the big results they are striving for."[48] In the posthumously published *Letters from the Earth* he wrote with disapproval that "woman's equality with man has never been conceded by any people, ancient or modern, civilized or savage."[49] ("Training," as Twain himself had written, "is everything. The peach was once a bitter almond; cauliflower is nothing but cabbage with a college education.")[50]

It remains to examine Mark Twain's responses to the real women in his life. Was Twain a Victorian patriarch through and through, forcing both his wife and his daughters into constricting, destructive prescribed roles? What was his response to women who were neither "wives" nor "daughters"? Was the septuagenarian writer a "dirty old man" at the end of his life? While there is not space here to offer an adequate response to these questions, some general points may be briefly raised.

Twain did, on many occasions, force the women closest to him – his wife and daughters – to play rather constricted roles within a conventionally patriarchal Victorian household. In many ways, he viewed Livy as the embodiment of Patmore's idealized "angel in the house"; obsessed throughout his life with the sanctity of female "purity" and chastity, Twain kept an abnormally tight rein on his daughters' social lives (even by standards of Victorian fatherhood, Twain's efforts to control were extreme); and he seems to have been insensitive to some of his daughters' deepest needs and desires. Both he and his wife, for example, seem to have been largely unaware of the intense importance Susy attached to her passionate relationship with Louise Brownell and to the pain that separation from Louise caused her.[51] It is also true that in his closing years, Twain's chief preoccupation, as he was the first to admit, was the coterie of prepubescent girls with whom he surrounded himself, his "Angel Fish."

But if Twain was insensitive to the women around him on some fronts, there is one area in which he deserves credit for being leagues ahead of most of his peers. At a time when the *Journal of the American Medical Association* was publishing editorials "proving" that "excessive mental labor is a cause of sterility" in women, Twain took women's intellects seriously.[52]

Reading had been Livy's chief passion for years before she met Twain; books and her responses to them dominated her correspondence and conversations.[53] While as a Victorian wife Livy took the expected interest in fashion, clothes, and home decoration, as Resa Willis has noted, "her first love was reading, and she preferred women who would discuss books rather than furnishings."[54] Twain, who wrote that he took "as much pride in her brains as I do in her beauty," wooed her from the start with a vision of married life that involved endless evenings of reading together.[55] For example, early in their courtship he mused, in a letter to Livy, "how pleasant it would be to sit . . . just us two, long winter evenings, & study together, & read favorite authors aloud & comment on them & so imprint them upon our memories."[56]

Twain also valued the intellectual exchanges he had with his daughters as they grew up, and would create opportunities for them to have weekly literary discussions with their peers.[57] The "Saturday Morning Club" (all of its members women except for Twain) addressed a range of complex and stimulating issues. Discussion topics during the year 1880–1, for example, included "Evolution and Society," "Conscience as Superior to Logic in Matters of Morals," and "The Knights of Labor." Occasional guest speakers, such as William Graham Sumner, led discussions of "Socialism" and "Banks." The 1890 list of topics included "Ibsen's Plays."[58]

At the dinner table at Twain's home in Hartford, New Orleans writer Grace King recalled, "talk was free and unconventional," with "Susy and Clara . . . expressing themselves boldly, without fear of criticism or correction," confident that their views were listened to and respected.[59] Twain appreciated and encouraged Susy's skills as a budding writer.

Susy was far from the only woman writer Twain encouraged. When King finished dramatizing her successful novel, *Monsieur Motte,* for example, Twain introduced her to theatrical manager and playwright Augustin Daly, "to see if he considered it worth producing."[60] Twain's easy, unaffected, egalitarian response to King surprised her. As she observed shortly after her visit to Hartford in 1887, Twain "treats ladies generally as if they were nice clever boys – like himself."[61] Twain served as mentor to Charlotte Teller, author of *The Cage* (1907), meeting with her daily about her work for almost three months, scribbling comments all over the manuscript's margins, and providing her with a "blurb."[62] Dorothy Quick, who met Twain when she was eleven, found Twain ready to stimulate her skills as a writer by creating unfinished stories and asking her "to write a solution for his hero's dilemma" and also by recording her dictations.[63] Quick, who found the "author's league for two" that Twain established soon expanded to include other girls her age, went on to become a professional writer and author of sixteen books.[64]

While admitting that no hard evidence exists to prove his case, Hamlin Hill imputes a "latently sexual" interest on Twain's part in some of the young girls of Dorothy Quick's age whose company Twain sought in his final years.[65] The hundreds of letters that Twain exchanged with these dozen or so "surrogate granddaughters" reveal nothing of the kind. Rather, they show an aging, lonely Twain plagued by declining health and waning literary power trying to recapture some of the energy and joy that characterized his household during the years of his own daughters' childhood – which were also, not coincidentally, his own most productive years as an artist. When "Angel Fish" came to visit, Twain frequently engaged them in "educational games and a battle of wits."[66] When they were away at school, Twain sent them books, as well as grandfatherly advice. In 1908, for example, he sent Frances Nunnally a copy of a novel centered on a precocious, imaginative, sometimes irreverent and rebellious twelve-year-old girl.[67] As Doris Lanier reminds us, "Twain was always interested in the intellectual development of his young friends."[68]

Sometimes Twain reinscribed the gender norms of his time; sometimes he transcended them. Just as Twain's own work embodies and reflects in key ways inconsistencies and ambiguities that inhered in the society that shaped him and that he, in turn, helped shape, the critical controversies that have grown up around Twain and women in the twentieth century reveal much about American society's complex responses to questions involving gender and culture, and to the role of real and imagined women in a canonical male writer's work.

There remains a whole range of questions on this subject that have never been asked, let alone answered. While we are beginning to probe the ways in which women influenced Twain's writing, we have yet to explore how Twain's work, in turn, shaped writing by women.[69] Twain served as a writing teacher for Gertrude Stein (according to Alice B. Toklas, he was her favorite writer), for Tillie Olsen (who admired the moral sharpness of his essays), for Elizabeth Spencer (who was intrigued by his evocation of a South that she was trying to limn on her own), and for Toni Morrison (who appreciated his ability to write books that "talked").[70] Reading *Huckleberry Finn*, did they and other women readers and writers find themselves identifying with Huck rather than with the female characters in the novel (much as Ralph Ellison found himself identifying with Huck rather than with Jim)? If so, were they "resisting readers" (to use Judith Fetterly's term)?[71] Or did they embrace, for the moment, an ungendered identity as "reader" or "fellow writer"? What other twentieth-century women writers found in Twain's vernacular picaresque hero or in his ironic authorial persona an empowering role model? Did Maxine Hong Kingston read Twain? Did Rita Mae Brown? Did Molly Ivins? Did Sherley Anne Williams? Did Dorothy Parker? Did Eudora Welty? Gloria Steinem? Peg Bracken? Gloria Naylor? Who was energized by his satire? Outraged by his limitations? Inspired by his wit? Irritated by his omissions? Excited by his rage? Energized by his prose style? Liberated by his irreverence? What Twain did they read, and what did they take from it? Who found her own voice by listening to his?

Perhaps, as the next century approaches, we will begin to understand more fully what Twain has meant to women readers and writers in this one. Like the book Huck thumbed through in the Grangerfords' parlor, this question promises to be "interesting but tough."

NOTES

1 Van Wyck Brooks, *The Ordeal of Mark Twain* (New York: Dutton, 1920), p. 151; Justin Kaplan, *Mr. Clemens and Mark Twain* (New York: Simon & Schuster, 1966).

2 Joyce W. Warren, "Old Ladies and Little Girls," *The American Narcissus: Individualism and Women in Nineteenth-Century American Fiction* (New Brunswick, N.J.: Rutgers University Press, 1984), pp. 149–50; see also Mary Ellen Goad, *The Image and the Woman in the Life and Writings of Mark Twain* (Emporia, Kans.: Emporia State Research Studies, vol. 19, no. 3, 1971); Judith Fryer, *The Faces of Eve: Women in the Nineteenth Century American Novel* (New York: Oxford University Press, 1976); Emmanuel Diel, "Mark Twain's Failure: Sexual Women Characters," *San Jose Studies* 5 (February 1979): 46–59; Wilma Garcia, *Mothers and Others: Myths of the Female in the Works of Melville, Twain and Hemingway* (New York: American University Studies/Peter Lang, 1984).

3 Hamlin Hill, *Mark Twain: God's Fool* (New York: Harper & Row, 1973); Guy Cardwell, *The Man Who Was Mark Twain* (New Haven, Conn.: Yale University Press, 1991).

4 Mark Twain, *The Autobiography of Mark Twain,* ed. Charles Neider (New York: Harper & Row, 1975), p. 190.

5 Brooks, *Ordeal of Mark Twain,* p. 157.

6 Peter Stoneley, *Mark Twain and the Feminine Aesthetic* (Cambridge University Press, 1992), p. 4; Bernard DeVoto, *Mark Twain's America* (Boston: Little Brown, 1935), p. 197; James Cox, *Mark Twain: The Fate of Humor* (Princeton, N.J.: Princeton University Press, 1966), p. 66.

7 Stoneley, *The Feminine Aesthetic,* p. 5; see Fred Lewis Pattee, *The Feminine Fifties* (New York: Appleton-Century, 1940).

8 Kaplan, *Mr. Clemens and Mark Twain,* p. 270.

9 Archibald Henderson, *Mark Twain* (1912; Philadelphia: Folcroft Press, 1969), p. 183.

10 Coventry Patmore, *The Angel in the House* (London: Dutton, 1905).

11 Laura Skandera-Trombley, "'The Mysterious Stranger': Absence of the Female in Mark Twain Biography," in *Mark Twain's Humor: Critical Essays,* ed. David E. E. Sloane (New York: Garland, 1993), pp. 576, 577, 576; Alan Gribben, "'It Is Unsatisfactory to Read to One's Self': Mark Twain's Informal Readings," *Quarterly Journal of Speech* 62 (1976): 55–56. For more on this topic see Laura Skandera-Trombley's *Mark Twain in the Company of Women* (Philadelphia: University of Philadelphia Press, 1994).

12 Shelley Fisher Fishkin, *Was Huck Black? Mark Twain and African-American Voices* (New York: Oxford University Press, 1993), pp. 8–9, 31, 36–8.

13 Michael Kiskis, "Susy Clemens as the Fire for Mark Twain's Autobiography," *Mid-Hudson Language Studies* 10 (1987): 44.

14 Ibid., p. 46.

15 Mark Twain, *Following the Equator* (1897; New York: Dover, 1989), pp. 209–12.

16 Alan Gribben, *Mark Twain's Library: A Reconstruction,* 2 vols. (Boston: G. K. Hall, 1980), vol. 2, p. 732.

17 Ibid., p. 788.

18 Stoneley, *The Feminine Aesthetic,* p. 5; Jane Tompkins, *Sensational Designs: The Cultural Work of American Fiction, 1790–1860* (New York: Oxford University Press, 1985), p. 123.

19 Stoneley, *The Feminine Aesthetic,* p. 8. See also Nina Baym, *Women's Fiction: A Guide to Novels by and about Women in America, 1820–1870* (Ithaca, N.Y.: Cornell University Press, 1978), and Cathy Davidson, *Revolution and the Word: The Rise of the Novel in America* (New York: Oxford University Press, 1986).

20 Skandera-Trombley, "'The Mysterious Stranger,'" p. 587.

21 Albert E. Stone, Jr., *The Innocent Eye: Childhood in Mark Twain's Imagination* (1961; Hamden, Conn.: Archon Books, 1970); Susan Harris, "Four Ways to Inscribe a Mackerel: Mark Twain and Laura Hawkins," *Studies in American Fiction* 13 (1985): 140; Gregg Camfield, "Sentimental Liberalism and the Problem of Race in *Huckleberry Finn,*" *Nineteenth Century Literature* 46.1 (1991): 97, 99. For additional comments on this subject, see Camfield's *Sentimental Twain: Samuel Langhorne Clemens in the Maze of Moral Philosophy* (Philadelphia: University of Pennsylvania Press, 1994).

22 Camfield, "Sentimental Liberalism," pp. 101, 109; Camfield, "A Funny Thing Happened on the Way to the Canon: The Suppressed Sentimental Side of *Adventures of Huckleberry Finn,*" Paper presented at the American Literature Association Convention, Baltimore, May 1993, p. 9.

23 Resa Willis, *Mark and Livy: The Love Story of Mark Twain and the Woman Who Almost Tamed Him* (New York: Atheneum, 1992), p. 23.

24 Kaplan, *Mister Clemens and Mark Twain,* 330; Louis J. Budd, *Our Mark Twain: The Making of His Public Personality* (Philadelphia: University of Pennsylvania Press, 1983), p. 123.

25 Willis, *Mark and Livy,* pp. 145–6.

26 William Dean Howells, *My Mark Twain* (New York: Harper Bros., 1910), p. 175; Bernard DeVoto, ed., *The Portable Mark Twain* (New York: Viking, 1968), pp. 18–19; Goad, "The Image and the Woman," p. 56; Fryer, *The Faces of Eve,* p. 26; Warren, "Old Ladies," p. 150.

27 Warren, "Old Ladies," p. 150; Harris, "Four Ways," p. 151.

28 Warren, "Old Ladies," pp. 152, 153.

29 J. D. Stahl, *Mark Twain, Culture and Gender: Envisioning America Through Europe* (Athens: University of Georgia Press, 1994).

30 Susan K. Harris, *Mark Twain's Escape from Time: A Study of Patterns and Images* (Columbia: University of Missouri Press, 1982), pp. 120, 122; Nancy

Walker, "Reformers and Young Maidens: Women and Virtue in *Adventures of Huckleberry Finn*," in *One Hundred Years of "Huckleberry Finn*," ed. Robert Sattelmeyer and J. Donald Crowley (Columbia: University of Missouri Press, 1985), p. 174; Camfield, "A Funny Thing," pp. 5, 7, 3, 9.

31 Harris, "Four Ways," pp. 146, 150.

32 Susan K. Harris, "Mark Twain's Bad Women," *Studies in American Fiction* 13 (1985): 161, 157.

33 Ibid., p. 165.

34 Christina Zwarg, "Woman as a Force in Mark Twain's *Joan of Arc:* The Unwordable Fascination," *Criticism* 27 (Winter 1985): 62; Margaret Thompson, "Between Good and Bad: The Female Outlaw in the Novels of Mark Twain," Unpublished paper, University of Texas, Austin, 1993, pp. 7–14; Stahl, *Mark Twain, Culture and Gender*, pp. 126, 149.

35 Carolyn Porter, "Roxana's Plot," in *Mark Twain's "Pudd'nhead Wilson": Race, Conflict, and Culture,* ed. Susan Gillman and Forrest G. Robinson (Durham, N.C.: Duke University Press), p. 124; Myra Jehlen, "The Ties That Bind: Race and Sex in *Pudd'nhead Wilson*, in ibid., pp. 114, 109.

36 Thompson, "Between Good and Bad," p. 2.

37 Howard G. Baetzhold, Joseph B. McCullough, and Donald Malcolm, "Mark Twain's Eden/Flood Parable: 'The Autobiography of Eve,'" *American Literary Realism* 24.1 (Fall 1991): 36.

38 Mark Twain, "Extract from Eve's Autobiography," in *New Uncensored Writings by Mark Twain: Letters from the Earth*, ed. Bernard DeVoto (New York: Harper & Row, 1991), p. 87. Henceforth referred to parenthetically in the text as EEA.

39 Mark Twain, "Introduction," in Susy Clemens, *Papa: An Intimate Biography of Mark Twain by Susy Clemens, His Daughter, Thirteen, With a Foreword and Copious Comments by Her Father,* ed. Charles Neider (Garden City, N.Y.: Doubleday, 1985), p. 82.

40 Shelley Fisher Fishkin, "'Making a Change': Strategies of Subversion in Gilman's Journalism and Short Fiction," in *Critical Essays on Charlotte Perkins Gilman,* ed. Joanne Karpinski (New York: G. K. Hall, 1992), pp. 240–8.

41 Mark Twain, "Hellfire Hotchkiss," in *Mark Twain's Satires and Burlesques*, ed. Franklin R. Rogers (Berkeley: University of California Press, 1967), pp. 185–6. Henceforth referred to parenthetically in the text as HH.

42 Mark Twain, "The 1002^d Arabian Night," in *Mark Twain's Satires and Burlesques,* ed. Rogers, p. 133.

43 Susan Gillman, *Dark Twins: Imposture and Identity in Mark Twain's America* (Chicago: University of Chicago Press, 1989), p. 125.

44 Mark Twain, ["Female Suffrage"] "Views of Mark Twain," in *Mark Twain: Collected Tales, Sketches, Speeches, & Essays, 1852–1890,* ed. Louis J. Budd (New York: Library of America, 1992), p. 214. Henceforth cited parenthetically in the text as FS.

45 Willis, *Mark and Livy,* p. 77.

46 Ibid., p. 78.

47 Mark Twain, *Mark Twain's Notebook*, ed. Albert Bigelow Paine (New York: Harper Bros., 1935), p. 256.

48 Quoted in Budd, *Our Mark Twain*, p. 188.

49 Mark Twain, *Letters from the Earth*, ed. Bernard DeVoto (New York: Harper & Row, 1991), p. 222.

50 Mark Twain, *Pudd'nhead Wilson* [1894] (New York: Bantam Books, 1959), p. 26.

51 Charles Neider, ed., Introduction to Susy Clemens, *Papa: An Intimate Biography*, pp. 13–37.

52 "The Higher Education of Women" (editorial), *Journal of the American Medical Association*, Sept. 4, 1886, pp. 267–9.

53 Willis, *Mark and Livy*, p. 32.

54 Ibid., p. 96.

55 Mark Twain, *The Love Letters of Mark Twain*, ed. Dixon Wecter (New York: Harper Bros., 1947), p. 68.

56 Mark Twain, *Mark Twain's Letters, Vol. 3: 1869*, ed. Victor Fischer and Michael B. Frank (Berkeley: University of California Press, 1992), p. 4.

57 Grace King, *Memories of a Southern Woman of Letters* (New York: Macmillan, 1932), p. 84.

58 I am grateful to Gregg Camfield for having shared this list of topics with me from the notes for his presentation, "Mark Twain and the Monday Evening Club," Mark Twain Circle, Modern Language Association Meeting, Toronto, December 29, 1993.

59 King, *Memories*, p. 84.

60 Robert Bush, "Grace King and Mark Twain," *American Literature* 54.1 (March 1972): 43.

61 Ibid., p. 40.

62 Gribben, *Mark Twain's Library*, vol. 2, p. 690.

63 John Cooley, ed., *Mark Twain's Aquarium: The Samuel Clemens Angelfish Correspondence, 1905–1910* (Athens: University of Georgia Press, 1991), p. 38.

64 Ibid.

65 Hill, *Mark Twain: God's Fool*, xxvii, 195–6, 260–1.

66 Doris Lanier, "Mark Twain's Georgia Angel Fish," *Mark Twain Journal* 24.1 (Spring 1986): 10.

67 Ibid.

68 Ibid.

69 While it focuses on the influence of Hawthorne rather than that of Twain, Emily Budick's *Engendering Romance: Women Writing in the Hawthorne Tradition* (New Haven, Conn.: Yale University Press, 1994) suggests some fruitful ways in which criticism may begin to explore interactions between male and female writers.

70 Gertrude Stein, cited in Richard Bridgman, *The Colloquial Style in America*, (New York: Oxford University Press, 1966), pp. 166–7, 243 n. 8. See also "Unique Tribute to Mark Twain from the Inimitable Gertrude Stein," *Mark Twain Journal* 15 (Summer 1971), front cover. Tillie Olsen, personal communication, June 1992; Elizabeth Spencer, personal communication, June 1993; Toni Morrison, personal communication, December 1991.

71 Judith Fetterly, *The Resisting Reader: A Feminist Approach to American Fiction* (Bloomington: Indiana University Press, 1978).

4

NEIL SCHMITZ

Mark Twain's Civil War: Humor's Reconstructive Writing

Humor, at its best, forgives and resolves a grievous wrong. It admits it, full measure, receives it, and expresses the immediate experience in humorous language. With verbal dexterity, in some comical voice, it economizes pain's impact. It speaks beautifully in Huck Finn's report of Buck Grangerford's death: "It made me so sick I most fell out of the tree. I ain't agoing to tell *all* that happened – it would make me sick again if I was to do that. I wished I hadn't ever come ashore that night, to see such things. I ain't ever going to get shut of them – lots of times I dream about them."[1] Humor doesn't deny, or defend; it transacts, it negotiates. Buck is dead, but there's Jim and the blessed raft, safety, survival. The Civil War section of the *Adventures of Huckleberry Finn* ends with Huck's euphoria, the sensation of escape, river and raft sweeping Huck away from the combat zone, ends with Huck's ecstatic rediscovery of Jim, the good food, the great stories. "You feel mighty free and easy and comfortable on a raft" (HF: 155). Briefly Huck sails free of the unreconstructed South. Its fight is not his fight. He's not a Grangerford, doesn't see himself in their narrative. His is the new narrative of the new (reconstructed) South, the solution for a still-dumbfounded post-bellum Southern writing, very shaky in its postwar fiction, its plots, its speeches.

In 1865 the principal Confederate armies, everywhere either hemmed in by General U. S. Grant or pursued by General W. T. Sherman, began to suffer major desertion. Manpower shortages were so critical, the Confederate government, in March 1865, too late, began to emancipate slaves for military service. There were casuistical Confederates (Jefferson Davis, Robert E. Lee, Judah Benjamin, Davis's secretary of state) who could parse the irony, but for most Southerners the decision was lunacy, and open admission that the South had lost the argument, lost the right to be at war. Slavery was the "chief stone of the corner," Alexander Stephens, Jefferson Davis's vice-president, had said in 1861. "Be it good or bad, [slavery] has grown up with our society and institutions, and is so interwoven with them, that to destroy it would be to destroy us as a people." This was the hard core of John C. Calhoun's Southern doctrine, the compact center of Southern ideology. "I hold," said Calhoun, "that in the present state of civilization, where two races of different origin, and distinguished by color, and other physical differences, as well as intellectual, are brought together, the relation now existing in the slaveholding states between the two, is, instead of an evil, a good – a positive good."[2] Hard-pressed by Grant and Sherman, unable to see God's favor in the turn of events, the cause seemingly fatally compromised (there was an argument for a selective Confederate emancipation), the Confederate South in 1865 could no longer convincingly assert its nationalist project. What was the expense of life and treasure for? R. M. T. Hunter, Davis's first secretary of state (1861–2), wrote, "I do not see, but I feel, that there is a righteous God in Heaven, who holds our destinies in his hand, and I do not believe He will allow us to be cast down and the wicked to prosper." But He did visibly seem to do so. "What have we done that the Almighty should scourge us with such a war?" General Josiah Gorgas asked in his diary. "Is the cause really hopeless? Is it to be abandoned and lost in this way?"[3] Everywhere there was isolation, stupefaction, silence. "We are shut in here," Mary Chesnut wrote, "turned with our faces to a dead wall. No mails. A letter is sometimes brought by a man on horseback, traveling through the wilderness made by Sherman. All RR's destroyed – bridges gone. We are cut off from the world – to eat out our own hearts."[4]

Substantially revised in the postwar period, 1881–4, but never brought into final book form, Chesnut's Civil War diary, even in its several modern editions, remains a mélange of contradictory thought and feeling. It contains many great lines and passages, but nothing ever adds up, gets larger or deeper, escapes the frame of the daily narrative. It is this massive unfinished text that is the consummate work of revisionary Confederate literature, not the massive finished apologetics of Jefferson Davis's *The Rise and Fall of the Confederate Government* (1881), of Alexander Stephens's *Constitutional View of the Late War Between the States* (1868–70). Chesnut freely expresses what they rigorously exclude in their text-based analyses, the real burden of Confederate nationalism, and does so early on, March 18, 1861.

> I wonder if it be a sin to think slavery a curse to any land. Sumner said not one word of this hated institution which is not true. Men and women are punished when their masters and mistresses are brutes and not when they do wrong – and then we live surrounded by prostitutes. An abandoned woman is sent out of any decent house elsewhere. Who thinks any worse of a negro or mulatto woman for being a thing we can't name? God forgive us, but ours is a *monstrous* system and wrong and iniquity.

Unlike Harriet Beecher Stowe, whom she read with hateful admiration, Chesnut couldn't locate a motive, moral, or plot for this antislavery position in her daily narrative. It was, after all, the damage slavery did to the marriages of respectable Southern white women that principally appalled her. "Thank God for my countrywomen," she writes in this same entry, "– alas for the men! No worse than men everywhere, but the lower their mistresses, the more degraded they must be." She didn't see the self-centeredness of her antislavery position in the sixties, and didn't see it in the eighties. "My Molly," her personal slave, exits the diary in June 1865, saying, "Never lef' Missis for no husband an' children in this world."5 "My Molly" says it all. This Confederate trope, Confederate Southern writing won't surrender.

What was her politics? What is the vision that informs her daily narrative? Chesnut scrupulously reported her reading: *Uncle Tom's Cabin*, Emerson, European histories, English and French literature. Whatever slavery was, monstrous or beautiful, the early narrative of Confederate nationalism brought to mind great histories, epic deeds. "While I was cudgeling my brain to say what kind of men we ought to choose," she writes in 1861, "I fell on Clarendon, and it was easy to construct my man out of this material." Many Confederates in 1861–2 looked into the *History of the Rebellion and the Civil Wars in England* (1702–4), pondered the mix of identifications: Cavalier/Puritan, tyranny/rebellion, Charles I/Cromwell. What story – English, biblical, classical – explained Southern defeat in 1865? At the end Chesnut was reading Byron's *Childe Harold's Pilgrimage;* Carlyle's *The French Revolution,* especially chapter 4, "The Loser Pays"; Sylvio Pellico's *Le Mie Prigioni* (1832), a political prisoner account; and Thomas Hood's "The Bridge of Sighs" (1844). In the C. Vann Woodward 1981 edition of Chesnut's diary, Mary Chesnut says finally, "Forgiveness is indifference. Forgiveness is impossible while *love lasts.*" She quotes Hood: "Make no deep scrutiny / Into our mutiny –."6

As Chesnut toiled over her diaries in the early 1880s, wanting dramatic coherence and intensity, wanting, but failing, to find a witty, far-seeing Cassandra in her text, the figure of conceptual order, a supple reconstructed Southern humorous writing came suddenly into the field and produced the first significant Southern reading of the Civil War. George Washington Cable's *The Grandissimes* (1880), Joel Chandler Harris's *Uncle Remus: His Songs and His Sayings* (1881), Mark Twain's *Adventures of Huckleberry Finn* (1884), Thomas Nelson Page's *In Ole Virginia* (1887) are interested in forgiveness, accept the humiliation and subjection of the Confederate South, undertake a therapy of disclosure, offer effective strategies of displacement and insulation, do the work of humor. Confederate generals surrendered to

Grant and Sherman. These Southern writers surrendered to Harriet Beecher Stowe. Uncle Tom was the opportune figure, his text, his speech, the place where the unspeakable (trust) could be entertained, the impossible (love) regarded. "My Molly" is fairly silent in Confederate writing, restricted in her speech. Uncle Tom speaks volumes, is the fount of story. He was the site of knowledge, where the deepest South revealed itself. Harris had put it together beautifully, the mis-en-scène, the words:

> One night, while the little boy was watching Uncle Remus twisting and wax-ing some shoe-thread, he made what appeared to him to be a very curious discovery. He discovered that the palms of the old man's hands were as white as his own, and the fact was such a source of wonder that he at last made it the subject of a remark. The response of Uncle Remus led to the earnest recital of a piece of unwritten history that must prove interesting to ethnologists.
>
> "Tooby sho de pa'm er my han's w'ite, honey," he quietly remarked, "en, w'en it comes ter dat, dey wuz a time w'en all de w'ite folks 'uz black – blacker dan me, kaze I done bin yer so long dat I bin sorter bleach out."[7]

All the principal Southern humorists (ethnologists of color and color differ-ences) knew how brilliant this was, this kind of writing with its tender exchanges, how appropriate the form and language. Here was a resource, fresh, interesting, extensive, a history not yet written, the turn Chesnut could not make, to My Molly, her subjectivity, her history.

In the 1880s, Mark Twain and Cable toured together, giving readings and lectures. Harris would have toured with them, but he had a fear of public speaking. When Page toured, he, too, wanted Uncle Remus in the act, and couldn't get him. All were variously published in the same powerful North-ern journals and magazines, often in the same issue. Harris and Page re-mained within the conceit of the sentimental, were formally and tonally reassuring whatever the grief their fiction bore. Page was the most sedative of the humorists. "Dem wuz good ole times, marster – de bes' Sam ever see! Dey wuz, in fac'! Niggers didn' hed nothin' 't all to do – jes' hed to 'ten' to de feedin' an' cleanin' de hosses an' doin' what de marster tell 'em to do; an' when dey wuz sick, dey had things sont 'em out de house, an' de same doctor come to see 'em what 'ten to de white folks when dey wuz po'ly."[8] The stories his black storytellers typically tell are about their beloved mas-ters and mistresses, "Marse Chan" and "Meh Lady: A Story of the War" in *Ole Virginia*. In Harris's text, the fable's frame, Uncle Remus's tender care of Miss Sally's seven-year-old boy, held the turbulent feelings set forth in the stories. "Food-sharing, sex-sharing – the Remus stories read like a cata-logue of Southern racial taboos, all standing on their heads," Bernard Wolfe tells us in his superb 1949 essay on Harris. "It was the would-be novelist in him who created Remus, the 'giver' of interracial caresses, but the trained journalist in him, having too good an eye and ear, reported the energetic folk blow in the caress."[9] Mark Twain and Cable set Stowe's figure and conceit at risk in different ways, confronted larger issues in their fiction. In *The Grandissimes,* where it is 1803–4, the lynching of a black woman, Clemence, is briefly described in cold documentary prose.

Of these writers, Mark Twain is the most problematic, the most distanced from the New South championed in Henry Woodfin Grady's *Atlanta Constitution,* a New South that still venerated its Confederate fathers, still insisted: "The South has nothing for which to apologize." Grady's famous 1886 speech, "The New South," given at a banquet in New York, spelled out the New South's perfect understanding of the prime dictate of Unionist discourse. It listened, this triumphant Unionist discourse, to Southern protestation, and then it asked: "But what of the negro?" The New South, Grady assured his public, understood what was to be done. "Our future, our very existence depends upon our working out this problem in full and equal justice." It affirmed the Unionist discourse of Lincoln and Sherman, their definitive versions. "We understand that when Lincoln signed the emancipation proclamation, your victory was assured, for he then committed you to the cause of human liberty, against which the arms of man cannot prevail – (while those of our statesmen who trusted to make slavery the corner-stone of the Confederacy doomed us to defeat as far as they could, committing us to a cause that reason could not defend or the sword maintain in the sight of advancing civilization." The New South went this far into Unionist discourse, but had its reservations, its obstinacies. At certain critical instances, the Confederate and Unionist narratives were still in conflict. The "late struggle between the States was war and not rebellion, revolution and not conspiracy." As Grady had it, the "new South presents a perfect democracy, the oligarchs leading in the popular movement." There were problems and paradoxes everywhere in Grady's speech, as there were in the New South itself. How does oligarchical democracy so perfectly work? What now was the status of black people in the New South? Of Harris's Uncle Remus and Page's Sam, the black men the New South chose to recognize and celebrate, it said: "To liberty and enfranchisement is as far as the law can carry the negro. The rest must be left to conscience and common sense." Harris wrote for the *Atlanta Constitution,* was its principal editorial writer. Why couldn't Harris do public readings of his Uncle Remus stories? In *Life on the Mississippi* (1883), Mark Twain saw through Harris's shyness, saw the whole rich irony of the New South's situation in Unionist discourse, of its humorous transactions in dialect poetry.

> [Harris] deeply disappointed a number of children who flocked eagerly to Mr. Cable's house to get a glimpse of the illustrious sage and oracle of the nation's nurseries. They said:
> "Why, he's white!"
> They were grieved about it. So, to console them, the book was brought, that they might hear Uncle Remus's Tar-baby story from the lips of Uncle Remus himself – or what, in their outraged eyes, was left of him. But it turned out that he had never read aloud to people, and was too shy to venture the attempt now.[10]

Mark Twain, it might be said, was the Southern humorist gone over, not just a deserter, a dissenter, but a literary scalawag, a Southern writer in Unionist discourse and narrative. Chapter 6 in Louis Budd's *Mark Twain: Social Philosopher* (1962) is entitled "The Scalawag." As Budd has it, this heavy term (its modern cognates are "quisling," "collaborator") aptly characterizes Mark Twain's political practice in the postwar period. There he was, at all those postwar Grand Army of the Republic banquets, happily toasting Union generals. The *Notice* posted at the head of *Huckleberry Finn* evokes Civil War/Reconstruction orders, the bills put up in the courthouse squares of occupied Southern cities and towns. "Persons attempting to find a moral in it will be banished; persons attempting to find a plot in it will be shot." For all its Southern speech, this text is in Unionist discourse. It abjures Sir Walter Scott, professes Uncle Tom.

How did Mark Twain get here, and how secure, how satisfying, is Huck's position? As late as 1954, the New South was still warily regarding Mark Twain. In his compendious *The South in American Literature, 1607–1900* (1954), Jay B. Hubbell, deriding Mark Twain's Scott thesis, argued that "Mark Twain had been out of touch with Southern life so long that, like many Northern travelers and historians, he had come to look for some simple formula which would explain the many differences between the two sections." As for Mark Twain's Jim: "There is in his picture of slavery a little too much of the old abolitionist legend of the Deep South."[11] I count as the classic texts in Mark Twain's Civil War writing "A True Story" (1874), *Life on the Mississippi* (1883), *Huckleberry Finn* (1885), and "The Private History of a Campaign That Failed" (1885). Mark Twain's reconstructive humorous reading of the Civil War gets essentially done in these texts, which were published in important national magazines – the *Atlantic Monthly*, the *Century Illustrated Monthly Magazine* – and immediately entered the major discursive networks in American literature. "An Adventure of Huckleberry Finn: With an Account of the Famous Grangerford–Shepherdson Feud" appeared in the November 1884 issue of the *Century*, which had just begun its monumental series, *Battles and Leaders of the Civil War*. Readers turned past Huck's account of Buck Grangerford's death, past E. W. Kemble's illustration, "Behind the Woodpile" (Grangerford farm boys shooting at Shepherdson farm boys), to find Warren Lee Goss's mud gritty "Recollections of a Private" and its illustration, a mounted federal cavalryman. It put Mark Twain figuratively right in the thick of things, though up a tree, onlooking, *hors de combat*.

To enter the cultural debate over the remembrance and meaning of the Civil War, to ponder the responsibility of the South for the Civil War, Mark Twain had bravely to come forward and admit he had no right to speak about such matters. He had spent the Civil War in Nevada, a sometime employee of the federal government, most of the time advancing his career as a comic journalist. What was he doing at all these military banquets, loving the toasts, the banter, the badinage, the blue coats and brass buttons? Mark Twain's love for the company of old soldiers betrayed him. His voice in this assembly of speakers, he realized, was "a sort of voice, – not a loud one, but a modest one; not a boastful one, but an apologetic one."[12] As early as 1877, in the Putnam Phalanx Dinner Speech, delivered in Hartford, Mark Twain had begun to address, humorously, at once the painful issue of his desertion and the present problem of his right to speak about the Civil War. "I did not assemble at the hotel parlors today to be received by a committee as a mere civilian guest; no, I assembled at the headquarters of the Putnam Phalanx, and insisted upon my right to be escorted to this place as one of the military guests. For I, too, am a soldier! I am inured to war. I have a military history."[13] This, too, was a sort of voice, facetious, protected.

"Putnam Phalanx" is the first draft of "The Private History of a Campaign That Failed," a suspiciously breezy first draft oozing anxiety. There is no traumatic shooting in this first piece. It is Ben Tupper, not young Samuel Clemens, who boyishly rationalizes his desertion: "Gentlemen, you can do as you choose; as for me, I've got enough of this sashaying around so's 't you can't get a chance to pray, because the time's all required for cussing" (MTS 108). And there was, too, as Justin Kaplan taught us in *Mr. Clemens and Mark Twain* (1966), the complex issue of Mark Twain's relation to U. S. Grant, the question "why a former Confederate irregular should be publishing, and ostensibly making a good deal of money doing so, the *Personal Memoirs* of the commander of all the Union armies."[14] In 1887, two years after the publication of the "Private History," addressing the Union Veterans Association of Maryland, Mark Twain was at his boldest: "You Union veterans of Maryland have prepared your feast and offered to me, a rebel veteran of Missouri, the wound-healing bread and salt of a gracious hospitality" (MTS 219). Tom Quirk and Richard E. Peck have written excellent essays on the relation of *Huckleberry Finn* to the "Private History." "This moving tale of Clemens shooting a stranger," Peck writes, "is, if you like, a lie, a most useful lie because it pulls into focus all the fragments comprising 'The History' in a dramatic conclusion that accounts for (and 'justifies'?) Clemens' desertion on grounds that it represented a moral act."[15] Yet there is a difference between young Samuel Clemens's retreat from his wartime duty in the Marion Rangers, his desertion of the cause of Confederate nationalism, and Huck's flight. *Huckleberry Finn* is not only about running away, it is also about the fright and guilt of changing sides.

In these Civil War texts, "A True Story," *Life on the Mississippi, Huckleberry Finn,* and "Private History," Mark Twain looks for ways to break out of the Southern imaginary (William Gilmore Simms, Sidney Lanier) into a Northern real (William Dean Howells, U. S. Grant), to break its narcissistic Sir Walter Scott trance, to open his text to the real, to difference, to the most radical of alterities. "Sir Walter," Mark Twain wrote in *Life on the Mississippi,* "had so large a hand in making Southern character, as it existed before the war, that he is in great measure responsible for the war. It seems a little harsh toward a dead man to say that we never should have had any war but for Sir Walter; and yet something of a plausible argument might, perhaps, be made in support of that wild proposition."[16] The Scott chapter is entitled "Enchantments and Enchanters." As Mark Twain saw it, there was no longer a usable Southern patriarchal literary tradition, a Confederate narrative. There was just the biracial Southern narrative Harriet Beecher Stowe had mothered in American literature, its complexities, its dreads, its horrors. Huck is in Unionist discourse, but only because where Jim is going, what Jim wants, is the Ohio, not the Mississippi. Such is the breakthrough of *Huckleberry Finn,* its stroke of genius. With Huck, Mark Twain sort of deserts Tom Sawyer, sort of chooses Jim. Mark Twain is a Southern writer in Unionist discourse, happily at work within its tenets, but always revising its terms, exploring its tolerances, its shortcomings, its practical meaning. Huck's speech is equivocal. His narrative isn't yet committed to a direction, isn't totally invested in a denouement. Hence we see in Mark Twain's Civil War writing this ongoing literary phenomenon, narratives interrupted, invaded, silenced. Huck is always on the move, now in Tom's story, then in Jim's, just as Tom and Jim come upon Huck's story and try to determine it. Huck's narrative is afloat, in passive suspense. Whose story is told here? Huck's? Tom's? Jim's? Humor reaches here its purest liquidity, its supplest resilience. What does Huck's speech do? It registers, it goes on.

All this discourse shifting and story breaching in *Huckleberry Finn* is remarkably foretold in "A True Story," which warns us about reading Jim as Uncle Remus, seeing in him what Misto C sees in Aunt Rachel: "She was a cheerful, hearty soul, and it was no more trouble for her to laugh than it is for a bird to sing."[17] The interlocutor is a Northern liberal gentleman who didn't request the story he receives, doesn't even want to hear it. "Why, I thought – that is, I meant – why, you *can't* have had any trouble. I've never heard you sigh, and never seen your eye when there wasn't a laugh in it" (TS 60). The title, "A True Story, Repeated Word for Word as I Heard It," still marks his incredulity and denial, as a Northerner, of any involvement or responsibility for Aunt Rachel's "trouble." He is here only as a scene setter, as asking the provocative question, as putting into play the decisive term, "trouble." It is in fact the outrageous ignorance/innocence of the interlocutor's casual remark that abruptly cuts Aunt Rachel's uproarious laughter off. "Aunt Rachel, how is it that you've lived sixty years and never had any trouble?" It is the lie of the euphemism that gives Aunt Rachel her sudden stab of pain, that snaps into sharp focus her relation to Misto C and his family, her alienated difference. "Trouble" is Misto C's cloaking term for slavery, his denial of its experience and its consequences. *How is it you're so merry – you who were once a slave? Slavery could not have been that bad since it has left you the joyous creature you are.* As the sketch begins, Aunt Rachel is "sitting respectfully below our level, on the steps, – for she was our servant, and colored." Into the narration of her story, word for word as he heard it, the interlocutor intrudes only once more, to reset the scene of narration. "Aunt Rachel had gradually risen, while she warmed to her subject, and now she towered above us, black against the stars" (TS 60). It has been an after-dinner sit on the porch, summertime, twilight, the company has been teasing Aunt Rachel, entertained by the rich exuberance of her Negro mirth, and then that explosively wrong phrase is uttered, "and never had any trouble." "Has I had any trouble? Misto C –, I's gwine to tell you, den I leave it to you" (TS 59–60). After Aunt Rachel towers, black against the stars, the interlocutor disappears. Aunt Rachel has the closing, the conversion of Misto C's term. "Oh, no, Misto C –, I hain't had no trouble. An' no *joy!*" (TS 63). This sentence is like a freeze-frame, Misto C's term in a wreckage of negatives.

To this extent, "A True Story" prefigures certain transactions in *Huckle-*

berry Finn, especially those in the pre-Cairo chapters. Jim will also speak up here, emerge in his threatening difference and counter Huck vigorously. "Doan talk to me 'bout Sollermun, Huck, I knows him by de back" (HF 95). "A True Story" thus redirects Southern writing, turns comic dialect sketch into serious testimony, a survivor's tale told in "'arnest," and does so with artful tact, inscribing the narrator's flawed appropriation, even though Aunt Rachel gives her story to him, leaves it with him. In that framework, Mark Twain's "A True Story" testifies to the literary value of Aunt Rachel's testimony. It realizes, as it were, that all the emergent complexities of African-American experience, the riches of its oral tradition, *His Songs and His Sayings* (Harris's subtitle), are properly the resources of Southern literature, as long as the Anglo-American writer inscribes Misto C. Liberated, enabled, this Southern writing already occupies in 1874 the fictive space Toni Morrison has come to define in *Song of Solomon* (1977) and *Beloved* (1987), African-American family history at the critical juncture of emancipation.

What are the familial traces? What are the documentary texts? In "A True Story," there is just a saying. A grandmother born in Maryland, a proud woman, would say: "I wa'nt bawn in de mash to be fool'd by trash. I's one o' de old Blue Hen's Chickens." And a scar, to recognize. Aunt Rachel's son, "my little Henry tore his wris' awful, and most busted his head, right up at de top of his forehead, an' de niggers didn't fly aroun' fas' enough to 'tend him" (TS 60). The grandmother angrily declares her saying, clears the kitchen, bandages the child's wounds. The family is sold at auction, broken up. Aunt Rachel loses her husband and her seven children. "– 'an six of 'em I hain't set eyes on ag'in to dis day, an' dat's twenty-two years ago las' Easter" (TS 61). When the Civil War comes, African-Americans begin searching for each other, children for parents, parents for children. Henry, who had run North and prospered, "sole out an' went to whar dey was recruitin', an' hired hisse'f out to de colonel for his servant; an' den he went all froo de battles everywhah, huntin' for his ole mammy" (TS 62). Saying and scar are finally matched, mother and son, a family line established, but there are ominous complications. A *"nigger* ridgment" on guard at the mansion where Aunt Rachel manages the kitchen holds a dance in that kitchen. Henry doesn't recognize his mother, treats her insolently, "smilin' at my big red turban, and makin' fun," has an attitude not unlike Misto C's, whereupon Aunt Rachel indignantly uses the grandmother's saying. In the rapture of the reunion, Aunt Rachel briefly exults: "Lord God ob heaven be praise', I got my own ag'in!" But what then? Where is she now? Where is Henry? "A True Story," as we've seen, abruptly closes.

"A True Story" gives us summarily an African-American account of the American midcentury, the 1850s, the Civil War, the Reconstruction. The three actions in *Huckleberry Finn* refer to these periods in Southern history. In the first section, chapters 1–16, written largely in 1876, runaway Huck suddenly finds himself in a slave narrative, a secondary character, reluctantly, anxiously, aiding and abetting Jim's flight to freedom in Illinois. We are here in actual time, in the 1850s. The middle section, chapters 16–22, written in 1879–80, begins with the Grangerford–Shepherdson feud, the chapter Mark Twain purposefully dealt into the series, *Battles and Leaders of the Civil War*, and ends with the humiliating overthrow of the king and the duke. The final section, chapters 32–43, written in 1883, concerns setting free an already freed Jim, symbolically enacts the Reconstruction as a nightmarish agony. For us the problem is the middle section, its gunfire, its bands and mobs of men. In this section we come upon the South as a place, a people, a nationality. Of the sections, it is the riskiest. It exposes Huck up his tree, keeps him in constant jeopardy, puts him in that hard place where he must finally choose sides. At these points, *Huckleberry Finn* intersects with *Life on the Mississippi*, with Mark Twain's reminiscences of his Civil War experience: "Putnam Phalanx," "Private History," "An Author's Soldiering." Complexes of pacifist/bellicose feeling swirl through the middle section of *Huckleberry Finn*. What *is* courage? The Grangerford episode seems to say one thing, the Bricksville episode another, the Wilks episode still another.

"The new South is simply the old South under new conditions."[18] In its ideological negotiation with the North, Grady's New South insisted that it be allowed to sanctify the memory of the old regime. "The sign of nobility in her families for generations to come will be the gray cap or the stained coat, on which, in the ebb of losing battle, God laid the sword of his imperishable knighthood." The New South would be progressive, would be in Unionist discourse, but it wouldn't recant, wouldn't criticize the fathers. "Slavery as an institution cannot be defended – but its administration was so nearly perfect among our forefathers as to challenge and hold our loving respect."[19] There is a lot of bad faith oozing in Grady's formulations; "its administration" simply lies on the page, blatant, palpable. The Confederate fathers "administered" slavery, and did the work of it so well as to "hold our loving respect." Could one retain Confederate articles, Confederate tropes, in Unionist discourse, perhaps even revise Unionist discourse, end the insistence of its punishing question: "But what of the negro?" In its early going, Grady's New South, Harris its principal writer, struggled with this question, worked in a humorous mode to resolve it. The human slaves and masters in

Page's *Old Virginia* are the very Brers in Harris's *Uncle Remus*. Slavery is foregrounded, sentimentalized. The newspaper that brings the tragic news of Lincoln's assassination to old Colonel Cameron in D. W. Griffith's *Birth of a Nation* (1915) is the *New South,* the name boldly printed. Griffith's film epic, which beautifully illustrates the jam and the jar of the two narratives, Confederate and Unionist, is at its most gloriously appropriative creating a Confederate Lincoln, a Lincoln sort of compelled to sign the Emancipation Proclamation.

Bad faith in *Huckleberry Finn* is rankest in the middle section. In the Old South you can't live without it, Huck discovers, offering that knowledge to us as a truism. "If they wanted us to call them kings and dukes, I hadn't no objections, 'long as it would keep peace in the family; and it warn't no use to tell Jim, so I didn't tell him. If I never learnt nothing else out of pap, I learnt that the best way to get along with his kind of people is to let them have their own way" (HF 165). Forrest G. Robinson writes, in *In Bad Faith: The Dynamics of Deception in Mark Twain's America* (1986), a dark Melvillean reading of *Huckleberry Finn,* "Bad Faith rules, by necessity, in all human affairs." Huck's phrase, "no use," is particularly telling. "Perhaps Huck's decision not to tell is the reflex of his fear that Jim will react to the truth by running away; perhaps, too, it expresses a fatalistic surrender to the inevitable failure of the quest. Whatever the case, the 'no use' that Huck appeals to cannot possibly speak for Jim, even though in declining to share what he knows Huck does just that."[20] No use, *now.* We are in and out of faiths, and narratives, in *Huckleberry Finn.* Jim, too, is withholding information. He has not told Huck that the reason for his flight no longer exists, that the cruel, murderous Pap Finn who is after Huck is dead. In the Old South of *Huckleberry Finn,* in the New South of *Life on the Mississippi,* everywhere, even among the best of friends, there is, at times, serious bad faith, significant withholding.

In what ways does the middle of *Huckleberry Finn,* so heavily freighted with Civil War experience, the bad feeling of that bad faith, humorously resolve its subject? Bad acting, always before us, is a major trope. The circus gives us good acting, we briefly see it, the fake drunk is a real acrobat, Huck is amazed, and then it is gone. The king and the duke, fabulators, mythologists, confidence men, bad actors, are in specific relation to those other two bad actors, Colonel Grangerford and Colonel Sherburn. These rule Huck's world, shore and river, in the middle section. Colonel Grangerford commands foolhardy courage, life-wasting bravery. Colonel Sherburn confronts riotous bravado, personal cowardice. They wear the planter's white suit, the white suit that would in time become Mark Twain's signature suit. When

Colonel Sherburn speaks, Mark Twain forces his way into Huck's text. It is the worst moment in *Huckleberry Finn*. Suddenly there is ugly writing, conflicted feeling, unresolved thinking, a spew of angry statements. It is as if Colonel Sherburn were addressing the Marion Rangers of "Private History." "But a mob without any *man* at the head of it, is *beneath* pitifulness. Now the thing for *you* to do, is to droop your tails and go home and crawl in a hole" (HF 191). Buck Grangerford, on the other hand, is ready to die, and his father is too. "I don't like that shooting from behind a bush," Colonel Grangerford tells thirteen-year-old Buck. "Why didn't you step into the road, my boy?" (HF 145). This is bad acting, as is the shooting of Buck floundering in the river, unable to defend himself, unarmed, in the open. But it is the king and the duke, the doctors of divinity and literature, who are always before us in the middle section, who deliver, at once lunatic and fraudulent, the ongoing dominant discourse.

In *Life on the Mississippi* Sir Walter Scott is the name of that discourse, of its romantic *a priori*, its faux medievalism. Scott enchains Southern thinking, Southern imagining, "with decayed and swinish forms of religion; with decayed and degraded systems of government; with the sillinesses and emptinesses, sham grandeurs, sham gauds, and sham chivalries of a brainless and worthless long-vanished society" (LM 242). He "made every gentleman in the South a major or a colonel, or a general or a judge, before the war," created "rank and caste down there, and also reverence for rank and caste, and pride and pleasure in them" (LM 242). He is the progenitor, the forefather, his faux medievalism the enabling mythos, its theology, its poetry. He is the killer of Southern writing. There is strenuous pursuit of Sir Walter Scott in *Life on the Mississippi*. Mark Twain stresses his radical disaffiliation. Chapter 46, "Enchantments and Enchanters," is the hottest chapter in the book, and still seething. Here, too, Mark Twain curiously inscribes the feminine, puts a mark on the manliness of Southern chivalry. "Take away the romantic mysteries, the kings and knights and big-sounding titles, and Mardi Gras would die, down there in the South. The very feature that keeps it alive – girly-girly romance – would kill it in the North or in London" (LM 241–2). In *Huckleberry Finn* the Duke of Bridgewater has about him a certain effeminacy, a certain intonation. Rehearsing the king as Juliet, the duke says: "You mustn't bellow out *Romeo!* that way, like a bull – you must say it soft, and sick, and languishy, so – R-o-o-meo! that is the idea; for Juliet's a dear sweet mere child of a girl, you know, and she don't bray like a jackass" (HF 177). It is there in the way the duke calls Looy the Seventeen by his familiar name, Capet, a misnomer, of course. The duke's carpetbag is much more interesting than the king's, which yields, besides clothes, only a "ratty deck of cards." The duke's bag is packed with convenient wonders, posters, costumes, wigs, theatrical face paint. The interesting question of how this squirmy bad acting relates to the straight bad acting of the Grangerfords and Sherburns Mark Twain merely exposes.

On board the raft, the king and the duke immediately establish rank and caste, place and position. Like Sir Walter Scott, they are blissfully blind to the plights of Huck and Jim. The king's first move as the executor of the Wilks estate is to sell the slaves, "two sons up the river to Memphis, and their mother down the river to Orleans" (HF 234). The duke's line: "jour printer, by trade; do a little in patent medicines; theatre-actor – tragedy, you know; take a turn at mesmerism and phrenology when there's a chance; teach singing-geography school for a change; sling a lecture, sometimes." The king's line: "I've done considerable in the doctoring way in my time. Layin' on o' hands is my best holt – for cancer and paralysis, and sich things; and I k'n tell a fortune pretty good, when I've got somebody along to find out the facts for me. Preachin's my line, too; and workin' camp-meetin's; and missionaryin' around" (HF 160–1). Mark Twain's critique of the patriarchal orders in Southern society is encompassing, though differently established. Huck merely registers the moral idiocy of the honor-bound colonels, the casualties of their disastrous leadership, then turns from them, to Jim and the raft, to a circus. He promptly sees through the king and the duke, discounts their fictions, despises their bad acting. Sir Walter Scott is a sunk concern in *Huckleberry Finn*.

In the Wilks episode, the sides are perfectly clear. Huck and Jim have come together on the issue of the king and the duke, shared their detestation of the "rapscallions." Yet Colonel Sherburn is still at large in the text, fearless, contemptuous, a figure not wholly in the brackets of censure, his speech not completely in Sir Walter Scott. He has killed a man with cool dispatch. He stares down Buck Harkness in the crowd, chooses Buck to confront individually. His challenge is – personal cowardice. He cocks his gun. Here's another Buck to be shot. "The crowd washed back sudden, and then broke apart and went tearing off every which way, and Buck Harkness he heeled it after them, looking tolerable cheap" (HF 191). Huck witnesses, makes the barest commentary: "I could a staid, if I'd a wanted to, but I didn't want to" (HF 191). Sherburn is not mentioned again in the narrative. The Colonel, so to speak, goes unanswered – until that is, Mark Twain's ingeniously worked-out formal response in the "Private History" appears in the *Century*, speaks modestly, humorously, among the war papers in its ongoing Civil War series.

Humor works very hard in this reminiscence. The text argues that it is autobiographical, to be held to the rules of evidence, but does so teasingly, is facetious from the start. There is still something smarmy about the "Private History," something totally unconvincing. It wants to make a pacifist argument (Huck's), wants to represent all the deserters, the Bull Run runners, the rabbits, the Buck Harknesses, the Hucks. It wants to show that Mark Twain left the war because, like Huck, he was horrified by killing, hated killing, but it can't finally face down its Colonel Sherburn, the grimly fearless, coolly self-controlled U. S. Grant. It turns abruptly from the pacifist pieties given over the corpse of the slain stranger to glorify Grant and the killing power of well-trained modern troops. The narrator exits with a nonsequitur, humorously put, cowardly speech par excellence, spoken from the safety of the subjunctive: "I could have become a soldier myself, if I had waited. I had got part of it learned; I knew more about retreating than the man that invented retreating" (PH 223). It echoes Huck's "I could a staid, if I'd a wanted to, but I didn't want to," but differently, is apologizing where Huck is not, is obsequious where Huck is simply decisive. In the text generally, extenuators and specifiers are not always immediately detectable. Here Mark Twain explains his family's relation to slavery: "I said, in palliation of this dark fact, that I had heard my father say, some years before he died, that slavery was a great wrong, and that he would free the solitary negro he then owned if he could think it right to give away the property of the family when he was so straitened in means" (PH 207). "Then" is the fixer in that sentence. The father in fact once dealt in slaves. As for the lugubrious death scene, Mark Twain scholarship has yet to corroborate its actual happening.

"In confronting that past in which the nation had reached its limits and been rent asunder, Mark Twain reached the limits of his humor, which is to say he reached the threshold of his disillusion." James M. Cox's reading of the situation in *Mark Twain: The Fate of Humor* (1966) still stands. "In *Huckleberry Finn* [Mark Twain] had come as near – and as far – as he was ever to do in reconstructing the Civil War past. The 'Private History' marked a second effort to encounter that past, but it was a smaller, safer effort."[21] Humor doesn't pull it off in the "Private History," is uncertain in its focus, doesn't admit the pain, evades it, puts into play the defense of the dead stranger, prevaricates, is contradictory. In *Huckleberry Finn,* Mark Twain's humor works purposefully. Huck says: "I reckon a body that ups and tells the truth when he is in a tight place, is taking considerable many resks; though I ain't had no experience, and can't say for certain; but it looks so to me, anyway; and yet here's a case where I'm blest if it don't look like the truth is better, and actuly *safer,* than a lie" (HF 239). Such is the difference between Huck Finn and Mark Twain. Huck never signed up, never pledged allegiance to Confederate nationalism. He is its witness, the doings of Sir Walter Scott, of the king and the duke. In the middle section, Huck has already, to some extent, gone over into Jim's narrative. Jim tells him the pitiful story of his deaf child, 'Lizabeth. He has a son, we learn, Johnny. This brief story from Jim's family history is beautifully arresting, and not at all self-serving. Huck will side, too, with Mary Jane Wilks and work to restore the African-American family the king has so callously broken up. This is where he comes into Unionist discourse, specifically into the allegiances of the Stowe variant. Huck signs up for women and blacks. Confiding in Mary Jane, spelling out a very complicated anti–king and duke strategy, Huck manfully swears his oath: "I don't want nothing more out of *you* than just your word – I'd druther have it than another man's kiss-the-Bible" (HF 239).

Apart from the problematic "Private History," Mark Twain's only other Civil War narrative is in *Life on the Mississippi,* "Vicksburg during the Trouble." Distinctly anti-Confederate, the chapter begins citing the euphemistic term "Trouble," uses the form of the dialect sketch again to do something like a documentary interview. There is no glorification of Confederate heroism here. Under bombardment, frantic women and children scurry for the cave shelters, "encouraged by the humorous grim soldiery, who shout 'Rats, to your holes!' and laugh" (LM 195). A civilian survivor of the siege, a married man, the father of children, remembers, in a flat prosaic voice, the awful tedium, and terror, of bomb-shelter life. He speaks, like Huck, in the language of reportage, seeing it all as it is, marking the absurdities. His wife, Maria, is caught outside as a bombardment begins. "When she was running for the holes, one morning, through a shell shower, a big shell burst near her and covered her all over with dirt, and a piece of iron carried away her game-bag of false hair from the back of her head. Well, she stopped to get that game-bag before she shoved along again!" (LM 196). Humor works very hard here, telling these funny truths. Another time a shell burst interrupts the narrator's inviting a friend to share a drink of rare whisky in his shelter. "A chunk of it cut the man's arm off, and left it dangling in my hand. And do you know the thing that is going to stick longest in my memory, and outlast everything else, little and big, I reckon, is the mean thought I had then? It was, 'the whisky *is saved!*'" (LM 197). In "Vicksburg during the Trouble," humor is almost exhausted, almost becomes the steeled irony of Stephen Crane and Ernest Hemingway, yet not quite, because it is the victim, the survivor, who speaks, not the interlocutory observer. "We always had eight; eight belonged there. Hunger and misery and sickness and fright and sorrow, and I don't know what all, got so loaded into them that none of them were ever rightly their old selves after the siege. They all died but three of us within a couple of years" (LM 196).

Mark Twain admires the National Cemetery outside Vicksburg, a "Mount Auburn" cemetery, modern, its grounds "tastefully laid out in broad terraces, with winding roads and paths; and there is a profuse adornment in the way of semitropical shrubs and flowers; and in one part is a piece of native wild-wood, left just as it grew, and, therefore, perfect in its charm" (LM 198). He particularly admires the touch of that remnant piece of wild-wood, "left just as it grew." There is no question here of Mark Twain's chosen side, his respect for the reach and power of the national government, its situation of this National Cemetery, its management of it. "The government's work is always conspicuous for excellence, solidity, thoroughness, neatness. The government does its work well in the first place, and then takes care of it" (LM 198). Unionist discourse empowers him, braces its monuments with metal, lets him interview outside the National Cemetery, an "aged colored man," another survivor of the siege. He

> showed us, with pride, an unexploded bombshell which had lain in his yard since the day it fell during the siege.
>
> "I was a-stannin' heah, an' de dog was a-stannin' heah; de dog he went for de shell, gwine to pick a fuss wid it; but I didn't; I says, 'Jes' make youseff at home heah; lay still whah you is, or bust up de place, jes' as you's a mind to, but I's got business out in de woods, I has!" (LM 198)

Unionist discourse was multifarious, supple, differently interested, competent in diverse speech. When "a Southerner of genius writes modern English," Mark Twain insisted, "his book goes upon crutches no longer, but upon wings; and they carry it swiftly all about America and England, and through the great English reprint publishing-houses of Germany – as witness the experience of Mr. Cable and 'Uncle Remus,' two of the very few Southern authors who do not write in the Southern style" (LM 243).

Life on the Mississippi is a charter for a new postwar Southern writing, *Huckleberry Finn* its first local masterpiece. Such writing abjures Sir Walter Scott, professes Huck and Jim. But what happens to Harris, to Cable? Only Page, the most apologetic, the most reverential, always lapsing into Sir Walter Scott, is fairly productive in that Southern writing. After *Huckleberry Finn,* nothing of comparable measure, until Griffith's *Birth of a Nation* (1915), which returns the Confederate relics, the Confederate tropes, to

American literature, brings formally to a close Mark Twain's radical program in the 1880s, his humorous resolution of the Civil War.

NOTES

1 Mark Twain, *Adventures of Huckleberry Finn,* ed. Walter Blair and Victor Fischer (Berkeley: University of California Press, 1985), p. 153. Hereafter cited parenthetically in the text as HF.

2 *Works of John C. Calhoun,* 6 vols., ed. Richard Cralle. (New York, 1854–7), vol. 2, p. 627.

3 Richard Beringer, Herman Hattaway, Archer Jones, and William N. Still, Jr., *Why the South Lost the War* (Athens: University of Georgia Press, 1986), p. 352.

4 *Mary Chesnut's Civil War,* ed. C. Vann Woodward (New Haven, Conn.: Yale University Press, 1981), p. 830.

5 Ibid., pp. 29, 39, 829.

6 Ibid., pp. 7, 836.

7 Joel Chandler Harris, *Uncle Remus: His Songs and His Sayings* (New York: Shocken Books: 1965), p. 163.

8 Thomas Nelson Page, *In Ole Virginia* (New York: Scribner's, 1887), p. 10.

9 Bernard Wolfe, "Uncle Remus and the Malevolent Rabbit: 'Takes a Limber-Toe Gem-mun fer ter Jump Jim Crow,'" in *Critical Essays on Joel Chandler Harris,* ed. R. Bruce Bickley, Jr. (Boston: G. K. Hall, 1981), pp. 74–5.

10 Henry W. Grady, *The New South* (New York: Bonner's, 1890), pp. 320, 316, 315, 320, 318, 316, 244.

11 Jay B. Hubbell, *The South in American Literature, 1607–1900* (Durham, N.C.: Duke University Press, 1954), pp. 832–3.

12 Mark Twain, "A Private History of the Campaign That Failed," in *Selected Shorter Writings,* ed. Walter Blair (Boston: Riverside Editions, 1962), p. 206. Henceforth cited parenthetically in the text as PH.

13 *Mark Twain Speaking,* ed. Paul Fatout (Iowa City: University of Iowa Press, 1976), p. 106. Henceforth cited parenthetically in the text as MTS.

14 Justin Kaplan, *Mr. Clemens and Mark Twain* (New York: Simon & Schuster, 1966), p. 274.

15 Richard E. Peck, "The Campaign That . . . Succeeded," *American Literary Realism, 1870–1910* 21.3 (Spring 1989): 10. See also Thomas Quirk, "Life Imitating Art: *Huckleberry Finn* and Twain's Autobiographical Writings," in *One Hundred Years of Huckleberry Finn: The Boy, His Book, and American Culture,* ed. Robert Sattelmeyer and J. Donald Crowley (Columbia: University of Missouri Press, 1985).

16 Mark Twain, *Life on the Mississippi* (New York: Hill & Wang, 1968), p. 243. Henceforth cited parenthetically in the text as LM.

17 Mark Twain, "A True Story, Repeated Word for Word as I Heard It," in *Selected Shorter Writings,* ed. Blair, p. 59. Henceforth cited parenthetically in the text as TS.

18 Grady, *The New South,* p. 146.
19 Ibid., pp. 148–9.
20 Forrest G. Robinson, *In Bad Faith: The Dynamics of Deception in Mark Twain's America* (Cambridge, Mass.: Harvard University Press, 1986), pp. 240, 139.
21 James M. Cox, *Mark Twain: The Fate of Humor* (Princeton, N.J.: Princeton University Press, 1966), p. 197.

5

MYRA JEHLEN

Banned in Concord: *Adventures of Huckleberry Finn* and Classic American Literature

As the home of Emerson, Thoreau, Hawthorne, and the Alcotts, the very name of Concord, Massachussetts, connotes sophisticated literary dissent. Yet a month after the publication of *Adventures of Huckleberry Finn*,[1] the committee in charge of Concord's public library voted to remove the book from its shelves, fearing that Huck Finn's irreverence would undermine the morals of young readers. In full agreement, Louisa May Alcott proposed a more radical ban: "If Mr. Clemens cannot think of something better to tell our pure-minded lads and lasses," she advised, "he had best stop writing for them." Jo March would not be allowed to play with Huck.

Thus far, the banning of *Huckleberry Finn* is a familiar sort of ironic anecdote whereby Alcott and the cultural guardians of Concord reveal their moral timidity, their literary obtuseness, or both. But the story does not end here with the self-exposure of an ostensibly enlightened authority. *Adventures of Huckleberry Finn* did go on, of course, to become *the* American classic, and generations of children were duly made to read it. What makes this turnabout remarkable, and unlike the elevation of, for instance, *Madame Bovary* after it too was to be banned or, nearer home, the ascension of *Pierre* into a classic and a cult, is that the canonization of Twain's novel has not involved significant rereading. The *Huckleberry Finn* celebrated as the archetypal American novel is acclaimed precisely for being, as the Concord critics charged, "rough, coarse, and inelegant," and especially for featuring a hero who lies, uses profanity, and steals besides, a boy who everyone agrees is, as to class and culture, the "veriest trash." When Bernard DeVoto declared *Adventures of Huckleberry Finn* the preeminent American novel (maybe approached but certainly not surpassed by *Moby-Dick*),[2] he took it as generally understood that jettisoning elegance and refinement through a vernacular narration was the novel's most spectacular achievement. "It is the one book in our literature," Leo Marx noted, "about which highbrows and lowbrows can agree."[3]

Hemingway, announcing that "all modern American literature comes from one book by Mark Twain called *Huckleberry Finn,*" dismissed the other possible ancestors – "Emerson, Hawthorne, Whittier, and Company" – for their lack of vulgarity: "All these men were gentlemen, or wished to be. They were all very respectable. They did not use the words that people always have used in speech, the words that survive in language. Nor would you gather that they had bodies. They had minds, yes. Nice, dry, clean minds."[4] Besides Mark Twain, according to Hemingway, there were two other "good writers," Henry James and Stephen Crane. Stephen Crane "wrote two fine stories" but died too young to play a substantial role in the American tradition. Linking James and Twain (never mind that Twain once declared he "would rather be damned to John Bunyan's heaven than read" *The Bostonians*)[5] is more than mischievous; for while failing to explain how James escapes the imputation of respectable language, Hemingway consolidates an American way of writing in the image of Mark Twain. Real American writers use real people's real words to tell the down and dirty of carnal lives.

This image of the quintessential American writing as not really literary goes along with a vision of the great American novel as not really literature but rather a sort of spontaneous telling of unmediated experience. In the same passage Hemingway explains that he has never been able to read Thoreau for being unable to read "literary" naturalists, only those who are "extremely accurate." "There ain't nothing more to write about, and I am rotten glad of it," remarks Huck at the end of his story, "because if I'd knowed what a trouble it was to make a book I wouldn't a tackled it and ain't agoing to no more" (912). And the famous last two sentences of the novel complete the picture: "But I reckon I got to light out for the territory ahead of the rest, because Aunt Sally she's going to adopt me and sivilize me and I can't stand it. I been there before." "I been there before" looks straight at the Concord Library Committee. The gentlemen and ladies of the committee have not got it wrong: Huck sets himself against respectability not in boyish innocence but knowingly, in fact like Hemingway.

How does a work justly seen to reject the achievements and values of high culture come to be the high culture's favored self-representation? It happens all the time that works of art are reviled when they are produced and later celebrated. But these recuperations turn on transformed understandings. The avant-garde looks iconoclastic to its age but the next recognizes it as, on the contrary, a reformation. The icons were false idols; their smashing purified the faith. A 1993 retrospective essay on Roy Lichtenstein's Pop paintings observes: "That those very early pictures in his signature style had anything to do with high style wasn't, at first, easy to see. They just looked like comics."[6] But Mark Twain's comedy always looked seriously defiant of high style.

While latter-day readers, careless of Huck's profanity and even of his tendency to "borrow" the occasional chicken and watermelon, differ that way from his contemporaries, Twain's audiences overall have always held to the literary faith. Unlike Huck, who lost all interest in Moses upon learning that the baby in the bulrushes was long grown up and gone, readers of *Huckleberry Finn* generally take great "stock in dead people" (626). The issue here is not the rejection of the traditional culture of books, this being a common motif of modernist writing. "What would we really know the meaning of?" asked Emerson sweeping aside the long descent of erudition. "The meal in the firkin; the milk in the pan; the ballad in the street; the news of the boat; the glance of the eye; the form and gait of the body."[7] Though he was indubitably "very respectable," Emerson anticipated Hemingway's preference for a quotidian and experience-based speech by a century. But Hemingway was probably right in implying that the sage of Concord would not therefore have embraced the style of *Huckleberry Finn*. For the simplicity and directness of idiom Emerson recommended and sought in his own writing was an ideal that actual vernaculars fulfilled little more than did conventional formalities.

In short, neither enlightenment nor retrospection elevates the style or the philosophy of *Huckleberry Finn*'s narrator into the high culture that has placed the work itself at its pinnacle. It might be argued that Huck's cultural authority is limited in that readers often exactly reverse his judgments – for instance, his judgment of the humbug Colonel Grangerford, who mightily impresses the naive Huck. But even as we overturn Huck's misunderstandings, we nonetheless endorse his more fundamental morality, which, indeed, eventually inspires his disillusionment with the whole senselessly violent Grangerford clan. Huck's lapses in authority thus don't mitigate the force of his challenge to the high culture, nor the puzzle of the high culture's embrace of his challenge. Let us be clear about this puzzle: Dickens wrote popular classics; the vernacular *Huckleberry Finn* is better described as a *populist* classic, a work animated by its defiance of high culture.[8]

It is possible that its anomaly is the source of the other peculiarity of Twain's novel, the fact that, despite its established status, it has been exceptionally controversial. *The Scarlet Letter, Moby-Dick* (once people learned how to read it), *Portrait of a Lady, Absalom, Absalom!,* to name four works likely to appear on any list of great American novels, are about controversial issues but have not been particularly controversial in themselves. Controversial at its publication, *Huckleberry Finn* is again today, and has been

for the past twenty years. Indeed, it is undergoing a second period of banning, this time for conforming too much to convention in a racist portrait of
the slave Jim. *Moby-Dick* and *Absalom, Absalom!* contain similarly offensive characters and events but they have not been cited. Perhaps *Huckleberry Finn*'s racism is more flagrant; but its targeting, given the rich possibilities for identifying racist writing among the classics, probably responds
also to its availability.

Moby-Dick clearly refers to *King Lear* and *Absalom, Absalom!* to the
biblical story of the son of David. These are elevating references that lend
authority to everyone concerned by identifying the authors, the novels, and
their audiences with high culture. The burlesque Shakespeare in *Huckleberry Finn* does require its readers to know enough to recognize that the
speeches recited by the duke and the dauphin are a senseless pastiche (of
Macbeth and *Richard III* along with *Hamlet*), thus to be themselves and to
recognize that the novel is of a higher culture than Huck.[9] At the same time,
any burlesque lowers its object. Twain's work *is* irreverent, and its lack of
respectability is more precisely a lack of respect. It is perhaps only fair that
its readers take their cue from it and treat *it* without reverence. No one feels
compelled to grant *Huckleberry Finn* artistic license, as many do, for instance, *The Merchant of Venice,* with even Jews interpreting Shylock as an
exposure of anti-Semitism rather than condemn Shakespeare.

Huckleberry Finn's lack of respect seems to have rendered it less sacro-
sanct than is common with classics; yet it has achieved, in Jonathan Arac's
term, a state of "hypercanonization."[10] Its banning is no surprise and not
unreasonable, but simultaneously it is the country's official text. What does
it say about America that is so telling, and how does its peculiar dissonant
voice enter into what it tells?

I want to propose that dissonance *is* the message of *Huckleberry Finn*. On
one level, this message is intentional or conscious and represents Mark
Twain's understanding of the world of Hannibal, Missouri, and late-
nineteenth-century America. Much of nineteenth-century literature projects
a similar vision of contradictions in the national culture. But Twain's novel
is not only about contradiction, it is itself radically contradictory – so
dissonant, indeed, that it finally fails to represent the contradictions it
means to address. At a deeper level than Twain controls, the great American
novel is itself literally incoherent. *Adventures of Huckleberry Finn* sounds
the contradictions of American culture so deeply that the novel drowns in
them, collapsing at the end into embarrassing slapstick and bad writing.

This final collapse has received considerable critical attention, which we will look at shortly. But before considering the explanations that have been offered, let me point to just the experience of reading through *Huckleberry Finn* and into its drastic decline. While the plot ends comically, the degeneration of the work evokes in the reader, on the contrary, something on the order of tragedy. One feels oneself in the presence of an artistic fatality. And since it is the work in itself that ends tragically, there is no catharsis: having exposed contradiction to an ultimate clarity, *Huckleberry Finn* stands witness to the impossibility of any acceptable resolution. It is, I think, this experience of artistic fatality at the close of the novel, following on the brilliant life of the preceding pages, that has rendered Twain's classic the most widely compelling of American classics and at the same time the most frequently and harshly attacked. *Huckleberry Finn* has been throughout its history peculiarly unsettling for being itself so unsettled.

It is unsettled, of course, for good reason, over issues its readers can no more resolve than could Mark Twain, for at the core of the contradictions that finally rend *Huckleberry Finn* is the ideal of individual freedom. The conflict between this ideal, which is fundamental to the nation's founding philosophy, and the founders' tolerance, in some cases their endorsement, of slavery needs no explication. *Huckleberry Finn* is about that conflict. It was written, however, not while that conflict was still clearly inscribed in the law of the land but after two events had greatly obscured it. First, the Civil War legally emancipated the slaves and in the judgment of many redressed the founding error; then Reconstruction failed to establish the conditions that would realize this emancipation, so that the former slaves returned to a servitude from which it would require a different sort of intervention to free them than any declaration. This new intervention would have to be positive, not only severing the bond of slavery but reconnecting the former slaves and masters in mutually responsible relations. Social responsibilities, however, tend, by the definition of self-reliant individualism, to come into conflict with both the theory and the practice of personal freedom. *Huckleberry Finn* is not only about slavery and the nation's compromised past but also, and in my view principally, about the contemporary dilemma of Reconstruction.

In a sentence, the two principal characters, Huck and Jim, represent the two sides of the dilemma: Huck strikes out for an absolute freedom, while Jim requires, in order to gain his own freedom, that Huck qualify his freedom by entering into the pursuit of Jim's. Signs that these two definitions of freedom pull the story in different directions are evident from the beginning, but their opposition becomes unmistakable at a fork in both the novel's plot and its physical terrain, as if the author had prefigured the trajectory of the work's own unfolding or were producing, along with his story, an allegory of its writing.[11] The fork, of course, is the meeting of the Mississippi and the Ohio where, I will now try to show, individual freedom for Huck reveals itself to be as different from what it is for Jim as North differs from South.

Very briefly, at the beginning of the story, freedom appears to be a single concept, in fact one that can unite individuals as different as black and white. And at this point, social engagement, defined globally as living inside society, is also a single concept that joins quite disparate persons in a generalized servitude. That civilization imprisons is not an unfamiliar theme in American literature, nor is the complementary theme of running away into nature. Escaping, Huck from family and Jim from society, they come together on the island and for the next six chapters forge an alliance of free individuals so without contradiction that it even recuperates the benefits of social engagement without its burdens. For in the first chapters, Jim and Huck have freedom in nature and live at home too. Forgotten are the tensions that had begun to emerge at the start of the story when Tom and Huck played practical tricks that shamed Jim. Instead, on an evening soon after they join forces on the island, with thunder rolling overhead and the rain coming down in sheets, Huck observes, " 'Jim this is nice, . . . I wouldn't want to be nowhere else but here. Pass me along another hunk of fish and some hot corn-bread.' " They have "got home all safe" (674).

Moreover, the next two chapters prove Jim's and Huck's home-bond solid *and* proof against society, as when Huck famously rushes back from reconnoitering the situation back in St. Petersburg to join Jim in his runaway status, " 'Git up and hump yourself, Jim! There ain't a minute to lose. They're after us!' " (685). And when they set out downriver, the raft is itself an idyllic home for which the river and the farms along its shores provide a cornucopia of waterfowl, chickens, watermelons, mushmelons, pumpkins, corn, and other "things of that kind" (689). But already a complication is emerging in the simple opposition between nature (natural human relations) and society. To Jim, a wrecked steamboat in their path seems best left alone; he cites the wisdom of heaven in support of his own down-to-earth good sense: " 'We's doin' blame' well, en we better let blame' well alone, as de good book says' " (690). But Huck answers to another authority: " 'Do you think Tom Sawyer would ever go by this thing? Not for pie, he wouldn't. He'd call it an adventure . . . and he'd land on that wreck if it was his last act. . . . Why, you'd think it was Christopher C'lumbus discovering Kingdom Come.' " " 'I wish,' " concludes Huck, " 'Tom Sawyer *was* here' " (690).

The problem is that Tom Sawyer *is* there, in spirit, a spirit difficult to reconcile with the spirit of Jim and Huck's antisociety.

Something new becomes apparent in this dispute: Huck's entire acquiescence, for all his social discomfort, in cultural conventions. Up to this point, only his rebellious side has been visible. Now Huck reveals what will become fully evident (in his admiration, for instance, of the Grangerfords' parlor) as a totally uncritical acceptance of the established culture. A conventionalism as instinctive as his rebellion, as well as the way this duality endangers Jim, emerges in the incident of the wreck. Huck wins this argument and boards the wreck, placing Jim, whose flight from society has nothing to do with adventure but with its opposite, survival, in dire peril.

This first time, however, the peril passes. Although Huck's tomfoolery briefly loses them the raft, the two runaways soon regain it and their unity, which grows even stronger. They now make Cairo the goal of the voyage; at this town on the river fork, Huck explains, "we would sell the raft and get on a steamboat and go way up the Ohio amongst the free States, and then be out of trouble" (704). Associating legal freedom with being out of trouble implies a newly political interpretation of Huck's rebellion, of course, and here the novel briefly adumbrates an internal social critique rather than a blanket rejection of society as such. As long as Huck and Jim have a common goal, the novel is inevitably political and cannot restrict itself to styles and mores.

The raft on which Huck and Jim float naked frees Huck from the itchiness of new clothes and Jim from shackles. The larger significance of Huck's bid for freedom in this first part of the novel comes willy-nilly from its association with Jim's escape. Withdrawing from slavery is not like withdrawing from the world, which leaves the world unchanged. A successful escape from slavery defeats it in that instance and in that way changes the world. The two runaways don't just leave Hannibal; as Huck guiltily realizes when Jim, anticipating his own freedom, begins to plot the escape of his two children, helping Jim subverts Mississippi society internally. Involvement is unavoidable: there is no world elsewhere, not the raft or the island to which Huck escapes with a cache of supplies and the dispossessed Jim with nothing. In the first part of the journey, the raft is not yet an alternative world but a world in opposition, instrumental to a political act and something to sell in exchange for still more useful steamboat tickets; nor is the Mississippi yet Nature but a particular river set in a political geography and to be left for the better-sited Ohio. Up to this point, therefore, until Huck and Jim run past Cairo, their escape connotes something very like a revolution.

In his classic essay entitled "Mr. Eliot, Mr. Trilling, and *Huckleberry Finn*" and addressing the problem of the ending, Leo Marx argued that when the raft floats past the mouth of the Ohio, the novel begins a long moral and political retreat from the rebellion that had inspired it and suffers a "failure of nerve." The trip downriver, Marx stresses, is "*away* from St. Petersburg," home of slave owners, pious hypocrites, petty tyrants, and abusive fathers. The road to freedom starts off down the Mississippi but takes a sharp left at the Ohio. When they miss this turn, Huck and Jim are heading due south, toward the heartland of slavery. It is only logical, Marx goes on, that at the end of *this* journey Huck reconnects with Tom and surrenders both his moral and his common sense to Tom's extravagant but entirely conventional fantasies. The political realities that had driven Huck and Jim to escape St. Petersburg fade out to be replaced by a hodgepodge of romances whose single unifying theme is the glory of Tom the Hero. To that glory, Jim's dignity is the first sacrifice and his very life could at any moment follow. Huck's dignity too is forfeit and, for Marx, so is the novel's when it ends in duplicity.

Now, there is little to dispute, I think, over the political offensiveness of Jim's reenslavement on the Phelps farm. This is especially apparent to a current reader, but insofar as the preceding chapters have revealed Jim's full-fledged manhood, his humiliation at the hands of the increasingly idiotic Tom must have made unpleasant reading at any time. Indeed, Jim's diminution thins the very fabric of the novel in that his reduction to an object of the two boys' connivance saps a linguistic agency that has been a major part of the novel's verbal wealth. In the often-cited dispute that ends with Huck's withdrawal because "you can't learn a nigger to argue," the essence of the humor and of the linguistic agility from which it arises comes from the reader's recognition that Jim has in fact won the argument. His syllogism proving that it makes no sense for a Frenchman to speak French demonstrates an exemplary logic. The premise is that all men speak English. "'Is a Frenchman a man?'" Jim asks. The answer being yes, then "'why doan' he *talk* like a man?'" (703). The premise is false, to be sure. But this is merely an error, not a fallacy; like Jim's superstitions in general, and unlike the prejudices of St. Petersburg worthies, the wrong premise reflects a superficial ignorance and does not impugn Jim's good sense. The incident reveals Huck's inability to argue, not Jim's.

But once returned to slavery, Jim seems incapacitated on even the most obvious points. His cabin filled with a slapstick assortment of rats, spiders, and snakes according to Tom's ideas of romantic imprisonment, Jim protests feebly and always in vain. For that matter, Huck is no more persuasive himself, as when he fails to carry an argument with Tom that there is no need to saw off the leg of the bed to free Jim's chain when it is perfectly easy to lift the bed and slip the chain off. The only absurd measure not taken is called off by Tom himself, who upon reflection decides not to saw off *Jim's* leg because " 'there ain't necessity enough for it' " (859). The destruction of Jim is complete when at the end of one chapter devoted entirely to Tom's harebrained schemes, Jim finally rebels only to apologize when "Tom most lost all patience with him": "So Jim said he was sorry, and said he wouldn't behave so no more" (884). The problem is that, entirely submissive to Tom, Jim no longer exists *for the novel* anymore than he does for himself; and Huck is not in much better shape.

But how did Jim and Huck slide to this ending from that beginning? We saw the first slip earlier in the incident of the wreck, which revealed a conflict between Huck's quest and Jim's, the former being to escape society, the latter to escape to a better society. The components of the conflict as they emerge at the wreck are, on one side, Huck's acceptance of Tom Sawyer culture, this in tandem with his impulse to free himself from culture as such and from the set life paths that culture projects, in short from all plots, and, on the other side, Jim's need to plot his life in minute detail, so that stepping anywhere to the side of his life path, for instance onto the wreck, is potentially fatal. At Cairo this conflict comes to a head and shows itself more radical than any political disagreement: Jim's path diverges not from Huck's path but from his *pathlessness*.

The incidents at the river fork are well known. Just as the raft's occupants are reluctantly admitting that they may have missed Cairo in the fog, a monstrous steamboat bears down on them coming upriver from the South. That a huge "black cloud" suddenly appears on the raft's horizon and resolves into a behemoth armed with "a long row of wide-open furnace doors shining like red-hot teeth" (717) just at the plot's moment of truth requires no comment. Twain, the novel, and the characters are all headed toward a potentially fatal crisis: one or the other of the two *Huckleberry Finn*s currently drifting along together will have to be sacrificed, either the story of Huck's escape or the story of Jim's. When the boat smashes through the raft, therefore, "Jim went overboard on one side and I on the other" (717).

As this moment of truth approaches, Huck is in an agony of indecision. Moments before, Jim's happy cry that they have reached their destination "went through me like a shot, and I thought if it *was* Cairo I reckoned I would die of miserableness" (711). He feels "so mean and miserable I most wished I was dead" at the thought that he has now done it – he has helped

Jim steal himself from a "poor old woman" who had "tried to be good to [Huck] every way she knowed how." He is tortured by the sense that at Cairo he becomes irremediably *engaged*: Jim is now talking about returning to St. Petersburg later, possibly to steal his children from slavery, "children that belonged to a man I didn't even know," "a man," Huck broods guiltily, "that hadn't ever done me no harm" (712). His better instincts prevail, of course, and immediately thereafter he finds himself protecting Jim from slave hunters. When Jim, from his fundamentally different perspective, thanks Huck and calls him " 'de ole true Huck; de on'y white genlman dat ever kep' his promise to ole Jim' " (712), he identifies Huck's problem exactly, namely that the association with an escaping slave is turning Huck into a reformer, a true white gentleman in a false genteel society.

But the hunters go off and Huck returns to the raft "feeling bad and low, because I knowed very well I had done wrong" (714). He is not a reformer; on the contrary, his rejection of society as such undercuts any more local criticisms. He performs all his brave acts on behalf of Jim out of his own desire for absolute freedom, not out of any antislavery conviction. The humor and pathos in the passage depend on the reader's recognition that Huck has done absolutely right. That he has done right while confronting an overwhelming social force for wrong is heroic; but it is also indecisive. He has succeeded in keeping things in suspense, with Jim and himself still runaways. Huck's unaware moral rectitude is also a state of suspense, however we may approve it, for at least part of our approval devolves on his personal disaffection while what it implies about social action remains uncertain. Huck's insurgency never aspires to establish itself; it wishes not to become established. Huck has no ambition to change the world; he just can't live in it.

The fork of the Mississippi and the Ohio in *Huckleberry Finn* represents an archetypal American choice between uncompromised individualism and responsible citizenship. Or more precisely, it forces the recognition that there is an absolute choice to be made between the two, that, contrary to some accounts of individualism at work for the improvement of society, one cannot be both. Huck's pursuit of individualism takes him into the deep South in the company of a runaway slave he has therefore failed to help free. The steamboat that smashes the raft at Cairo is headed right back to St. Petersburg. The pastoral idyll is over, and Jim and Huck are no longer bound on a common quest.

Huckleberry Finn is Huck's book, not Jim's. It starts out as a comedy, an "As You Like It" with a hero drawn from the bottom of society rather than the top. But whereas the Forest of Arden is to be the setting for the reform of society, the world of the raft becomes an alternative to St. Petersburg, not its better self. While "As You Like It" implies, in the journey away from a corrupt court, a restorative return, *Huckleberry Finn* would imagine returning, either north or south, either toward freedom or slavery, only as defeat. Thus, it threatens to end as a tragedy. The ending, which returns Jim to slavery and Huck to the domesticity of the Phelps household and his role as Tom's sidekick, replaces a possible tragedy by a second version of the comedic beginning. This then concludes the same way as the first beginning, with Huck's escape and in fact Jim's as well. The circle overcomes the threatening line of the river plot, which can only lead in the south to tragedy and in the North to a social involvement that would be equally annihilative for Huck. Hemingway's praise for *Huckleberry Finn* extended only to the point of Jim's recapture; the rest, he thought, was "just cheating." It is cheating, in that Jim's prior emancipation obviates the thorny problem of freeing him in the south. It is also probably a failure of nerve and even a defeat, as Marx contends, in its abandonment of the challenge to racism. But through those very failures, the ending reaffirms the morality of an individual commitment to freedom in the face of society's entrapments and to transcendent truths against the world's inevitable duplicities.[12]

Moreover, the ending is disturbing because it is all three: a cheat, a defeat, and an affirmation, and makes their connection too evident for philosophical comfort. Through this ending rather than despite it, *Huckleberry Finn* uncovers a contradiction that is not as visible in other major novels. It is not absolutely clear that Ahab *has* to drown the entire crew of the *Pequod* to fulfill his individual vision; and it is the less clear in that he is himself drowned. But the necessity of sacrificing Jim's freedom to Huck's independence is inscribed in the novel's very geography, in the river fork that heads one way to Jim's emancipation and the other to the continuation of Huck's outsider status. When in the end Jim too is freed, this further frees Huck, for Jim's reenslavement would have embroiled his friend in continuing guilt. Freed through no act either of his own or of Huck's, Jim embroils Huck in neither history nor future obligation.

The steamboat comes crashing through the raft in full symbolic throttle and elicits a commensurately resonant reaction: "I dived," Huck explains, "and I aimed to find the bottom, too, for a thirty-foot wheel had got to go over me, and I wanted it to have plenty of room" (717). From this dive he resurfaces alone and drifts with the current, which now heads toward shore. Landing near a log cabin, he feints a continuation of his flight but it is for now at an end: "I was going to rush by and get away but a lot of dogs jumped out and went to howling and barking at me, and I knowed better than to move another peg" (718). Huck has reentered the world and, contrary to Hemingway, Marx, and the tradition that sees the ending as a sudden debacle, his encounter with the society centered in this log cabin already marks his return to the world of St. Petersburg.

This version of St. Petersburg centers on male violence but as the complement, not the opposite, of female domesticity. The Grangerfords greet Huck with guns at the ready until they determine that he is not associated with their archenemies, the Shepherdsons, whereupon they embrace him as family. Calling off dogs and guns, the Grangerford patriarch "told me to make myself easy and at home," and home is the province of the Grangerford matriarch, "the sweetest old gray-headed lady," who takes over: "The poor thing's as wet as he can be," she chides her husband, and "it may be he's hungry." The Grangerford girls are made to run around and get him something to eat while Buck, a boy just about Huck's size, age, and name, is instructed to "take this little stranger and get the wet clothes off from him and dress him up in some of yours that's dry" (720-1). Huck is back with Miss Watson and Tom, with a twist: the murderous father is no longer the outcast pap but a magisterial colonel. This father doesn't threaten his own son, but he kills sons he designates as enemy as ruthlessly as ever pap did. In fact, Grangerford is only more successful in bringing about the death of his sons: three of an original six have already been killed in the family feud. The opposite of pap, the Colonel is also pap come back as his own ideal fantasy.

"Col. Grangerford was a gentleman," Huck begins his description. "He was well born, as the saying is, and that's worth as much in a man as it is in a horse, so the Widow Douglas said, and nobody ever denied that she was of the first aristocracy in our town; and pap he always said it, too." As prepossessing in his linen suit "so white it hurt your eyes to look at it" as pap was disreputable in his rags, Grangerford has perfected the art of the menacing temper. He gets the kind of respect in seconds that eludes pap in hours of rampaging: "When [the Colonel] turned into a cloud-bank it was awful dark for a half a minute and that was enough; there wouldn't nothing go wrong again for a week" (728). Grangerford is also a drinker, starting at breakfast when his two eldest sons mix him his first glass of bitters. As irrational and deadly in his hatreds as pap, the Colonel is far more dangerous. The society in which Huck lands just the other side of the Ohio fork is a corrected version of St. Petersburg, its flaws perfected and made fully operative. So once again fleeing for his life, Huck regains the river, the raft, and Jim. Drifting down the Mississippi, they hang up their lantern and celebrate exactly as they had earlier. Jim cooks up "corn-dodgers and buttermilk, and pork and cabbage, and greens . . . and whilst I eat my supper we talked, and had a good time." They've gotten away again. "We said there warn't no home like a raft, after all. Other places do seem so cramped up and smothery. You feel mighty free and easy and comfortable on a raft" (739).

Except that every minute the raft floats deeper into slave territory. As the journey proceeds, the best Jim and Huck can hope for is not to arrive anywhere; it is now that life on the raft becomes most idyllic. Jim and Huck go naked and lie about dangling their feet in the water, smoking their pipes and talking "about all kinds of things." To avoid being apprehended, they travel at night and tie up days under sheltering banks in an Edenic landscape of "song-birds just going it," cool breezes, and sweet smells. In the midst of a lyrical description of this enchanted world, Twain suddenly pulls back to caution that the smells wafting from land are not always sweet "because they've left dead fish laying around, gars, and such, and they do get pretty rank" (740). This touch of realism only underlines its suppression as the runaways run toward their prisons.

But the idyll doesn't last. While Twain seems to keep his eyes averted from the Deep South looming ahead as determinedly as Jim and Huck, he is nonetheless clearly worried. The duke and the dauphin are commonly taken to represent Twain's increasingly uncertain hold on his story.[13] At a loss about how to restore some sort of reasonable purpose to the journey downriver ("'Goodness sakes, would a runaway nigger run *south*?'" retorts Huck when queried about Jim's status), Twain, according to this reading, gave up on Jim and Huck as captains and handed the tiller to two new characters who would at least provide new topics of conversation and occasion some diversionary adventures. The duke and the dauphin do qualify as replacements in that they too are runaways; in fact, when Huck first hears the sounds of the chase he is certain he is himself the target, "for whenever anybody was after anybody I judged it was *me* – or maybe Jim" (742). The new escapees, however, have been forced to flee by their own duplicity, not society's, and they bring this redoubled duplicity to the raft.

Already in the Grangerford episode, Twain had focused on fakery. The gentlemen in that episode kill one another without reason and the ladies weep as senselessly, both acting out a debased cultural script. The duke and the dauphin are the proper poets of such a society. Emmeline Grangerford's odes to death expose the superficiality of the conventional culture but not the corruption in its depths. To plumb those depths we need a longer fish line, as it were a measure for measure, a standard in the measure of the outrage: the quintessential standard, Shakespeare. The duke and the dauphin make their first fraudulent foray from the raft bearing a sham Shakespeare. Hamlet's soliloquy is the classic of high writing in Anglo-American literature. Bilgewater explains to the king, who has never heard of it, "'Hamlet's soliloquy, you know; the most celebrated thing in Shakespeare. Ah, it's sublime, sublime!'" (757). The English classic of classics is appropriately invoked in the American classic of classics – invoked and burlesqued, which brings our discussion back to the issue of *Huckleberry Finn*'s irreverence.

For while the counterfeit soliloquy exposes Bilgewater's own falseness, the burlesque inevitably bleeds onto the real thing. It is difficult after reading the duke's speech not to laugh a little at Shakespeare's. By a sort of Gresham's law of literature, parody has a tendency to drive out the authentic, or at least to demote it. Once the duke has taken hold of *Hamlet* and shown that the tragedy of moral compunction can be adapted to the purpose of a comic imposture, the demolition of conventional and traditional culture begun in St. Petersburg with Huck's telling commentaries on the Old Testament, continued in the Grangerford parlor (where Huck sums up *Pilgrim's Progress* as being "about a man that left his family it didn't say why" [724], an accurate and devastating account), is complete. In this work of literature, finally, there is nothing to be hoped for from literature.

Not surprisingly, the episode of the Shakespeare burlesque also contains what may be finally the most disturbing incident in the novel, although oddly, as Forrest Robinson, who has dealt with it at length, points out, it has received little critical attention.[14] Huck and his companions land at a small town called Bricksville to hold a "Shaksperean Revival!!!"[15] Bricksville is the grimmest of the river settlements Huck visits. Little luxury has been displayed elsewhere, but the houses of St. Petersburg, for instance, had a certain snugness and comfort. In Bricksville, "the stores and houses was most all old shackly dried-up frame concerns that hadn't ever been painted"; a failure at mastering the accoutrements of civilization, the town is no better at harnessing the energies of nature: "The houses had little gardens around them, but they didn't seem to raise hardly anything in them but jimpson weeds, and sunflowers, and ash-piles, and old curled-up boots and shoes, and pieces of bottles, and rags, and played-out tin-ware." In front of the stores that have produced this sterile refuse, the people lounging are even more blighted than their town. Long conversations unfold on such themes as chewing tobacco, as follows: "'Gimme a chaw' v tobacker, Hank.' 'Cain't – I ain't got but one chaw left. Ask Bill.'" These exchanges can wax witty, as when the donor of a "chaw" considers the quantity returned and quips: "'Here, gimme the *chaw*, and you take the *plug*.'" Twain's humor is here particularly agile in turning on the feebleness of the joke. At the same time, nothing is more damning to a character in a work of wit than displaying his lack of it. The inhabitants of Bricksville are the dregs of a never impressive world.

One of the few entertainments life in Bricksville affords is the monthly drunken spree of old Boggs, a cantankerous but wholly harmless codger everyone even in that town takes humorously. Huck encounters Boggs lurching about threatening to kill everyone he meets but especially Colonel Sherburn, the owner of the biggest store in town and "a heap the best dressed" as well. When Boggs begins boozily to insult Sherburn, the Colonel unexpectedly takes it all seriously and threatens to kill the drunken fool if he doesn't cease his rantings forever after one o'clock that day. Out of control with drink and stupidity, Boggs is quite unable to quit and Sherburn carries out his threat, Boggs pleading, " 'O Lord, don't shoot!' " a pathos reinforced by the cries of Boggs's young daughter, who runs weeping to throw herself on her dying father.

All this naturally riles up the lethargic populace, who now threaten to lynch the murderer. Contemptuously facing this mob, Sherburn delivers a speech of, as Henry Nash Smith pointed out, an oddly ambiguous morality. The Colonel begins ("slow and scornful," observes Huck): " 'The idea of *you* lynching anybody! It's amusing. The idea of you thinking you had pluck enough to lynch a *man*. . . . Why, a *man's* safe in the hands of ten thousand of your kind – as long as it's day-time and you're not behind him.' " As he warms to his harangue, the remarkable thing is that Twain clearly does too, to the point that Smith suggests Sherburn is the only character in the book besides Huck with whom Twain seems to identify, animating the speech with his own sentiments.

" 'Do I know you? [Sherburn asks the crowd.] I know you clear through. I was born and raised in the South, and I've lived in the North; so I know the average all around. The average man's a coward. In the North he lets anybody walk over him that wants to, and goes home and prays for a humble spirit to bear it. In the South one man, all by himself, has stopped a stage full of men, in the day-time, and robbed the lot. Your newspapers call you a brave people so much that you think you *are* braver than any other people – whereas you're just *as* brave, and no braver. Why don't your juries hang murderers? Because they're afraid the man's friends will shoot them in the back, in the dark – and it's just what they *would* do.' "

There is more in this vein until, having declared that " 'the pitifulest thing out is a mob,' " Sherburn waves it away and "the crowd washed back sudden, and then broke all apart and went tearing off every which way."

Sherburn's speech (the murder seems to be just its pretext) enters the story without preamble and ends without aftermath. It seems disconnected from the plot, a sort of rupture in the narrative as if some impulse that could neither be contained nor translated into a plausible addition to the story had overtaken Twain and he had blurted it out. This impression is strengthened by the fact that the speech rings with conviction and is, against one's expectations and principles, entirely persuasive. When he delivers this attack on the cowardice of the average man, Sherburn has just killed a helpless buffoon. He doesn't defend this murder; he doesn't even mention it. Instead, he accuses the mob of being unable to carry out its own murders. An incident in which a rich and powerful man has claimed and exercised the right to kill at will anyone weaker than he ends with his denouncing his inferiors; and the novel clearly approves of him.

I would read Sherburn's speech as a soliloquy inspired by the proximity of Hamlet's, and the Nietzschean accents of Sherburn's speech as a response to the decadence of cultural value represented by the duke's travesty. Hamlet, who also lives in a corrupt world, finds conscience a source of cowardice, reflection an impediment to action. Sherburn denounces a world where an absence of moral conviction makes cowards who are indecisive only because they wait for others to tell them what to do. Hamlet shies from "enterprises of great pitch and moment" out of an excess of complexity; Sherburn kills his man, not a fratricidal king but a foolish lout, in simple rage. Nothing in the universe of the duke's travesty or in the degenerate village that is to be its stage can command humanity or even common decency. In that context, untrammeled and unmediated by any traditional system of values, Twain speaks through two characters, one an outcast, the other a strongman. This is another side of the same contradiction that paralyzes Twain at the fork at Cairo, between a vision of uncompromised personal integrity and another of moral effectiveness in society.

Sherburn is a merchant and a military man, a double pillar of society – but in a society that does not deserve to be supported. On the contrary, it merits being brought crashing down, for all the reasons Huck has been exposing through the incidents of his journey. This is not a reformable society; one can only curse it and leave. Sherburn curses it and stays, and Twain finds himself approving the cursing and not knowing what to think of the staying. Does he see something of his own situation in Sherburn's furious isolation among idiots and knaves? Sherburn, moreover, is not merely an inhabitant of society; as storekeeper and military man, he is presumably one of those who shape it. In Huck, Twain depicts on the contrary someone who has no power at all. Homeless and a child, soon an orphan, Huck is a complete outsider. The real question is not whether he will leave society but whether he will enter it and to what end? From his ontological distance, Huck looks at the world of men with natural detachment. At his most critical he feels "ashamed of the human race" (784). Instead, Sherburn sets about shaming the damned human race, inveighing against its odious weakness to its face, hating its inescapable presence. The murder of Boggs, who is in Sherburn's eyes the lowest representation of humanity, expresses that hatred: he tells Boggs to be gone, but Boggs stays and Sherburn can't stand his presence another moment. What Sherburn cannot do is himself leave, so as to be, like Huck, peacefully and even compassionately ashamed of the human race – away from it.

Robinson treats the Sherburn episode as an instance of acute bad faith in which the townspeople abandon their moral responsibilities to the ferociously individualistic Sherburn. His speech, according to Robinson, is a jeremiad and to that extent proffers certain truths. Bad faith, however, is reciprocal and Sherburn for his part seeks from his audience confirmation that he is beyond them. I disagree only on this last point. The bad faith of the Bricksville mob is evident, but Sherburn's may not be. There is too little dramatic development in the scene to indicate that he is drawing his self-image from the mob. Indeed, as Robinson observes, critics have generally dealt with Sherburn by complaining that his speech is aesthetically unintegrated into the novel. The harangue stands out by its departure from Huck's idiom, although he is presumably its reporter. This failure to translate Sherburn's speech into Huck's language seems to me to reflect an incompatibility between the two. Nor is Sherburn as a character any better able to enter *Huckleberry Finn*. Instead, the speech and the Colonel bespeak an authorial position outside the novel from or against which the novel may be written but which cannot itself be encompassed. As a part of the novel's world, Sherburn's position, that since the average man is a petty coward sneaking about in fear of his worthless life, killing one is good riddance, would invalidate Huck's moral dilemma and collapse the novel into a diatribe.[16] Indeed, Sherburn's town of Bricksville owes its extreme dreariness, beyond not only the necessity but also the possibility of mockery, I would suggest, to the extremity of Sherburn's vision.

It is also impossible in the Mississippi River towns through which Huck and Jim journey to imagine being a hero. This in turn makes Sherburn a cold-blooded killer and Huck a saint (and Tom a fool). Let me repeat that as a saint, however, Huck is no more bent on social reform, no more optimistic about it, than is Sherburn. That is, his radical liberalism, not unlike Emerson's, is also conservative. He never reacts to social iniquities by imagining them reformed; they appear to him natural, ineluctable parts of a system as fixed as the system of nature. You either stay inside the system, bathe every day and wear tight collars, or you leave. Colonel Sherburn has stayed inside and the recognition that the bathwater is dirty causes him unendurable disgust. In Sherburn's soliloquy, irreverence has turned to bitter revulsion.

Though extraneous, the Sherburn episode marks a turning point. The Shakespeare fraud does little overt harm to anyone in the story. It's a second-degree fraud, an opportunistic deceit exploiting real and therefore more dire vulnerabilities in the people it cons. To Jim's astonishment that "dese kings o' ourn is regular rapscallions," Huck explains calmly that "it's in the breed. . . . all kings is mostly rapscallions." Huck has read history: "Look at Henry the Eight; this'n 's a Sunday-School Superintendent to *him*. And look at Charles the Second, and Louis Fourteen, and Louis Fifteen, and James Second, and Edward Second, and Richard Third, and forty more; besides all them Saxon heptarchies that used to rip around so in old times and raise Cain" (775). Compared with these, he concludes, the duke and the king "ain't nothing" (776). But their next exploit, as if this one had been an overture, *is* something and sets its own standard.

The Wilks family are good people; though others have been good to Huck, like Miss Watson and the Grangerfords, they have been clearly implicated in bad things. One touchstone of the Wilkses' real goodness is their grief at the sale of their slaves. Twain never undercuts Mary Jane's sincerity when she tearfully tells Huck that "she didn't know *how* she was ever going to be happy . . . knowing the [slave] mother and the children warn't ever going to see each other no more" (807). " 'Miss Mary Jane,' " says Huck, " 'you can't abear to see people in trouble and *I* can't – most always.' " The humor comes from Huck's wry self-awareness and implies no qualification of the girl's kindness.

On the other side, the king and the duke wax seriously evil; indeed, the long Wilks episode is not funny. Had a lawyer named Levi Bell, a precursor of Puddn'head Wilson, not intervened, the outcome would have been dark in the measure of Sherburn's misanthropy – darker, in that in Sherburn's world there are no good people to be ruined. In the Wilkses' world, however, the good people are as powerless as the cowards in Bricksville. The helpless lambs offer no hope of betterment; they only measure its absence. Huck and Jim had left St. Petersburg with high hopes of freedom that are badly set back at Cairo. The Wilks episode ends in the utter defeat of these hopes. There seems to be no way to escape the duke and the king, who now on the contrary complete their takeover by turning Jim in. The rest we have already discussed. Jim's captivity is paralleled by Huck's in thrall to Tom.

It is on the very verge of the collapse of all possibility of freedom that

Huck places his highest bid for it. Indeed, Jim has already been recaptured when Huck finds himself at last making the decision Twain had not been able to make at Cairo: "It was a close place," he realizes. "I was a trembling, because I'd got to decide, forever, betwixt two things, and I knowed it. I studies a minute, sort of holding my breath, and then says to myself: 'All right, then, I'll *go to hell*'" (834–5). Let us say the obvious: Twain has chosen the route of social engagement when it's too late in the story to take it. Huck has decided he is willing to go to hell, but the harder decision was whether to go to Ohio.

Though he never makes this harder decision, though indeed he evades it in a way that implies he would have been unlikely to choose the Ohio route – unlikely, that is, to write the story so as to indicate this was the right direction – the fact that it emerges as a decision already distinguishes *Huckleberry Finn* from its cohort of great American novels. *Huckleberry Finn* represents the characteristic American theme of the conflict between the individual and society more penetratingly than its peers do: more commonly, the conflict of individual versus society appears only as it does at the very end of *Huckleberry Finn,* not as it does earlier at the fork of the two rivers. Why does *Huckleberry Finn* go deeper? My suggestion has been that precisely its irreverence – the reason it was banned in Concord – uncovers for it a conflict *within* society that is more or less invisible in works such as *Moby-Dick.* The chapter in Melville's novel entitled "Knights and Squires" raises the issue of intrasocial differences but makes nothing of them to qualify the global representativeness of Ahab and Ishmael. The formal, aesthetic, as well as thematic premise of *Huckleberry Finn* is that class difference matters, that in the course of their lives individuals continually encounter forks where their own fate is inextricably joined with that of others they either succor or sacrifice.

For the centuries since it was written and in all the European-engendered cultures of which America's may be the ultimate embodiment, Hamlet's soliloquy is the ideal representation of heroic self-scrutiny and of the examination of one's life in the world. Hamlet, Prince of Denmark, queries his soul in a way that speaks directly to many souls, but not everyone's. One has to be able, reading it, to imagine oneself apart, therefore free to choose one's way of being, yet at the center of things and thus able to choose: a self-image that is actually available only to a minority of people. This limitation is not evident when one reads the soliloquy. On the contrary, reading it at all, one reads it as universally applicable; otherwise one does not read it. One can emerge from the reading in despair at the state of things, disgusted with the world and especially with one's own role in it. But this response is not as radical as it seems or may feel, for the very act of reading and thus manifesting one's place in the community of Hamlets provides a considerable consolation. Reading and understanding *Hamlet* brings one to doubt the world; by the same token, in the same process, it also earns the reader a certain dispensation from resolving those doubts. One simultaneously, dialectically escapes, by reading *Hamlet,* the truths revealed by it. This power to partly absolve or at least console is embedded in the very language of the play, which makes transcendent order out of disorder.

The burlesque soliloquy in *Huckleberry Finn* disorders the Shakespeare text and leaves its readers with no dispensation, no escape, nothing to mediate their recognition of Denmark's rot. Worse, the burlesque doesn't just remove; it mocks the dispensation others have found in the soliloquy. Colonel Sherburn's soliloquy is one result of the fall to the very bottom that results; the conflict of individual and society appears in his speech as absolute and hopeless. Worse yet, the burlesque enacts an aspect of Hamlet's speech that is otherwise invisible, the fact that it is class-bound. This is a concrete effect. The distance between the real text and the travesty is the distance between the educated individual who knows the real text and the populace that doesn't. My point will have become evident: the burlesqued soliloquy exposes the myth of universal individualism in nineteenth-century America. Or perhaps it does something a little less absolute: it opens up the question of universal individualism and enables us to look deeper to where that question arises in a context of social relations.

I am using the parody of Hamlet's speech, of course, to represent the relation of the novel generally to high culture. That relation, which has been seen widely to render *Huckleberry Finn more* universally resonant, while it makes the work more broadly accessible, tends almost in the opposite direction to give it more social specificity, to bring to the surface the ways in which universality is socially specific. When this specificity surfaces, it brings with it something we have already traced out in the plot, the recognition that the universal individual is not only a limited being but a dependent one: Huck will get to light out once more for the territory only by *not* going up the Ohio with Jim – in general by not involving himself in his society. His individual freedom is not simply an evasion of social engagement; it involves a negative engagement, a sacrifice of Jim because Jim would implicate him, and elsewhere a conservativism that precludes other implications. Sherburn's creed of the superman is the other side of this coin.

The end of *Huckleberry Finn,* which has disturbed and continues to disturb virtually everyone who reads it, is neither cheating nor a failure of nerve. It presents the ugly truth that to be Huck Finn and stay Huck Finn you have to let Jim be returned to slavery. Mark Twain found this truth as unbearable to acknowledge as anyone, so (here is the cheat and the failure of nerve) he freed Jim anyway. But this evasion actually deepened his critique of individualism by revealing how much it depends on political quietism, for in order to save Huck, Twain has to depict the slave society as relatively humane and quite capable of self-reform. There is no need for a civil war in St. Petersburg – nor for reconstruction.

A recent and very influential recasting of Huck's vernacular voice has identified it as in fact black.[17] Shelley Fisher Fishkin has argued that Huck's dialect is taken not from Tom Blankenship, a poor-white boy on whom Twain wrote he had modeled Huck, but from Jimmy, a black child who waited on the author at a hotel supper. The conclusions Fisher Fishkin draws from her discovery are, first, that the roots of American writing are sunk deep in African-American culture and, second, that *Huckleberry Finn* is "multiracial and multicultural." But while the first seems undeniable, the second does not necessarily accompany it. It is Mark Twain and by projection Huck Finn who speak in Jimmy's accents, not Jimmy; and an impersonated voice doesn't speak in its own words or express its own thoughts. Is Twain's novel "multicultural" or does it represent a culture that has successfully appropriated a multitude of accents into its own language? It seems important that despite the central place of Jimmy's voice in constituting the story, the black character Jim could not be imagined as narrator. Huck's narration of Jim's story in Jimmy's idiom only extends Huck's cultural power: Twain controls poor-white Huck, who controls black Jim/Jimmy. This is of a piece with Huck's moral breakthrough at the moment Jim is reenslaved: it is Huck who is made better and stronger by deciding to go to hell rather than turn Jim in, not Jim. I can sum up the preceding discussion in terms of this recent influential rereading of *Huckleberry Finn* by suggesting that if in fact Huck speaks with Jimmy's voice, Jimmy's voice, like Jim's freedom, has been sacrificed to Huck's enlarged democratic persona.

Why is *Huckleberry Finn the* American classic? Because almost uniquely it probes the lowest and most sensitive layer of the American mind, where individualism takes a first purchase on the world in some degree cognizant that the community will have to pay for it. Classics typically mediate a culture's founding contradictions. The *Iliad* celebrates and abhors war. *Huckleberry Finn* celebrates and abhors individualism. Other American classics share that ambivalence, of course, but perhaps none see the contradiction between the generals and the soldiers in the individualist war as clearly as Twain, who, perversely, made his individualist general someone who should have been cannon fodder and then had him enlist his own sacrifice. Not all readers see that this is cause for despair, as Twain ultimately did, but that this funny book for boys has glimpsed the heart of the national darkness is, I think, generally felt; and one essential power of a classic is to see in the dark.

NOTES

1 All references are to the Library of America edition of *Mark Twain: Mississippi Writings*, ed. Guy Cardwell (New York: 1982), pp. 615–912. Page references are cited parenthetically in text.

2 Bernard DeVoto, *Mark Twain's America* (New York: Houghton Mifflin, 1932), see pp. 308, 310–20.

3 "Mr. Eliot, Mr. Trilling, and *Huckleberry Finn*," *American Scholar* 22 (Autumn 1953): 423–40.

4 Ernest Hemingway, *Green Hills of Africa* (New York: Scribner's, 1935), pp. 22, 21.

5 Cited in DeVoto, *Mark Twain's America*, p. 308.

6 Adam Gopnik, "The Wise Innocent," *New Yorker*, November 8, 1993, p. 119.

7 "The American Scholar," in *Emerson: Essays and Lectures*, ed. Joel Porte (New York: Library of America, 1983), p. 69.

8 The date of *Huckleberry Finn*'s publication, 1885, is in fact a likely one for a populist work. Although the People's Party was not established until later (running its first presidential candidate in 1892), anti-Northern industrialist agitation in the agrarian South and Southwest had already given rise to Farmers' Alliances and other populist movements in the 1880s.

9 Nineteenth-century readers need not have been very well educated to know Shakespeare, who was the most popular playwright on the circuit. On the breadth of Shakespeare's nineteenth-century audience see Lawrence Levine, *Highbrow/Lowbrow: The Emergence of Cultural Hierarchy in America* (New York: Oxford University Press, 1988), chap. 1.

10 Jonathan Arac, "Nationalism, Hypercanonization, and *Huckleberry Finn*," *boundary2* 19:1 (1992): 14–33.

11 See in this respect Neil Schmitz, "Twain, *Huckleberry Finn*, and the Reconstruction," *American Studies* 12 (1971): 59–67.

12 The writing of *Huckleberry Finn* was prolonged and difficult. Albert Bigelow Paine, who was Twain's first literary executor, and Bernard DeVoto, who was the second, both described exceptional problems in the composition of the author's masterpiece, but the definitive account is probably Walter Blair's "When Was *Huckleberry Finn* Written?" (*American Literature* 30 [1958]: 1–25). Of particular relevance to this essay is Blair's proof that Twain had not initially planned to have the entire story unfold on the river but decided to do so about halfway through the writing.

13 In an essay on Benjamin Franklin's *Autobiography*, I have traced Franklin's formulation of a civic morality explicitly in response to the organic duplicity of

the modern self and its opaque interiority. Civic morality in *Huckleberry Finn* is a mockery, a burlesque like those the duke and the dauphin make of Shakespeare.

14 Forrest G. Robinson, *In Bad Faith: The Dynamics of Deception in Mark Twain's America* (Cambridge, Mass.: Harvard University Press, 1986).

15 All citations to this episode are from chapters 21 and 22, pp. 757–72.

16 This is essentially the perspective of Twain's last and uncompleted work, *The Mysterious Stranger.*

17 Shelley Fisher Fishkin, *Was Huck Black? Mark Twain and African-American Voices* (New York: Oxford University Press, 1993).

6

DAVID LIONEL SMITH

Black Critics and Mark Twain

The title of this essay raises a vexing set of questions: What justifies the racial categorization of critical opinion? Do all black critics share a critical consensus on Twain, or at least a range of opinions, that distinguishes them from other critics: "white" critics, "brown" critics, and so on? If so, how is it that race constitutes the basis for a critical consensus; and if it does not, what is the point of surveying critical perspectives on the basis of race? Are there not some white critics who agree with some black critics; and if so, should they not be included in the discussion? The effect of treating black critics as a group separate from other critics is to segregate them from the majority of critics and criticism concerned with Mark Twain. However instructive it may be to regard such critics as a separate group, the troubling implications of segregation remain.

This being the case, is there anything, apart from social convention, that justifies the topic "black critics and Mark Twain"? Perhaps not. Such a question can always be qualified, however, by the criteria that define justification. In ideal terms, race ought not matter as a way of categorizing critical literature. Unfortunately, social conventions cannot be dismissed simply because they are intellectually spurious. In criticism, as well as in every other aspect of American life, our perceptions and attitudes are indelibly race-coded. Conceptually, racial categories make no sense, but in actual experience, race continues to be definitive. Regrettably, race continues to matter.

To testify for a moment autobiographically, I have been confronted with this issue a number of times regarding my essay "Huck, Jim, and American Racial Discourse."[1] My racial identity apparently matters a great deal to readers of that essay. This point has been brought to my attention by a surprising assortment of people: blacks and whites, senior scholars and students, college professors and high school teachers, Americans and foreigners. The common element in these encounters has not been the kind of people making the statements, nor shared opinions or political perspectives, nor even their assessments of the article. Rather, they have been united by a virtually uniform structure in their narratives, suggesting an odd sort of subgenre. Sometimes these persons report their own experience of reading the essay, and sometimes they describe the experience of one of their students. The reader likes the essay but feels troubled about liking it, not knowing whether the author is black. Meeting me is a great pleasure because now my informant feels reassured or can convey reassurance to his or her students. Smith is black. It's OK to like his essay. When my informant is a black graduate student, this familiar narrative has one kind of resonance for me. When she is a white professor from Canada, it has another resonance. I have never quite fathomed, however, what I wrote in the essay that would have been less acceptable from the keyboard of a white scholar. Nor have I ever had the cheek to ask.

My intention in relating this personal experience is neither confession nor complaint. The point is to illustrate that even in contemporary literary criticism, our presuppositions about racial identity and the discursive standpoints prescribed or permitted or precluded by racial identity shape not only what and how we write but also how we regard and interpret what we read. If this is an issue in the works of literary critics, it is certainly an issue in the reception of Mark Twain's fiction. To say this is not to imply that the category "black critics" is conceptually valid, but it is to suggest that we are obligated to consider what the category "black critics" might be understood to entail. We ought not be satisfied merely to assert, "These are Negroes and here is what they thought." Yet perhaps there is something to be learned by considering how a consciousness of racial identity has shaped some responses to the work of Mark Twain.

One of the earliest appraisals of Mark Twain by a prominent black writer was the work of someone we do not remember as a literary figure. After the death of Samuel Clemens in 1910, Booker T. Washington published a tribute to him in the *North American Review.* In it he comments on Clemens as a writer and friend, and he also discusses the portrayal of Jim in *Adventures of Huckleberry Finn.* Regarding the latter, he says:

> I do not believe any one can read this story closely, however, without becoming aware of the deep sympathy of the author in "Jim." In fact, before one gets through with the book, one cannot fail to observe that in some way or other the author, without making any comment and without going out of his way, has somehow succeeded in making his readers feel a genuine respect for "Jim," in spite of the ignorance he displays. I cannot help feeling that in this character Mark Twain has, perhaps unconsciously, exhibited his sympathy and interest in the masses of the negro people.[2]

Regarding Clemens, Washington extolls him as "rare and unique," declaring his conviction that "his success in literature rests largely upon the fact that he came from among the common people. . . . he stuck close to nature and to the common people, and in doing so he disregarded in a large degree many of the ordinary rules of rhetoric which often serve merely to cramp and make writers unnatural and uninteresting."[3]

This is an interesting assessment of Mark Twain, especially for what it reveals of Booker T. Washington – a man who was notoriously elusive. The qualities that he praises in Twain are ones he likes to assert regarding himself: origins among and commitments to common folk and a contempt for the affectations of effete culture. We do not generally consider any particular class background to be a precondition of literary greatness; and we certainly know that Washington was not a devotee of literary or any other art. His praise of Twain, however, reflects the intensity of his own class feelings. Clearly, he saw in Samuel Clemens the sort of man he considered himself to be.

Washington's comments regarding Jim contain several errors of detail, suggesting that he had not read the book recently. For instance, he remembers Jim as a boy. What seems more noteworthy, however, is how he describes Twain's achievement in the portrayal of Jim. He notes that the portrayal conveys Twain's general sympathy with African-Americans – a perception that many subsequent critics have not shared. Even more intriguing is his cryptic insinuation that Twain moves his readers to sympathize with Jim "somehow" and "without making any comment and without going out of his way." These observations, too, are very revealing of Washington himself. As the preeminent "race leader" in an extraordinarily bigoted era, he was acutely aware of the limitations imposed on racial discourse. In that depraved moment of our history, to speak kindly of African-Americans was less acceptable socially than to abuse and disparage them. Washington was a virtuoso at negotiating the negrophobic mine field of American public discourse at the turn of the century, winning white support for black institutions without ever offending whites by representing black people as full partners in humanity. For Washington, an archpragmatist in a pragmatic age, the final result was what really mattered. Thus, when he praises Twain for achieving the effect of sympathy without revealing his intentions or strategies, he is once again identifying Twain with himself. In the sense that Twain generally masked his seriousness behind comedy and satire – a point that Washington astutely notes in this eulogy – Washington's identification with Twain is startlingly apt. Nevertheless, given Washington's untroubled propensity to prefer expediency over honesty, it is hard to imagine that Mark

Twain would have seen himself in Washington the way that Washington clearly sees himself in Twain. Though these two eminent men shared strategies of public role playing and dissembling, they were of profoundly different sensibilities.

Washington praises Twain for two other things that seem worthy of note. First, he acknowledges Twain's passionate work on behalf of the Africans who were so viciously exploited by Belgian imperialism in the Congo. "In his letter to Leopold, the late King of the Belgians, in his own inimitable way he did a service in calling to the attention of the world the cruelties practised upon the black natives of the Congo that had far-reaching results."[4] Washington seldom involved himself with controversial issues and never publicly criticized white people. Thus, his endorsement of Twain's bitterly satirical "letter" is a bit surprising. Finally, he mentions Twain's participation in a fundraiser for Tuskegee Institute at Carnegie Hall in 1906. (A photograph of Twain and Washington onstage is included in Shelley Fisher Fishkin's *Was Huck Black? Mark Twain and African-American Voices*).[5] Washington's mentioning this is significant because it underscores his argument that Twain was a friend of African-American people.

Washington's comments focus on matters of character, which is appropriate in a eulogy. Nevertheless, this concern with the personal attitudes of Samuel Clemens regarding racial matters, not just with the attitudes expressed in his writings, has remained a characteristic feature of Twain criticism. Washington's essay anticipates the preoccupation of both black and white critics with this question. Most of what it says about Mark Twain sounds perfectly obvious, and as was characteristic of Washington, the obviousness masks the astuteness and subtlety of his insights. Still, this is a eulogy, not a work of criticism. It reveals a surprising affinity between these two men, but is it actually pertinent to a discussion of black critics and Twain? I think so. The questions of how one judges the racial attitudes of Samuel Clemens and how one interprets the portrayal of Jim have remained central to this debate. Washington declares himself forcefully and succinctly on both issues.

Unlike Washington, Sterling Brown was a literary man: a poet, scholar, and professor. In temperament and sensibility, he was perhaps the exact opposite of Washington. Bluntly honest and unhesitant to confront racists insult for insult, Brown was an heir of W. E. B. Du Bois, not Booker T. Washington. Brown's *The Negro in American Fiction* (1937), still the most thorough work of its kind, is an exhaustive survey of virtually every novel or story that included Negro characters, from colonial times to the 1930s. Though he addresses the works very briefly, Brown offers clear, incisive, and sometimes pungent assessments of the texts. Thus, Twain receives only two pages, but Brown gives very high praise to his portrayal of Jim:

> Jim is the best example in nineteenth century fiction of the average Negro slave (not the tragic mulatto or the noble savage), illiterate, superstitious, yet clinging to his hope for freedom, to his love for his own. And he is completely believable, whether arguing that Frenchmen should talk like people, or doing most of the work on the raft, or forgiving Huck whose trick caused him to be bitten by a snake, or sympathizing with the poor little Dauphin, who, since America has no kings, "cain't git no situation."[6]

In contrast to so many African-American intellectuals, Brown both relished black vernacular culture and appreciated the realistic representation of it in literary works. Thus, he regards Jim's superstition and his ignorant notions (regarding Frenchmen, for example) as amusingly realistic and not as embarrassments to the race.[7]

Like most Twain critics, Brown describes *Pudd'nhead Wilson* as a deeply flawed novel. In part, he sees the technical execution of the novel as deficient, commenting, for example, that "Roxy is a first-rate preliminary sketch."[8] More vexing to him, however, is the tangled irony of the book that leaves many readers uncertain whether Twain agrees with Roxy's equation of her son's bad character with his "Negro blood." Essentially, Brown values Twain's realism over his irony, even when the latter works effectively. For example, "grimly realistic" is his term of approbation for Roxy's fear of being sold down the river. This emphasis on realism is crucial to Brown, because it represents the counterbalance to and refutation of a racist ideology that characteristically manifests itself in stereotypes and inaccurate or implausible descriptions of black people. In this context, the metaphor "preliminary sketch" serves the same purpose, indicating work that is moving toward a laudably accurate depiction. For black critics such as Sterling Brown, the espousal of realism has been a strategy in the struggle against racial stereotypes and Eurochauvinism.

Many other black critics, however, have rejected realism – some realities are embarrassing, after all – insisting instead on idealism, propriety, and the depiction of only what they consider complimentary to the race. The motivations for such a stance are easy enough to understand, but the inadequacies ought to be equally obvious. Carried to its logical extremes, this view of literature leads its adherents to reject much of our great literature and to embrace trite and tepid works of no enduring value. As Brown well understood, the ultimate complaint of most such critics is not that Jim is inaccurately rendered but rather that uneducated Negroes like Jim are embarrassments who should not be depicted at all. Brown, by contrast, advocates an unflinching honesty in the representation of black history, social behavior, and culture. He therefore applauds the manifestations of such honesty in the work of Mark Twain.

Despite their many obvious differences, Washington and Brown agree in regarding Mark Twain as a writer who is unusual in his sympathetic portrayal of black characters. Other black critics have taken the opposite view of Twain's work, viewing him as a purveyor of racial stereotypes and humiliating racial depictions. In recent times, no one has articulated this perspective more vigorously and persistently than John H. Wallace, a public school administrator who has campaigned vociferously against the teaching of *Adventures of Huckleberry Finn* in primary and secondary schools. Wallace's essay, "The Case Against *Huck*," for example, begins with the assertion that Twain's novel "is the most grotesque example of racist trash ever written."[9] Wallace has frequently used this line in his interviews, editorials, and essays regarding the book. Given this description of *Huckleberry Finn*, one must wonder how he would describe the novels of Thomas Dixon. Furthermore, it is not clear how one should regard the ironic fact that Wallace has produced his own sanitized version of the novel, minus the words "nigger" and "hell," *The Adventures of Huckleberry Finn Adapted*, thereby attaching his own name to a work of "grotesque racist trash."

In any case, earnestness, not irony, has been John Wallace's forte. Despite his reductive approach to the text, his argument does reflect the concerns of many parents and teachers who have objected to the assignment of the novel in schools. Wallace summarizes his view as follows:

> My own research indicates that the assignment and reading aloud of *Huckleberry Finn* in our classrooms is humiliating and insulting to black students. It contributes to their feelings of low self-esteem and to the white students' disrespect for black people. It constitutes mental cruelty, harassment, and outright racial intimidation to force black students to sit in the classroom with their white peers and read *Huckleberry Finn*. The attitudes developed by the reading of such literature can lead to tensions, discontent, and even fighting.[10]

This approach focuses almost exclusively on the racial attitudes that readers bring with them to the text. As Wallace's obsessive preoccupation with the word "nigger" suggests, this is a sociology of the classroom and not a form of critical exegesis. For that reason, Wallace's declarations undoubtedly have greater immediacy and pertinence to many secondary school educators and parents' organizations than more sophisticated responses to the novel sometimes achieve. Nevertheless, the mere exclusion of troubling material constitutes an evasion, not a solution, of fundamental problems. We might do well to question an educational philosophy that values comfort over understanding. These issues notwithstanding, John H. Wallace deserves to be mentioned in this discussion because his work provides such a direct link to the broader public debate over this novel.

Very few serious scholars would endorse Wallace's declarations unequivocally, but many share his view that the novel does more to promulgate than to subvert racist views. A number of critics address this problem in terms of racial stereotypes. For example, Fredrick Woodard and Donnarae MacCann argue in their article, "Minstrel Shackles and Nineteenth-Century 'Liberality,'" that "Twain's use of the minstrel tradition undercuts serious consideration of Jim's humanity beyond those qualities stereotypically attributed to the noble savage; and Jim is forever frozen within the convention of the minstrel darky."[11] This argument is predicated in part upon the assumption that the portrayals of blacks in minstrelsy were altogether false and devoid of any content except the intention to disparage and demean. This assumption contains a great deal of truth, but there is also a significant body of scholarship that advocates more complex and ambiguous readings of minstrelsy.[12] It is important to note, for example, that there were numerous conventions of depicting blacks within minstrelsy. When Woodard and MacCann speak of a singular "convention," they imply a uniformity that was not, in fact, the case. Thus, one might agree with Woodard and MacCann that Twain uses minstrel stereotypes and yet disagree with them about what to infer from that fact. We shall return to this point momentarily when we consider Ralph Ellison's comments on Twain and *Huckleberry Finn*.

For critics who seek to interpret Mark Twain's fiction by studying his letters, lectures, and nonfiction for clues regarding the racial attitudes of Samuel Clemens, there is ample evidence of both exceptional liberality and commonplace racist attitudes. The man who paid the expenses of a black law student at Yale, Warner McGuinn, also proclaimed his passion for "the old-fashioned nigger show."[13] Such extratextual evidence is interesting to consider, but it does not enable us to answer the interpretive questions posed by Mark Twain's fiction. What Twain said about minstrel shows does not in fact clarify the ironic ambiguities of Roxy's declarations about racial character; it does not even help us to reconcile the low-comic Jim with the compassionate mentor Jim. The irreconcilable inconsistencies within texts like *Adventures of Huckleberry Finn* and *Puddn'head Wilson* guarantee that critics, both black and white, will continue to interpret the racial implications of these texts in conflicting ways. In my own view, these inconsistencies are not authorial failings. Rather, they are accurate reflections of an irreducibly heterogeneous social reality. That these texts defy our attempts to reduce them to simplicity is part of what makes them great and enduring works that remain productive for us to study and debate. For black critics, this ambiguity regarding racial questions poses a particular kind of problem that we ought to consider before proceeding.

While "black" as a category of identity does not entail any specific opinions or perspectives, it does, within a broad cultural context, define a certain range of rhetorical options and constraints. In other words, we cannot predict the attitudes or opinions of any critic merely on the basis of his or her race, but since race, or at least "blackness," does have prescribed entailments within our culture, there is always an implicit racial "politics" in taking a public stance on any given question. In other words, to interpret *Huckleberry Finn* as a racist book, an antiracist book, or a mixed bag of liberal and racist tendencies is to align oneself politically with one faction or another. While this is in some sense true for all critics, it is a consideration that impinges upon black critics with a particular urgency.

Thus, when John Wallace condemns *Adventures of Huckleberry Finn,* he implicitly aligns himself with the interests of anguished black children. When Woodard and MacCann emphasize the stereotypical depictions in the novel, they align themselves with black people aggrieved by a continuing persistence of racist portrayals. Washington and Brown, from different ends of the political spectrum, both distinguish Twain as a unique exception to the racist rule in American culture. Implicitly, they both represent traditions of black activism that espouse cooperation with white allies: Washington, the conservative tradition, and Brown, the progressive tradition. My own reading of Twain as an antiracist writer is oriented toward the latter tradition. Whether one chooses to emphasize the persistence of racism or the struggle against it is a fundamental issue. One may be in sympathy with all of these positions, but practically speaking, one cannot give equal weight to all of them. One must choose, and the choice, we know, will be perceived as a gesture of self-declaration. For black critics, then, the work of Mark Twain is an especially fraught topic.

The great fame of Ralph Ellison as a novelist has overshadowed his work as a critic. Nevertheless, Ellison's small body of critical work is unsurpassed for the quality of its insights into American literature, especially regarding the relationship between aesthetic values and the social issues of freedom, democracy, and race as these concerns manifest themselves in our literary tradition. Not surprisingly, Ellison has shown a strong affinity for Mark Twain, and he has expressed an acute awareness of the issues described in the preceding paragraph. He comments:

It is not at all odd that this black-faced figure of white fun is for Negroes a symbol of everything they rejected in the white man's thinking about race, in themselves and in their own group. When he appears, for example, in the guise of Nigger Jim, the Negro is made uncomfortable. Writing at a time when the blackfaced minstrel was still popular, and shortly after a war which left even the abolitionists weary of those problems associated with the Negro, Twain fitted Jim into the outlines of the minstrel tradition, and it is from behind this stereotype mask that we see Jim's dignity and human capacity – and Twain's complexity – emerge.[14]

For Ellison, Mark Twain's greatness is manifested in his sophisticated understanding of the moral dilemmas posed by race. Ellison's comments regarding Jim reflect his own multifaceted appreciation of Twain's work and also place him in sharp contrast to many other African-American critics.

One of the enduring reasons for African-American discomfort with Jim is reflected in the language of Ellison's comments. Referring to Jim as "Nigger Jim," he echoes the common practice of critics, including African-Americans, in his generation. Indeed, this designation remains all too common among critics of our own time. There is no legitimate basis for it within the text of *Huckleberry Finn*. When he first appears in the novel, Huck describes him as "Miss Watson's big nigger, named Jim."[15] This alone hardly justifies calling him "Nigger Jim," especially since he is not thus described elsewhere in the novel. Nonetheless, Twain critics from Albert Bigelow Paine onward have persisted in using this offensive sobriquet. Even if Twain himself used this nickname in conversation, in letters, or in public performances, that would not mandate critics to do the same. Rather, the tradition of saying "Nigger Jim" reflects a certain casualness, perhaps even a secret pleasure, in the critics' own use of the word "nigger." Attaching the word to Jim's name allows its use in public contexts that would otherwise preclude such language. This being the case, entering the critical discussion surrounding *Adventures of Huckleberry Finn* required (and requires) of black critics a high tolerance for the word "nigger" in the mouths of whites. This is a challenge that many talented black critics have been pleased to decline.

That Ellison speaks so easily of "Nigger Jim," however, is not surprising. Ellison is universally recognized as a writer with a profound appreciation of irony and a secure, unapologetic attitude regarding his African-American identity. He also is a writer deeply grounded in black vernacular culture, and he is therefore thoroughly aware of the various ways in which African-Americans have toyed with and reappropriated the use of this word. In black vernacular usage, "nigger" reflects an ironic consciousness that the word is an insult in the mouths of whites. Thus, when black folk use it, they often parody white presumption. Sometimes, however, they use it to be hurtful, and in those cases the term becomes a double insult – a put down from the put down. The implications of this word depend upon who uses it, under what circumstances, and with what intentions. Consequently, though Ellison refers to "Nigger Jim," we know from his other comments that he has no implicit intention to dehumanize Jim. Nevertheless, his use of this deplorable nickname helps to legitimize it. Such are the paradoxes of American racial discourse.

We should not underestimate the singularity of Ellison's insight that from behind a minstrel mask "Jim's dignity and human capacity emerge." Such an insight requires a deeply ironic sensibility. Many African-American critics, for whatever reason, have been disinclined, or perhaps unable, to extend their appreciation of irony into their encounters with racist stereotypes. This constitutes a significant disadvantage in addressing the work of an ironist like Mark Twain. Ellison, on the other hand, never forgets that simple appearances often conceal complex realities:

> Huckleberry Finn knew, as did Mark Twain, that Jim was not only a slave but a human being, a man who in some ways was to be envied, and who expressed his essential humanity in his desire for freedom, his will to possess his own labor, in his loyalty and capacity for friendship and in his love for his wife and child. Yet Twain, though guilty of the sentimentality common to humorists, does not idealize the slave. Jim is drawn in all his ignorance and superstition, with his good traits and his bad. He, like all men, is ambiguous, limited in circumstance but not in possibility. . . . Jim, therefore, is not simply a slave, he is a symbol of humanity, and in freeing Jim, Huck makes a bid to free himself of the conventionalized evil taken for civilization by the town.[16]

Ellison's reading of Jim, which resonates with that of Sterling Brown, turns the conventional understanding of minstrelsy on its head. As conventionally understood, minstrelsy renders black people comical by caricaturing them as subhuman. In Ellison's reading, the comic mask of blackness is a form of artifice that serves to accentuate the universal humanity beneath the mask. He argues in the final sentence of the essay, "Mark Twain knew that in *his* America humanity masked its face with blackness."[17] In these terms, when Huck makes his commitment to Jim, he embraces his own humanity.

Ellison's recognition of Jim as the moral center of the novel allows him to offer an elegant explanation of why the troubling final section of the novel is both formally and thematically necessary and not an unfortunate deviation, as some critics, including Hemingway, have argued.[18] The ultimate point of Ellison's argument, however, is not merely to solve critical puzzles with clever solutions. Ellison's larger agenda is to align himself within the liberal humanist tradition and to redefine that tradition, making African-American culture and concerns central to it. The great moral issues of freedom and democracy in America cannot be understood, he insists, without taking into account the place of slavery and of black people in America. If not for the presence of African-Americans, he argues in "What America Would Be Like Without Blacks," there would be no American language as we know it, no American novel, and American history would be wholly different.[19]

The appeal of this argument is immediately obvious. Nevertheless, it is an argument that many black critics would neither make nor endorse. By emphasizing shared values and common humanity, Ellison implicitly advocates a liberal pluralist vision in which mutual respect and cooperation across racial lines are both possible and desirable. For many other black critics, the more important point to assert is the continuity of white racism. To portray Twain as a purveyor of stereotypes emphasizes this latter point. In effect, the difference between these two perspectives is a matter of priorities. Ellison commits himself to articulating an ideal. Others prefer bearing witness to bitter experience. The work of Mark Twain lends itself to both agendas.

In assessing *Adventures of Huckleberry Finn,* critics are obligated to address or to evade the meanings of race, slavery, and freedom in American culture. Many white critics have elected to evade these questions, and our intellectual culture is such that they could make this choice without dishonor. Such freedom has not extended to black critics. Indeed, black critics who discuss this novel without addressing the portrayal of Jim and the racial issues posed by the novel risk appearing personally deficient, ashamed to admit their own racial identity.[20] White critics may engage the text however they wish, while black critics, if they comment on it at all, are expected to declare their own racial politics. Such declarations, however, make black critics vulnerable to charges that they are politicizing the critical discussion of Twain's work for personal, not scholarly, reasons. Obviously, these discursive expectations and entailments are unequal for black and white critics. This is yet another example of what race, in operational terms, means.

Perhaps this helps to explain why black critics have been much less involved in Twain criticism than one might expect, given the nature of his greatest work. Indeed, when the *Mark Twain Journal* decided to mark the centennial of *Huckleberry Finn* by publishing a special issue featuring the responses of black critics to the novel, it dramatically increased the quantity of work on this novel by black critics. Despite the impact of that issue and its republication in book form as *Satire or Evasion,* very few black critics have become active in the circles of Mark Twain scholarship. This fact

perhaps suggests that Ralph Ellison's vision of a pluralist cultural discourse
remains more an ideal than a reality.

NOTES

1 This essay was first published in the *Mark Twain Journal*. It has been reprinted
   in M. Thomas Inge, ed., *Huck Finn Among Critics* (Frederick, Md.: University
   Publications of American, 1985), pp. 247–65; James S. Leonard, Thomas A.
   Tenney, and Thadious M. Davis, eds., *Satire or Evasion? Black Perspectives on
   "Huckleberry Finn"* (Durham, N.C.: Duke University Press, 1992), pp. 103–
   20; Eric Sundquist, ed., *Mark Twain: A Collection of Critical Essays* (En-
   glewood Cliffs, N.J.: Prentice-Hall, 1994), pp. 90–102.
2 Louis R. Harlan and Raymond W. Smock, eds., *The Booker T. Washington
   Papers, Vol. 10: 1909–11* (Urbana: University of Illinois Press, 1981), pp. 348–
   50. Reprinted from *North American Review* 191 (June 1910): 828–30.
3 Ibid., pp. 349–50.
4 Ibid., p. 349.
5 Shelley Fisher Fishkin, *Was Huck Black? Mark Twain and African-American
   Voices* (New York: Oxford University Press, 1993), p. 106.
6 Sterling Brown, *The Negro in American Fiction* (Washington, D.C.: Associates
   in Negro Folk Education, 1937), p. 68. Reprinted by Arno Press, New York,
   1969.
7 The conflict regarding acceptable forms of racial humor has been one of the
   sharpest and most enduring rifts in black intellectual culture. The controversy
   over the *Amos 'n Andy* television show in the 1950s, a radio favorite among the
   black masses that was reviled by the black elites and ultimately suppressed by a
   successful NAACP campaign, exemplifies the class politics of this issue. The
   history of these conflicting responses has been most recently addressed by Mel
   Watkins in *On the Real Side: Laughing, Lying, Signifying – The Underground
   Tradition of African-American Humor That Transformed American Culture,
   from Slavery to Richard Pryor* (New York: Simon & Schuster, 1994).
8 Brown, *The Negro in American Fiction*, p. 69.
9 John H. Wallace, "The Case Against *Huck Finn*," in *Satire or Evasion?* ed.
   Leonard et al., p. 16.
10 Ibid., p. 17.
11 Fredrick Woodard and Donnarae MacCann, "Minstrel Shackles and
   Nineteenth-Century 'Liberality,' " in *Satire or Evasion?* ed. Leonard et al., p. 142.
12 One strain of scholarship emphasizes the use of universal comic archetypes in
   minstrelsy and argues that minstrelsy presents a complex interplay between
   notions of racial difference and acknowledgments of common humanity. Such
   critics include Constance Rourke and Ralph Ellison, who was deeply influenced
   by Rourke's work. Robert Toll's work, based on a more thorough survey of the
   traditions within minstrelsy, distinguishes among the various kinds of portrayals and the contrasting social and political perspectives among minstrel
   troupes and performers. Toll's detailed account of the evolution of minstrelsy

over many decades undercuts the conflation of minstrelsy into a single, simple phenomenon; and his consideration of African-American minstrels explodes the common misconception that blackface comedy was merely a white man's game. Most recently, Eric Lott has brought the subtle tools of contemporary cultural studies to bear on minstrelsy, examining its appropriations of black culture, the complexly ambivalent dynamics between contempt for and fascination with African-Americans, and the role of minstrelsy in creating a multicultural consciousness in America. The work of these scholars enables us to understand minstrelsy in much more subtle, detailed, and sophisticated terms. See Constance Rourke, *American Humor: A Study of the National Character* (New York: Harcourt, Brace, 1931); Ralph Ellison, *Shadow and Act* (New York: Vintage Books, 1972); Robert C. Toll, *Blacking Up: The Minstrel Show in Nineteenth-Century America* (New York: Oxford University Press, 1974); and Eric Lott, *Love and Theft: Blackface Minstrelsy and the American Working Class* (New York: Oxford University Press, 1993).

13 Bernard DeVoto, ed., *Mark Twain in Eruption* (New York: Harper Bros., 1940), p. 110. Regarding Twain's support of McGuinn, see Fishkin, *Was Huck Black?* pp. 90–1.
14 Ellison, *Shadow and Act,* p. 50.
15 Samuel Clemens, *Adventures of Huckleberry Finn,* 2d ed. (New York: Norton, 1977), p. 10.
16 Ellison, *Shadow and Act,* pp. 31–2.
17 Ibid., p. 44.
18 Ralph Ellison, *Going to the Territory* (New York: Random House, 1986), pp. 267–8.
19 Ibid., pp. 109–10.
20 A rare exception is Arnold Rampersad's splendid, objective, and original article, ."*Adventures of Huckleberry Finn* and Afro-American Literature," *Mark Twain Journal* 22.2 (Fall 1984): 45–52. Reprinted in *Satire and Evasion?* ed. Leonard et al., pp. 216–227, and *Mark Twain: A Collection,* ed. Sundquist, pp. 103–12.

7

ERIC LOTT

Mr. Clemens and Jim Crow: Twain, Race, and Blackface

Soon after leaving Hannibal for New York in 1853, Sam Clemens wrote home to his mother: "I reckon I had better black my face, for in these Eastern States niggers are considerably better than white people."[1] As the youth who would be Mark Twain wrote these words, Christy's Minstrels were at the peak of their extraordinary eight-year run (1846–54) at New York City's Mechanics' Hall, and many other blackface troupes battled them for public attention. Meanwhile, the new phenomenon of the "Tom show" – dramatic blackface productions of Harriet Beecher Stowe's *Uncle Tom's Cabin,* published the year before – was emerging to (briefly) displace and reorient the minstrel tradition; by 1854 there were several such shows running in New York alone. Probably the prominence of blackface in New York only clinched Clemens's love of minstrelsy, which extended back to his Hannibal childhood.

Blackface minstrelsy – "the genuine nigger show, the extravagant nigger show," Twain calls it in the autobiography he dictated in his last years – had burst upon the unwitting town in the early 1840s as a "glad and stunning surprise."[2] Usually involving a small band of white men armed with banjo, fiddle, tambourine, and bone castanets and arrayed in blackface makeup and ludicrous dress, the minstrel show, from the 1830s to the early years of the twentieth century, offered white travesties and imitations of black humor, dance, speech, and music. It most often opened with assorted songs, breakdowns, and gags, followed by an "olio" portion of novelty acts such as malapropistic "stump speeches" or parodic "lectures," and concluded with a burlesque skit set in the South. In his *Autobiography* Twain averred: "If I could have the nigger show back again in its pristine purity and perfection I should have but little further use for opera" (AU 64). This quite unguarded attraction to "blacking up" perhaps made it inevitable that in a letter to his mother Twain would reach for the blackface mask to finesse his response to racial difference in the northern city. For the rest of his life, Twain's imaginative encounters with race would be unavoidably bound up with blackface minstrelsy.

If Sam Clemens's class- and race-conscious recoil from free blacks sounds a lot like Huck Finn's pap – "And to see the cool way of that nigger – why, he wouldn't a give me the road if I hadn't shoved him out o' the way"[3] – it also reminds us that such consciousness, as in minstrelsy, often acknowledged the lure to *be* black ("I reckon I had better black my face"), to inhabit the cool, virility, humility, abandon, degradation, and *gaité de coeur* that were the prime components of white fantasies of black manhood. Pap himself, in Twain's sly depiction of his rage against the black professor, is actually as black as the hated "mulatter," since he is, as Huck says, "just all mud" after a drunken night lying in the gutter (HF 26). These subterranean links between black and lower-class white men called forth in the minstrel show, as in Mark Twain's work, interracial recognitions and identifications no less than the imperative to disavow them. Certainly nineteenth-century blackface acts sought to deny the idea that blacks and whites shared a common humanity. Their racist gibes and pastoral gambols asserted that slavery was amusing, right, and natural; their racial portrayals turned blacks into simps, dupes, and docile tunesmiths.

> Come listen all you galls and boys
> I'se jist from Tuckyhoe,
> I'm going to sing a little song,
> My name's Jim Crow.

> Weel about and turn about
> And do jus so,
> Eb'ry time I weel about
> And jump Jim Crow.[4]

Exhibited before tradesmen, teamsters, and shopkeepers (and, in the 1850s and after, their female counterparts) in Northern entertainment venues such as New York City's Mechanics' Hall, minstrel shows were in part the cultural flank of a generalized working-class hostility to blacks. This hostility was evinced in public slurs and violent acts – the casual racial policing that produced innumerable brawls and forced indignities as well as the organized racial panic that fomented New York's terrible 1834 antiabolitionist race riots.

Yet the minstrel show very often twinned black and white, equating as much as differentiating them. The sources of this equation lay in exactly the same social conditions that gave rise to racist violence. One glimpses in the violence a severe white insecurity about the status of whiteness. To be lower class and white in the early nineteenth century, as the industrial revolution began to grind into high gear, was to be subject to remorseless assaults on one's independence and livelihood. The terms and conditions of work were steadily and alarmingly deteriorating; the status and character of white manhood struck masculinist workingmen as increasingly like that of women and blacks. The term "wage slave" came into being to denote this social drift, implying a defiant, "manly" outrage about the common condition of slaves and workingmen as well as a primacy of concern for the status of white wage workers. Blackface minstrelsy was founded on this social antinomy. On one hand, it basked in what one historian has called the "wages of whiteness"; on the other, it reveled in the identifications between white men and slaves.[5] As for the latter, the very form of blackface acts – an inhabitance of black bodies, clothing, and gesture – records the literal white "investment" in black culture and an implicit desire to cross the color line. Blackface burlesque skits such as T. D. Rice's *O Hush! or, The Virginny Cupids* (1834) assumed, however contradictorily, a white audience alliance with "'spectable" black mechanics onstage even as they ridiculed supercilious black "dandies" – a racist designation that nonetheless reveals the class animus fueling much of the minstrel show's racial disdain.[6] The interracial recognition on which minstrelsy often called was visible in the artisan abolitionism that competed with artisan racism for the hearts and minds of workingmen; working-class antislavery feeling was intermittently strong in the antebellum years and may have aided blackface minstrelsy's turn toward a liberating sentimentalism in the late 1840s.[7] Stephen Foster's "Old Folks at Home" (1851) and "My Old Kentucky Home, Good-Night!" (1853), sung from behind the blackface mask, unquestionably evoked sympathy for separated slave families and generally implied the feeling humanity of slaves, though in doing so it relied on the old racial stereotypes. As Ralph Ellison has remarked, even when the intentions of minstrel performers were least palatable, still "these fellows had to go and listen, they had to open their ears to [black] speech even if their purpose was to make it comic."[8] The complex and active exchanges of white self and black Other in blackface performance, however derisive, opened the color line to effacement in the very moment of its construction.[9]

Twain's own response to blackface minstrelsy illustrates the ambivalence of lower-class white racial feeling, which suffuses his greatest novelistic treatments of race and slavery. Twain wrote of the minstrel show:

The minstrels appeared with coal-black hands and faces and their clothing was a loud and extravagant burlesque of the clothing worn by the plantation slave of the time; not that the rags of the poor slave were burlesqued, for that would not have been possible; burlesque could have added nothing in the way of

extravagance to the sorrowful accumulation of rags and patches which constituted his costume; it was the form and color of his dress that was burlesqued.

(AU 64)

Twain proceeds here with some caution and not a little sympathy for the
slave; he senses, perhaps uncomfortably, that the pleasures of stage burlesque have been wrought out of the quotidian violence of slavery. He even
observes that blackface minstrels had "buttons as big as a blacking box,"
collapsing blackface masquerade, the means of its artifice, and an echo of
one of its literal models – Negro bootblacks – in a single self-conscious
figure. But Twain easily abandons such self-consciousness, as his reference
to the slave's "costume," a clearly aestheticizing gesture, might lead us to
expect:

> The minstrel used a very broad negro dialect; he used it competently and with
> easy facility and it was funny – delightfully and satisfyingly funny. . . . [Min-
> strels'] lips were thickened and lengthened with bright red paint to such a
> degree that their mouths resembled slices cut in a ripe watermelon. . . . The
> minstrel troupes had good voices and both their solos and their choruses were
> a delight to me as long as the negro show continued in existence.   (AU 64–6)

Twain is undeniably attracted to and celebratory of black culture. Yet just
what that culture *is* to him is not altogether easy to make out, distorted and
filtered as it is by white fantasy, desire, and delight. When views like Twain's
do not simply fall into ridicule, they are certainly the patronizing flip side of
it, suggesting Twain's ability to lose sight of the sorry circumstances that
underlie his mirth and his continued and unexamined interest in racial
exoticism. Ralph Ellison once observed that *Huck Finn*'s Jim rarely emerges
from behind the minstrel mask; reading Twain's remarks on the minstrel
show lends a great deal of force to that observation.[10]

Already in *Tom Sawyer* (1876), Twain had called on the pleasures of
minstrelsy in his portrayal of Jim; in chapter 2 Jim comes "skipping out at
the gate" singing "Buffalo Gals" – a blackface tune previously known as
"Lubly Fan" (1844):

> Den lubly Fan will you cum out to night,
>   will you cum out to night,
>   will you cum out to night,
> Den lubly Fan will you cum out to night,
> An dance by de lite ob de moon.
>
> I stopt her an I had some talk,
>   Had some talk,
>   Had some talk,

But her foot covered up de whole side-walk
An left no room for me.

. . . .

Her lips are like de oyster plant,
   De oyster plant,
   De oyster plant,
I try to kiss dem but I cant,
Dey am so berry large.[11]

It may well be that blacks picked up even outrageously untoward songs from the blackface theater and adapted them to their own uses, as the long history of black "signifying" on such white productions, and the rowdy misogyny of much black oral culture, suggest.[12] Conversely, Twain's own intent might have been irony rather than realism: Jim, a black man, sings this blackface ditty as Tom whitewashes his aunt's fence in punishment for his truancy, the heightening of racial markers working up a certain self-consciousness here. There may even be an implied equation between Tom and Jim, since Tom's frequent disappearances mimic the escapes of fugitive slaves (which Jim would soon become in *Huck Finn*) and require a constant whitening or chastening in order to distinguish Tom from such a status. Or perhaps Aunt Polly is merely the "lubly" object of a veiled blackface joke on Twain's part (if so, this puts Twain himself in blackface). Just as surely as all of these conjectures, however, Twain saw the character of Jim through lenses the minstrel show had afforded – he let a racist song go out of Jim's heart. The minstrel show's influence on Twain oddly redoubled over the next eight years, the years of *Huck Finn*'s composition.

Blackface minstrelsy indeed underwrote one of the nineteenth century's most powerful antiracist novels – a tribute to the political fractures of minstrelsy and *Huckleberry Finn* both. This is no simple matter of minstrel show "trappings" or "residues" in Twain's novel (as we often hurry to say), an issue of unfortunate, merely historical formal qualities in the portrayal of Jim disrupting Twain's liberal thematic intentions. The text is shot through with blackface thinking. Written as well as situated in the minstrel show's boom years, *Adventures of Huckleberry Finn* (1884), as Anthony J. Berret has argued, relies on comic dialogues between Huck and Jim (much of the humor at Jim's expense), many and various novelty acts (the king and the duke's scams, the circus, etc.), and riotous burlesques of social and cultural matters (Emmeline Grangerford's sentimental poetry, the final setting-free of an already free Jim). The whole book may thus conform to a tripartite minstrel show structure of comic dialogues, olio, and Southern burlesque.[13]

And circumstances surrounding *Huck Finn*'s writing only clarify its indebtedness to the minstrel tradition.

In 1882 Twain got the idea for a lecture tour (which he termed a circus or menagerie) to include himself, William Dean Howells, Thomas Bailey Aldrich, George Washington Cable, and Joel Chandler Harris. This authorial circus seems hardly more than the variety acts of a minstrel show, and the reading tour that came out of the idea, featuring Cable's straight man and Twain's clown, was in a sense precisely one, since both authors read the roles of black characters onstage, Cable even singing black songs.[14] This was the tour during which Twain first read parts of *Huck Finn,* significantly the "King Sollermun" and "How come a Frenchman doan' talk like a man?" passages, whose blackface resonances are very clear. These passages may in fact have been written to be so performed after *Adventures of Huckleberry Finn* was already completed.[15] The political complexity of this affair is compounded by Cable's having published, midtour, "The Freedman's Case in Equity," a forthright attack on Southern racism that appeared in the same issue of *Century Magazine* that ran an excerpt from *Huck Finn.* Somehow the authors' views did not arrest the blackface tones of their readings, or Twain's naming of one of his selections "Can't Learn a Nigger to Argue," a title he changed only when Cable requested it.[16] These events no doubt put a highly ambiguous spin on *Huck Finn,* but they indicate as well that the contradiction between the book's overt politics and its indebtedness to the minstrel show was less cumbrous in the nineteenth century. Even the most enlightened nineteenth-century political thinkers, for example, adhered to "romantic racialism," as historian George Fredrickson has termed it, which celebrated the supposedly greater emotional depth and spiritual resources of black people even as it postulated innate differences between the races, just as the minstrel show seemed to do.[17] *Huck Finn*'s limitations can surely be laid at the minstrel show's doorstep, but its strengths are oddly imbricated with strains of thought and feeling that inspired blackface performance.

We are thus led to a rather scandalous conclusion. The liberatory coupling of Huck and Jim *and* the gruesome blackface sources of Jim's character are the unseparate and equal results of minstrelsy's influence on the work of Mark Twain. Writers who have rightly denounced the minstrel show aura of *Huck Finn* miss the extent to which even the best moments have a blackface cast.[18] True enough Twain's lapses are easy to spot, and we ought to remark on a few of these. There is, for instance, the slave down on the Phelps farm who at the end of *Huck Finn* tends to Jim in his reenslavement. Named Nat in what one can only assume is jocular homage to Nat Turner, this character is so reminiscent of Jim's portrayal at the novel's beginning that he undermines the steady commitment Jim exhibits in the final chapters; the blackface aspersions against him taint Jim as well. Possessed of what Huck/ Twain calls a "good-natured, chuckle-headed face," obsessed with fending off the witches he says have been haunting him, Nat is a sort of hysterical paranoiac (HF 186). (The reference to Nat Turner's obsessive, visionary Christianity works to discredit both men.) Nat observes that Jim sings out when he first sees Huck and Tom, and says so; but the boys flatly deny having heard it, pushing Nat to resort to mystical explanations. " 'Oh, it's de dad-blame' witches, sah, en I wisht I was dead, I do. Dey's awluz at it, sah, en dey do mos' kill me, dey sk'yers me so' " (HF 187). Even if we remark that Nat is forced to this conclusion by the boys' denial, his squirms are rendered with infantilizing exactitude. Shortly after, amid one of Tom's stratagems in the digressive freeing of Jim, some hounds rush into the hut and Nat is again afrighted: "You'll say I's a fool, but if I didn't b'lieve I see most a million dogs, er devils, er some'n, I wisht I may die right heah in dese tracks. I did, mos' sholy" (HF 196). Tom offers to make Nat a witch pie to ward them off, to which Nat responds: "Will you do it, honey? – will you? I'll wusshup de groun' und' yo' foot, I will!" (HF 197). Twain may have intended us to pick up on Tom's callousness in fanning the flames of Nat's fear: we note, for instance, that Nat has never heard of the now-implanted idea of a witch pie and indeed that Nat promises not to disregard Tom's request that he let alone the witch preparations, "not f'r ten hund'd thous'n' billion dollars" (HF 197) – a sum that would probably free Nat from his fetters. But the very uncertainty of Twain's intentions, together with his seemingly happy blackface depiction of Nat's self-abasement, undercuts all but racist meanings from the scene.

At the same time, moments very like this one may reveal more sympathetic dimensions. At the beginning of *Huck Finn* Tom Sawyer can't help playing a trick on Jim while he sleeps; he puts his hat on a branch above his head. Jim believes he's been bewitched and put in a trance and ridden by witches. Huck says Jim tells demonstrably self-serving tales of his adventures:

> Jim was monstrous proud about it, and he got so he wouldn't hardly notice the other niggers. Niggers would come miles to hear Jim tell about it, and he was more looked up to than any nigger in that country. Strange niggers would stand with their mouths open and look him all over, same as if he was a wonder. . . . Jim was most ruined, for a servant, because he got so stuck up on account of having seen the devil and been rode by witches. (HF 11)

In one sense this is standard "darky" fare. Huck even supplies the proper white exasperation with such charlatanism. Yet as several scholars have shown, this moment of apparent blackface foolishness is in fact an occasion in which Jim seizes rhetorical and perhaps actual power. Despite Huck's rather harsh judgment of Jim's self-investment, the fact is that he becomes a "wonder" within the black community and is "most ruined" for a servant – unsuited for slavery – in the wake of his tales. The superstition to which we are encouraged by Huck to condescend has real and potentially subverting results in the world of the novel. One notes that Jim's actual words are not rendered here, which in the orthographic hierarchy of white dialect writing might have had the effect of reducing their impact. This is a moment when Jim, as he does in other ways throughout *Huck Finn,* uses tricks and deceits to his advantage.[19] We may call this a kind of blackface antiracism, of whose political duplicity and indeed variability Twain was not always the complete master.

This may even be a moment, as Shelley Fisher Fishkin has argued, that reveals Twain's intimacy with black life. For beliefs and stories such as Jim's were present and alive within black culture, which coded terrifying "night rides" by patrolling whites or Ku Klux Klan brigades as those of ghouls and spirits.[20] Tales of such night rides, says Gladys-Marie Fry, duly suffered and survived by resilient blacks, allowed the heroic exploits of a subject people free expression.[21] Yet Twain leaves his white readers to divine for themselves the pressing uses of such tales as Jim tells, and in doing so steps again into the uncharmed circle of blackface – for it is, after all, Twain who is deploying black lore for his own ambiguous uses. Ambiguity arises also in scenes where racialist assumptions seem to be under the novelist's scrutinizing gaze. Soon after Huck and Tom arrive on the Phelps farm, with Jim still to be located, Tom suddenly realizes that the dinners the boys see regularly transported to a certain hut seem suspicious:

> "Looky here, Huck, what fools we are, to not think of it before! I bet I know where Jim is."
> "No! Where?"
> "In that hut down by the ash-hopper. Why, looky here. When we was at dinner, didn't you see a nigger man go in there with some vittles?"
> "Yes."
> "What did you think the vittles was for?"
> "For a dog."
> "So'd I. Well, it wasn't for a dog."
> "Why?"
> "Because part of it was watermelon."

"So it was – I noticed it. Well, it does beat all, that I never thought about a dog not eating watermelon. It shows how a body can see and don't see at the same time."

(HF 183)

Working on the assumption that, as Tom puts it, "watermelon shows man," Huck and Tom detect Jim's whereabouts. This is a craftily constructed scene, one that makes some of Twain's largest political points. Huck's recognition that one can see and not see simultaneously is perhaps the aptest self-description in his whole twisted history of antislavery antiabolitionism. The scene pointedly distinguishes man from dog. And yet the means of this distinction is the clichéd watermelon reference, as though that stereotypical food in particular were the one to best locate Jim. It is true that Tom's words suggest only that dogs do not eat watermelon, not that black people do; and even if the latter is implied, it is Tom and Huck, not Twain, speaking. But Twain is joking around here even in the midst of one of his most earnest moral observations. I think we are justified in concluding that the closer Twain got to black cultural practices and to racially subversive meanings, the more, paradoxically, his blackface debts multiplied. Blackface was something like the device or code or signifying system through which Twain worked out his least self-conscious and most sophisticated impulses regarding race in the United States. Jim's triumphs and Twain's ironies have to be as elaborately deciphered as Huck's future through Jim's hair ball, so self-evident are their minstrel roots.

What is more, scenes we always take as Twain's most enlightened strokes suggest a surprising complicity with the minstrel show. Jim's emotionalism and the fugitives' several joyous reunions on the raft call on the romantic racialism that underwrote minstrelsy's sentimental strain – its broken-family nostalgia and long-suffered separations. Stephen Foster's "Old Folks at Home" (1851), for instance, depends for its effect on the pathos culled from black families forced to split up:

> Way down upon de Swanee ribber,
> Far, far away,
> Dere's wha my heart is turning ebber,
> Dere's wha de old folks stay.
>
> All up and down de whole creation,
> Sadly I roam,
> Still longing for de old plantation,
> And for de old folks at home.

Foster's "Oh! Susanna" (1848) exploits the poignance of black attempts to reunite:

I came from Alabama wid
my banjo on my knee,
I'm g'wan to Lousiana
My true love for to see,
It rain'd all night the day I left,
The weather it was dry,
The sun so hot I frose to death;
Susanna, dont you cry.

Oh! Susanna,
Oh! dont you cry for me,
I've come from Alabama,
wid my banjo on my knee.[22]

Twain's novel relies on similar familial predicaments whose resonance derives from the slave's stereotyped emotionality, his deeper well of feeling. Jim does not ache for the old plantation but he does miss his children, from whom he has been separated: "He was often moaning and mourning that way, nights, when he judged I was asleep, and saying, 'Po' little 'Lizabeth! po' little Johnny! its mighty hard; I spec' I ain't ever gwyne to see you no mo', no mo'!' He was a mighty good nigger, Jim was" (HF 125). This moment demonstrates to Huck that Jim "cared just as much for his people as white folks does for their'n" (HF 125), one of Twain's heavier-handed interventions, but in calling on the black types evident in minstrelsy the scene qualifies the very point it wants to make. Investing black people with human feeling, in the minstrel show or in *Huck Finn,* was no doubt an advance over other less charitable views. Yet doing it by way of the postulated inequality of romantic racialism troubled the commitment to American freedom.

In their flight down the river Jim and Huck are themselves occasionally separated, whereupon the two are placed in the longing position of the lovers in "Oh! Susanna" (as Leslie Fiedler somewhat anxiously suspicioned long ago).[23] The most famous of their reunions, after Huck and Jim lose each other in a fog, is an aesthetic and political triumph. Adrift in a canoe on the foggy river with no idea as to Jim's and the raft's whereabouts, Huck falls into uneasy sleep. When he wakes up, it takes him a moment to recall his dilemma. The fog is gone, and in no time Huck has made it to the raft. Jim is asleep, the raft littered with evidence of its difficult passage in the fog. Huck decides to play a trick on Jim – shades of Tom Sawyer – by telling him that he dreamed the whole thing. Jim rouses: "'Goodness gracious, is dat you, Huck? En you ain' dead – you ain' drowned – you's back agin? It's too good for true, honey, it's too good for true. Lemme look at you, chile, lemme feel o' you. No, you ain' dead! you's back agin,' live en soun', jis de same old Huck – de same ole Huck, thanks to goodness!" (HF 70). Huck mutes Jim's gladness as he gets him to adopt the theory that the fog was all a dream. Once convinced, Jim sets out to interpret the dream, to Huck's considerable derision. Huck lets on that it was a joke after all, and Jim's response to Huck's prank apportions most of the humanity on the raft to himself:

> "When I got all wore out wid work, en wid de callin' for you, en went to sleep, my heart wuz mos' broke bekase you wuz los', en I didn' k'yer no mo' what become er me en de raf'. En when I wake up en fine you back agin', all safe en soun', de tears come en I could a got down on my knees en kiss' yo' foot I's so thankful. En all you wuz thinkin' 'bout wuz how you could make a fool uv ole Jim wid a lie. Dat truck dah is *trash;* en trash is what people is dat puts dirt on de head er dey fren's en makes 'em ashamed."　　　(HF 72)

Jim gets to call Huck white trash. Jim's concern for Huck transcends mere worry over his own safety as a fugitive; it is a concern that is not visibly reciprocated by Huck. Indeed Huck, whose experience of the fog curiously resembles that of Jim – he is lost and lonely, falls asleep and feels like he is dreaming, then is glad to see Jim – denies his vulnerability by projecting it onto the slave. Unable to deal with his own experience, treat Jim like a human being, or express his feelings, Huck concocts a trick that makes Jim do all the work – first of articulating Huck's joy at reuniting, then of experiencing Huck's puzzlement and frustration. The "solid white fog" (HF 68), that apt metaphor for white supremacy, which separated Huck and Jim even from the sight of each other, now dissolves only to find Huck reerecting racial barriers. It takes Jim's speech to make Huck "humble myself to a nigger" (HF 72). We might remark, however, that Twain himself is leaning heavily on Jim in this scene to do his work for him. Even as he exposes Huck's racist failings he needs the pathos that minstrel shows in the 1840s and 1850s had begun to pin to the slaves to make his case. Not only does Jim's joy reiterate the steadfast urge to reunion of "Oh! Susanna," his delivery of Huck's comeuppance is swelled by its air of brokenhearted disappointment. Twain knew well the aggregated sources of racial guilt, racial desire, and racial longing that make just the kind of emotional strategy Jim uses irresistibly effective to whites, whether Huck, Twain himself, or his white reader; and his working of the white audience through his manipulations of Jim's character is not the least of *Huck Finn*'s convergences with the minstrel tradition. That Twain may have come to know the appeal of racial emotionalism from the minstrel show itself only shows how variable the political work of minstrelsy could be. If, in other words, some of *Huck Finn*'s best scenes come close to blackface minstrelsy, this hardly cancels their impact (though it does show how little literature transcends its cultural moment). The duplicity of these scenes simply evidences how implicated we remain in the contradictions of North American racial life.

Perhaps Twain was remarking on the absurd consequences of this fundamental cultural fact when he put Jim in what can only be called Arabface. In order to free the fugitive slave from being tied up all day while the king, the duke, and Huck go ashore, the duke disguises Jim as an insane Arab to keep the curious at bay. Attired in a King Lear outfit and horse-hair wig and whiskers, and his face and hands theater-painted a "dead dull solid blue" (HF 126), Jim's appearance surely recalls the art of blackface at the same time that it explodes the very idea of racial performance. Twain no doubt means to lampoon the racial thinking behind forms such as blackface when he has the duke tell Jim that should anyone draw near the raft, Jim must "hop out of the wigwam, and carry on a little, and fetch a howl or two like a wild beast" (HF 126). Savage injuns and niggers and A-rabs too are invoked here as figments of the white supremacist imagination. The effect of Jim's costuming, we note, is to make him look, as Huck puts it, "like a man that's been drownded nine days" and "like he was dead" (HF 126–7) – racist caricature is itself a kind of death.

Despite Twain's self-consciousness, though, the evidence suggests we take Huck's admiring remark about Jim in chapter 40 – that he "knowed" Jim was "white inside" – as the crowning statement on the centrality of blackface's contradictions to Twain's imagination. The remark is a perfect specimen of the imperial psychological orientation Homi Bhabha calls "ambivalence."[24] Convinced of the humanity and identity of American blacks, Twain seems nonetheless to have been haunted by their difference. Hence he returned over and over to the actual practice and literary trope of blackface, which hedges by imagining the Other as black only in exterior, still white inside. A delicate balance must be maintained here. To think of blacks as altogether the same – as all white – threatens white supremacist identity; to think of them as altogether different – as all black – raises the specter of white annihilation and superfluity. As in many societies with subject populations at home or abroad, the Other must be rendered not quite black and yet not white. "They" must be versions of "us," caught in a cycle of mimicry (usually construed as "civilizing" or benevolent rule), and yet perennially unable to make the grade. Racist ideologies, even the relatively gentle ones Twain deploys, insert the boundaries that ever threaten to evaporate between the kinds of human beings stuck in such a hierarchical relationship. Why should it surprise us that, even in a dissenter like Twain, the colonial mentality, so routinely unsettled by an anxiety of otherness, produced a need to preserve the differentness of blacks through blackface gestures even as it nervously asserted that "they" were like "us" after all?

Exploring as well as enacting this logic, Twain anticipated Antonio Gramsci's remarks on "national-popular" literature – that it emerges out of extant popular materials rather than artificially refined or imposed ideas.[25] Twain took up the American dilemma not by avoiding popular racial representations but by inhabiting them so forcefully that he produced an immanent criticism of them. It is not just that Huck more or less fulfills Twain's intention of making nonsense of America's racial strictures (including those of Twain's readers) by living up to them the best anyone can; Twain himself pushed his blackface devices so far that they turned back on themselves, revealing the contradictory character of white racial feeling.[26] It is this simultaneous inhabitance and critique that makes *Huck Finn* so scabrous, unassimilable, and perhaps unteachable to our own time. I don't think Twain chose to work within the popular racial codes of his day out of calculation, as a way of exploiting racist entertainment for antiracist uses, though that often turns out to be *Huck Finn*'s effect. He did it with an odd relish, out of a sense of inwardness and intimacy with the mass audience who shared his love of minstrelsy – the "mighty mass of the uncultivated" he said he wanted to reach with his novel (sold door to door by canvassing agents) and with whom he felt the greatest kinship.[27] It is worth noting here Twain's own willingness in effect to put on the blackface mask. After dinner one night at an 1874 Twain dinner party in Hartford, Twain dropped into his version of several slave spirituals, which had begun to be disseminated by black university singing groups in the early 1870s. Later, an overimbibed Twain mimicked a black man at a hoedown, dancing black dances for his guests in his drawing room.[28] Out of this sensibility came writing based on Twain's immersion in lower- or working-class racial feeling: writing that still resists attempts to tame down or clean up its engagements with race and class in America and that is as partial, flawed, and disturbing as it is penetrating, emblematic, and current.

It is such contradictions that allow *Huck Finn* and many other Twain writings yet to grate on our nerves. These same contradictions, however, make Twain's work valuable, if hard to take. Ecstatic in blackface, Twain touched on a form that conveyed exactly the brutality, insecurity, omnipotence, envy, condescension, jealousy, and fascination that characterize popular white racial responses to black people. Arguments either pro or con Mark Twain and race flatten out this complexity. Much of Twain's work enacts (Twain's own) white lower- or working-class affective racial alliances, which have always been more ambiguous and variable than bourgeois culture and its educational apparatuses can safely admit. Working-class whites negotiate the color line demonstratively, intimately, with a sort of rowdy, wisecracking wonder; this structure of feeling eludes middlebrow aesthetics (see any film version of *Huck Finn*) no less than it exceeds the proper boundaries of "respectable" political discourse. In this sense Twain scandalizes liberal racial moralizers of our day as he scandalized the complacent racists of his own. *Huck Finn's* narrator and even more its author suggest the capacities for antiracist transformation that lie far more promisingly in the popular classes than in their enemies, for whom manners only hide the privilege of blaming racial "insensitivity" on those they dominate.

The contradictions of lower-class racial feeling inform the notorious quip Twain made in a letter to William Dean Howells in 1872 after reading Howells's review of *Roughing It*. "I am as uplifted and reassured as a mother who has given birth to a white baby when she was awfully afraid it was going to be a mulatto."[29] This is an unfortunate remark from the author of "The United States of Lyncherdom" (1901). Yet we ought to reflect on its complex provenance. For the remark puts Twain in the position of a white woman unsure about the consequences of what in the nineteenth century would have been called her "past." No doubt this anxiety speaks to Twain's own past as, two years after marrying Olivia Langdon, a coal magnate's daughter, he battled still to establish himself in the ways of Eastern respectability. In his joke to Howells, Twain imagines his own rural, artisan-class upbringing, however obliquely, coming back in his brainchild *Roughing It* to haunt him as a curiously racial specter – and he imagines his work itself to be the offspring of a miscegenated culture. This mapping of class matters by way of race metaphors indicates the degree of commonality that could be imagined between blacks and lower-class whites even as Twain feared the effects of that commonality in respectable society. Twain's occasional "black" *self*-representations, for instance the 1882 black-dialect note he wrote to his publisher, James Osgood, may bear out this duality.[30] Certainly the sympathy necessary for a piece such as Twain's "A True Story" (1874), told almost entirely in the voice of a black mother who has lived through slavery, could only have come from some deep source of interracial identification such as lower-class life might have afforded.

And yet if we follow out the speculative logic of Twain's quip, we find his genteel wife, Olivia, put in the place of a white woman suffering Twain's own "black" intrusions into the respectable East. From this angle Twain is the black man whose unholy past traduces the unsullied and unmixed literary whiteness he wants to inherit. This tendency – no less a part of Twain's racial contradictions – points up the unselfconscious and frightening index

of white racial emotional life suffusing Twain's writing. The radical egalitarianism of that work is compromised by the unwarranted reliance on blackface gags and black gulls. Even the impressive evidence in Twain's life of
transgressions against the color line runs up against the pale gaze through
which Twain absorbed black cultural practices and the inevitably partial
character of all such crossover dream-work.[31] Staying true to the complexities of Mark Twain also means recognizing the whiteness of his tales, a
quality illuminated by another of Twain's encounters with the minstrel
show. In the *Autobiography* Twain tells us he once took his mother and one
Aunt Betsey Smith to see Christy's Minstrels in St. Louis. Twain's anxiety
about being sullied by race, as with the "mulatto" *Roughing It,* takes him
again into the area of sexuality and gender; this anxiety surfaces in the
oedipal hostility he vents toward his mother in what is, after all, a relatively
minor episode. The comic situation Twain constructs centers upon getting
his mother to attend a minstrel show, since she is a religious woman who
takes her dissipation, Twain notes, only when it can be proved not to be
irreligious. One almost senses Twain rubbing his hands together as he prepares to sink his mother into some real dissipation – a desacralizing impulse
on the part of the son inspired by the unease minstrelsy has provoked in the
writer.

Twain tells his mother and Aunt Betsey Smith that they are attending an
exhibition of African music by some lately returned missionaries:

> When the grotesque negroes [Twain here gets carried away with his own
> conceit] came filing out on the stage in their extravagant costumes, the old
> ladies were almost speechless with astonishment. I explained to them that the
> missionaries always dressed like that in Africa.
> But Aunt Betsey said, reproachfully, "But they're niggers."   (AU 67–8)

Very soon, of course, the newcomers begin to enjoy themselves, "their
consciences . . . quiet now, quiet enough to be dead," Twain writes. They
gaze on "that long curved line of artistic mountebanks with devouring eyes"
(AU 68), and in the end revivify the show by laughing at a stale pun from the
endmen. Twain jokes in this account not only at the expense of blacks but at
that of his mother. The linking of race and motherhood as objects of Twain's
aggression is registered in the syntactical ambiguity as to who possesses the
devouring eyes, a double threat Twain assuages through degradation of
both. This retreat to the haven of whiteness is triggered by Twain's response
to his mother, which somehow, here and elsewhere, so raises the frightening
bar of race as to become confused with it. Blackness and motherhood stand
as suffocating obstacles to Twain's most intimate and unconscious feelings

of white manhood, and they occasionally call forth from him vivid disavowals. Maternity, race, and blackface revealingly unsettle Twain's novel *Pudd'nhead Wilson* (1894).

The premise of *Pudd'nhead Wilson* is the switching at birth of a slave boy, Valet de Chambre (called Chambers), and a scion of a distinguished white family, Thomas a Becket Driscoll (called Tom). The boys are switched by Roxy, the slave mother of Chambers, who has sole care over the two and who, like her son, is virtually white in appearance. As Twain trenchantly puts it: "To all intents and purposes Roxy was as white as anybody, but the one-sixteenth of her which was black out-voted the other fifteen parts and made her a "negro."[32] This kick at the one-drop "fiction of law and custom" (PW 9) persists throughout the novel; indeed, Twain's hackneyed plot device is there to explore questions of blood and breeding, racial genetics and social conditioning. But Twain's inquiry into American racial customs is confused by the ambiguities incident to the category of race itself, by other plot devices (such as a pair of visiting Italian twins – originally Siamese twins whose story Twain wrenched from the novel and published as *Those Extraordinary Twins*), by generic swerves (a detective story that involves failed lawyer Pudd'nhead Wilson's interest in fingerprinting), and by the maternal role of Roxy.[33]

Roxy's relationship with her son after she enters him into the world of whiteness is the first ambiguous intrusion on Twain's investigation of the color line. Having renamed her son Tom (and conducted a similar reversal on the real Tom), she no longer feels so heavily the weight of slavery. Her master dies, setting her free in fact, and both the rechristened Tom and Chambers go to live with an uncle while Roxy leaves the Missouri town of Dawson's Landing to work aboard Mississippi steamboats. Tom turns out a gambler forever in debt, a wretched, purposeless, and mean specimen who treats his mother with all the viciousness of the white master he has become; Chambers, the former heir, grows up a courageous, strong, but perforce submissive youth who functions as both whipping boy and bodyguard for Tom. Roxy's return has all the earmarks of the maternal power Twain attacks in his minstrel show episode and in *Tom Sawyer*'s whitewashing scene. Rankled by Tom's way with her and attempting to reform at least this part of his behavior, Roxy essentially blackmails her son with the knowledge that he is black: "'You is a *nigger! – bawn* a nigger en a *slave!* . . . en if I opens my mouf, ole Marse Driscoll'll sell you down de river befo' you is two days older den what you is now! . . . you's my *son –*" (PW 41). If earlier Tom lorded over his mother in a fantasy of filial domination, he now suffers subjugation by her; this oedipal distress is triggered once again by the eruption of race, as though the categories of "son" and "nigger" inevitably overlapped and together best named the abjection of a white male child's relation to his mother.[34] The exceedingly odd thing about this turn is that Roxy threatens Tom with the very evidence of blood that Twain at first and intermittently questions – and that Roxy herself has subverted in switching the babies in the first place. Tom's one drop is made visible, as it were, by Roxy's presence (one thinks of Twain on the verge of "blacking up" in the letter to his mother), a conjoining of maternity and race that confounds the former emphasis on nurture. Roxy returns to cancel with blood the racial masquerade she set in motion. If this perhaps seems inevitable given Twain's fear of female power – the family romance that mixes up this work on racial categorizing – it is nonetheless strange when one recognizes how alive Twain is in *Pudd'nhead Wilson* to precisely the racial masquerade produced by law and custom and theatricalized by blackface minstrelsy. Indeed, this novel is Twain's most sustained blackface production – one that is inspired but ultimately destroyed by the racial contradictions on which blackface rests.

Blackface perfectly mediates the implicit argument in *Pudd'nhead Wilson* between social and genetic explanations for "racial" behavior. Emphasizing race as theater, blackface speaks to the performative and manufactured character of identity; emanating from racist ideologies of blood, it continually threatens to collapse race into biology. This is by and large what happens to Twain's novel, and its interest in blackface, an apt expression of the dilemmas it wants to expose, finally traps Twain in retrograde racialist thinking. Much of *Pudd'nhead Wilson* attends to the fictionality or theatricalizing of race. When Tom returns from his stint at Yale, for example, the town boys have a "negro bellringer . . . tricked out in a flamboyant curtain-calico exaggeration of his finery, and imitating his fancy eastern graces" (PW 24). This act is a sort of minstrel gag in reverse; the black man burlesques Tom's acquired graces, and does so at the behest of an audience of village white boys. While the absurdity of the act assumes an insuperable barrier between black and white, it also suggests that Tom's whiteness is itself an act, a suggestion that is truer than either the bell ringer or Tom can know since Tom's identity is precisely a black man's whiteface performance. Racial theater is here and throughout Tom's plot a way for Twain to rebut or interrogate the claims of blood – the assigning of attributes and traits according to racial lineage. It is true enough that social conditioning goes so deep that its effects are more than mere theater, in some sense difficult to distinguish from biology. But Twain plays on its humanly constructed character even when he may seem to be giving in to blood. After Roxy tells Tom he is black, and Tom wakes up a Negro like Godfrey Cambridge in Melvin Van Peebles's film *Watermelon Man* (1970), all of his old habits begin to wither and he begins to act the part. "It was the 'nigger' in him asserting its humility," writes Twain, just as Tom finds "the 'nigger' in him involuntarily giving the road, on the sidewalk, to the white rowdy and loafer" (PW 44–5). Twain's seemingly geneticized insistence is qualified by the scare quotes he wraps around the racial indicator, and indeed an adjacent passage Twain inexplicably cut from the published novel so crosses blood with circumstance that biologism is in effect rejected.[35] At the very least the status of Tom's new attitude – blood legacy? psychological metaphor? racial fiction? – remains in doubt.

At the same time, Twain rightly acknowledges the way racial fictions such as blackface assume the status of truth. Soon after Roxy switches the black and white babies, she comes to think of her own son, "by the fiction created by herself" (PW 19), as legitimately her master. Practicing the forms of submission becomes habit, then nature; "the little counterfeit rift of separation between imitation-slave and imitation-master widened and widened, and became an abyss, and a very real one – and on one side of it stood Roxy, the dupe of her own deceptions, and on the other stood her child, no longer a usurper to her, but her accepted and recognized master"(PW 19). Roxy has indeed become an imitation slave – a minstrel performer. But as Twain's narrator hints, this is no easy act: it is a world. When Roxy returns after eight years on steamboats, broke after a bank failure and in need of some form of income, she hopes to appeal to Tom: "She would go and fawn upon him, slave-like – for this would have to be her attitude, of course – and maybe she would find that time had modified him, and that he would be glad to see his long forgotten old nurse and treat her gently" (PW 34). There is, to be sure, some distance between Roxy and her slave-*like* act. The very need for blackface formality, however, indicates the foregone conclusion. Race is theater but race is real, and no amount of blackface accoutrements wins Tom's pleasure:

> "Look at me good; does you 'member ole Roxy? – does you know yo' ole nigger mammy, honey? Well, now, I kin lay down en die in peace, caze I's seed –"
>
> "Cut it short, damn it, cut it short! What is it you want?"
>
> "You heah dat? Jes' de same old Marse Tom, allays so gay and funnin' wid de ole mammy. I 'uz jes' as shore –"
>
> "Cut it short, I tell you, and get along! What do you want?"   (PW 37)

Roxy's self-minstrelizing has become the rule, and only her threat of exposing Tom changes his view of her. The great irony of Roxy's later blackface cross-dressed masquerade (PW 89), put on to deflect her capture after Tom (per Roxy's selfless request) sells her to pay his debts, is that blackface both disguises and reveals her. Too light-skinned to be noticed in black makeup, Roxy in blackface comes out, though paradoxically in secret, as a black woman and a slave.

This is the sense in which Chambers is right to refuse Roxy's description of him as an "imitation nigger." Amid a minstrel show dialogue that does Twain little credit, Roxy labels Chambers, born to a first family of Virginia, a "misable imitation nigger dat I bore in sorrow en tribbilation" (PW 35). She means blackface, quite literally, but Chambers, who can know nothing of this meaning, responds with sense: "If I's imitation, what is you? Bofe of us is imitation *white* – dat's what we is – en pow'full good imitation, too – Yah-yah-yah! [This is incidentally a standard ejaculation from the minstrel show.] – We don't 'mount to noth'n as imitation *niggers*" (PW 35). The last remark is apt commentary on the way racial fictions like blackface and the law amount to reality for black people, whatever their genetic provenance. (Twain ironically bears this out in observing the interaction between these two black characters through the blackface glass, darkly.) Not only do "imitation niggers" not amount to much in fact, Chambers and Roxy pointlessly imitate because by "fictional" decree they already occupy the despised category in question. Indeed the suggestion here is that blood actually confounds the color line upheld by racial fictions, since blacks can on occasion look "pow'full" white. This is the double bind of American racial demarcation: for Roxy and Chambers to be imitation black is to *be* black and gird racial boundaries; for them to be imitation white is to be mere mimics, once removed, "mulatto."

The chief tribute to the forceful sway of such instituted fictions is Roxy's and possibly Twain's resort to explanations of blood in glossing Tom's behavior. Racial acts so easily seem acts of racial predisposition that even those aware of this fact succumb to myths of racial biology. Pudd'nhead Wilson is of course the most notable believer in a genetics of race; as he says to himself when Roxy refuses to have her fingerprints taken, "The drop of black blood in her is superstitious" (PW 23). Wilson's ultimate triumph, his discovery through his eccentric interest in fingerprinting that Tom has murdered his uncle – a conclusion that "corrects" the racial identities of Tom and Chambers, redrawing the color line, and results in Tom being sold down the river – allies his belief in blood with white supremacy even as it causes one to doubt Twain's clarity and allegiances on matters of racial definition. Roxy herself plumps for blood. As she says to Tom of his rascal nature, countering Twain's earlier wariness: "It's de nigger in you, dat's what it is. Thirty-one parts o' you is white, en on'y one part nigger, en dat po' little one part is yo' *soul*" (PW 70). My reader may well object that Roxy's racial genealogy includes not only Tom's white father, Colonel Cecil Burleigh Essex, and other white men ("ole Cap'n John Smith") but also Pocahontas and "a nigger king outen Africa." And Roxy later mutters, "Ain't nigger enough in him to show in his finger-nails . . . yit dey's enough to paint his soul" (PW 70), perhaps a succinct bit of irony about the "painted" and put-on nature even of racial "blood." But when profligate, swindling Tom enters the house of the man everyone thinks is his uncle and murders him *in a blackface disguise,* it is difficult to escape the conclusion that Twain has himself painted not only Tom's soul but his face the color ordained by his one drop of black blood.

The murder of Judge Driscoll is the last in a long line of actions that prove Tom's ill character, the shiftless, fruitless existence that leads him to kill for money and the casual viciousness he sows generally. Tom seems to be acting on his one-thirty-second of black blood, acting racially rather than racially acting – motivated, that is to say, by heredity. Twain suggests early on that Tom's upbringing among the planter class accounts for his failings (PW 18–19), but no one of that gentry comes close to Tom's sorry history. Tom is a "bad baby" (PW 17) from the cradle, before much conditioning at all has taken hold; later, he stabs Chambers with a pocketknife in a scene straight out of the "coon show," blackface minstrelsy's 1890s legacy on the black stage (PW 21). Twain underscores Tom's difference by alluding to his youthful plan to have his father sell Chambers down the river, at which point Judge Driscoll steps in to buy him – "for public sentiment did not approve of that way of treating family servants for light cause or for no cause" (PW 22). Tom even sells his own mother, once at her behest, admittedly, but that sale delivers Roxy (contrary to their agreement) down the river, and when she escapes with a bounty on her head Tom comes very close to turning her in. It is worth noting that in Twain's working conception of the novel Tom began as a scoundrel and was given a mulatto mother only after the fact, as though to explain his devilry.[36] The textual gaps and lapses owing to the notoriously chaotic composition of *Pudd'nhead Wilson* surely account for some of its inconsistencies of racial definition, but not even these explain the curiously inherent nature of Tom's flaws amid a self-conscious context of racial masquerade and play.

Tom's murder of his supposed uncle caps his unwholesome career. Of course, telling historical resonances crowd this scene. Tom in blackface, killing Judge Driscoll as he counts his money, is the avenger of his race against the planter class, who, as Twain writes earlier in the novel, "daily robbed [the slave] of an inestimable treasure – his liberty" (PW 12). Tom's escape in female dress adds to the killing an element of black female revenge for the master's rape of slave women, one of whose issue is Tom himself. Tom's murder with the knife owned by one of the Italian twins, a knife previously used, we are told, in the twins' self-defense (PW 52–3), reinforces the sense of justifiable homicide. However, such resonances make sense only if heredity, not history, is the cause of Tom's crime. He is, after all, so alienated from blackness that he finds oppressive even occasional intimacies with Roxy (Roxy's love makes him "wince, secretly – for she was a 'nigger'" [PW 80]). He has spent far more of his life white than black, and his blackness is still a secret. In this sense he kills his uncle not out of a sense of oppression but to prevent his mixed heritage from being revealed. Tom's hatred of his uncle does increase after Roxy's disclosure that he is black, and in killing the judge he strikes at the legal representative whose juridical fictions would consign Tom to the black side of the color line. Yet the blackface disguise achieves a kind of transparency when Pudd'nhead Wilson secures Tom's "true" racial identity. Not Tom's fingernails but his fingerprints betray his blackness. This "sure identifier," as Wilson calls it, this "mysterious and marvelous natal autograph," reinstitutes the racist fictions of law and custom. The bearer of its physiological truth cannot mask it, "nor can he disguise it or hide it away, nor can it become illegible by the wear and the mutations of time" (PW 108–9). Racial crossing and masquerade, performance and play founder on Wilson's restored hierarchy of racial biology, a restoration in which Twain seems to acquiesce.

Twain's decision to put Tom in blackface during his uncle's murder let minstrelsy's legacy of blood cloud minstrelsy's racial theatrics. As in most of his experiments along the color line, Twain in *Pudd'nhead Wilson* was so attuned to the racial complexities of his time as to be incapable of critical distance from them. Twain's devotion to the minstrel show, recorded autobiographically a decade after the publication of *Pudd'nhead Wilson*, was in no small part responsible for his racial ambivalence and the confusions thereof. "It seems to me that to the elevated mind and the sensitive spirit the hand organ and the nigger show are a standard and a summit to whose rarefied altitude the other forms of musical art may not hope to reach" (AU 64). Blackface furnished Twain's very language of race, a language riddled with ambiguities Twain did not so much illuminate as reiterate.

NOTES

1   Mark Twain, *Mark Twain's Letters,* ed. Edgar Marquess Branch et al. (Berkeley: University of California Press, 1988), vol. 1, p. 4.

2   Mark Twain, *The Autobiography of Mark Twain,* ed. Charles Neider (New York: Harper & Row, 1959), pp. 63–4. Henceforth cited parenthetically in the text as AU.

3   Samuel Langhorne Clemens, *Adventures of Huckleberry Finn* (1884; rpt. New York: Norton, 1977), p. 27. Henceforth cited parenthetically in the text as HF.

4   "Jim Crow" (New York: E. Riley, early 1830s); for this song and some of its variations, see Sam Dennison, *Scandalize My Name: Black Imagery in American Popular Music* (New York: Garland, 1982), pp. 51–7.

5   David Roediger, *The Wages of Whiteness: Race and the Making of the American Working Class* (London: Verso, 1991).

6   For the text of *O Hush!* see Gary Engle, ed., *This Grotesque Essence: Plays from the American Minstrel Stage* (Baton Rouge: Louisiana State University Press, 1978), pp. 1–12.

7   John B. Jentz, "The Anti-Slavery Constituency in Jacksonian New York City," *Civil War History* 27.2 (1981): 101–22; Williston Lofton, "Abolition and Labor," *Journal of Negro History* 33.3 (1948): 249–83; Joseph G. Rayback, "The American Workingman and the Antislavery Crusade," *Journal of Economic History* 3.2 (1943): 152–63; Eric Foner, "Abolitionism and the Labor Movement in Ante-Bellum America," *Politics and Ideology in the Age of the Civil War* (New York: Oxford University Press, 1980), pp. 57–76; Herbert Shapiro, "Labor and Antislavery: Reflections on the Literature," *Nature, Society, and Thought* 2.4 (1989): 471–90.

8   Interview with Ralph Ellison, quoted in Shelley Fisher Fishkin, *Was Huck Black? Mark Twain and African American Voices* (New York: Oxford, 1993), p. 90.

9   For more on the minstrel show, see Eric Lott, *Love and Theft: Blackface Minstrelsy and the American Working Class* (New York: Oxford, 1993).

10 Ralph Ellison, *Shadow and Act* (1964; rpt. New York: Vintage, 1972), p. 50.

11 "Lubly Fan," in S. Foster Damon, comp., *Series of Old American Songs* (Providence, R.I.: Brown University Library, 1936), no. 39.

12 For examples of each tendency see Lawrence Levine, *Black Culture and Black Consciousness: Afro-American Folk Thought from Slavery to Freedom* (New York: Oxford University Press, 1977), pp. 190–366.

13 Anthony J. Berret, "*Huckleberry Finn* and the Minstrel Show," *American Studies* 27.2 (1986): 37–49.

14 Paul Fatout, *Mark Twain on the Lecture Circuit* (Carbondale: Southern Illinois University Press, 1960), pp. 204–31.

15 Fredrick Woodard and Donnarae MacCann, "*Huckleberry Finn* and the Traditions of Blackface Minstrelsy," *Interracial Books for Children Bulletin* 15.1, 2 (1984): 5.

16 Guy Cardwell, *Twins of Genius* (East Lansing: Michigan State College Press, 1953), p. 105; Steven Mailloux, *Rhetorical Power* (Ithaca, N.Y.: Cornell University Press, 1989), pp. 57–99; Forrest G. Robinson, *In Bad Faith: The Dynamics of Deception in Mark Twain's America* (Cambridge, Mass.: Harvard University Press, 1986), pp. 111–211.

17 George M. Fredrickson, *The Black Image in the White Mind: The Debate on Afro-American Character and Destiny, 1817–1914* (New York: Harper & Row, 1971), pp. 101–2.

18 Woodard and MacCann, "*Huckleberry Finn* and the Traditions of Blackface Minstrelsy"; Woodard and MacCann, "Minstrel Shackles and Nineteenth-Century 'Liberality' in *Huckleberry Finn*," in *Satire or Evasion? Black Perspectives on Huckleberry Finn*, ed. James S. Leonard, Thomas A. Tenney, and Thadious M. Davis (Durham, N.C.: Duke University Press, 1991), pp. 141–53; Bernard Bell, "Twain's 'Nigger' Jim: The Tragic Face Behind the Minstrel Mask," *Mark Twain Journal* 23.1 (1985): 10–17.

19 David L. Smith, "Huck, Jim, and American Racial Discourse," in *Satire or Evasion?* ed. Leonard et al., pp. 103–20; James M. Cox, "A Hard Book to Take," in *One Hundred Years of "Huckleberry Finn,"* ed. Robert Sattelmeyer and J. Donald Crowley (Columbia: University of Missouri Press, 1985), pp. 386–403.

20 Fishkin, *Was Huck Black?* pp. 83–4.

21 Gladys-Marie Fry, *Night Riders in Black Folk History* (1975; rpt. Athens: University of Georgia Press, 1991), pp. 9–10.

22 Richard Jackson, ed., *Stephen Foster Song Book* (New York: Dover, 1974), pp. 101–2, 89–91.

23 Leslie Fiedler, "Come Back to the Raft Ag'in, Huck Honey!" *The Collected Essays of Leslie Fiedler* (New York: Stein & Day, 1971), vol. 1, pp. 142–51.

24 Homi Bhabha, "The Other Question: The Stereotype and Colonial Discourse," *Screen* 24.6 (1983): 18–36.

25 Antonio Gramsci, *Selections from Cultural Writings*, ed. David Forgacs and Geoffrey Nowell-Smith, trans. William Boelhower (London: Lawrence & Wishart, 1985), pp. 207, 209–11.

26 On immanent criticism see Theodor Adorno, "Cultural Criticism and Society," *Prisms*, trans. Samuel and Shierry Weber (Cambridge, Mass.: MIT Press, 1967), p. 32.

27 Justin Kaplan, *Mr. Clemens and Mark Twain* (New York: Simon & Schuster, 1966), p. 270.

28 Ibid., p. 174.

29 Mark Twain and William Dean Howells, *Mark Twain–Howells Letters: The Correspondence of Samuel L. Clemens and William Dean Howells, 1872–1910*, ed. Henry Nash Smith and William Gibson (Cambridge, Mass.: Harvard University Press, 1960), vol. 1, pp. 10–11.

30 Mark Twain, *Mark Twain's Letters to His Publishers, 1867–1894*, ed. Hamlin Hill (Berkeley: University of California Press, 1967), pp. 152–3.

31 See Fishkin, *Was Huck Black?* passim.

32 Samuel Langhorne Clemens, *Pudd'nhead Wilson and Those Extraordinary Twins*, ed. Sidney E. Berger (1894; rpt. New York: Norton, 1980), pp. 8–9. Henceforth cited parenthetically in text as PW.

33 In thinking about *Pudd'nhead Wilson*, I am indebted to several essays collected in *Mark Twain's "Pudd'nhead Wilson": Race, Conflict, and Culture*, ed. Susan Gillman and Forrest G. Robinson (Durham, N.C.: Duke University Press, 1990): James M. Cox, "*Pudd'nhead Wilson* Revisited," pp. 1–21; Forrest G. Robinson, "The Sense of Disorder in *Pudd'nhead Wilson*," pp. 22–45; Eric J. Sundquist, "Mark Twain and Homer Plessy," pp. 46–72; Michael Rogin, "Francis Galton and Mark Twain: The Natal Autograph in *Pudd'nhead Wil-*

son," pp. 73–85; and Myra Jehlen, "The Ties That Bind: Race and Sex in *Pudd'nhead Wilson,"* pp. 105–20.

34 On the predicament of abjection, which produces unstable and permeable borders of the self in its separation from the mother and a consequent, repetitive search for stability and borderedness, see Julia Kristeva, *Powers of Horror: An Essay on Abjection,* trans. Leon Roudiez (1980; New York: Columbia University Press, 1982), pp. 1–13.

35 For a discussion of this excised passage, see Fishkin, *Was Huck Black?* pp. 122–3.

36 Hershel Parker, *Flawed Texts and Verbal Icons: Literary Authority in American Fiction* (Evanston, Ill.: Northwestern University Press, 1984), pp. 123–5.

8

EVAN CARTON

Speech Acts and Social Action:
Mark Twain and the Politics
of Literary Performance

During the past decade or more, the field of literary studies has been a notoriously embattled one. The battles within and around it, sometimes referred to as "the culture wars" or "the canon wars," have expressed in various ways the deepening identity conflict not only of this academic discipline but of the contemporary American society and culture of which it is a part. In literary studies, the conflict has centered around an issue that may be broadly characterized as the politics of literary performance. This issue has arisen out of powerful challenges – often posed by women and ethnic minorities, who have only lately entered the professoriate in significant numbers – to the dominant view among academic critics since the Second World War that literary works, their authors, and the activity of evaluating and interpreting them transcend, or at least are separable from, matters of partisan politics and considerations of the marketplace. With increasing influence, the challengers of this view have insisted on the political and economic determinants, values, and consequences of "literary performance," a term I mean to encompass both what literary works express and, more generally, what their authors and their interpreters do. The practices of literary authorship and literary instruction and criticism, that is, are themselves kinds of literary performance. And according to the discipline's recent insurgents (now, arguably, its elite), literary studies must interrogate the political conditions and capacities not only of literary objects but of these practices as well.

Defenders of the challenged cultural vision and disciplinary model that assigns aesthetics and politics to separate spheres and holds great writers and responsible critics to be super- or extrapolitical have charged that the new "politicization" of literature and literary study means the sacrifice of aesthetic standards and the abandonment of cultural commonality. Lynne V. Cheney, for instance, the former chair of the National Endowment for the Humanities, argues in a 1988 report to the president and Congress that English professors now occupy themselves with considerations of gender, race, and class, while "truth and beauty and excellence are regarded as irrelevant."[1] Columnist George F. Will sounds the warning of social dissolution in a 1991 *Newsweek* column that represents contemporary literary critics as "forces . . . fighting against the conservation of the common culture that is the nation's social cement."[2]

Cultural conservatives inside and outside the academy often take the established (but now endangered) literary canon – the select group of "classic" works and writers, celebrated in national mythology and routinely assigned in the nation's classrooms – to embody America's "common culture" and to exemplify its standards of "truth and beauty and excellence." Many among the "forces" that the conservatives oppose, however, have observed that this group of celebrated writers representing the national essence and artistic excellence overwhelmingly consists of upper- or middle-class white men. Consequently, these critics have questioned whether aesthetic judgments have not always involved – and concealed – race, class, and gender politics. Moreover, they have questioned two related assumptions of those who would *conserve* a common culture exemplified by the work of transcendent artists who somehow represent the whole: the assumption that a writer (or any other individual) can rise above the particular dimensions and circumstances of his or her identity to imaginatively possess or represent the country at large, and the assumption that there exists a coherent, shared, and representable national culture or "American" identity at all.

My essay proposes to examine the person and the performances of Mark Twain in the context of these questions and challenges, these battles in the field of literary studies. I wish to consider the different statuses assigned him by the two cultural visions that now compete for primacy within that field and the ways in which his writings themselves inscribe and engage these visions. I am interested, too, both in what the contemporary critical concern with the politics of literary performance might have to say about Twain and in what Twain might have to say to it.

Twain is a peculiarly appropriate candidate for this sort of consideration. To begin with, he is the canonical author around whom the modern critical notion of a common American culture took shape. He is the figure whom journalists and critics heralded, during his life and after his death, as America's quintessential representative, a figure who transcended the facts of his personal experience and yet incarnated the experience of the American everyman. Twain's double status as transcendent writer and representative American man was officially established in 1905 at his gala seventieth birthday dinner, a 160-guest literary love feast and coronation, hosted at Delmonico's by publisher George Harvey. Ratified by the popular press at Twain's death five years later ("no other author" was so "curiously and intimately American," the *New York American* pronounced, in a eulogy entitled "Chief of American Men of Letters," whose counterparts appeared as lead news stories and editorials in almost every major newspaper in the country),[3] this double status would be famously reaffirmed in the years to follow.

Later, in 1910, Twain's friend and fellow novelist William Dean Howells wrote that Twain was "without a rival since Cervantes and Shakespeare" and dubbed him "the Lincoln of our literature."[4] In 1915, literary historian Fred Lewis Pattee identified Twain as the original creator of a truly national American literature, a view that Ernest Hemingway endorsed and extended when he wrote, twenty years later, that "all modern American literature comes from one book by Mark Twain called *Huckleberry Finn.* . . . it's the best book we've had."[5] Perhaps the titles of two Twain biographies, published half a century apart, most richly convey the critical tradition in which Twain stands at once as the nation's supreme literary proprietor and its common literary property: one is *Mark Twain's America,* the other *Our Mark Twain.*[6]

Challengers of the doctrines of the representative artist and the common culture might detect a privileged complacency in the referentially vague first-person plural pronouns that support the claims made for Twain and for America in the passages just cited. Who exactly, they might ask, is included in the community of ownership and representation that is designated by the phrases "our literature" and "our Mark Twain"? To put the question another way, whose experience and opinions are *excluded,* for instance, by the "we" of Hemingway's ubiquitously quoted remark that *Adventures of Huckleberry Finn* is "the best book we've had"? Clearly, the black parents and activists who in the late 1950s and again in the 1980s lobbied to have the novel removed from public school curricula because they felt it stereotyped and denigrated blacks would not count themselves among Hemingway's ostensibly national community of judgment. But once this is said, it must be acknowledged that Hemingway's "we" no more represents the white Americans who, decades earlier, also campaigned against Twain's novel, citing the "endemic lying, the petty thefts, the denigration of respectability and religion, the bad language, and the bad grammar" as the grounds of their objections, but revealing deeper motives through references to Twain's "hideously subversive" depiction of brutal, corrupt, and exploitative white characters and of a heroic, morally superior black one.[7]

In fact, although the American icon "our Mark Twain" has been venerated for almost a century, there has rarely been a moment when any of the claims of his admirers has gone uncontested. Claims for his literary artistry have been met by a host of countercharges: he was a mere humorist, a popular entertainer, a writer of boys' books; he combined and recombined a slim repertoire of formulaic plots and comic devices; he wrote mainly for money, which he sometimes needed or wanted so badly that he sent to press hastily composed manuscripts whose narrative flaws and compositional errors he left editors and printers to correct or not. The view that his greatness lies in his social criticism and moral vision has elicited equally vigorous opposition. Van Wyck Brooks's provocative *The Ordeal of Mark Twain,* published in 1920, argued that Twain had squandered his potential as an artist and as a powerful social critic, that, in contrast to his greatest European contemporaries, he had failed to rise "to the conception of literature as a great impersonal social instrument," becoming instead the "manacled servant" of a bourgeois society that at once restricted the creative spirit to the crass pursuit of material wealth and smothered it in genteel sentimentality.[8] Justin Kaplan's Pulitzer Prize–winning 1966 biography, *Mr. Clemens and Mark Twain,* also presented a psychologically divided writer, who both scorned and envied the gentility of the cultural elite and the wealth and power of the captains of industry, and who lived in increasing self-contempt.[9] And, especially in the 1930s, leftist literary historians such as Granville Hicks discounted Twain as a social critic by pointing out that except for the early co-authored novel, *The Gilded Age,* Twain's work is set in the past or in Europe and does not directly deal with "movements and events of American life in the latter half of the nineteenth century."[10] Even the claim that Twain is distinguished by his ordinary humanity and common sympathy has been challenged by characterizations of his behavior as vain, manipulative, and imperious and of his literature, particularly the late work, as subtly elitist and authoritarian. Twain's public and literary performances elicit all of these critical claims and counterclaims. But what is even more interesting and instructive is that they themselves make them.

A year after the birthday dinner that had confirmed him not only as America's preeminent cultural symbol but as a veritable "oracle on the human race," Twain appeared at a White House reception in a white flannel suit. To astonished reporters, Twain confided that his suit was the "uniform of the American Association of Purity and Perfection," an organization to which he was the "only man in the country eligible" to belong.[11] Twain's comment wittily ascribes opposing significances to his fashion statement. Unveiled at the symbolic center of American representative democracy, the pure and perfect white suit, on the one hand, announces Twain's identification with the nation, its aspirations, and its idealized self-image (even as it ironizes America's and Twain's own moral pretensions) and, on the other hand, distinguishes Twain from, even elevates him over, everyone else, both symbolically and – since convention categorically dictated black dress suits for men – materially. This play of democratic commonality against personal distinction in the significances of Twain's white suit is at once enhanced and complicated by the immediate purpose of Twain's visit to Washington that day and by the subsequent public response to his defiance of convention. Twain had come to the capital to lobby for copyright reform, legislation to strengthen authors' private property rights in their work. In that context, the suit signified his literary originality and claim to self-possession. But Twain's gesture, which in the following year became his regular sartorial signature, also invited an entranced press and public to see it (as they frequently did) as a blow against artificial and undemocratic constraint by a champion of American-style individual freedom, populist informality, and common comfort – this, despite the fact that Twain's trademark suits, often cut from the finest French fabric and lined in silk, were priced well beyond the means of the average American.

Thus far, my reading of the whiteness of the suit and of Twain's initial commentary on it has suggested that this performance enacted both national identification and national critique as it both displayed Twain and, in some respects, concealed him. The suit indeed performs these double operations, but I want to propose now that their meanings are much deeper than has yet been indicated. During his last trip to England in 1907, Twain spoke again about his now-habitual mode of public dress at a banquet at London's Savage Club, to which he had been elected a member more than thirty years before. Twain told his dinner companions:

> When I find myself in assemblies like this, with everybody in black clothes, I know I possess something that is superior to everybody else's. Clothes are never clean. You don't know whether they are clean or not because you can't see. . . . I am proud to say that I can wear a white suit of clothes without a blemish for three days. . . . I do not want to boast. I only want to make you understand that you are not clean.[12]

As he had done at the White House, Twain here associates his clothing with purity and cleanliness and hints that moral as well as material cleanliness is at issue. But now he calls attention less to the symbolism than to the actual color of what he wears. His motive in wearing the white suit, he claims, is to show that, unlike the other members of the Savage Club, he has nothing to hide. Yet even as Twain's explanation asserts that the suit manifests his stainlessness, it also invites – almost challenges – his audience to examine him for a "blemish." Indeed, an observation he had made ten years earlier – in a circumstance that, though quite different, also involved the conjunction of clothing, whiteness, and "savages" – supports the suspicion of an ironic countermotive in Twain's self-display, a countermotive of which he may not have been conscious when he began to clothe himself in white but of which, at some point and at some level, he could not have failed to be aware. In *Following the Equator,* the narrative of his travels on a lecture tour through Asia, Australia, and South Africa, Twain tells of passing a missionary school in Ceylon and feeling suddenly outraged by the English clothing prescribed for the black pupils and by the clothing of his own party of American tourists, which he characterizes as "barbarous" and "repulsive as a shroud." However, he continues:

> [our clothes] have their reason for existing. They are on us to expose us – to advertise what we wear them to conceal. . . . Yes, our clothes are a lie, and have been nothing short of that these hundred years. They are insincere, they are the ugly and appropriate outward exposure of an inward sham and a moral decay.[13]

Following the Equator, along with a good deal of the journalism and commentary that Twain published (and some that he did not) at the turn of the century, was in fact much concerned with the ways in which white men clothed themselves. Occasionally, as in his 1905 essay, "The Czar's Soliloquy," Twain's subject is the power of clothes themselves to confer illegitimate authority, but more often it is figurative clothing – the concealments, self-deceptions, and pretenses to purity of the "civilized white" in his dealings with the "savage." These terms could be drawn from almost anywhere in the writings of this period, but I have taken them from a passage in *Following the Equator* that hails "the spirit which the civilized white has always exhibited toward the savage" in the case of an Australian settler who on Jesus' birthday invited the blacks living around the land he claimed to a banquet that featured a great arsenic-laced Christmas pudding (FE 1: 213). Twain sardonically salutes this creative and honest squatter, whose deed was "better, kinder, swifter, and much more humane than a number of the methods which have been sanctified by custom," yet who earns the disapproval of his fellow settlers for so displaying the true colors that they tried to mute, for advertising what is meant to be decorously concealed. Concluding the chapter, in language that might almost be imagined to provide a prefigurative commentary on his own performance at the Savage Club a decade hence, Twain charges the squatter only with "the indiscretion of introducing a novelty which was calculated to attract attention to our civilization" and pronounces: "There are many humorous things in this world; among them the white man's notion that he is less savage than the other savages" (FE 1: 215–16). Like his verbal representations of the horrors of white imperialism and colonialism, in which his habitual use of the first-person plural insistently marks him with the stain he exposes, Twain's white suit bears the blemish that it imputes to others, the blemish that is not an adulteration of whiteness but the fact and history of whiteness itself.

After Twain's death, Howells wrote that his friend had "held himself responsible for the wrong which the white race had done the black race in slavery," and that when he had paid the tuition for a black student to attend Yale, Twain had said "he was doing it as his part of the reparation due from every white to every black man."[14] But it is not merely the residual guilt of a reconstructed white Southerner about slavery, nor even penitence for his two-week service in 1861 as a Confederate Marion Ranger, that accounts for Twain's lifelong performative device of self-implication and self-exposure. This device is also a reflexive commentary on the history, and on the continuing social and economic dimensions, of his own career as a literary performer, as well as a way to interrogate, more generally, the nature of literary performance itself.

Twain's illustrious career as a novelist, essayist, moralist, and lecturer was shot through with specific situational ironies and with broadly historical ones. The equatorial lecture tour of 1895–6, for instance, which touched off some of his most scathing indictments of the greed and power-lust that drove what he called "the civilization trust," was a trip Twain undertook to rescue himself from the personal bankruptcy he had brought on through ruinous investment in an innovative, but ultimately unworkable typesetting machine that he had dreamed would make him "one of the wealthiest grandees in America."[15] But from its outset, Twain's literary enterprise did not just partake of the historical moment that it criticized, a moment of wild national and international scrambling for capital accumulation that Twain himself would label "The Gilded Age"; it also enacted, Twain sensed, some of that moment's characteristic forms of exploitation and evasion.

Twain's first significant financial success as a literary performer came on the lecture platform. There Twain discovered the full extent of his ability, as he punningly put it, "to make comic capital of everything I saw and heard,"[16] and although he claimed to dislike it, he returned often to this lucrative forum. In 1869, the year of the publication of his first extended work, *The Innocents Abroad,* Twain proposed to capitalize on his recent celebrity with a lecture tour of the West. Wanting a popular co-performer to fill out an attractive evening's program, he asked his friend "Petroleum V. Nasby" (David Ross Locke) to join him on the tour and to present "Cussed be Canaan" – a stirring antislavery monologue that had made Nasby one of the most famous circuit lecturers. Nasby declined the invitation, writing to Twain: "You know that lemon, our African brother, juicy as he was in his day, has been squeezed dry. Why howl about his wrongs after said wrongs have been redressed? . . . You see, friend Twain, the Fifteenth Amendment busted 'Cussed be Canaan.'"[17] Nasby's response unwittingly frames what would be the central paradox of Twain's professional life and anticipates the central form of his self-critique.

Twain probably recognized in 1869 what he would observe and howl about again and again in the next forty years: that his African brothers and sisters had not in the least been squeezed dry by those who would wring illicit wealth and privilege from their sufferings. In the terrorization and effective reenslavement of Southern blacks after Reconstruction's abandonment, in the exploits of Cecil Rhodes's South African Company, in Belgian King Leopold's genocidal rule over the black inhabitants of the Congo, a rule officially recognized by the United States and partly bankrolled by American capitalists such as J. P. Morgan, John D. Rockefeller, and Daniel Guggenheim, the wrongs done to Africans continued unabated. Still, Twain's social and literary imagination was principally informed by his experiences of and reflections on the institution of legal African slavery in the American South – an institution that no longer existed but that he nonetheless continued performatively and profitably to exploit. In the late novel *Pudd'nhead Wilson,* Twain's "imitation white" villain, Tom Driscoll, needing cash to pay his gambling debts, sells his mother Roxy down the river into the harshest plantation slavery, despite the fact that Roxy is no longer legally a slave. Roxy manages to run away, but not before she has observed of New Englanders like her overseer and, inescapably, her Connecticut Yankee creator, "Dey knows how to work a nigger to death."[18] However vivid his displays of America's historic stain, it was also true that, from his invitation to Petroleum V. Nasby, to his own popular lecture piece – a Negro ghost story called "The Golden Arm," through his major novels and beyond, Twain, like the nation, was enriched by the practice – in one case literal, in the other literary – of "work[ing] a nigger to death."

Public speech, the profit motive, and exploitation are closely linked throughout Twain's writings. At a 1907 dinner (which, Twain explained, he accidentally happened to attend) for the notoriously corrupt Montana senator William Andrews Clark, these elements were most nakedly conjoined: "I had believed that in my time I had seen at banquets all the different kinds of speechmaking animals there are and also all the different kinds of people that go to make our population, but it was a mistake. This was the first time I had ever seen men get down in the gutter and frankly worship dollars and their possessors."[19] Thirty-four years earlier, the same elements had been brought together in a satirical letter that Twain published in the *New York Tribune* in support of U.S. efforts to annex Hawaii: "We must annex these people," he wrote. "We can afflict them with our wise and beneficent government. . . . We can give them railway corporations who will buy their Legislatures like old clothes, and run over their best citizens. . . . We can furnish them some Jay Goulds who will do away with their old-time notion that stealing is not respectable. . . . We can give them lecturers! I will go myself."[20] Even earlier than this, in perhaps his first effort at extended fictional narrative, Twain had playfully yet strikingly aligned the professional lecture with the history of the European colonization of the Americas and displacement of peoples of color. In "An Extract from Captain Stormfield's Visit to Heaven," originally drafted in 1868 but published, as fragments, only in 1907 and 1908, Twain's protagonist, touring "the American corner of heaven," exclaims, "I hardly ever see a white angel; where I run across one white angel, I strike as many as a hundred million coppercolored ones – people that can't speak English." Stormfield's companion explains that "America was occupied a billion years and more by Injuns and Aztecs, and that sort of folks, before a white man ever set foot in it," and that even during "the first three hundred years after Columbus's discovery, *there wasn't ever more than one good lecture audience of white people, all put together, in America*. . . . You can't expect us to amount to anything in heaven, and we don't."[21]

Twain's reflexive interrogation of American public speech and of his own literary performances as writer and lecturer, then, stemmed in part from his recognition that economic interest and racial exploitation – whether as explicit motives or collateral effects – were common to both. But it was not only the external circumstances and the visible content of such performances that implicated them in exploitative social relations. More profoundly, it was their form. For Twain, all acts of communication, even invitations to democratic communion, simultaneously enact the will to mastery and domination. Speech acts are forms of rhetorical imperialism, campaigns to colonize the consciousnesses and destroy the volition of their targets. The use of military metaphors and images of aggression to describe verbal performances and their effects pervades Twain's writings. A notable instance is his characterization of his 1877 speech at a Chicago banquet honoring general and former president Ulysses S. Grant. "I fetched him! I broke him up utterly," Twain wrote to his wife about the effect of his comic speech (in which he had imagined Grant as an infant "trying to find some way of getting his big toe in his mouth") on the greatest warrior of the age. And to Howells he added: "I knew I could lick him. I shook him up like dynamite. . . . my truths had wracked all the bones of his body apart."[22] Readers of the 1889 novel *A Connecticut Yankee in King Arthur's Court* will recognize this imagery as a key feature of the expressive style of Twain's Yankee, Hank Morgan. Morgan, the bearer of American democracy, enlightenment, progress, and industrial capitalism, begins his career in Arthurian England as a platform speaker who literally survives by his ability to create "gaud[y] effects."[23] Over the course of the novel, Morgan assumes a number of social roles, but he is centrally and repeatedly a literary performer who leaves his audiences, whether in laughter or in terror, "collapsed by platoons" (CY 158). The unacknowledged imperialism that informs Morgan's performances is the silent lie that ultimately vitiates his democratic "truths."

Twain acknowledges the implicit will to power that both motivates and structures his literary performances, but he also resists it. From early on in his lecture career, he developed techniques of exposing and undercutting his own gaudy effects. This practice, as the *Boston Daily Advertiser* reported in 1869, often perplexed his listeners: "The audience gets into a queer state after a while. It knows not what to trust. . . . Even when Mr. Clemens has made a really fine period, or introduced a brilliant descriptive passage, he takes pains to turn the affair into a joke at the end."[24] As Henry Nash Smith reports, Twain experimented with other disruptive devices as well. To betray the representational illusion of his words, Twain might conclude a passage with the line, "Let someone beat that for harnessing adjectives together." To reveal the narcissism of the performer, he would interrupt himself with his own wild applause. "More subtly, toward the end of the description he would pretend to forget a word so as to break the spell in which he held the audience and prevent the tempest of applause that would otherwise have followed."[25]

Smith argues that Twain's inability "to achieve a stable attitude toward his own exalted rhetoric" and an "integrated vision" of his society was a failing that he overcame only in moments of his vernacular frontier narratives and, most completely, in *Adventures of Huckleberry Finn*.[26] Yet along with a number of more recent critics, such as James M. Cox, Laurence B. Holland, Stanley Brodwin, and Forrest G. Robinson, I believe that rhetorical and attitudinal instability was a consistent strategy for Twain and one that, in a way, constituted a coherent vision of his society – as viewed from his particular place in it – and of his own vocation.[27] For the deepest truths told by that society and that vocation were also lies, and their most exalted rhetoric of freedom was also enslaving. I have already indicated some of the ways that Twain understood these paradoxes to inhere, and I will elaborate on them in discussing Twain's major fiction. That discussion may be usefully prefaced, however, by a consideration of an essay in which figures of truth and falsehood, and of freedom and slavery, playfully yet suggestively converge, an essay in which Twain also links himself directly to the nation.

Twain called his 1899 Christmas feature for the *New York World* "My First Lie and How I Got Out of It," but he stated at the outset that his first lie was, in fact, "too far back" for him to remember. His second, however, occurred when, at nine days old, he feigned injury by a diaper pin in order to get extra love and attention. As he looks back on this lie, he finds it representative of the "seldom noticed fact . . . that almost all lies are acts, and speech has no part in them"; the most common, most dangerous, and most widely accepted lie, he explains, is *"the lie of silent assertion."*[28] Twain's trivial, seemingly instinctive infant lie thus serves as a curious springboard to what is redescribed, later in the essay, as "the silent colossal national lie that is the support and confederate of all . . . tyrannies and shams and inequalities and unfairnesses," a lie whose first and central instance for Twain is the long complicity of "humane and intelligent" white Americans in the institution of slavery through their "silent assertion that there wasn't anything going on in which humane and intelligent people were interested."[29]

As a young man, of course, Twain had participated in this national lie, although it was one whose origins lay "too far back" for him personally to recall. I am suggesting that the logic of the essay demands that we read Twain's and the nation's tolerance of slavery – in fact, not only their tolerance of it, but their unacknowledged yet constitutive dependence on it – as the "first lie" of Twain's title, a lie only indirectly recalled and confessed. Indeed, the identification of Twain's original, inherited lie with the "colossal national lie" is supported by the unexpected turn, at the conclusion of this essay on lying, to the famous tale of the colossal national truth teller and stainless father, George Washington.

> As regards that time that George Washington told the truth, a word must be said, of course. It is the principal jewel in the crown of America, and it is natural that we should work it for all it is worth, as Milton said in his "Lay of the Last Minstrel." It was a timely and judicious truth, and I should have told

it myself in the circumstances. . . . I think it was not premeditated but an inspiration. With his fine military mind, he had probably arranged to let his brother Edward in for the cherry tree results, but by an inspiration he saw his opportunity in time and took advantage of it. By telling the truth he could astonish his father; his father would tell the neighbors; the neighbors would spread it; it would travel to all firesides; in the end it would make him President, and not only that, but First President. He was a far-seeing boy and would be likely to think of these things. Therefore, to my mind, he stands justified for what he did. But not for that other tower; it was a mistake. Still, I don't know about that; upon reflection I think perhaps it wasn't. For indeed it is that tower that makes the other one live. If he hadn't said "I cannot tell a lie" there would have been no convulsion.[30]

Twain's childhood deception and Washington's childhood confession structurally as well as historically frame the national lie at the essay's center. In Twain's retelling, moreover, these paired opposites converge. Both Twain's lie and Washington's truth are strategic bids for recognition. But more significantly, both conceal a prior lie – Twain's unconfessed original lie and Washington's dramatic "tower," the claim that he is incapable of lying. Twain writes that "that [preliminary] tower makes the other one live," but the deeper suggestion of his essay is that it is the explicit, strategic truth telling that conceals both its true motive (approval, fame, a reputation for virtue) and the lie that is its stated motive ("I cannot tell a lie"). And, by extension, the celebrated, yet only partial, truth of the nation that Washington fathers – the freedom and democracy that Washington wins for it and emblematizes – conceals the "colossal national lie" with which it is twinned.

Here, one founding American myth, Washington's categorical truth telling, stands in for another, "liberty and justice for all," a myth motivated and exploded by slavery and racism. That this national myth, and not the cherry tree story, is the "principal jewel in the crown of America" is implied by Twain's otherwise incomprehensible remark that "work[ing] it for all it is worth" is enjoined by a mock-Miltonic text called the "Lay [lie?] of the Last Minstrel." In juxtaposing Washington's truth with the lie of the minstrel show, in which white men worked black stereotypes for all the laughs and profits they were worth, this strange sentence exposes the entanglement of the nation's ideal of freedom in its practice of "work[ing] a nigger to death." As I suggested earlier, Twain felt himself to be vocationally implicated in this practice and, of course, Washington, a slaveholder, was also implicated. More particularly, Twain and Washington both silently profited at the expense of blacks and "got out of it" on the basis of a reputation for freedom loving and truth telling.

Twain's essay at once confesses this shared lie and, in the opacity and indirection of its confession, gets out of it again. For while his social criticism is clear in the essay's middle section, it is possible to read the passages on Washington and himself, such as the following extension of the diaper-pin narrative, and make nothing more of them than "comic capital."

> It was human nature to want to get these riches, and I fell. I lied about the pin
> – advertising one when there wasn't any. You would have done it; George
> Washington did it, anybody would have done it. During the first half of my life
> I never knew a child that was able to raise above that temptation and keep
> from telling that lie. Up to 1867 all the civilized children that were ever born
> into the world were liars – including George. Then the safety pin came in and
> blocked the game. But is that reform worth anything? No; for it is reform by
> force and has no virtue in it; it merely stops that form of lying, it doesn't
> impair the disposition to lie, by a shade.[31]

Is this seemingly innocuous passage an oblique variation on Twain's central theme? Does Twain's historicization of his lie about the diaper pin and generalization of his indictment to include George Washington and all "the civilized children" up until 1867, none of whom could resist these illicit "riches," suggest that the passage may be a clothed representation of the complicity with slavery that shaped "the first half of [Twain's] life" and of the "reform" – the Civil War – that forcibly ended the national lie of silent assertion when it ended slavery but did not "impair the disposition to lie, by a shade"? Or is the passage in fact nothing more than a joke about infant con artists and the invention of the safety pin?

In a burst of creative energy in the summer of 1883, Twain drafted the concluding sections of his long-suspended novel, *Adventures of Huckleberry Finn*. Exuberantly, he wrote to his mother, "This summer it is no more trouble for me to write than it is to lie."[32] The story that he was completing would stake powerful claims to moral truth telling that generations of readers would recognize and honor. But from its first paragraph, when Huck identifies "Mr. Mark Twain" as a writer who "told the truth, mainly" yet adds that he's "never seen anybody but lied, one time or another," Twain signals that the truths and the lies of his novel are inseparable and interdependent.[33] Early in the novel, Huck sustains his voyage with Jim through a series of lies. But these small situational evasions are called forth by the colossal societal lie that holds human beings to be chattel. Thus, on the principle that a culture whose constitutional reality is a fiction forces truth telling into the outward form of lies, they seem to be enactments of a larger moral truth. After the raft is smashed, Huck and Jim's story is supplanted by a string of fraudulent performances, beginning with the sartorial perfor- mance of Colonel Grangerford – the patriarch of a savage clan who, none- theless, "every day of his life . . . put on a clean shirt and a full suit from head to foot made of linen so white it hurt your eyes to look at it" (HF 89) – and continuing through the dramatic scams of the king and the duke. Yet these lies also do not at first seem to implicate the principals, author, or reader of the novel so much as they unite them in implicit moral opposition to the fakes and usurpers.

The silent lies of the conclusion that Twain was working on when he wrote to his mother, however, were more fundamental – and more shatter- ing – to his book's truth-telling claims. Many readers and critics have been disturbed by the extended charade of the novel's last ten chapters, in which Tom Sawyer stage-manages a stylishly dire imprisonment for Jim on the Phelps farm and masterminds a ludicrously complicated escape plot. Tom's burlesque robs Jim of the dignity he had earlier been accorded in his poig- nant quest to free himself and his family and in his physical, intellectual, and moral superintendence of Huck on the raft. Now Jim is set to work writing in blood on shirts, breaking his teeth on purposeless but romantic contra- band hidden in his corn pone, sharpening candlesticks into pens to scratch his coat-of-arms on the shed wall, and fending off the snakes, rats, and insects with which Huck and Tom have stocked his room to make it more authentically dungeon-like. The black man humbly endures these indignities at the hands of children; as Huck reports: "Jim couldn't see no sense in the most of it, but he allowed we was white folks and knowed better than him" (HF 208). Twain's revelation at the end that Tom's entire scheme to liberate Jim had been predicated upon a lie of silent assertion – Tom's concealment of the fact that Jim was already legally free – only magnifies the cruelty and exploitativeness of the charade. But by this revelation Twain also squarely indicts his own novelistic enterprise, in some degree the twin of Tom's plot. Neither is an actual liberation quest but a pursuit – as Twain's title and Tom's explanations specify – of "adventures." Tom's performance, too, like Twain's, is a thoroughly literary one, and Tom's motive describes Twain's vocation: to "make . . . talk" (HF 195). Moreover, the ending of *Adventures of Huckleberry Finn* confesses that Twain's performance has shared all along the comfortable propriety and assured inefficacy of Tom's. Writing after the Civil War, Twain, as Huck says of Tom, has "sure enough . . . gone and took all that trouble and bother to set a free nigger free!" (HF 242).

Tom's mock liberation of Jim stands in sharp apparent contrast to an earlier moment of high moral drama, the passage – probably the most famous in Twain's work – in which Huck tears up the letter informing Miss Watson of her runaway slave's whereabouts and pronounces, "All right, then, I'll go to hell" (HF 180). If Tom's silence about Jim's status conceals the lie beneath his stated purpose to free him, Huck's silence about Jim's status – his refusal to inform Miss Watson – in the earlier scene reveals the truth of his goodness beneath his stated purpose to go to hell. In this scene, readers have felt, Huck recognizes and honors Jim's humanity against the combined force of law, social convention, and what he has been taught to understand as Christianity itself. Thus, Huck's blithe participation shortly afterward in a game that dehumanizes Jim, prolongs his enslavement, and jeopardizes him needlessly has seemed the most troubling aspect of the Phelps farm episodes. But Huck's moment of moral truth itself is not free of the taint of narcissistic performance, not for Huck and certainly not for Twain and his readers. It is, to begin with, a highly self-conscious and distinctly *literary* moment that revolves around two competing texts – the written words that Huck tremblingly holds in his hand and the spoken words that he dramatically holds on his tongue and in his thoughts.

> It was a close place. I took [the letter] up, and held it in my hand. I was a trembling, because I'd got to decide, forever, betwixt two things, and I knowed it. I studied a minute, sort of holding my breath, and then says to myself:
> "All right, then, I'll go to hell" – and tore it up.
> It was awful thoughts, and awful words, but they was said. And I let them stay said; and never thought no more about reforming.   (HF 179–80)

However genuine the feelings for Jim that prompt Huck to destroy his letter to Miss Watson, the language of this passage suggests that, for Huck, the sheer romance of the grand defiant gesture and the grander pronouncement is itself a powerful inducement. Huck's resolution to be a moral pariah, moreover, is the vehicle by which Twain achieves supreme moral communion with a postwar audience that can be assumed to believe that protecting a slave is the opposite of damnable. We know, reads the unspoken subtext of Huck's declaration, that for this deed Huck's place in heaven is ensured. Thus, Huck's moment of greatest moral risk is, for Twain and his readers, a moment of moral comfort, even complacency. This is the complacency that Twain exposes by having Huck assume the identity of Tom Sawyer in the very next chapter and soon, under the direction of the actual Tom Sawyer, resume the business of adventure as usual, at Jim's expense, as if the stirring commitment to Jim that Huck had just proclaimed were but a passing bit of rhetorical self-indulgence. For, as James M. Cox has written, the critical judgment that readers are invited to render upon the novel's young adventurers "is surely the judgment rendered upon the moral sentiment on which the book has ridden." Cox continues:

> If the reader sees in Tom's performance a rather shabby and safe bit of play, he is seeing no more than the exposure of the approval with which he watched Huck operate. For, if Tom is rather contemptibly setting a free slave free, what after all is the reader doing, who begins the book after the *fact* of the Civil War? This is the "joke" of the book – the moment when, in outrageous burlesque, it attacks the sentiment which its style has at once evoked and exploited.[34]

I would argue that this is the joke not only of *Adventures of Huckleberry Finn* but of Twain's literary career, and that the author himself is its prime target. It is the same joke that Twain played on his lecture audiences, the same attack that he mounted against his own exalted platform rhetoric, when he applauded or congratulated himself for an especially illusionistic stringing together of adjectives. It is the joke that exposes the lie that is the business of the literary performer: the passing off of representation as reality. More specifically, for Twain, it is the joke that exposes the paradox of his identity as social critic and truth teller: that "Mark Twain" is a creation of the very institutions, ambitions, and privileges that have produced and driven the stratified, capitalist culture he rails against: most notably, slavery, the lust for wealth emblematized by the gold rush, and whiteness.

Both *A Connecticut Yankee in King Arthur's Court* and *Pudd'nhead Wilson* enact versions of the same joke – on their main characters, on their readers, and on their author – that concludes *Adventures of Huckleberry Finn*. Hank Morgan is ostensibly a late-nineteenth-century machinist knocked back into Arthurian England, but in the overarching geography of Twain's imagination, he is another prospective liberator of the inhabitants of a slave state. Again and again, Morgan equates his sixth-century environment with the slaveholding American South of Twain's youth, about whose social and psychological dynamics this Connecticut Yankee seems peculiarly knowledgeable. "The most of King Arthur's British nation were slaves, pure and simple" (CY 54), he observes, later articulating the novel's informing principle that "a privileged class, an aristocracy, is but a band of slaveholders under another name" (CY 171). One might say that Hank Morgan figures as the solitary white man in the Dark Ages and that, like Tom Sawyer, he assumes the role of emancipator in response to an unexpected opportunity to play a dramatic role into which he can throw a great deal of anachronistic style.

Morgan's disquisition on "Sixth Century Political Economy" led many

contemporary readers to hail *A Connecticut Yankee* as a ringing endorsement of the young movement for organized labor in the United States.
Indeed, during his composition of the novel, Twain had interested himself in
the embattled Knights of Labor and had studied its 1878 Manifesto of
Wrongs and Demands. In a speech to the Hartford Monday Evening Club in
1886, Twain asked his audience of businessmen and professionals: "Who
are the oppressors? The few: the king, the capitalist, and a handful of
overseers and superintendents. Who are the oppressed? The many." Typically, he implicated himself and his audience among the oppressors: "[Their
manifesto] impeaches certain of *us* of high treason against the rightful sovereignty of this world, . . . and you will assuredly find counts in it which not
any logic of *ours* can controvert."[35] Like his author, Hank Morgan turns in
a dramatic and progressive performance on the subject of wages, prices, and
labor relations, one so powerful that it stuns his resistant interlocutor, a
blacksmith, and allows Morgan "to drive him into the earth – drive him *all*
in – drive him in till not even the curve of his skull [showed] above ground"
(CY 233).

Here, and throughout the novel, Morgan's metaphors belie the ostensible
democratic sentiments and purpose of his literary performance. In this instance, too, Morgan's language recalls the actual relations that he had enjoyed with his laboring subordinates in Hartford, relations that literally
catapulted him to Camelot in the first place. At the Colt factory, Morgan
had not been one of the many but the "head superintendent" with "a couple
of thousand men under [him]" who had maintained personal dominance
and shop order by physical intimidation until he "got [his] dose . . . during a
misunderstanding conducted with crowbars" (CY 15). And in Camelot,
these relations are replicated with the entire populace when Morgan becomes "the Boss." For although he declines an aristocratic title and takes
democratic pride in pointing out that his position is one to which he has
been "elected by the nation" (CY 57), Morgan does not reflect that the vote
may be compromised by the electorate's belief that he possesses the power
to blot out the sun. The novel's broad humor – and its invitation to its
American audience to bask in the manifestly destined triumph of a modern
American-style civilization over a backward European one – discourages
any such troubling reflections on the part of the reader as well.

Henry Nash Smith wrote of Twain that his very "capacity for entering
imaginatively into modes of experience at second hand . . . exposed him to a
long series of contagions" to which his progressive principles and critical
acumen did not render him immune. "When he read the orators of Manifest
Destiny," for instance, "he surrendered himself to the plaster-and-gilt opu-

lence of their lofty utterances and came under the spell of their self-hypnosis."[36] This is the spell that the combination of Twain's narrative performance and the imaginative experience of U.S. nationalism casts over the reader of *A Connecticut Yankee,* a spell whose nightmarish consequences are revealed only in the climactic battle of the Sand Belt. An updated and grander version of Tom Sawyer's plan to free Jim, Morgan's carefully orchestrated final confrontation with the aristocracy promises to liberate a nation of slaves. But what the plan's execution exposes and literalizes is an arrogance and brutality that more than match the arrogance and brutality of the enslavers and that have contaminated the Boss's promise from the start. Morgan's orgy of grand effects – land mines, high-voltage electric fences, floodgates, Gatling guns – touches off a holocaust that momentarily renders his band of technocrats complete "masters of England" (CY 317) but that soon consumes them as well, as they are poisoned by the prison of rotting bodies in which they have immured themselves. Thus, the bringer of civilization to the savages dies the greatest savage of them all.

The lie of American exceptionalism that I take the ending of *A Connecticut Yankee* to expose is at the same time a lie of intellectual exceptionalism – the fiction that the intellectual stands above and apart from the society he or she observes and criticizes, unblemished by its failings and insusceptible to its self-delusions. Twain's last major novel, *Pudd'nhead Wilson,* even more vividly exploits and exposes this fiction of intellectual exceptionalism. On his first day in the slaveholding town of Dawson's Landing, David Wilson – Eastern-educated lawyer, man of letters, interpreter of obscure signs, nonslaveholder – is marginalized by a community that cannot read his dry humor. Wilson's identification as a pudd'nhead by his intellectual and, presumably, moral inferiors secures for him the role of detached and ironic cultural observer and, thus, makes him the white, liberal, educated reader's representative in the novel. Twain structurally enforces Wilson's ironic detachment from the community, and invites the reader to partake of this privileged position, by placing an entry from Pudd'nhead Wilson's calendar above each chapter, where it constitutes a kind of inside joke on the action about to be narrated.

In assuming this position, however, both Wilson and the reader ignore or forget the deepest meanings of Wilson's original joke, precisely those meanings that the town of Dawson's Landing could not afford to acknowledge. Wilson's remark about a howling invisible dog – that he wished he owned half of it so that he could kill his half – is experienced as profoundly troubling by a community that depends upon its ability to make clear determinations of human property, to distinguish between black slaves and white masters even when the physical difference may be invisible, and to deny collective responsibility for the violence that pervades it. When one of the townspeople observes, in support of the general verdict of Wilson's idiocy, that "if you kill one half of a general dog there ain't any man that can tell whose half it was" (PW 59–60), his statement foreshadows the novel's central event in which the slave mother Roxy, black only by "a fiction of law and custom" (PW 64), exchanges her even whiter infant son for the son of her master, thus – since no one can tell the two apart – giving her child a life of freedom and consigning the other to a slave's social death. But all evidence of the incoherence of the town's racial classification system, of the interdependency of its owned and its free halves, and of its collective implication in the fate of the body politic or "general dog" is stricken from the official record in Wilson's final joke – a joke that has the force of law and that ratifies Wilson's exchange of the title "Pudd'nhead" for the title "Mayor."

Soon after Roxy reverses the names and the fates of her son, Valet de Chambre, and the scion of the white aristocracy, Thomas a Becket Driscoll, the imitation slave is consigned to the kitchen and forgotten by the narrative. "Tom," corrupted by his social privilege and unearned power, grows up cruel, cowardly, and deceitful, selling his mother down the river after she informs him of the secret of his birth and ultimately murdering his uncle and guardian. When Pudd'nhead Wilson rises to defend the visiting Italian twins, Luigi and Angelo Capello, whom Tom has framed for the murder of Judge Driscoll, he is a man who has been ostracized and underestimated by the town throughout the novel. Pudd'nhead's prime tormentor has time and again demonstrated his own reprehensibility, and while the reader knows his biological identity, he has been called Tom for so long that he can only be imagined as Tom. Wilson unveils his evidence slowly and theatrically, relishing his hour of revenge against the small-minded citizens of Dawson's Landing, whom he has at last indisputably outwitted. Masterfully, he prepares the revelation that his ridiculed hobby of fingerprinting, practiced twenty years ago on two infants, holds the key both to the murder and to the more shocking crime – a revelation that will redeem his intelligence (and the reader's) as it relieves the gathering tension of the well-wrought courtroom scene. For all these reasons, the reader is likely to enjoy and endorse Pudd'nhead's literary performance.

When Pudd'nhead proclaims, "Valet de Chambre, negro and slave – falsely called Thomas a Becket Driscoll – make upon the window the fingerprints that will hang you!" (PW 222), the novel at once attains its formal resolution, Dawson's Landing restores and reaffirms its social order, and the reader clearly and devastatingly perceives the significance of the plot that he has abetted. It is "Tom" (the character regularly referred to as a dog, a cur, a pup) who has murdered; it is "Chambers" who is convicted. This invisible and undifferentiable double identity is split in half – like the severed Siamese twins, the Capello brothers – and the nominally black half is condemned for the savagery of the experientially white. Even in Chambers's apparent absence, the novel has held his place in its narrative economy, just as a place has been held for him in the slave economy by the creditors of the Driscoll estate, who, once he is no longer Tom, sell him down the river. And Pudd'nhead, once he has dispatched his half of the man, expects the other half to live. To everyone's great satisfaction, he promises that the real Tom, an abused and illiterate kitchen slave, will "within a quarter of an hour . . . stand before you white and free!" (PW 222). With this performance, David Wilson becomes "a made man for good" (PW 224), an outcome that emphasizes the curious equivalence between the ending of this novel and that of *A Connecticut Yankee*. "We had conquered; in turn we were conquered," writes Hank Morgan's protégé for his comatose boss (CY 318). In both cases, an elite intellectual minority – represented in *Pudd'nhead Wilson* by the alliance of title character, narrator, and reader – vanquishes a corrupt majority against which it has defined itself, only to discover in that victory the limits of its transcendence, its share in the common character and fate of the "general dog."

A fiction of transcendence – aesthetic on one side, critical or ideological on the other – has often united the opponents in the recent "culture wars." The literary performer as exalted artist represents "our common culture" yet rises above it, producing original literature that is not bound to the stock conventions and sentiments of mass entertainment or blemished by commercial motives. The literary performer as righteous critic exposes the division, deception, and oppression that the American myth veils and perpetrates, yet somehow avoids the positional limitations and the ideological blindnesses and contradictions that are exposed as unavoidable. Both as an artist and as a social critic, Twain writes this fiction of transcendence and unwrites it, denying himself and his reader a "stable attitude toward his . . . exalted rhetoric." For the professional literary performer, his work insists, making art or making political opposition remains for better or worse an act of language – of ordinary communication, of word play, of making talk. And making talk is also the word monger's way of making money.

Such insistence is a means of bringing to crisis the tension between the position that a speaker or writer articulates and the position that he or she occupies. This is Twain's characteristic commitment and device. It appears, as I have attempted to show, in the confrontations he stages between the political content of his literary performances and the politics of their form. And it appears in his dramatization of the race and class privilege, and even the element of exploitation, that informs his most eloquent critiques of racism and gestures of solidarity with the exploited. The prevalence of this commitment and device, too, accounts for the conflicted relations that twentieth-century American literary intellectuals, especially political progressives, have had with Twain. It is as if he has served for many as a second self – in some instances a kind of ego ideal to be embraced and in others a burdensome Siamese twin to be detached; here the figure who represents one's most powerfully imagined truth, there the figure who belies it. But these opposing significances in the end are interdependent. For to give the lie to imagined or performed truths that would obscure the position of the imaginer or the work of performance is, in a way, to honor these truths and to sustain the act of truth telling.

NOTES

1 Lynne V. Cheney, *The Humanities in America: A Report to the President, the Congress, and the American People* (Washington, D.C.: National Endowment for the Humanities, 1988), p. 21.
2 George F. Will, "The Politicization of Higher Education," *Newsweek*, April 22, 1991, p. 72.
3 "Chief of American Men of Letters," *New York American*, April 22, 1910, p. 20.
4 William Dean Howells, *My Mark Twain* (New York: Harpers, 1910), pp. 161, 101.
5 Fred Lewis Pattee, *A History of American Literature Since 1870* (New York: Century, 1915), p. 45; Ernest Hemingway, *Green Hills of Africa* (New York: Scribner's, 1935), p. 22.
6 Bernard DeVoto, *Mark Twain's America* (Boston: Little, Brown, 1932); Louis J. Budd, *Our Mark Twain* (Philadelphia: University of Pennsylvania Press, 1983).
7 Quoted in Philip S. Foner, *Mark Twain: Social Critic* (New York: International, 1958), p. 209.
8 Van Wyck Brooks, *The Ordeal of Mark Twain* (New York: Dutton, 1970), pp. 178, 128.
9 Justin Kaplan, *Mr. Clemens and Mark Twain* (New York: Simon & Schuster, 1966).
10 Granville Hicks, *The Great Tradition* (New York: Macmillan, 1935), p. 45.
11 Budd, *Our Mark Twain*, pp. 193, 207.
12 Quoted in Janet Smith, ed., *Mark Twain on the Damned Human Race* (New York: Hill & Wang, 1962), pp. 232-3.

13 Mark Twain, *Following the Equator* (New York: Harper Bros., 1903), vol. 2, pp. 21–2. Henceforth cited parenthetically in the text as FE.

14 Howells, *My Mark Twain*, p. 35.

15 Foner, *Mark Twain: Social Critic*, p. 31.

16 Ibid., p. 41.

17 Ibid., p. 216.

18 Mark Twain, *Pudd'nhead Wilson* (Harmondsworth: Penguin Books, 1969), p. 182. Henceforth cited parenthetically in the text as PW.

19 Mark Twain, *Mark Twain in Eruption*, ed. Bernard DeVoto (New York: Harper Bros., 1940), p. 76.

20 Foner, *Mark Twain, Social Critic*, pp. 241–2.

21 J. Smith, ed., *Damned Human Race*, p. 222, my emphasis.

22 Kaplan, *Mr. Clemens and Mark Twain*, pp. 226–7.

23 Mark Twain, *A Connecticut Yankee in King Arthur's Court* (New York: New American Library, 1963), p. 272. Henceforth cited parenthetically in the text as CY.

24 Quoted in Henry Nash Smith, *Mark Twain: The Development of a Writer* (Cambridge, Mass.: Harvard University Press, 1962), p. 19.

25 Ibid., pp. 19, 20.

26 Ibid.

27 See James M. Cox, *Mark Twain: The Fate of Humor* (Princeton, N.J.: Princeton University Press, 1966); Laurence B. Holland, "A 'Raft of Trouble': Word and Deed in *Huckleberry Finn*," in *American Realism: New Essays*, ed. Eric J. Sundquist (Baltimore: Johns Hopkins University Press, 1982), pp. 66–81; Stanley Brodwin, "Mark Twain and the Myth of the Daring Jest," in *The Mythologizing of Mark Twain*, ed. Sara deSaussure Davis and Philip D. Beidler (Birmingham: University of Alabama Press, 1984), pp. 136–57; and Forrest G. Robinson, *In Bad Faith: The Dynamics of Deception in Mark Twain's America* (Cambridge, Mass.: Harvard University Press, 1986).

28 J. Smith, ed., *Damned Human Race*, pp. 28, 29.

29 Ibid., pp. 35, 29.

30 Ibid., p. 34.

31 Ibid., p. 28.

32 Kaplan, *Mr. Clemens and Mark Twain*, p. 251.

33 Mark Twain, *Adventures of Huckleberry Finn* (Boston: Houghton Mifflin, 1958), p. 3. Henceforth cited parenthetically in the text as HF.

34 Cox, *The Fate of Humor*, p. 175.

35 Foner, *Mark Twain: Social Critic*, pp. 169, 172, my emphasis.

36 H. N. Smith, *Mark Twain*, p. 16.

9

JOHN CARLOS ROWE

How the Boss Played the Game: Twain's Critique of Imperialism in *A Connecticut Yankee in King Arthur's Court*

Shall we bang right ahead in our old-time, loud, pious way, and commit the new century to the game; or shall we sober up and sit down and think it over first? Would it not be prudent to get our Civilization-tools together, and see how much stock is left on hand in the way of Glass Beads and Theology, and Maxim Guns and Hymn Books, and Trade Gin and Torches of Progress and Enlightenment (patent adjustable ones, good to fire villages with, upon occasion), and balance the books, and arrive at the profit and loss, so that we may intelligently decide whether to continue the business or sell out the property and start a new Civilization Scheme on the proceeds?

> Mark Twain, "To the Person Sitting in Darkness,"
> *North American Review*, February 1901

Twain is famous for his jeremiads against European imperialism and the fledgling efforts of the United States at colonial expansion in the Philippines. As scholars have pointed out, most of Twain's anticolonial zeal dates from the late 1890s and early 1900s, provoked by such international crises as the Spanish–American War (1898), the Boxer Rebellion in China (1900), and the Boer War in South Africa (1899–1902). Twain's rage over U.S. annexation of the Philippines in "To the Person Sitting in Darkness" (1901) and "A Defense of General Funston" (1902), the cruel despotism of Belgium's Leopold II in the Congo Free State in "King Leopold's Soliloquy" (1905), and Czar Nicholas II's exploitation of Russians, Poles, and Finns in "The Czar's Soliloquy" (1905) belongs to the historical period in which "imperialism" had entered the popular vocabulary as a term of opprobrium.[1]

Powerful as Twain's anticolonial writings from this period are, they seem to be different from the more ambivalent sentiments regarding the uses and abuses of "civilization" Twain had articulated as late as 1897 in *Following the Equator*. Despite frequently expressed sympathies with native peoples throughout his global lecturing tour, Twain also appears to acknowledge the inevitability of Euroamerican hegemony over the modern world. Richard

Bridgman concludes in *Traveling in Mark Twain* that such a destiny did not in 1897 disappoint Twain: "For all the abuses of conquest that Twain had documented and lamented, his conclusive feeling was that 'all the savage lands in the world are going to be brought under the subjection of the Christian governments of Europe. I am not sorry, but glad.' He was not being ironic. He believed, he wrote, that India demonstrated that after much bloodshed the result would be 'peace and order and the reign of law.' "[2]

To be sure, Twain was powerfully impressed by historical events, from the Spanish–American War to the Russo-Japanese War, that underscored the brutality of Euroamerican colonialism and foreshadowed the violence of the First World War. Yet these historical events alone were not the primary reasons for the changes in Twain's views on colonialism from *Following the Equator* to the anti-imperialist tracts he wrote between 1898 and 1905. What Bridgman confidently decides to be Twain's preference for imperial order, British India over the "misrule" of the Thugs, for example, by no means applies generally to Twain's often contradictory attitudes in this travel book regarding the uses and abuses of Western civilization both at home and abroad. The strict periodization of the "anti-imperialist" Mark Twain of the fin de siècle as distinct from the apparently patriotic and nationalist Twain of the 1870s and 1880s, has prevented us from recognizing how anticolonial and anti-imperialist attitudes inflect virtually all of Twain's writings.[3]

One of Twain's most obvious literary treatments of imperialism, indeed one of the most obvious in nineteenth-century literature in general, is *A Connecticut Yankee in King Arthur's Court*, but it is not customarily approached in terms of its serious reflections on imperialism. One reason for this neglect is that *Connecticut Yankee*, published in 1889, belongs to the decade preceding Twain's overt "change of mind" about the dangers of colonialism and imperialism. Another reason, of course, is the formal distraction of the historical romance. Arthurian England "invaded" by a nineteenth-century Yankee does not seem to be a fictive *donnée* likely to encourage discussion of the dangers of Euroamerican colonialism in the modern period. Yet more familiar literary indictments of Western imperialism, such as Conrad's *Heart of Darkness* (1899), often recall the colonial origins of the European colonizers, as Marlow does at the beginning of his tale: " 'Imagine the feelings of a commander of a fine – what d'ye call 'em – trireme in the Mediterranean, ordered suddenly to the north. . . . Imagine him here – the very end of the world, a sea the colour of lead, a sky the colour of smoke. . . . Sandbanks, marshes, forests, savages – precious little to eat fit for a civilised man, nothing but Thames water. No Falernian wine here, no going ashore.'"4 At times, such invocations of Roman conquerors work to rationalize European or American ventures abroad, either by connecting the modern nations with a great tradition or by encouraging resignation to the "inevitability" of men's will to conquest and expansion.5 In other cases, previous colonial projects are recalled to remind us that history repeats itself primarily when we refuse to acknowledge the fundamental theft involved in colonization. Melville's *Typee* (1846) makes frequent reference to Roman generals and legions in Europe, and *Benito Cereno* (1856) revives the imperium of the Holy Roman emperor both in Europe and in the New World to warn us that the nominally democratic United States is following the lead of the European imperium against which it claimed to have rebelled.6

The most convincing argument for excluding *Connecticut Yankee* from a consideration of Twain's anti-imperialism is the relative novelty of the terms "imperialism" and "anti-imperialism" in the United States at the end of the 1890s, primarily as a result of the public debates over the Spanish–American and Philippine–American Wars. Rudyard Kipling's poem "The White Man's Burden" (1899), in which Kipling specifically urges the United States to assume its "responsibilities" in the Philippines as the European powers had done elsewhere, is often considered a sort of historical marker for the infection of public discourse in the United States with the jingoism of conservative European imperialists.7 In the 1896 presidential campaign, William Jennings Bryan ran on a free-silver platform and, after his defeat by McKinley, served as colonel of a Nebraska regiment of volunteers in the Spanish–American War. In the 1900 campaign, Bryan combined free-silver with anti-imperialism to challenge McKinley once again, recognizing that the incumbent president was closely associated with expansionist foreign policies.8

This sort of historical specificity regarding the popular use of the terms "imperialism" and "anti-imperialism" in political debates in the United States seems to be reinforced by Twain's own statements regarding the "change" in his position on our foreign policies between 1898 and 1902. In his 1947 essay, "Mark Twain and Howells: Anti-Imperialists," William Gibson restricts his consideration of Twain's anti-imperialism to this period in large part because of Twain's public declarations that he has changed his mind about U.S. expansionism after our betrayal of Aguinaldo and the Philippine people's revolution. Responding to a *Chicago Tribune* reporter's statement in 1900, "'You've been quoted here as an anti-imperialist,'" Twain replied, "'Well, I am. A year ago I wasn't. I thought it would be a great thing to give a whole lot of freedom to the Filipinos, but I guess now that it's better to let them give it to themselves."[9] Gibson and others have pointed out that Twain, like Henry Adams, supported our foreign policy in the nominal "liberation" of Cuba from Spain, but changed his mind about U.S. foreign policy when it shifted from one of aiding republican movements to annexing foreign territory, as it did, however "accidentally," at the end of the Philippine–American War.[10]

Twain's public statements about his "change of mind" belie, however, the continuity of his thinking about imperialism from *Connecticut Yankee* to his overtly anti-imperialist satires of the period 1898–1905. His ambivalence regarding Euroamerican imperialism is also quite consistent throughout his career, as I shall argue *Connecticut Yankee* demonstrates. What appears at times to be Twain's equivocation regarding the changing foreign policies of the great powers can usually be attributed to his strong and consistent conviction that *all* people throughout history are prone to conquer and colonize their neighbors. As he writes in *Following the Equator*:

> All the territorial possessions of all the political establishments in the earth – including America, of course, consist of pilferings from other people's wash. No tribe, however insignificant, and no nation, howsoever mighty, occupies a foot of land that was not stolen. When the English, the French, and the Spaniards reached America, the Indian tribes had been raiding each other's territorial clothes-lines for ages, and every acre of ground in the continent had been stolen and restolen five hundred times.[11]

The only solution to this vicious historical cycle of conquest and exploitation seems to be the emancipation that Twain identified with the American and French Revolutions, both of which turned crucially on war and conquest in the interests of the people's rule. Twain's problem throughout his writings, whether he is questioning domestic politics or foreign policies, is finding a standard for judging correctly the degree to which republican aims and their emancipatory struggles can be distinguished from the tiresome old business of conquest by kings, priests, and tycoons.

It is just this division between the republican sentiments of Hank Morgan and his bid for despotic power in sixth-century England that organizes the dramatic action and social criticism of *A Connecticut Yankee in King Arthur's Court*. In the course of negotiating this fundamental division in his protagonist's character, Twain anticipates most of the anti-imperialist views he would make so explicit in his satires between 1898 and 1905. In exposing the ways that the usual tyrants would learn to disguise themselves as bearers of enlightenment and thus emancipation from both despotic rule and the drudgery of everyday labor, Twain anticipates the more modern critique of neoimperialist strategies of "winning hearts and minds" in the course of shaping consumers – the sort of neoimperialism we associate with today's global corporations, proper heirs both of Hank Morgan's late-nineteenth-century capitalist feudalism and of the Euroamerican colonial "missions" into the earth's "hearts of darkness."

For all this modernity, however, Twain's anti-imperialism remains fully grounded in older definitions of imperialism as "the personal sovereignty of a powerful ruler over numerous territories, whether in Europe or overseas."[12] What Twain likes to call the "game" in his anti-imperialist writings remains much the same as it has been for centuries. In "To the Person Sitting in Darkness," Twain writes: "The Blessings-of-Civilization Trust, wisely and curiously administered is a Daisy. There is more money in it, more territory, more sovereignty, and other kinds of emolument, than there is in any other game that is played. But Christendom has been playing it badly of late years."[13] In *Following the Equator,* his metaphor for the masquerade of colonial exploitation as "enlightenment" is clothing, in terms of what has been hung out to dry on the clothesline, stolen wash, and "fashionable" dress of the day:

> In one hundred and fifty years England has beneficently retired garment after garment from the Indian lines, until there is hardly a rag of the original wash left dangling anywhere. In eight hundred years an obscure tribe of Muscovite savages has risen to the dazzling position of Land-Robber-in-Chief; she found a quarter of the world hanging out to dry on a hundred parallels of latitude, and she scooped in the whole wash.[14]

In his attacks on Chamberlain's conduct in the Boer War and McKinley's annexation of the Philippines, Twain equates these democratic leaders with the German kaiser and Russian czar in their willing deception of the people they represent and conquer: "We all know the Business is being ruined. The reason is not far to seek. It is because our Mr. McKinley, and Mr. Chamberlain, and the Kaiser, and the Tsar and the French have been exporting the Actual Thing *with the outside cover left off.* This is bad for the Game. It shows that these new players of it are not sufficiently acquainted with it" ("Person" 295). In *A Connecticut Yankee,* he anticipates this indictment of imperialism by showing how despotism secures its power by controlling people's attitudes and values, either by encouraging their superstitions, as the Church and Merlin do, or by manipulating public opinion, as Hank and Clarence do with their weekly newspaper. When Twain writes in 1901 that "Mr. Chamberlain manufactures a war out of materials so inadequate and so fanciful that they make the boxes grieve and the gallery laugh" ("Person"

295), we are reminded that the "theatricality" of the publicity used by Chamberlain to disguise the real motives of the Boer War is anticipated by the "theatricality" of Hank Morgan's republican postures in *Connecticut Yankee*.

Numerous scenes of such political "theater" are enacted by the Boss, from the eclipse and the restoration of the holy well to his penultimate "duel" with the Knights of the Round Table. I want to focus now on that "duel" both to typify Twain's treatment of political theatricality in *Connecticut Yankee* and to connect it with one of the most legendary "events" of nineteenth-century British colonialism: "Chinese" Gordon's death at the hands of the Mahdi and his "dervishes" in Khartoum. In chapter 39, Twain deliberately confuses the contemporary Western street fight, the "last-stand" of the heroic frontier officer overwhelmed by "Indians" or "natives," the Southern duel of honor, and the chivalric jousting tournament. Calmly standing before the charge of mounted knights in full armor, Hank uses his Colt "Dragoon" revolvers to demonstrate his military power. Shooting Sir Sagramour out of his saddle, he calmly fires nine more shots and kills nine more of the five hundred knights massed against him. This scene obviously anticipates the genocide at the end of the narrative, as well as the failure of Hank's revolution, "trapped" as it is both by its own fortifications and by its own perverse logic. Hank's "bluff" in facing down five hundred knights with two Colt revolvers holding twelve cartridges is the sort of scene repeated countless times in the dime novels of Western adventure and in the "heroic" exploits of British and European adventurers in exotic colonial sites. Not only is Chinese Gordon's tragic bravura recalled ironically here, but the equally legendary stand of General Custer at the Little Big Horn in 1876 echoes through the scene for the contemporary reader.

Twain "conceived, composed, and finally revised *Yankee* during five years of intermittent work between December 1884 and September 1889."[15] One of the most celebrated events of European colonialism in that period was the death of Charles George Gordon, "Chinese Gordon," on January 26, 1885, in Khartoum, Sudan, where he had returned in February 1884 to put down the rebellion led by the Moslem leader, Mohammed Ahmed (the Mahdi), whose forces had destroyed British General William Hicks's Egyptian force of ten thousand. Like the final battle between the Church's knights and the Boss's boys, the fabled end of Chinese Gordon, besieged by the rebels at Khartoum, was the result of a religious "revolt." Like Hank Morgan's, Chinese Gordon's "progressive reforms" in Egypt and North Africa had helped "precipitate the inevitable disaster," as Lytton Strachey would put it in his apt conclusion to *Eminent Victorians* (1918), "The End of General Gordon."[16] Among the reforms Gordon had accomplished while serving as governor of the equatorial provinces of central Africa (1873–80) was the "suppression of the slave trade," which is the first reform Hank Morgan makes after he has made public his revolution against knight-errantry, following his shooting of ten knights out of their saddles in chapter 39.

Contemporary accounts of Chinese Gordon's death at Khartoum are typically legendary; not surprisingly they range from saintly forbearance to martial valor. Strachey's account captures just this legendary quality of the "progressive" European colonizer sacrificing himself in the cause of Civilization:

> Another spear transfixed him; he fell, and the swords of the three other Dervishes instantly hacked him to death. Thus, if we are to believe the official chroniclers, in the dignity of unresisting disdain, General Gordon met his end. . . . Other witnesses told a very different story. The man whom they saw die was not a saint but a warrior. With intrepidity, with skill, with desperation, he flew at his enemies. When his pistol was exhausted, he fought on with his sword; he forced his way to the bottom of the staircase; and, among a heap of corpses, only succumbed at length to the sheer weight of the multitudes against him. (EV 190)

Strachey concludes that these contradictory accounts of Chinese Gordon's end typify just what he represents in the European imperial project at the end of the Victorian age: "But General Gordon had always been a contradictious person – even a little off his head, perhaps, though a hero; . . . At any rate, it had all ended very happily – in a glorious slaughter of 20,000 Arabs, a vast addition to the British Empire" (EV 192).

Chinese Gordon's "contradictions" are, of course, just what subsequent literary representations of the Eurocolonial adventurer would stress, as Conrad's Kurtz and even his narrator, Marlow, attest. In a similar manner, Hank Morgan combines contradictory impulses favoring emancipation of the people from their slavery and the conventional conqueror's desire for absolute power.[17] Interpreted in this way, the Yankee "Boss" – Gordon assumed the title "Gordon Pasha" – can be linked with the imperialist projects of European monarchs and the Church's missionaries, but in a manner that is at once notably farsighted for 1889 and curiously archaic. Interpreting the Yankee entrepreneur and his alter ego, the Barnum-like promoter, as a version of the frontier military or political representative of imperial power – Custer or Gordon – Twain makes the equation between capitalist expansion and Euroamerican imperialism that does not enter the public debate until several decades later. On the other hand, Twain's appar-

ent equation of the frontier hero, colonial adventurer, and capitalist entrepreneur with the feudal despot seems to ignore the important changes that
had occurred in the intervening thirteen centuries, especially in terms of how
these different fictions are marketed and consumed.

In connecting Morgan with Gordon, capitalism with political imperialism, Twain seems to anticipate early modern critics of capitalism such as
Lenin, who in *Imperialism, the Highest Stage of Capitalism* (1916) argued
that capitalism had entered its "last" phase in the imperial expansion that
had temporarily saved the industrial nations, only to plunge them into the
sort of world conflict (the First World War) that would ensure their final
collapse.[18] There is little evidence in *Connecticut Yankee* that Twain fully
comprehends what the shift from the older forms of political imperialism to
the newer modes of economic domination involves. All the evidence works
in the contrary direction to argue that Twain hopes to show that the Yankee
capitalist is simply a revival of the feudal monarch, who claims his power
either by force of arms or by theatrical display of "divine right." Rather
than viewing the new modes of economic and political power – what Lenin
considered the inevitable expansion of capitalism by whatever means – as
significant transformations of such older modes of domination as hereditary
wealth and title, Twain treats capitalism as simply a repetition in different
dress of the same old story of the will to power of the "damned human
race." Despite much attention to economics in *Connecticut Yankee*, the
actual *theory* of political economy is quite simple and involves little transformation of economic conditions from Arthur's sixth-century Britain to
Morgan's nineteenth-century America. Hank does attempt to "enlighten"
the feudal peasantry regarding their rights to their own labor power and to
explain how wages for such labor must be determined in relation to prices,
endorsing a "free-trade" economic philosophy that, while lost on the serfs
he lectures, appears to be Twain's answer to imbalances of international
power occasioned by older forms of political imperialism.

In chapter 33, "Sixth Century Political Economy," Hank uses the differences of wage–price ratios in the several tributary kingdoms of Arthur's
disunited England to condemn protected trade and endorse free-trade economies in ways unmistakably relevant to the late nineteenth century and the
increasingly global economy stimulated in large part by imperialism. At the
end of the elaborate banquet that Hank has staged to help Marco impress
his neighbors, but that ends up merely glorifying the disguised Boss, Hank
assumes his willful place as ruler by lecturing the peasants while Arthur
"went off to take a nap." The substance of his lesson is the promise of free
trade: "At first glance, things appeared to be exceeding prosperous in this

little tributary kingdom – whose lord was King Bagdemagus – as compared with the state of things in my own region. They had the 'protection' system in full force here, whereas we were working along down towards free trade."[19] Morgan's endorsement of free trade is preparatory to his pitch for trade unions and the rights of the worker to "take a hand in fixing his wages himself" – the familiar late-nineteenth-century bid for "free labor" (CY 330). Whatever doubts we may have about Morgan representing Twain's views elsewhere, there can be no such doubt here. In his March 22, 1886, address to the Monday Evening Club of Hartford, "The New Dynasty," Twain lends powerful support to the cause of organized labor, and he does so by linking exploited workers with such "victims" as "the nations of the earth":

> Now so far as we know or may guess, this has been going on for a million years. Who are the oppressors? The few: the king, the capitalist, and handful of other overseers and superintendents. Who the oppressed? The many: The nations of the earth; the valuable personages; the workers; they that MAKE the bread that the soft-handed and the idle eat.[20]

Henry Nash Smith argued many years ago that Twain's analysis of economics in *Connecticut Yankee* is one of the several failures of the book, attributable to Twain's inability to provide the "concrete detail" for a "complex of institutions that had previously been little more than a vague abstraction for him."[21] Twain's problem in representing modern economic theories is not, however, his confusion over the "concrete detail," but his endorsement of a "progressive" free-trade theory that was already showing in the 1880s its adaptability to the new modes of imperial domination. Since the seventeenth century, free-trade advocates had argued that tariffs and economic parochialism only "wasted" economic energies that should be used to increase the world's wealth. "Free-trade" theory is central to enlightenment political economies, and Adam Smith's *Inquiry into the Nature and Causes of the Wealth of Nations* (1776) is the classic text, especially in its advocacy of the coordination of free trade with what might be termed a global "division of labor," or specialization by region or nation in modes of production best suited to it.[22] Hank Morgan and Twain clearly agree that free trade will help maximize the wealth of a united "England," bring an end to its sixth-century division into many "tributary kingdoms" (i.e., "colonies"), and do so by awakening serfs (i.e., "workers") to their rights over their own labor and thus to their roles in negotiating appropriate wages for that labor.

If this is the "enlightenment" that Hank Morgan brings to the "colony" of sixth-century England, it is nonetheless a wisdom that did not prevail in the course of early modern imperial expansion. Insofar as Twain links "free trade" and "trade unionism" in chapter 33, we may conclude that *Connecticut Yankee* deals with the important relationship between domestic and international economies, between the rights of labor in the United States and the rights of colonized peoples in the various Euroamerican empires Twain would satirize so explicitly between 1898 and 1905. What Twain does not take adequately into account in *Connecticut Yankee* or in his later anti-imperialist writings is what subsequently came to be termed "free-trade imperialism." Mommsen traces "free-trade imperialism" to a "pioneer study" in 1953 by Ronald Robinson and John Gallagher, "The Imperialism of Free Trade."[23] As Mommsen summarizes their argument:

> By developing the theory of "informal empire" Robinson and Gallagher broke decisively with the tradition which defined imperialism exclusively in terms of formal territorial colonial rule, and instead emphasized the importance of imperialist factors of a non-governmental character. The true motive force of Victorian expansion was economic, and the imperialists were at first content to exercise informal control from a few coastal stations. Political methods were in the main used only to open up previously closed markets to the ostensibly free operation of Western competitive capitalism. . . . "The usual summing up of the policy of the free trade empire as 'trade, not rule' should read 'trade with informal control if possible; trade with rule when necessary.' "[24]

Robinson and Gallagher's theory of "free-trade imperialism" was developed in light of the process of decolonization taking place in the years following the Second World War. Twain could hardly have been farsighted enough to "predict" the neocolonial dangers that could be seen as still operative even as former colonies were being granted their nominal "independence" in this much later process of decolonization.

What Twain *does* anticipate, even as he relies on an older theory of imperialism, is the degree to which capitalism will be involved in global domination and the reinscription of the old evils of the "damned human race" in the new texts of economic and technological exploitation and control. When Hank Morgan does begin to play the "Game" on his own, making public his revolution against knight-errantry and the Church, his admirable social reforms are explicitly linked with his own colonial practices:

> Slavery was dead and gone; all men were equal before the law; taxation had been equalized. The telegraph, the telephone, the phonograph, the type-writer,

the sewing machine, and all the thousand and handy servants of steam and electricity were working their way into favor. We had a steamboat or two on the Thames, we had steam war-ships, and the beginnings of a steam commercial marine; *I was getting ready to send out an expedition to discover America.*

(CY 228, my emphasis)

The Boss's ultimate revolution, "a rounded and complete governmental revolution without bloodshed . . . a republic," to be declared "upon Arthur's death," seems to accord well with Twain's advocacy in his anti-imperialist satires of republican revolutions in colonized countries like Cuba and the Philippines (CY 229). But the failure of the Boss's project – a failure that in the context of the historical romance occasions thirteen centuries more of despotism, slavery, and suffering – is already inscribed in the reforms of which he is so proud.[25]

Cataloging the weaknesses of *Connecticut Yankee,* Henry Nash Smith adds Twain's "meager" development of the "theme of technological advance": "Despite Mark Twain's occasional efforts to give fictional substance to the Yankee's mechanical prowess, he actually performs no constructive feat except the restoration of the holy well; and it will be recalled that the technology of this episode does not go into repairing the well, but into the fraudulent display of fireworks with which he awes the populace."[26] Actually, Twain provides considerable details about the technologies he considers basic to Morgan's capitalist and free-trade economy. In addition to Hank's talents with munitions (including fireworks, of course), he is adept at the new modes of transportation and communication he introduces into sixth-century England ostensibly to end feudal provincialism and encourage national unity, secretly to secure his power and influence. What his various mines and factories serve is, after all, the development of the telegraph lines, newspaper and publishing enterprises, and steam-powered transport that enable him to "unite" and, of course, thereby rule an "England" soon to become the "British Empire," as Hank prepares to "send out an expedition to discover America."

I cannot review here all that has been written about Twain's own contradictory attitudes toward the new technologies, except to point out how perfectly *Connecticut Yankee* expresses those contradictions. This is not to claim that Twain took no intellectual position on the new technologies of "electricity and steam," or that he condemned them in print while hypocritically trying to develop and market the Paige typesetter and other inventions in which he invested. Twain's views in *Connecticut Yankee* about the role of capitalism in the old styles of political imperialism may be somewhat archaic, but he understands quite clearly that *control* not only of the means of communication but also of the *technology* of such communicative instruments would become increasingly crucial factors in determining social, political, and economic power in the modern age.

If the republican revolutions he supported in his anti-imperialist writings were to succeed, they would have to take into account the new modes of communication and transport – modes of "colonization" that extended from everyday life at home and in the workplace to the most distant and exotic "foreign territory." Yet *how* the "people" were to control these means of communication eludes Twain in *Connecticut Yankee,* as well as in his anti-imperialist satires. The Boss's vocational training schools (boy and man factories) and his normal schools ("Teacher-Factories") are unsatisfactory solutions in two respects. First, he provides little insight into the curricula and pedagogy of these schools – that is, their basic modes of production. Second, Warner and Twain had already exposed in *The Gilded Age* the vulnerability of such educational institutions to control by the usual political despots and confidence men.[27] Among those educated by the Boss and his new social system, only Clarence displays the independence of mind, healthy disrespect for authority, and creative imagination required to control the new technologies rather than simply "operate" the machines. Clarence's qualifications for such authority are already apparent when Hank Morgan first meets him. With the exception of his quick aptitude for technical training, Clarence gains little from the modern education provided by the Boss. There is little evidence that the boys and teachers "trained" under the new educational regime have learned anything beyond the mere manufacture and operation of the new technologies; they are still profoundly dependent on the ruler, who has simply exchanged his crown or miter for the scientist's laboratory coat.

The failure of conventional education often signals in Twain's writings the alternative of Twain's special brand of satiric "instruction." Twain's subtle, artistic solution to the despair his own social criticism encourages is to teach the reader how to expose truth behind the ceaseless lies of those in power. In his anti-imperialist writings, he teaches us to recognize the "Actual Thing" those in power have for millennia tried to "sell" to "the Customer Sitting in Darkness" as "Civilization." In place of that false "enlightenment," Twain offers the "many" who are "oppressed" the means to bring their own light into the shadowy game played by those in power ("Person" 295). He knew quite well how to teach us to subvert the pretensions of language and other signs of power that allow kings to assume their arbitrary powers.

Yet the new technologies of communication that were already replacing the dominant medium of print and the new modes of transportation that were drastically changing global geography and commerce in the 1880s were far more difficult to comprehend and control than even the infamously deceptive language of power and pretense that Twain had learned to subvert with such genius. At the end of *Connecticut Yankee,* Hank Morgan is trapped within Merlin's Cave by the very military technology he has employed to defend his forces and annihilate knight-errantry. Electrocuting, drowning, and machine-gunning "twenty-five thousand men," the Boss enacts in the sixth century the special horrors of modern, mechanized warfare as they were revealed in the unequal battles between European imperial powers and preindustrial peoples: "Within ten short minutes after we had opened fire, armed resistance was totally annihilated, the campaign was ended, we fifty-four were masters of England! Twenty-five thousand men lay dead around us" (CY 440). Terrible as the cost of this imbalance of power between colonizers and colonized would be throughout the Victorian period, Twain's criticism hardly begins to address what were already becoming the new means of economic imperialism that would employ in far subtler and more pervasive ways the new technologies Twain treats here as mere instruments of military conquest.

During the week of waiting for the Battle of the Sand-Belt to begin and then as he convalesces from his wound, Hank Morgan "was writing all the time . . . turning my old diary into this narrative form," writing letters to Sandy, and later bringing the story we are reading to the abrupt end requiring Clarence's P.S. (chapter 44) and Twain's "Final P.S." (formally beyond the "End of the Manuscript") (CY 426). From the site of feudal superstition and tyranny to the site of modern technological terror, the Cave continues to function, as it had in *The Adventures of Tom Sawyer,* as Twain's metaphor for the cultural unconscious. Throughout his career, Twain himself always tried to write himself out of that Cave, but something always seemed to block the entrance. In *Tom Sawyer,* it is the corpse of Injun Joe; in *Connecticut Yankee,* it is the disease-breeding mass of rotting corpses that hang from or float in the Boss's fortifications.

Twain imagines at the very end that he *has* escaped the Cave, insofar as the Boss's manuscript is both protected and "postscripted" by Clarence, then "framed" by the modern storyteller, "M.T.," who in turn leaves this fictive history to the reader. Such literary circulation is often Twain's answer to the determinant power structures he so abhorred, and the collaborative project of "writing" our own history offers a charming, if sentimental, answer to the question of how the true republic should employ technology in the interests of democratic representation. Yet even as Twain wrote *Connecticut Yankee,* the neoimperialist policies that would lead the United

States from the Philippines to Vietnam and the Persian Gulf were already being developed in the marketing strategies of global capitalism and the technologies of the telegraph and steamship.

The formal political empires of the nineteenth-century European powers metamorphosed at the turn of the century into the "informal imperialism" that combines "commercial penetration and political influence" so characteristic of the First World's global power in our own age.[28] Crucial to what some have termed the contemporary process of *recolonization* under the conditions of "informal" or "new" imperialism is control of the means of communication and thus representation.[29] Twain imagines in *Connecticut Yankee* that the bodies heaped at the mouth of the Cave, like the colonial atrocities exposed by "that trivial little kodak" in King Leopold's Congo Free State, will at last become visible as the "Actual Thing." In our own age, Third and Fourth World peoples and countries are increasingly rendered "invisible," even as their everyday fields of vision are saturated by the consumer products and media technologies of the First World.[30] This commercial and technological penetration of every corner of the globe, which at the same time renders invisible the others so dominated, begins with the well-intentioned republican and progressive rhetoric epitomized by Hank Morgan and historically performed by turn-of-the-century diplomats, like John Hay, secretary of state in the McKinley and Roosevelt administrations (1898–1905). In his 1901 address, "American Diplomacy," Hay endorses the free-trade philosophy that Twain himself appears to endorse in *Connecticut Yankee*: "We have kept always in view the fact that we are preeminently a peace-loving people; that our normal activities are in the direction of trade and commerce; that the vast development of our industries imperatively demands that we shall not only retain and confirm our hold on our present markets, but seek constantly, by all honorable means, to extend our commercial interests in every practicable direction."[31] With little variation, perhaps a few more rhetorical "flowers" and many more printer's errors, this might have been published in Camelot's *Weekly Hosannah and Literary Volcano* under the Boss's byline.

In *Connecticut Yankee*, Twain warns the reader that the United States is already following the lead of the European imperial powers, a message he would repeat with growing volubility in the anti-imperialist writings from 1898 to 1905. Twain did not understand, however, what he had himself written, or perhaps what had been telegraphed by the cultural unconscious that worked so fantastically through Twain: that the very medium which he had protected so jealously for its capacity to resist tyranny and build republic consensus had already been invaded, if not conquered. Unable to explain how the nineteenth-century "man of letters" might leap into the communications expert – both spin doctor and computer scientist – of our postmodern age, Twain could only condemn the instrumentality of the new technologies and the repetition of the older forms of despotism under the conditions of modernity. In this respect, his critique of Euroamerican imperialism failed to account for the transformation from the nineteenth-century modes of political domination to twentieth-century modes of commercial and technological domination. Yet by imagining in *Connecticut Yankee* the curious intersection of feudal modes of domination with the progressive claims of nineteenth-century capitalism – the uncanny resemblance of Merlin and Morgan – Twain sent yet another of his prophetic warnings from the mouth of the Cave.

NOTES

1 Wolfgang Mommsen, *Theories of Imperialism,* trans. P. S. Falla (Chicago: University of Chicago Press, 1980), p. 4: "It was Disraeli's opponents, especially Gladstone, who used the opprobrious term 'imperialism' to describe his policy of external aggression inspired by domestic motives," in response to the British foreign policies announced in Disraeli's famous Crystal Palace Speech of 1872.

2 Richard Bridgman, *Traveling in Mark Twain* (Berkeley: University of California Press, 1987), p. 143. Bridgman goes on to acknowledge that if "these hopeful sentiments . . . represented Mark Twain's best judgment as he came to the end of his last extensive journey, in fact he would shortly be obliged to repudiate them, and did, with unparalleled indignation, in a series of critiques of imperialist policy" (pp. 143–4).

3 William Gibson, "Mark Twain and Howells: Anti-Imperialists," *New England Quarterly* 20 (December 1947): 470, tries to reconcile Twain's anti-imperialism with his general criticism of America's failure to realize its democratic and republican promise: "Throughout the Gilded Age, Twain and Howells were aware of the problems implicit in democratic government in the United States, and critical of what they held its shortcomings to be, but at no time were they more jealous of its preservation than at the end. At the turn of the century they attacked imperialism as Emerson and Thoreau had attacked slavery. Like Emerson and Thoreau before them, they also wrote in a major tradition in American letters."

4 Joseph Conrad, *Heart of Darkness,* ed. Robert Kimbrough (New York: Norton, 1971), pp. 5–6.

5 Yeats, Pound, and Eliot helped revive classical traditions in the early modern period, even as they ironized their sources, blasted traditionalists, and claimed avant-garde status for their new "classicism." There is nevertheless a certain cultural narrative linking Victorian "medievalism" with early modern "classicism" that becomes more readable if we understand its function to be the reconsolidation of the cultural resources of the European and American nation-states as they shifted from political to economic and cultural modes of colonial domination in the same historical period.

6 See my "Imperialism at Home and Abroad in Melville's *Typee*," in *National Identities and Post-Americanist Narratives*, ed. Donald E. Pease (Durham, N.C.: Duke University Press, 1994), and "Romancing the Stone: Melville's Critique of Ideology in *Pierre*," in *Theorizing American Literature*, ed. Bainard Coward and Joseph Kronick (Baton Rouge: Louisiana State University Press, 1991), pp. 195–232, for a more detailed discussion of Melville's anticipation of early modern critiques of the role of the United States in colonial expansion.

7 Rudyard Kipling, "The White Man's Burden: The United States and the Philippine Islands," *Rudyard Kipling's Verse* (Garden City, N.Y.: Doubleday, 1940), pp. 321–3.

8 At the beginning of the Spanish–American War, McKinley claimed not to have known the location of the Philippines within two thousand miles. To this day, standard reference books, like the *Encyclopedia Americana*, treat our annexation of the Philippines as an "accident" of history, thus thrusting us unwillingly and unexpectedly into the role of imperial power. McKinley assumed this role quite well, but Twain makes clear in "To the Person Sitting in Darkness" (1901) that McKinley was following quite consciously the European plan.

9 As quoted in Gibson, "Mark Twain and Howells," p. 446.

10 See my "Henry Adams and Imperialism," in *New Essays on Henry Adams's "Education,"* ed. John Carlos Rowe (New York: Cambridge University Press, forthcoming).

11 Mark Twain, *Following the Equator: A Journey Around the World*, 2 vols., in *The Writings of Mark Twain* (New York: Collier, 1899), vol. 16, pp. 298–9.

12 Mommsen, *Theories of Imperialism*, p. 4.

13 Mark Twain, "To the Person Sitting in Darkness," *Selected Shorter Writings of Mark Twain*, ed. Walter Blair (Boston: Houghton Mifflin, 1962), p. 295. Henceforth cited parenthetically in the text as "Person."

14 Twain, *Following the Equator*, vol. 16, p. 299. Western political analysts had worried about the unpredictable role Russia would play in the struggles for territory among the European imperial powers since the Russo-Turkish War of 1877–8, during which Russian troops had driven as far as Constantinople in their support of the Serbs and Bulgarians. The new threat posed by Russia to the established nineteenth-century European empires, especially in Asia Minor and the Far East, explains in part Twain's begrudging endorsement of the rule of British order and law elsewhere in *Following the Equator*. Like other Westerners, Twain tended to demonize the colonial and expansionist policies of non-Euroamerican powers, as his reference to Czar Nicholas II's descent from "an obscure tribe of Muscovite savages" indicates.

15 Robert Hirst, "Note on the Text," *Connecticut Yankee*, Mark Twain Library, (Berkeley: University of California Press, 1983), p. 477.

16 Lytton Strachey, *Eminent Victorians* (New York: Weidenfeld & Nicolson, 1988), p. 149. Henceforth cited parenthetically in the text as EV.

17 There are many parallels between Hank Morgan and Chinese Gordon. Although he died representing the British government, Gordon was a new kind of foreign adventurer and diplomat, who served rulers other than Victoria, but always (it would appear) with the larger interests of the British Empire in mind.

He had served the Khedive Ismail of Egypt before returning to Africa, and he had been invited by King Leopold II to serve as his representative in the Congo Free State (an assignment Gordon declined). In a similar fashion, Hank Morgan serves Arthur, even as the Boss knows that his best interests lie in serving the higher authority of modern U.S. interests – both commercial and political. Gordon's disdain for British bureaucracy and his insistence on accomplishing tasks on his own is another quality he shares with Hank (as well as with later figures, like T. E. Lawrence, who modeled themselves after his overtly anti-imperialist cosmopolitanism). In the final siege of Khartoum, Gordon ordered the cellar of the palace to be loaded with gunpowder, so "that the whole building might, at a moment's notice, be blown in the air," anticipating the Boss's and Clarence's plans to blow up their factories should they fall into the hands of the Church and the Boss's earlier "demonstration" of his power by blowing up Merlin's Tower (EV 188). Finally, Gordon's one constant in all his adventures was a curious sense of missionary zeal, that he was doing "God's" work. One of Hank Morgan's major projects – and differences from Mark Twain – is his plan to begin the Reformation "early," substituting the Protestant Church for Catholicism.

18 V. I. Lenin, *Imperialism, the Highest Stage of Capitalism*, in *Collected Works* (London: International, 1964), vol. 22, pp. 185–91.

19 Mark Twain, *A Connecticut Yankee in King Arthur's Court*, ed. Allison R. Ensor, Norton Critical Edition (New York: Norton, 1982), p. 323. Henceforth cited parenthetically in the text as CY.

20 Mark Twain, "The New Dynasty" (March 22, 1886), in ibid., pp. 284–5.

21 Henry Nash Smith, *Mark Twain's Fable of Progress: Political and Economic Ideas in "A Connecticut Yankee"* (New Brunswick, N.J.: Rutgers University Press, 1964), p. 100.

22 See Adam Smith, *Inquiry into the Nature and Causes of the Wealth of Nations* (1776; New York: Random House, 1937), pp. 440–65, for the classic discussion of advantages of free trade and the division of international labor (book 4, "Of Systems of Political Economy," chap. 3).

23 Ronald Robinson and John Gallagher, "The Imperialism of Free Trade," *Economic History Review*, 2d ser., 6 (1953): 1–25. See Mommsen's discussion of Robinson and Gallagher in *Theories of Imperialism*, p. 87–90.

24 Mommsen, *Theories of Imperialism*, p. 88.

25 The failure of Hank Morgan's revolution is anticipated in Twain's "The Great Revolution in Pitcairn," which was first published in *Atlantic Monthly* 43 (1879): 295–302, and included by Ensor in "Backgrounds and Sources" in his Norton Critical Edition of *Connecticut Yankee*. Not only does "The Great Revolution in Pitcairn" suggest that Americans, like Hank Morgan and Butterworth Stavely, are just as prone to imperial power as the British and Europeans, it also establishes the continuity of Twain's anti-imperialist thinking from the 1870s to the early twentieth century.

26 H. N. Smith, *Mark Twain's Fable*, p. 86.

27 See my discussion of Twain's critique of American higher education in *The Gilded Age* in "Fatal Speculations: Murder, Money, and Manners in Twain's *Pudd'nhead Wilson*," in *Mark Twain's "Pudd'nhead Wilson": Race, Conflict,*

and Culture, ed. Forrest G. Robinson and Susan Gillman (Durham, N.C.: Duke University Press, 1990), pp. 137–46.

28 Mommsen, *Theories of Imperialism,* p. 89.

29 Bernard Nietschmann, "The Third World War," *Cultural Survival Quarterly* 11 (1989): 6.

30 In ibid., p. 3, Nietschmann provides a helpful definition of Fourth World nations as "the nation peoples and their countries that exist beneath the imposed states. . . . Fourth World nations may be surrounded, divided or dismembered by one or more international states. The Fourth World encompasses most of the world's distinct peoples, about a third of the world's population and approximately 50 percent of the land area." These "nation peoples" are notoriously "invisible," because of their relation to "one or more international states."

31 John Hay, "American Diplomacy," *Addresses of John Hay* (New York: Century, 1907), p. 122.

IO

SUSAN GILLMAN

Mark Twain's Travels in the Racial Occult: *Following the Equator* and the Dream Tales

Mark Twain was always intensely engaged by two important nineteenth-century cultural conversations, one addressing issues of race, the other theories of the unconscious. His later writings in particular are known both for their explicit anti-imperialism, and the charged racial awareness it produced, and for their flirtation with spiritualism, dream theory, and a variety of occult phenomena. Each of these cultural arenas, the racial and the psychological, has been recognized individually as a major force shaping Twain's imagination, but how they might have interacted to produce his large body of late, mostly unfinished (and some unpublished) writings has yet to be determined. The later works, the group of fantastic, quasi-philosophical pieces, now published in volumes with such titles as *Which Was the Dream? and Other Symbolic Writings of the Later Years* and *Mark Twain's Fables of Man*, all written around the time of Twain's 1895–6 world lecture tour and after, are themselves part of the challenge, in that they have always raised for readers and scholars a range of fundamental problems: at issue are their textual status and generic location, their aesthetic "incoherence," and their apparent "retreat" from both the humor and the social and political engagement that make Mark Twain one of our best-loved national authors.

Twain himself made the kind of loose association among these various elements – race, spiritualism, imperialism – that is characteristic of his autobiographical dictations in a series of entries for March 1906. Moving from Monday, March 12, to Wednesday, March 21, he touches on newspaper reports of the "slaughter" of six hundred Moros, men, women, and children, by U.S. troops in the Philippines ("'Slaughter' is a good word. . . . They were mere naked savages, and yet there is a sort of pathos about it when that word 'children' falls under your eye, . . . and by help of its deathless eloquence color, creed, and nationality vanish away"), to boyhood memories of "the first Jews" he had ever seen ("It took me a good while to get over the awe of it"), to what he calls "mental telegraphy" ("I imagine that we get most of our thoughts out of somebody else's head, by mental telegraphy – and . . . in the majority of cases, out of the heads of strangers; strangers far removed – Chinamen, Hindus, and all manner of remote foreigners whose language we should not be able to understand, but whose thoughts we can read without difficulty").[1]

Despite intriguing evidence of this free-associative sort, as well as the similarly suggestive evidence of the whole of Twain's later writings, it has not been easy to see how, or even that, the arenas of the racial and the psychological intersect for Twain. But following the lead of two of his African-American contemporaries, Pauline Hopkins and W. E. B. Du Bois, both of whom applied the vocabulary of double or divided consciousness to the race question, we may ask: if the New Psychology, as it was known, proved in their adaptations a racialized science, then why not for Twain too?[2] Following their lead, we may even take as a given the occulted presence of "race" in much of Twain's late writing, ranging from the travel narrative *Following the Equator*, the record of his 1895–6 world lecture tour and of his views of race and colonial relations on the "hot belt of the equator"; to the "dream tales," the fables of nightmarish voyages to alternate worlds and states of mind, only one of which (entitled "Which Was It?") charts the kind of openly racial nightmare characteristic of his explicit narratives of passing and hidden racial identity; to the last and greatest dream tale, *The Mysterious Stranger*, a collection of texts in which an angelic stranger, the young nephew of Satan, draws on an array of psychic powers to offer a series of dreamlike meditations on the fallen human race.

It is rare to group these works together, except in the form of their footnotes, which are like a series of cross-references to their shared cultural context: the repeated, but often unincorporated and unelaborated allusions throughout Twain's late writing to the various imperial ventures of the 1890s (including those of Great Britain in India, the United States in Cuba and the Philippines, and most of the world's powers in China). What connects these works, however, goes beyond even the context of empire and its underlying racial practices. Far from being simply the literary manifestations of Twain's retreat into personal despair that they are so often made out to be, the dream tales, like their companion travel narrative, *Following the Equator*, written during the same period, invoke and adapt the notions of spirit communication and disembodied space-and-time travel, made newly respectable at this time by the investigations of psychical researchers, as a means of revisiting the old terrain of U.S. slavery and linking it to the newer global imperialism, the worldwide nationalism, nativism, and racism of the late 1890s.

These "travel" writings transform a variety of locales, from the American South both before and after the war, to the equatorial colonies of Africa, to Austria of both 1490 and 1702, to the veins of a "tramp" named Blitzowski, into the worlds elsewhere through which Twain reimagines the "Negro Question" – now located both at home and abroad, in the empires of the world, as a continuation of the U.S. past into the global present. Starting with "Which Was It?" and several other little-known, unfinished stories of racial passing and ending with The Mysterious Stranger, the late, unfinished series of manuscripts on the youthful Satan's travels among the human race, Twain variously reimagines "race": as a tragic family romance of denied kinship, role reversal, and revenge; as a hidden source of taint and disease; as a set of customs deforming both slave and master, native and colonizer; and ultimately as a particular subset of what he called the "damned human race," universally enslaved to necessity and its own nature.

In arguing that Twain's late writings return, via the occult, to the familiar subject of race, I am myself going back over the literary terrain of the dream tales that I have already described both as broadly historicized and escapist: immersed in the contexts of the New Psychology and global empire, the tales are divided between the twin impulses to acknowledge racial issues and to turn away from them.[3] But Twain goes much farther here in his engagement with contemporary politics than I first recognized. His transformation of the occult into a specifically racial register in these late works underscores the different uses, ranging from the personal to the cultural, to which he put the available psychological discourses. Theories of spiritualism and occult phenomena gave Twain a particularly rich access to questions of authorship and selfhood, as I argued earlier, but also, and more important in this context, to cultural images of otherness.

That is, when in Following the Equator he uses as the epigraph to a chapter on South African politics the maxim from "Pudd'nhead Wilson's New Calendar," "Everyone is a moon, and has a dark side which he never shows to anybody," he is not thinking simply of double personality or the hidden side of the mind, as it is usually read.[4] Rather he is speaking explicitly in the chapter of his own inability, as a "stranger," to understand the Boer "side of the quarrel" with the British over control of the Transvaal – the ruling Boers themselves in conflict with their native-born subjects, known as Uitlanders (which Twain translates as "strangers, foreigners") in their own land (FE 657). The point here is that there are actually many more than two sides, the light and the dark, to the "Political Pot" of imperial politics in South Africa, as an accompanying Dan Beard illustration of that title suggests with the following labels on the wooden logs stoking the boiling pot of "Africa": "Syndicate, Trusts, Spanish, French, Dutch, English, Negro, Half Breed, Gold Bugs" (FE 655). Complicating this already overflowing, not to say overdetermined, usage of the "dark side" is our discovery a few chapters later that it may also apply to Cecil Rhodes, premier of the British Cape Colony and architect of British expansionist policy in South Africa, who is described as "deputy-God on the one side, deputy-Satan on the other, . . . an Archangel with wings to half the world, Satan with a tail to the other half" (FE 708, 710). The rich, even perplexing, constellation of meanings that Twain associates with the notion of the dark side demonstrates at the very least how culturally, and politically, mobile a metaphor it was. Extending the "dark side" to include the occult, as it was being investigated, theorized, and popularized by a variety of researchers at the time, from Charcot and Bernheim to Freud to William James, we can begin to see the complex system of cultural references that Twain is constructing in what we might call his travels in the racial occult.

The question of genre is also key to reading this group of Twain's late writings, for as so many readers, following his lead, have recognized, the series of unfinished manuscripts that he left largely unpublished at his death reflect repeated efforts to find a form adequate to his later vision – to what he called his "pen warmed up in hell." Even if few (then or now) have found Twain's views on God and the "damned human race" as shocking as he thought they were, still the formal question he raises is a telling one. If, as I will argue, the classic American narrative of racial passing proved a dead end for Twain, then it was a cross between the travel narrative, the form with which he made his literary reputation, and the occult-oriented dream tale that produced the richest of his late writing on the race question.

Twain's most successful narrative approach to the problem of U.S. race slavery was always through voice: the counterposed comic and poignant vernaculars of Huck and Jim, the vernacular outrage of Roxana in *Pudd'nhead Wilson* (1894), next to *Huckleberry Finn* (1885) Twain's best-known novel on race. Almost equally central to his representation of the "Negro Question" was the context of institutional, medico-juridical discourses on race, those that enabled him to grapple in *Pudd'nhead Wilson* with the "fictions of law and custom" constituting racial identity. Yet simultaneous with both of these strategies was another, competing racial narrative which I call that of the "avenging mulatto," Twain's adaptation of the conventional tragic mulatto tale, as figured in works by white "romantic racialists" (Harriet Beecher Stowe, George Washington Cable, and Kate Chopin, for example) as well as by some black writers (William Wells

Brown, Charles Chesnutt, and Nella Larsen, for example). Between the 1880s and the early 1900s, Twain wrote three little-known, unfinished sketches of racial tragedies in which the son of a white master-father and slave mother takes revenge on the father, culminating in patricide. While essentially operating within the conventional narrative boundaries of the tragic mulatto, Twain's tales reverse the terms of that plot. Rather than himself – and the gender is part of the reversal – coming to a tragic end, typically death, separation from a love revealed to be incestuous, or deportation to Europe, Twain's mulatto responds aggressively to his biracial heritage by inflicting the tragic fate not on himself but on his own white father. At this point in the plot, the story breaks off, unconcluded.

What stands out here is the problem of Twain's apparently constitutional inability to complete this particular racial story. It has always been something of a related critical puzzle that *Pudd'nhead Wilson,* a novel that raises textual questions of aesthetic "coherence," or completeness, originally contained in manuscript form much racial material that never appeared in the published editions.[5] Indeed, of Twain's various, little-known "avenging mulatto" sketches, the most "widely" circulated is a series of passages written in the manuscript but deleted by him from the published version, which outline a vestigial patricide plot hatched by the vengeful "white" Tom Driscoll, following his slave-mother Roxana's revelation that he is a black slave, son of an aristocratic white man. These cancelled passages, appended to the Norton *Pudd'nhead Wilson,* confirm what several readers and critics have always asserted, that though the novel culminates in Tom's murder of his supposed white uncle and benefactor, Judge Driscoll, from the "standpoint of imaginative coherence," Judge Driscoll is Tom's father just as clearly as Roxana is his mother. And the suppressed patricide plot thus remains in the novel, barely disguised despite Twain's double stratagem, recognized by Henry Nash Smith and others, of making Roxana the slave of a shadowy brother of Judge Driscoll at the time of Tom's birth and then creating an even more shadowy figure, Colonel Cecil Burleigh Essex, to be Tom's biological father.[6] In fact, in the working notes for the novel, to return once again to the repressed, Twain made Judge Driscoll himself the father of Tom.

What are we to make of this almost impossibly thin disguise? Consulting a range of contemporary writings on the race question may help here, by telling us what people in the late nineteenth century could say about race relations and how they could say it. Put another way, Twain's personal difficulties with saying what he wanted to say reveal as much about the limits and possibilities of American racial rhetoric as they do about him.

Most readers have read Twain's well-recorded self-censorship biographically and psychologically rather than culturally, seeing it in either his squeamishness about the fact of miscegenation between master and female slave or his ambivalence toward his own father, John Marshall Clemens, whom he clearly identified with the gentlemanly Driscolls, Essexes, and other "F.F.V.'s" (First Families of Virginia) humorously and lovingly satirized in the novel. If we place Twain's suppressed patricide plot in the context of other possible plots offered by contemporary race narratives, it emerges strikingly as a telling variant of the tragic mulatto story.

Blackness is conceived in this story as hidden taint, with the conventions of the search for origins and the revelation of kinship that are central to much African-American fiction resulting here in fearful exposure, identity destroying rather than affirming. *Pudd'nhead Wilson* only touches on this process, briefly representing the volcanic "irruption" in Tom Driscoll's psyche upon being made aware (by his mulatto mother) of "the 'nigger' in him." But the manuscript plays with extended moments of realization in passages such as these:

> I must begin a new life to-day – but not outside; no, only inside. I must be the same slangy, useless youth as before, outside, but inside I shall be a nigger with a grievance – . . . I wish I knew my father . . . I will wheedle it out of her some day; and if he is alive, then let him not go out at night.
>
> He loathed the "nigger" in him, but got pleasure out of bringing this secret "filth," as he called it, into familiar and constant contact with the sacred whites. . . . [And there was one thought that sang always in his heart. He called that his father's death-song.] (MMS 234–5, 246–7)

Even in the manuscript the bracketed last sentences are crossed out, emphasizing that the repeated references to the son's killing the father are both the object and the threat. Similarly problematic is the revelation of Tom's "blackness," which brings not the conventional resolution of ambiguous identity but rather a continuation, and intensification, of the former disjunction between "white" outside and "black" inside. In Twain's fantasy that culminates in the specter of violence against the white father, the knowledge of hidden blackness becomes, if anything, a greater threat to white dominance, and indeed to the boundaries of whiteness itself, which so readily harbors the "secret filth" of blackness.

Race is envisioned here almost entirely as a structure of domination and subordination, as relations of power between familial power brokers, father and son. The slave mother is subordinated in the role of victim to the master-father, the source and object of the primary emotion. So, too, are racial-sexual relations almost entirely suppressed, not simply, however, due to Twain's prudery but also because the whole focus of the narrative is on the filial relation, figured as filial taboo. This is the vision Twain pursued in the two other race narratives, one a four-page outline, dated in the 1880s, for a story about a mulatto ("1/16 negro"), "his father his master & mean," who, after the war, "at last, seeing even the best educated negro is at a disadvantage, . . . clips his wiry hair close, wears gloves always (to conceal his telltale nails) & passes for a white man." He falls in love with his cousin – "he used to 'miss' her on the plantation" – and then the notes break off at the climactic moment of revelation:

> At the time of the climax he is telling the stirring story of the heroic devotion of a poor negro mother to her son – of course not mentioning that he was the son & that *his* is the mother who bears the scar which he has described. Then she steps forward and shows the scar she got in saving him from his own father's brutality. So this gassy man is *his* father, & it is his niece whom XX loves, & who with (perhaps) his daughter, supports him.[7]

Though the genealogical ramifications of the plot are confusing – again, the revelation of kinship is far from clarifying – they seem to suggest that others in the story are also exposed as living under the illusion that they are white – shared illusion, the sketch suggests, that is part and parcel of the protagonist's knowing, aggressive passing.

The latest and longest race narrative comes, significantly, at the end of an unfinished novel – "Which Was It?" – published in a collection of Twain's late dream writings.[8] The basic plot resembles that of Twain's major dream tales: a respected and successful family man has a momentary dream of disaster, seeming to last for many years, in which he experiences financial reversal, social disgrace, and, in this case, the accusation of murder. All of the stories break off before the dreamer finally awakens, but only "Which Was It?" concludes with a specifically racial nightmare: the specter of black supremacy, the total reversal of racial power relations.

The protagonist, George Louisiana Purchase Harrison ("It is a curious name, but in a way patriotic. He was born on the date of the signing of the Purchase-treaty"), respectable community leader, reveals what his middle name suggests is the criminal side of American Manifest Destiny when he commits forgery and murder, evidence of which is obtained by the free mulatto Jasper, who then blackmails Harrison for the rest of the story (WWD 179). The payment exacted: Jasper, whose slave-mother is sold down the river and who is swindled out of his freedom by his white master-father, George Harrison's uncle, takes revenge on the nephew by "enslaving" him. Publicly master and servant, in private they exchange roles. "You b'longs to me, now. You's my proppity, same as a nigger, . . . Get up and fetch yo' marster a dram!" (WWD 413), exults Jasper, exposing Harrison's self-image as upright citizen in control of his family's destiny for the illusion Harrison himself already knows it to be. "I was proud of my invincible uprightness . . . and all the time was rotten to the soul. . . . I am an exposed sham; I have found myself out" (WWD 219). Jasper is a projection of unresolved guilt, not simply Harrison's own for the murder he has committed, but more broadly a collective guilt for the national hypocrisy of slavery and, more pointedly, of the postemancipation reinstitution of slavery in the form of legalized segregation. Jasper's predicament as a slave who, having bought himself from "the meanest white man dat ever walked," ends up in his "second slavery" due to the treachery of that master ("he took 'vantage of me en stole [my freedom] back") mimics precisely the national betrayal of the ex-slaves – even to the complicity of the law ("that sells and banishes free niggers") and the courts ("a white man's court") in eroding the rights of the ex-slaves (WWD 415, 320, 308).

To this racial nightmare the story envisions only one response: another nightmare, the master's fantasy of his victim's revenge, the exchange of roles between black and white. Jasper inflicts upon George Harrison the masquerade of freedom that he himself had experienced: "When dey's anybody aroun', I's yo' servant, en pow'ful polite . . . ; en when dey ain't nobody aroun' but me en you, you's *my* servant, en if I don't sweat you!" (WWD 417). Harrison's response, "Slave of an ex-slave! it is the final degradation," underlines the extent to which central insight into race relations here involves the desire for, and certainly the threat of, the absolute exchange of power from white to black. As early as the 1880s, in a notebook entry Twain had predicted "Negro supremacy – the whites underfoot in a hundred years."[9] Jasper embodies narratively the fulfillment of that prediction: "The meek slouch of the slave was gone from him. . . . He *looked* the master; but that which had gone from him was not lost, for his . . . humble mien had passed to his white serf, and already they seemed not out of place there, but fit, and . . . at home" (WWD 415).

At this point of completed racial role reversal, of "Negro supremacy," the narrative breaks off. To pursue the narrative logic beyond this moment would inevitably expose the moral dilemma that the slave must now become like the master and the past repeat itself. Of course, this is a dilemma only from the standpoint that assigns one-dimensionality to blackness, dividing docility from aggression – the white response to black vengefulness. It is as if there was simply no more that could be said on race conceived through this binary, as if Twain had reached a dead end in the limits both of his own moral dilemma and of this particular narrative form. Despite the numerous gestures made in these three pieces toward rewriting the story of the tragic mulatto – the cruel master-father, the heroic slave-mother, the vengeful mulatto son – Twain's racial vision, itself bifurcated, ultimately could not be accommodated by that popular form. It would take the global vision of international travel as well as the increasing pressures of world imperialism for Twain to return, with a new, more expansive vision, to the American racial scene.

Following the Equator (1897), the travel book based on Twain's 1895–6 around-the-world lecture tour, which took him from the Pacific Northwest to Australia, New Zealand, Ceylon, India, and South Africa, announces its connection to the U.S. racial context of *Pudd'nhead Wilson* with the maxims from "Pudd'nhead Wilson's New Calendar" that head each chapter. But the travel narrative, engaging a variety of racial and national groups, moves beyond the claustrophobic world of the prewar South in more than simply a geographical sense. Here the black–white binary that defines the U.S. racial system and the master narrative of U.S. race relations gives way to the complexities of race and nation in the colonial context: like Du Bois, who equated race and nation in "The Conservation of Races," Twain is struck by the variety of "nationalities and complexions" in Mauritius ("island under French control"), including "French, English, Chinese, Arabs, Africans with wool, blacks with straight hair, East Indians, half-whites, quadroons – and great varieties in costumes and colors" (FE 617). And here the race–sex nexus that Twain largely shies away from in the avenging mulatto sketches emerges more fully, in the images of blackness and sexuality that are repeatedly associated in his focus on the sensuality of black skin, bodies, and clothing. Most important, however, this around-the-world travelogue establishes a mode of occult travel, of travel across time and space, that links the U.S. and global racial contexts. The result is a penetrating, and often exuberant, satiric meditation on the racial practices that undergird the institutions of empire and U.S. race slavery alike.

When Twain crosses the equator and arrives in Ceylon, he enters a dreamlike state of "Oriental charm and mystery" that forms, in one respect, the heart of *Following the Equator* (FE 336). Much as in mediumistic trance, Twain cultivates a susceptibility to the spirit(s) of the place, a sensitivity that signals ironically not simply otherworldly escape, but also engagement with the cultures confronting him – extending back to the world of his own American past. Twain's mode of occult travel oscillates between, on the one

hand, dreamy nostalgia for the past and an exoticizing orientalism in the
present and, on the other hand, confrontation with the criminality and
corruption of both. And race is central to both modes as well, to the attraction and the threat of past and present.

Ceylon is "utterly Oriental" in comparison with the "tempered Orient"
of Cairo, "an Orient with an indefinite something wanting," much, we are
told in the kind of cross-cultural comparison that will become increasingly
frequent, as Florida or New Orleans is "a modified South, a tempered
South" (FE 339). One hallmark of Twain's orientalism is the exotic aura of
black and brown skin: in Ceylon "that wilderness of rich color, that incom-
parable dissolving-view of harmonious tints, and lithe half-covered forms,
and beautiful brown faces"; in Bombay the "sprinkling of white people"
among the million inhabitants is "not enough to have the slightest modify-
ing effect on the massed dark complexion of the public" (FE 340–3, 345).
Another hallmark is the explicit dreaminess – the sense of a distant and
decaying world – of the oriental, or "tropical," experience: in Ceylon, "this
dream of fairyland and paradise," "there was that swoon in the air . . . , and
in the remoteness of the mountains were the ruined cities and mouldering
temples, the mysterious relics of a forgotten time and a vanished race"; in
India, "a bewitching place, a bewildering place, an enchanting place," we
enter "the land of dreams and romance, of fabulous wealth and fabulous
poverty, of splendor and rags, of palaces and hovels" (FE 339–40, 343, 345,
347). Here, on the "hot belt of the equator," we have clearly arrived at the
very center of the voyage, Twain's own paradoxical heart of darkness,
where this remote orientalized land of dream and romance merges, both
pleasurably and disturbingly, with memories of Twain's boyhood in the
antebellum South (FE 339).

The drowsy, dreamy atmosphere itself that heralds the "real" Orient for
Twain should be familiar to his readers as the incantation of Hannibal, the
same means by which he summons up all the images of his boyhood village
in his fiction, from *Huck Finn*'s St. Petersburg to *Pudd'nhead Wilson*'s
Dawson's Landing to *The Mysterious Stranger*'s Eseldorf.[10] Even more explicitly, however, Twain links "your long-ago dreams of India rising in a sort
of vague and luscious moonlight above the horizon-rim of your opaque
consciousness" to "a thousand forgotten details which were parts of a
vision that had once been vivid to you when you were a boy, and steeped
your spirit in tales of the East" (FE 357). The elements of this oriental vision – "the princely titles," "the romances" of the exchange of princes
and paupers in their cradles – are all also familiar parts of the world of
Pudd'nhead Wilson, where aristocratic Southerners with pretentious,

English-sounding names and pseudomilitary titles are confronted with robberies and murder originating in the exchange of "black" and "white" babies in their cradles (FE 357–8). Indeed, at one point, in a series of chapters on native crime in India, Twain humorously insists that criminality, in the form of "Indian Thuggee," forms a fundamental space–time continuum between his American past and the equatorial present. Remembering how fifty years ago, as a boy in "the then remote and sparsely peopled Mississippi valley," he had heard "vague tales and rumors of a mysterious body of professional murderers come wandering in from a country which was constructively as far from us as the constellations blinking in space – India," he then recounts how he has just now on his trip come across a copy of the very "Government Report" that originated the Thug tales: "It is full of fascinations; and it turns those dim, dark fairy tales of my boyhood days into realities" (FE 426–7).

Among those dim, dark tales of professional murderers was the story of Murell's Gang, American Thugs "once celebrated," Twain says in his 1883 travel book *Life on the Mississippi,* as "a colossal combination of robbers, horse-thieves, . . . and counterfeiters," who were most notorious, however, for trading in slaves, stealing and then reselling them along the Mississippi River. Twain immortalizes Murell as a "wholesale" rascal to Jesse James's "retail" rascal in *Life on the Mississippi,* specifically because of Murell's exploitation of both the profits and fears engendered by slavery. Engaged in the slave trade, Murell and his associates also planned to foment "negro insurrections and the capture of New Orleans." A long passage quoted from the account of "this big operator" (as Twain calls him) in Marryat's *Diary in America* documents how the gang would sell the same slave three or four times over (inciting him to run away from each master with promises of money and freedom) and then murder him (to get rid of the only possible witness against them), while their "ultimate intentions" were "on a very extended scale, having no less an object in view than raising the blacks against the whites, taking possession of, and plundering New Orleans, and making themselves possessors of the territory."[11] This specifically racial criminality, predicated on slave rebelliousness, is reiterated in *Tom Sawyer,* where the vengeful half-breed Injun Joe's buried treasure is said to have been the booty of Murell's Gang. The dim, dark fairy tales of Twain's boyhood are revealed, in the context of Indian Thuggee, to be just that, as dreams as dim and dark as the nightmare of black revenge in *Which Was It?*.

If we continue to pursue the notion that criminality marks an occult, racialized connection between Twain's oriental present and American past, then the paradigmatic episode establishing the occult mode in *Following the Equator* is his recounting of the beating of a native servant that he witnesses on the first night at his hotel in Bombay. The hotel is full of "dark native servants," all looking as though "dressed for a part in the Arabian Nights," "turbaned, and fez'd and embroidered, cap'd, and barefooted, and cotton-clad" (FE 348). A white man, "a burly German," dissatisfied in some way with one of the natives, gives him a "brisk cuff on the jaw," which, Twain notes, the native took with "meekness," showing no apparent resentment (FE 351). The sight triggers the return of a long series of repressed memories, again of his boyhood in the antebellum South:

> I had not seen the like of this for fifty years. It carried me back to my boyhood, and flashed upon me the forgotten fact that this was the *usual* way of explaining one's desires to a slave. I was able to remember that the method seemed right and natural to me in those days, I being born to it and unaware that elsewhere there were other methods; but I was also able to remember that those unresented cuffings made me sorry for the victim and ashamed for the punisher.   (FE 351)

The punisher is none other than Clemens's father. Here, rather than demonize the father, as Twain does in the mulatto tales, in order, fundamentally, to reject his own past, he cultivates the more forgiving cultural relativism induced by the "elsewhere" of travel. Continuing his environmental line of argument on his own warped, childhood sense of what seemed "right and natural," he explains that his father was "'a refined and kindly gentleman, very grave . . . and upright," who rarely laid a hand on his family; however, he "had passed his life among the slaves from the cradle up, and his cuffings proceeded from the custom of the time, not from his nature" (FE 352). The father and son share the same flawed birthright, the "custom of the time," which the son unequivocally rejects as an adult and yet which enables his identification with his father and his past.

Why are the sins of the Southern father viewed so sympathetically in this travelogue? More than simply the comparative cultural perspective or the relativism of actual travel, it is the mode of occult travel that makes the difference here. Twain concludes his long meditation on the punishment of natives and slaves by saluting the thrill of mental travel, of space-and-time travel:

> It is curious – the space-annihilating power of thought. For just one second, all that goes to make the *me* in me was in a Missourian village, on the other side of the globe, vividly seeing again these forgotten pictures of fifty years ago, and wholly unconscious of all things but just those; and in the next second I

was back in Bombay, and that kneeling native's smitten cheek was not done tingling yet! Back to boyhood – fifty years; back to age again, another fifty; and in a flight equal to the circumference of the globe – all in two seconds by the watch! (FE 352)

The sheer exuberance of this representation of the experience of occult travel nearly outweighs the pain, and the implied condemnation, of the triggering event, the beating of the native. Indeed, we might say that the time travel enables both a recovery of the past, steeped in conflict and guilt as well as dreamy nostalgia, and a retreat from it. It is precisely the oscillation from the dream vision of the Missouri village, itself a source of both pleasure and anxiety, to the reality of Bombay, itself divided between both the exoticism and the otherness of the racialized Orient, that enacts the central rhythm of *Following the Equator*: the movement, alternately reassuring and unsettling, between U.S. race slavery and global imperialism, both social structures that Twain condemns absolutely even as they bring into focus ambivalent desires (simultaneous attraction and repulsion for the other and for the father).

Of the racial practices that connect these institutions, Twain focuses, as we have seen, on the role of custom in deforming the master as well as the slave and, by implication, the colonizer as well as the colonized. Even some of the book's best-known, most overt anti-imperialism appeals, ironically, to the "law of custom" as the justification for the "laying on" of European civilization around the world:

Dear me, robbery by European nations of each other's territories has never been a sin, . . . All the territorial possessions of all the political establishments in the earth – including America, of course – consist of pilferings from other people's wash. . . . In Europe and Asia and Africa every acre of ground has been stolen several millions of times. A crime persevered in a thousand centuries ceases to be a crime, and becomes a virtue. This is the law of custom, and custom supersedes all other forms of law. (FE 623–4)

We are now in a global version of the world of *Pudd'nhead Wilson*, where the "custom" of territorial robbery becomes analogous to the practice of racial classification, defined in the novel as a "fiction of law and custom." The question of racial grouping by skin color forges a final, important relationship between Twain's antebellum past and the imperial present.

The orientalizing of blackness throughout *Following the Equator* does not go much beyond a conventional exoticizing of difference until Twain constructs a comparative vision of white and black complexions. In India, struck once again by the sight of native costume and color, Twain muses on the comparative disadvantage of "Christian" clothing and white skin color. "Where dark complexions are massed, they make the whites look bleached-out, unwholesome, and sometimes frankly ghastly. I could notice this as a boy, down South in the slavery days before the war" (FE 381). Then, in a classic moment of occult travel, Twain looks outside his window in London, where he is writing the book, and compares the white passers-by with the picture in his mind of "the splendid black satin skin of the South African Zulus of Durban" ("I can see those Zulus yet . . .") (FE 381). The result is a list of the gradations of whiteness, complete with cartoon-like illustrations of various deformed-looking white faces, entitled "The Passers-By," that comes close to parodying the racial classifications of degrees of blackness that were standard throughout most of the colonial world, from Latin America to South Africa – almost everywhere, in fact, except in the United States. Ranging from "complexion, new parchment" and "old parchment," to "grayish skin, with purple areas" and "whitey-gray," to "unwholesome fish-belly skin" and "ghastly white," the list of the "tint which we miscall white" brings to mind nothing so much as the terms for fractional degrees of racial mixture, which Twain satirizes in his description of the French colony of Mauritius, the very place, we remember, whose variety of "nationalities and complexions" he also so admired (FE 382–3):

> The majority [of the population] is East Indian; then mongrels; then negroes . . . ; then French; then English. There was an American, but he is dead or mislaid. The mongrels are the result of all kinds of mixtures; black and white, mulatto and white, octoroon and white. And so there is every shade of complexion. (FE 620)

The passage concludes with another list of skin colors, this one the mirror image of the white passers-by, ranging from "ebony" and "horse-chesnut," to "molasses-candy," and ending finally with "fish-belly white – this latter the leprous complexion frequent with the Anglo-Saxon long resident in tropical climates" (FE 620). The repetition of "fish-belly white," best remembered as Twain's immortal term of disgust for the abusive, poor-white Pap Finn, forges the final occult link between the antebellum South and the imperial Orient. The logic of U.S. racial division, based on the "one-drop rule" and therefore assuming degrees of blackness only – white is a "pure" category – is exploded within the context of colonial race relations, where nation competes and blurs with race, and whiteness is made to appear alien, defamiliarized by the "massed dark complexion of the public."

If *Following the Equator* moved Twain away from the notion of blackness as hidden taint, so central to the tragic mulatto plot, he returned to that vision, with a different, spiritualist-inflected angle in the long, unfinished "Three Thousand Years Among the Microbes," written in 1905, just before the end of yet another imperial conflict, the Japanese defeat of czarist Russia.[12] Narrated by the human subject of a failed experiment that has transformed him into a microbe, specifically a cholera germ, "infesting" the blood of a "tramp" named Blitzowski – a Hungarian immigrant! – this bizarre travel narrative catalogs the microbe's journey among the "swarming nations of germ-vermin" within the "planet" of the tramp's body. Although it may seem strange to place this fantastic tale in the context of *Following the Equator,* it was on that trip, in Sydney, that Twain says he dreamed his "large" microbe dream: "that the vast worlds that we see twinkling millions of miles apart in the fields of space are the blood corpuscles in [God's] veins; and that we and the other creatures are the microbes that charge with multitudinous life the corpuscles" (FE 132). This particular dream, which Twain had first recorded in his notebook in August 1884, when he was preparing *Huck Finn* for publication, establishes a series of links between the microbe story and Twain's various narratives of travel and race relations. First, elaborating on the notion of the diseased, hidden self that constitutes one version of the racial unconscious for Twain, he stresses how unaware the microbes are that their planet ("their world, their globe, lord of their universe") is the "mouldering" body of an undesirable Hungarian tramp ("he was shipped to America by Hungary because Hungary was tired of him") and that they are themselves infecting his blood and tissue (WWD 436, 504). And then, extending this notion outward, into a further response to the increasing pressures of global imperialism, particularly the U.S. annexation of the Philippines in 1899 and the subsequent military occupation of the islands, he makes all of the microbic nations into thinly disguised versions of the world's empires and colonies, one "feeding on" another, just as, Satan explains in *The Mysterious Stranger,* England has "swallowed" India and Europe is "swallowing" China.[13]

Even more pointedly and exuberantly, "Microbes" refashions the mode of occult travel in *Following the Equator*'s dream work by inverting the spiritualist notion of out-of-body travel: instead of multiple personalities or levels of consciousness inhabiting one mind, we get alternate worlds coexisting within the tramp's body. Moreover, this is a spiritualist's paradise where alternate forms of life continue on after death. To the microbe-narrator, who can see molecular activity invisible to the human eye, the "charnel house" of the tramp's body is not full of death but life and motion: ". . . with my microbe-eye I could see *every individual* of the whirling billions of *atoms* that *compose* the speck. . . . Many have wandered away and joined themselves to new plasmic forms, and are continuing their careers in the bodies of . . . other creatures. . . . And so our people here have no word to signify that either a person or his spirit is *dead,* in our sense of that term" (WWD 447, 457, Twain's emphasis). In part a reference to one of Twain's favorite objects of satire, Mary Baker Eddy's Christian Science ("Kitchen Science"), this spiritualist's fantasy alludes explicitly, the narrative acknowledges, to the work of "a man like Sir Oliver Lodge," well-known British physicist and original sponsor of the British Society for Psychical Research (SPR), of whom the microbe-narrator asks rather sardonically, "What secret of Nature can be hidden from him?" (WWD 447). As a member of the SPR's Committee on Physical Phenomena, Lodge conducted a series of experiments with the notorious medium Mrs. Piper, designed in part to verify the so-called phenomena of "psychic excursions" or "travelling clairvoyance," in which, the theory goes, a spirit from outside can enter the organism or the spirit from inside can go out – both of which Twain transforms into his own mode of occult travel in the microbe story.[14]

Published in the 1968 collection *Which Was the Dream?,* the microbe story not only adapts the spiritualist psychic excursion but also inverts Twain's own dream plot by beginning with the narrator's having awakened into another existence, this one incorporating a mirror image of America, his former country, in the "Republic of Getrichquick." "Under its flag is the whole of Blitzowski's stomach, which is the richest country, . . . the most prodigally and variously endowed with material resources in all the microbic world" (WWD 442). Here, the dream frame clearly serves as a window on the world rather than on the mind, as an avenue not so much to the individual unconscious, as it is for example in the theory of waking and dream selves adumbrated in the "Print Shop" manuscript of *The Mysterious Stranger,* but rather to the cultural unconscious of the late-nineteenth-century world of empire.

Parodying a variety of anti-immigrant sentiments, the microbe-narrator, an "instantly naturalized" citizen, calls himself "Huck" ("an abbreviation of my American middle name, Huxley") but compensates for this foreignness by his microbic "patriotism" that "out-natived the natives themselves": "I was become intensely, passionately, cholera-germanic; . . . I was the germiest of the germy" (WWD 435, 471). This assimilation does not stop him from trading on his exoticism, entertaining his microbe-family with a program of "sentimental music" from the minstrel shows of his past ("I don't 'low no Coon to Fool roun' Me"; WWD 462). In a further parody of the nativist view of the immigrant as permanently alien, he straddles the borders of his two worlds, constantly translating, linguistically, chronologically, and otherwise, between them, and amusing the microbic "boys" (among them a friend of his, a yellow-fever germ with an unpronounceable name that he "had to modify to Benjamin Franklin") with Old World stories of the "Cuban skirmish" and the "Jap–Russian War" (WWD 448, 538–9). In Twain's larger satire, of course, the international aggressions of the early twentieth century correspond to their mirror images in the "planet Blitzowski": a particular focus is the Republic of Getrichquick, which ends an era of "selfish isolation" with the "high and holy policy" of "Benevolent Assimilation," in which a "collection of mud islets inhabited by harmless bacilli" "was first ingeniously wrested from its owners, by help of the unsuspicious owners themselves, then it was purchased from its routed and dispossessed foreign oppressors at a great price" (WWD 443). Thus did Twain articulate, in barely disguised form in this fantastic narrative of 1905, his by then well-known criticism of the ongoing U.S. intervention in the Philippines.

The spotlight on U.S. imperialism in "Microbes" raises a number of questions. One, to which I will return in my conclusion, is the problem of the submerged history throughout Twain's dream writings, sometimes submerged as it is here, just below the surface, but sufficiently so that the dream tales are generally misread as escapist, retreating from the world of history and reality. Another is the question raised by William Gibson, the textual editor of *The Mysterious Stranger*, about the complete absence of the Spanish–American War from those stories, many of which are permeated by equally submerged allusions to world empires, past and present. "Microbes" was written in May–June 1905, just as Twain was returning to further work on the last *Mysterious Stranger* manuscript, "No. 44, The Mysterious Stranger," or the "Print Shop" version, where he would add chapters burlesquing a minstrel show and satirizing both Mary Baker Eddy and imperial Russia – all of which material he had just included in some form in "Microbes," along with the long section on Getrichquick's Benevolent Assimilation of the archipelago of the Philippines. It is as though the two works, "Microbes" and *The Mysterious Stranger*, like so many of Twain's later writings, are intertwined, each partaking of the imaginative and cultural engagements of the other. Reading them together, along with several other contemporary, allied texts, as a kind of continuous work enables us to see the three unfinished manuscripts of *The Mysterious Stranger* as an ensemble, if not a "coherent whole," joining the "Matter of Hannibal" to world empire at the turn of the century and moving toward a broad-ranging meditation on ethnic, religious, and nationalist violence throughout world history.

Written between 1897 and 1908, *The Mysterious Stranger* consists of at least four versions that survive in three manuscripts, all set in either ante-bellum Hannibal or Austria during what Twain considers the Middle Ages (whether 1702 or 1490). The settings tend to blend together, in part all variants on the "Matter of Hannibal," as Henry Nash Smith long ago noted: the Austrian settings of the two longest manuscripts, "Chronicle of Young Satan" and "No. 44," are both initially invoked through identical dream openings, evocations of the same willed state of drowsy, partial consciousness that was always essential to Twain's literary representations of boyhood, whether in *Tom Sawyer, Huck Finn,* or *Pudd'nhead Wilson.* "Austria was far from the world, and asleep, and our village . . . drowsed in peace in the deep privacy of a hilly and woodsy solitude where news of the world hardly ever came to disturb its dreams" (MS 35, 221).[15] This is also, of course, virtually the same dreamy sensibility that Twain cultivates in *Following the Equator,* not, however, as a mode of remote distancing but as one of occult connection, a summoning up of the worlds of both his U.S. past and global present. Similarly, the *Mysterious Stranger* settings add up to more than a series of images of Hannibal, for they signal a new link between U.S. race slavery of the past and global imperialism of the present: crudely put, Hannibal brings up the "Negro Question," Austria brings up the "Jewish Question," and Twain draws once again on the occult matter of spiritualism, embodying it in the array of psychic powers attributed to Satan, the "spirit control" (in the parlance of psychical research) of all the *Mysterious Stranger* stories in order to bring together the two questions, and their separate times and places, in a vision of universal human enslave-ment. Indeed, as we will see, the *Stranger* manuscripts, together with several allied texts, forge a matrix of associations: between the "mild domestic slavery" of Hannibal and the more brutal racism of turn-of-the-century empire, between the ancient bondage of the Jews and the contemporary enslavement of blacks, particularly African-Americans, between race and the occult (MTA 1: 124). Finally, all of these references, like so much of the history permeating Twain's late, dream writing, are articulated not directly or explicitly, but in a fragmented, associative mode characteristic of the cultural life of stereotypes, racial and otherwise.

Twain began *The Mysterious Stranger* in Vienna in the winter of 1897, when anti-Semitism was reaching new extremes on the Continent, with both the notorious Dreyfus case in France (which made world headlines for more than ten years after Dreyfus was convicted of treason in 1894 and which Twain discussed frequently) and periodic attacks on Austrian Jews, scape-goats for the many political and nationalist conflicts between Austria and

Hungary. The Austrian context, identified with the "Jewish Problem," clearly found its way into the first, and, some believe, most influential, of the *Stranger* manuscripts, "Chronicle of Young Satan," a reworking of an earlier fragment set in St. Petersburg of the 1840s, now transmuted into the Austrian village of Eseldorf, site of the adventures of three young boys, their good and evil priests, and the stranger known both as Philip Traum and as Satan, after his uncle. Several textual scholars have noted that Twain derived his portrait of the evil priest, Father Adolf, from several of the Austrian political figures whom he lambasted, in part for their anti-Semitism, in "Stirring Times in Austria," an essay published in *Harper's Magazine* of March 1898.[16]

But a far more substantive link between the Hannibal and Austrian contexts, and, by extension, between the black and Jewish questions, emerges in a better-known companion article, "Concerning the Jews," written in the summer of 1898 in response to letters from Jewish readers alarmed by Twain's report of persecution of Austrian Jews and published in September 1899 in *Harper's Monthly*.[17] What Twain called "the Jew article," and what I see as one of the allied texts of *The Mysterious Stranger*, invokes Satan as a figure of the persecuted Jew.[18] The connection would, of course, have been ready-made in the nineteenth century, given the long tradition of condemning the Jews as murderers of Christ. Twain, however, rings his own change on that connection, reclaiming both Satan and the Jews as victims of religious hatred. Beginning with the question of his own "race, color, caste, and creed prejudices," Twain asserts that he is not even prejudiced against Satan and perhaps even "leans a little his way on account of his not having a fair show." As a persecuted innocent, Satan explicitly raises the context of the Dreyfus case. Condemned by "all religions" without having presented his "side" or his "case," Satan provides the "precedent" for Dreyfus's condemnation – Dreyfus whom Twain elsewhere consistently defended as an "innocent man," "a persecuted and unoffending man" ("Concerning" 236–7).[19] If Satan here is virtually identified as a Jew, at the end of the essay the Jew – meaning, Twain specifies, "both a religion and a race" – becomes an analogue for Satan ("Concerning" 237). Characterizing the eternal race prejudice against the Jew as rooted in his being a "foreigner in the German sense – *stranger*," Twain notes that "even the angels dislike a foreigner. . . . You will always be by ways and habits and predilections substantially strangers – foreigners – wherever you are, and that will probably keep the race prejudice against you alive. But you were the favorites of Heaven originally" ("Concerning" 248).

As if this were not enough to re-create the Jew in the image of Twain's own fallen angel and stranger, he concludes the essay with an extravagant, world-historical vision of Jewish immortality that sounds for all the world like the cosmic displays of the angelic immortal mind in several versions of *The Mysterious Stranger*: the first version, "Chronicle," culminates with young Satan's "history of the progress of the human race" from the Egyptian, Greek, and Roman wars to the present, and the last version with No. 44's "Assembly of the Dead," a procession of skeletons throughout history (MS 134, 400):

> The Egyptian, the Babylonian, and the Persian rose, filled the planet with sound and splendor, then faded to dream-stuff and passed away; the Greek and the Roman followed, and made a vast noise, and they are gone; . . . The Jew saw them all, beat them all, and is now what he always was, exhibiting no . . . infirmities of age, . . . no dulling of his alert and aggressive mind. All things are mortal but the Jew; all other forces pass, but he remains. What is the secret of his immortality? ("Concerning" 249)

If on one level this tribute to the Jews inadvertently trades on the anti-Semite's stereotypical image of the successful Jew, still Twain's "Jew article" was a powerful enough defense to elicit attempts in Germany, from his death in 1910 through the Nazi era, to prove that he was a Jew, "Salamon Clemens."[20]

During the years of writing *The Mysterious Stranger*, under the pressure of world events – the "despotisms and aristocracies and chattel slaveries, and military slaveries, and religious slaveries, . . . all about the globe" – the Jewish Question came, ironically, even closer to home, to Hannibal itself.[21] In Twain's autobiographical dictations for March 1906, we recall, he moved from discussions of the U.S. military occupation of the Philippines to childhood memories of the Levin boys, "the first Jews I had ever seen." The rest of the entry suggests first, and most directly, how Hannibal's Jews were linked, in Twain's imagination, to U.S. race slavery and, second, though far less explicitly, to his meditation on universal human enslavement in the *Stranger* stories. Of those "first Jews," he says:

> To my fancy they were clothed invisibly in the damp and cobwebby mold of antiquity. They carried me back to Egypt, and in imagination I moved among the Pharohs. . . . The name of the boys was Levin. We had a collective name for them. . . . We called them Twenty-two – and even when the joke was old and had been worn threadbare we always followed it with the explanation, to make sure that it would be understood, "Twice Levin – twenty-two."
> (MTA 2: 218)

To locate these Jews, with their special aura of biblical enslavement, in the midst of Hannibal, "a slave-holding community," as Twain calls it elsewhere in the autobiography, that is, in the heart of the antebellum South, is to gesture toward the identification between the pharaonic bondage of the Israelites and U.S. chattel slavery that is characteristic of the nineteenth-century American racial imagination, both black and white. A number of narratives, mythical and historical, were used, especially in the elaboration of slave identity, to bring into focus the black–Jewish parallel: biblical tales of cooperation between blacks and Jews, the stories of Solomon, the queen of Sheba, and the Exodus, in particular the heroic figure of Moses.[22] But if the analogue in most abolitionist and postbellum African-American writing was to the deliverance of the Jews from Egypt, for Twain the identification between Jewishness and blackness focused specifically on the fact of enslavement itself.

This is the analogical or allegorical association made in two nearly identical stories, written during the late 1890s but set in the 1840s, in which a young Jew rescues a slave girl who has been won in a poker game by a notorious gambler and is to be sold away, not from her family, but from her white mistress. In both "Newhouse's Jew Story" and "Randall's Jew Story," the slave girl is nearly white, and beautiful, maid and mistress are as close as sisters, and the Jew's defeat of the gambler in a duel marks him as "a man." The Jew's story is thus expressed through a series of racial stereotypes by a frame narrator whose stated intention is to tell a tale of one Jew that explains why the narrator, himself once a Jew "hater," can no longer tolerate such prejudice.[23] Like the Levin entry, these stories mobilize a number of ethnic and racial stereotypes of both Jewishness and blackness in the service of rejecting the body of those stereotypes.

All of Twain's Jew stories, then, including the Levin entry, forge a partially articulated connection between anti-Semitism and race slavery. This is also how the Jewish question enters *The Mysterious Stranger*: through indirection and analogy, as Henry Nash Smith acknowledged in his tentative suggestion that Satan's name of "Quarant-quatre or Forty-four" (in both "Schoolhouse Hill," actually set in Hannibal, and "No. 44, The Mysterious Stranger") may derive from extending the Levin joke to twice twenty-two.[24] But the Satan-as-Jew analogue need not rely only on Smith's ingenious numerical argument, or only on the Satan-Dreyfus figure of "Concerning the Jews." The *Stranger* manuscripts themselves, as well as the working notes, provide a series of equally suggestive, equally tentative allusions to a black–Jewish association, one that ultimately crosses or intersects with the occult as that specific ethnic pairing is generalized into the work's universal vision of human enslavement to the "Moral Sense," God, and history.

Although, or perhaps because, Satan is endowed with virtually every psychic power ever investigated by spiritualists, from clairvoyance and telepathy, to the mediumistic ability to summon spirits of the dead, he is the stranger, misunderstood and feared by most human authorities, the priests in particular. As the stranger, he is both exoticized (by the boys he befriends) and outcast (by the rest), in the classic division of attraction and repulsion toward the other. Twain's working notes make Satan almost more of an explicit figure of otherness than the *Stranger* stories themselves do, persistently associating him with "disease-germs" – "he is to find the diseases & tortures & microbes" – in a fantasy that found expression in "Three Thousand Years Among the Microbes" (MS 416, 421). At the same time these notes touch on numerous references to Jews. Planning "Chronicle of Young Satan" while he lived in Vienna, he listed the following in close proximity: a set of apparently parallel settings, "Village," "Castle on heights," "Ghetto, Jew J. Goldschmidt, I. Nussbaum," "New Jerusalem"; Satan's decline ("disease invades him, . . . he is persecuted, but remains a heretic; so they torture him, convict him, damn him & burn him"); and, finally, "Stoning the Jews (passing remark)" (MS 418, 421). Without making too much of too little evidence, I would suggest that the various faces of Twain's Satan, as a long-standing icon of his imagination, reflect what Sander Gilman calls the protean nature of stereotypes, the tendency of such major categories of difference as race, sexuality, and pathology to become associated, to stand in for one another, even when "their association demands a suspension of common sense." So that Satan, the fallen angel, is the Jew, at once the persecuted, the diseased, and the chosen, just as, we will see, as No. 44 he transforms himself into the specter of a black slave playing both Bones and Banjo in a minstrel show.[25] In the context of this genealogy, one of the most striking of Twain's various lists of ideas for the *Stranger* starts with "Old Ship of Zion" and moves to "Mesmerism, Nigger Minstrels, Spirit rappings, Materializing" (MS 436).

Thus, Satan becomes Twain's medium, his conduit to the racial spirits haunting both his present and his past. It is telling that "Schoolhouse Hill," the only manuscript set in Hannibal and the only one to address directly the question of U.S. slavery, is also explicitly steeped in the occult. A village among whose citizens are a "'nigger' trader" and a newly converted spiritualist, this fictionalized Hannibal provides the setting for the manuscript described by textual editor William M. Gibson as "apparently . . . both an essay in the correction of ideas and a comedy set in the world of Tom

Sawyer and Huck Finn, whose boy-hero would like to reform and save it" (MS 8). Gibson also speculates that there is even a possible Jewish connection in this story of the village that needs reforming: in his notebook for June and July 1897, Gibson says, Twain wrote "some notes for a 'New Huck Finn' in which the 'Lev'n' boys were to be suspiciously regarded by the town"; then Twain has, "Instead of 11, call them 9 (Nein) and 18" (MS 473). This protean black–Jewish association, locating the Jewish Question in the world of Hannibal, where the Negro Question was paramount, was never fully realized, but in the story as Twain wrote it, not only is "Marse" Oliver Hotchkiss, the slave-owning head of the household in which young "Forty-four" appears (and a figure of the Clemens brother Orion), a sometime spiritualist ("the latest thing in religions was the Fox-girl Rochester rappings; so he was a Spiritualist for the present"), but also during a snowstorm he stages a séance to materialize the spirit of the lost Forty-four during which "slave-State etiquette" is breached: as a newly converted abolitionist, he insists that all around the table hold hands, including his two slaves (MS 191, 205). This promising foray into the racial occult breaks off just as the slaves Aunt Rachel and Uncle Jeff are arguing with Marse Oliver about what he calls their "ignorant prejudice" against devils like Forty-four (MS 219).

In the last *Stranger* manuscript, however, the cross between matters racial and spiritual becomes for Twain a means of extended identification with the enslavement and suffering of African-Americans. Near the end of "No. 44," in yet another exhibition of 44's supernatural powers, he materializes as a "black man," "Cunnel Bludso's nigger fum Souf C'yarlina" and performs the traditional song and dance of the minstrel show. Simultaneously a figure of humor and pathos, he plays the banjo and sings ("in a sort of bastard English") "Buffalo Gals," addresses the young boy-narrator as "honey," and, finally, sings (in "a sweet voice, such a divine voice") "Swanee River" (MS 354–5).

> And so on, verse after verse, sketching his humble lost home, . . . and the black faces that had been dear to him, and which he would look upon no more – and by the magic of it that uncouth figure lost its uncouthness and became lovely like the song, . . . whereas a silken dress and a white face and white graces would have profaned it, and cheapened its noble pathos. (MS 356)

The narrator concludes by stressing the spiritualist side of this racial vision. Closing his eyes to try to picture that lost home, he opens them to find himself right there, in front of a log cabin in "a mellow summer twilight," only to feel the vision "fading, fading, . . . like a dream," as his room and furniture dimly reappear, "spectrally, with the perishing home showing vaguely, through it, as through a veil" (MS 356). We do not really need the reminder of Du Boisean double consciousness, with its similarly racialized invocation of the veil, to affirm the meaning of Twain's location in the racial occult here. For in the very next chapter he himself makes explicit the significance of the minstrel show vision with the plea of the narrator's Duplicate, his "dream-creature," named appropriately Emil Schwarz, linking blackness and Jewishness in the German, to "free me from . . . these bonds of flesh." Asserting that, like other dream spirits, "we do not know time, we do not know space – we live, and love, and labor, and enjoy, fifty years in an hour, while you are sleeping, snoring, repairing your crazy tissues," he pleads with the narrator to "be my friend and brother" and "take away this rotting flesh and set my spirit free!" "Oh, here I am a servant! – I who never served before; here I am a slave – slave among little mean kings and emperors made of clothes, the kings and emperors slaves themselves, to mud-built carrion that are *their* slaves!" (MS 369–70, Twain's emphasis). This is the work's final vision of universal human enslavement, containing and collapsing within it all of the historically specific nationalist, religious, and ethnic persecutions encompassed by *The Mysterious Stranger,* from the medieval witch-hunt, to the French Revolution, to European missionary and colonial violence in China and India.

What is at stake in paying so much critical attention to a body of writing that Mark Twain never completed? And why focus particularly on the presence in this collection of fragments of a history of race and colonial relations that is so easy to miss? Despite the aspersions cast on Twain's personal inability to confront or acknowledge issues of slavery, miscegenation, and race, what he and his late writings have to teach us is not idiosyncratic to him. Rather, in both their generic and formal "messiness" – the critical and aesthetic challenges they pose – these texts are, strange to say, characteristic of much "race literature" of the period. From Du Bois's *Souls of Black Folk,* to black women's "sentimental fiction," to the historical romances of George Washington Cable, Thomas Dixon, and others, these works present Twainian problems of unusual, or mixed, generic boundaries: in a word, are they art or propaganda? In their blending of poetics and politics, they embody rather Du Bois's famous dictum that "all Art is propaganda." Much of this writing alternates, as Twain's does, between fictional and factual discourses: the highly conventional, "melodramatic" plots often combined, or even competing with, the network of allusions to and representations of contemporary events and debates. Like his, the "history" in many of these other texts tends then to be problematic, either awkwardly incorporated into the fictional plot or partially submerged in the form of thinly disguised references to actual people and events, or, at the other extreme, too dominant, leading to the propaganda-not-art label. Perhaps we might even say that the generic and historical problems in the literature are actually symptoms of the race problem itself: the struggle to produce alternative racial discourses testifies to the pervasiveness of nineteenth-century racist ideology and its very limited rhetorics. Finally, the very aesthetic difficulties that have led so many readers to dismiss both Twain's late writings as products of personal despair and most late-nineteenth-century race literature as propaganda place him at or near the very center of the literary effort to represent the "race question" at this time – exactly where we always knew Mark Twain belongs.

NOTES

1 *Mark Twain's Autobiography*, 2 vols., ed. Albert Bigelow Paine (New York: Harper, 1924), vol. 2, pp. 193, 218, 222. Henceforth cited parenthetically in the text as MTA.

2 Several critics have recognized the Hopkins–Du Bois connection to the New Psychology. See Thomas J. Otten, "Pauline Hopkins and the Hidden Self of Race," *ELH* 59 (1992): 227–56; Eric J. Sundquist, *To Wake the Nations: Race in the Making of American Literature* (Cambridge, Mass.: Harvard University Press, 1993), pp. 569–74; Dickson Bruce, Jr., "W. E. B. Du Bois and the Idea of Double Consciousness," *American Literature* 64 (1992): 299–309; Cynthia D. Schrager, "Pauline Hopkins and William James: The New Psychology and the Politics of Race" (unpublished paper, University of California, Berkeley). On the New Psychology, see Robert Fuller, *Freud and the American Unconscious* (New York: Oxford, 1986).

3 See my *Dark Twins: Imposture and Identity in Mark Twain's America* (Chicago: University of Chicago Press, 1989).

4 Mark Twain, *Following the Equator: A Journey Around the World* (Hartford, Conn.: American, 1897), p. 654. Hereafter cited parenthetically in the text as FE.

5 The "Morgan Manuscript" of *Pudd'nhead Wilson* is in the J. Pierpont Morgan Library, New York. Hereafter cited parenthetically in the text as MMS. On the textual issues raised by *Pudd'nhead Wilson*, see Hershel Parker, *Flawed Texts and Verbals Icons: Literary Authority in American Fiction* (Evanston, Ill.: Northwestern University Press, 1984), pp. 115–36.

6 I take my language here directly from Henry Nash Smith, *Mark Twain: The Development of a Writer* (Cambridge, Mass.: Harvard University Press, 1962); rpt. in Sidney E. Berger, ed., *Pudd'nhead Wilson and Those Extraordinary Twins* (New York: Norton, 1980), pp. 248–9.

7 ["The Man with the Negro Blood,"] four manuscript pages (Box 37), The Mark Twain Papers [hereafter MTP], Bancroft Library, University of California, Berkeley.

8 Mark Twain, "Which Was It?" in John S. Tuckey, ed., *Which Was the Dream? and Other Symbolic Writings of the Later Years* (Berkeley: University of California Press, 1968), pp. 179–429. Hereafter cited parenthetically in the text as WWD.

9 Notebook 18, Typescript p. 19, MTP.

10 On the "Matter of Hannibal," see Henry Nash Smith, "Mark Twain's Images of Hannibal: From St. Petersburg to Eseldorf," *Texas Studies in English* 37 (1958): 3–23.

11 Mark Twain, *Life on the Mississippi*, intro. John Seelye (New York: Oxford, 1990), pp. 199–202.

12 "Microbes" is published in Tuckey, ed., *Which Was the Dream?* pp. 433–553.

13 Mark Twain, *The Mysterious Stranger*, ed. William M. Gibson (Berkeley: University of California Press, 1969), pp. 134, 136. Hereafter cited parenthetically in the text as MS.

14 On Lodge's relation to psychical research, especially to the work of F. W. H. Myers, see Alan Gauld, *The Founders of Psychical Research* (New York: Schocken Books, 1968), pp. 142, 255–8, 289–93. On Twain's relation to Myers's theory of the "subliminal self" in particular and to psychical research in general, see Gillman, *Dark Twins*, pp. 136–162.

15 For one of the best recent commentaries on the conjunction of the dream mode and the topic of slavery in *The Mysterious Stranger*, see Forrest G. Robinson, *In Bad Faith: The Dynamics of Deception in Mark Twain's America* (Cambridge, Mass.: Harvard University Press, 1986), pp. 228–37.

16 See Gibson, ed., Introduction to *Mysterious Stranger*, p. 12; John S. Tuckey, *Mark Twain and Little Satan: The Writing of "The Mysterious Stranger"* (West Lafayette, Ind.: Purdue University Press, 1963), pp. 17–23.

17 Mark Twain, "Concerning the Jews," in *The Complete Essays of Mark Twain*, ed. Charles Neider (Garden City, N.Y.: Doubleday, 1963), pp. 235–250. Hereafter cited parenthetically in text as "Concerning."

18 Twain used the phrase in a letter to Henry Huttleston Rogers, quoted in Philip S. Foner, *Mark Twain: Social Critic* (New York: International, 1958), p. 297.

19 The two Dreyfus phrases come from "My First Lie, and How I Got Out of It" (1899), in *The Writings of Mark Twain*, 25 vols. (New York: Harper, 1907–18), vol. 23, pp. 147–8.

20 Janet Smith, ed., *Mark Twain on the Damned Human Race* (New York: Hill & Wang, 1962), p. 159.

21 This phrase comes from Twain's "My First Lie, and How I Got Out of It," p. 148.

22 On the black–Jewish connection, see Sundquist, *To Wake the Nations*, pp. 559, 574, and, especially, Paul Gilroy, *The Black Atlantic: Double Consciousness and Modernity* (Cambridge, Mass.: Harvard University Press, 1993), pp. 574–8.

23 The two stories are published in John S. Tuckey, ed., *Mark Twain's Fables of Man* (Berkeley: University of California Press, 1972), pp. 280–9.

24 See H. N. Smith, "Mark Twain's Images of Hannibal," p. 20.

25 For my thinking on stereotypes here, and earlier in *Dark Twins*, I am indebted to Gilman's fascinating work in *Difference and Pathology: Stereotypes of Sexu-*

ality, Race, and Madness (Ithaca, N.Y.: Cornell University Press, 1985). The phrase I quote is in the Preface, p. 12. More recently, Gilman has written on Twain's relation to the cultural iconography of the Jew, in "Mark Twain and the Diseases of the Jews," *American Literature* 65 (March 1993): 95–115.

STANLEY BRODWIN

Mark Twain's Theology: The Gods of a Brevet Presbyterian

Humor, by definition, becomes a polemical factor in the Christian view
of life. . . . The Comic is always based on contradiction.

Kierkegaard, *Journals and Papers*, vol. 2, pp. 264, 266

Father Adam & the apple – he didn't know it was loaded.

Mark Twain

EXPLORING THE JOKE OF JOKES:
THE NATURE OF RELIGIOUS BELIEF

"Place yourself at the centre of a man's philosophic vision," William James
counseled, "and you understand at once all the different things it makes him
write or say. But keep outside, use your post-mortem method, try to build
the philosophy out of simple phrases, first taking one and then another in
seeking to make them fit and of course you fail. You crawl over the thing
like a myopic ant over a building, tumbling into every microscopic crack or
fissure, finding nothing but inconsistencies, and never suspecting that a
centre exists."[1] Unfortunately, the critic cannot wholly disregard the "post-
mortem" method, and so it is inevitable that "inconsistencies" – even radical contradictions – will frustrate any attempt to find that satisfying artistic
wholeness or philosophical unity we seek – or sometimes never suspect
exists – in a writer of Mark Twain's complexity and stature. This does not
mean that the critical struggle to place ourselves at the "centre" can be
dispensed with; rather, we must pursue the task in the expectation that any
judgment we make of what that "centre" finally is will at least yield us a
measure of consistency in all the inconsistencies we are bound to discover.

To be sure, the search by critics for the absolute center of Mark Twain's
mind and imagination has gone on almost from the time he delighted America with his self-described "villainous backwoods sketch" of "The Jumping
Frog of Calaveras County" in 1865. The ensuing years saw the unfolding of

the spectacular career of a truly "charismatic" personality who seemed to put on and take off one tantalizing mask after another: consummate comic lecturer, spawned by the American frontier, travel writer, "jackleg" novelist of childhood or the contemporary scene of the multilayered corruptions of the Gilded Age, romancer, social critic, satirical journalist, watchdog of his culture's moral health and creeping diseases.

After a while the Mark Twain–Samuel Clemens "split" puzzled and amused almost everyone caught in his spell, including Twain himself, who apparently entered into the mystification in order to create consciously the ultimate protective mask of psychic security, a security paid for by the knowledge that in the end he would be often judged a "buffoon," however lovable, by those who bought and reviewed his books. He wrote a self-justifying letter to Andrew Lang, responding to harsh British reviews of his comic reduction of the Arthurian myth in A Connecticut Yankee in King Arthur's Court (1889) that "I have never tried in even one single instance, to help cultivate the cultivated classes."[2] His words reveal an anxiety quickened into life by the probe that unmasked and rejected a dimension of his mind that he did not wish to be scorned, although he was fully aware that his burlesque treatment of the sacred Arthurian myth and its Christian images would evoke such a response.

But there are profounder dimensions to his "centre" than his urge to deflate the sacred, perhaps the most important being his virtually lifelong engagement with the religious ethos of his culture, his personal struggles with theology and with the way theological concepts and beliefs shaped a humanity ultimately (and justifiably) "damned." This complex issue is intensified by the fact that a mere tracing of Twain's literary sources and patterns of thought gleaned from his fiction, travel books, letters, and notebooks, however vital to our understanding of his imaginative life, cannot fully illuminate Twain's center. It well may be that this core lies not in any particular strand of thought, no matter how earnestly held, but rather in his radical sense of contradiction, his comic and satiric epistemology, which consistently revealed the brutal gap between illusion and reality, belief and behavior, the ideal and the "real" in art, politics, social life, and, above all, what he would eventually regard as the false "principles" of a Christian civilization. That center may be described as a cluster of dynamically interrelated nodes: his comic and burlesque reflexes, his intense sense of history and its meaning, his profound identification with biblical storytelling and mythology, especially the Adamic myth, his tenacious eighteenth-century deistic rationalism, and, finally, his pervasive sense of guilt from whose grip he could not free himself, even though he transferred the responsibility to a

Calvinistic God or to his theory of environmental determinism. Most important, there is his own self-revealed stance as a "moralist in disguise" as well as his impulse to preach, indeed, to *be* a preacher even as he recognized the absurdity of the ambition in the face of his lack of religious faith and his authentic "calling," as he communicated in a letter to Orion in 1865:

> And now let me preach *you* a sermon. I never had but two *powerful* ambitions in my life. One was to be a pilot, & the other a preacher of the gospel. I accomplished the one & failed in the other, *because* I could not supply myself with the necessary stock in trade – i.e. religion. I have given it up forever. I never had a "call" in that direction, anyhow, & my aspirations were the very ecstasy of presumption. But I *have* had a "call" to literature, of a low order – i.e. humorous. It is nothing to be proud of, but it is my strongest suit, & if I were to listen to that maxim of stern *duty* which says . . . that to do right you must multiply the one or the two or the three talents which the Almighty entrusts to your keeping.[3]

That this problem was not of a mere "moment," we know from Twain's letter a full year later to Samuel E. Moffett:

> Dear Sammy – Keep up your lick & you will become a great minister of the gospel someday, & then I shall be satisfied. I wanted to be a minister myself – it was the only genuine ambition I ever had – but somehow I never had any qualification for it but the ambition. I always missed fire on the ministry. *Then* I hoped *some* member of the family would take hold of it & succeed. Orion would make a preacher, & I am ready to swear he will never make anything else in the world. But he won't touch it. I am utterly & completely disgusted with a member of the family who *could* carry out my old ambition & won't. If I only had his chance, I would make the abandoned sinner get up & howl. But you may succeed, & I am determined Pamela shall make you try it anyhow.
>
> (*Letters* 367)

That Twain genuinely pondered becoming a preacher of the gospel alerts us to a quality of his mind that is essential for understanding the spiritual dynamics at the core of his psyche. For in him there contested the imperative of "stern *duty*" to develop his talents. To waste them would violate the divine purpose of giving each human being a significant part in the providential scheme of things, even the "call" to low, humorous literature. There is a tense contradiction here that was the source of his creative energy and the controlling factor charging his evolving philosophic "center." Trapped in his contradictions, he is forced to question the time he has spent meddling with things he feels unfit for. He had been an apprentice printer, a miner out West, a steamboat pilot, and a journalist in Nevada. Were all these activities, including his "serious" attacks on the "shams" of his society, merely diversions? Of course, all these experiences were to form the very substance of his mature work, but of what final value could they be if his "inner Self," that radical disposition to be an *artist* of the comic, were denied or dissipated in a frenzy of uncertain economic expectations and occupations? Somehow, his "talent" for humorous writing would have to find expression. But the decision to "excite the *laughter* of God's children" did not prevent him from befriending clergymen. Fortunately, Mark Twain developed his comic art at a time in American culture when theological problems were gradually becoming the subjects of novelists. The reader, Twain affirmed, would be better served by *"narratives of generous deeds that . . . augment the nobility of the nation . . . and* NOT *from the drowsy pulpit!"*[4] Twain thus justified his "low" calling, and occupied his own special pulpit. The authentic preacher is still to be honored, however. But even the well-meaning minister bores, "with uninflammable truism about doing good . . . bores them, chloroforms them, stupefies them with argumentative mercy without a flaw in the grammar, or an emotion which the minister could put in the right place if he turned his back and took his finger off the manuscript" (WIM 54). Not so the author of *Innocents Abroad;* can we not hear charged in his indictment and language his own moral and satiric soul preparing "sermons" that will rarely bore? And so we can grasp his partiality to clergymen, his long and fruitful friendship with Joseph Twichell and other ministers at Nook Farm during his triumphant Hartford years.[5]

Surely Twain found in these good men a part of himself, a function he could never fulfill – to make those sinners howl – and to carry the essence of Christianity sans "ceremonies and wire-drawn creeds" (WIM 53) to the masses.

As it turned out, the Wild Humorist of the Pacific Slopes would reach the masses whether or not he truly aimed for them. He honed frontier art forms, mastered Victorian rhetoric, and used them to expose the world's shams. Institutional religion and its doctrines became one of his major targets from the 1860s on. Decades later, on November 5, 1908, he made this quietly sardonic analysis, obviously the result of years of observation:

> All schools, all colleges have two great functions: to confer, and to conceal valuable knowledge. The Theological knowledge which they conceal cannot justly be regarded as less valuable than that which they reveal. That is, if, when a man is buying a basket of strawberries, it can profit him to know that the bottom half of it is rotten.[6]

Of this odd and complex statement, one may ask: To what kinds of "knowledge" is Twain alluding? What is being conferred and what is being concealed? Concealed is the fact that man is an unjustly "banished Adam," exiled into a universe that ultimately loses any cosmic or providentially divine order. It is the universe that becomes for Mark Twain a solipsistic dream, an endless succession of subjective "realities," or a nihilistic world. In his emergent view, humanity has *descended* rather than ascended the evolutionary ladder; it is weighted with lies, self-deception, and shams of every kind. History not only is a litany of barbarities, with Christianity the greatest offender, but is also controlled by different antithetical images of God. Therefore, we live in an ontologically contradictory universe, yet are exhorted to act against our God-created instincts. Authentic morality becomes impossible because, in Twain's view, the conscience is trained by environment and external circumstances that plunge us into an existential anguish of guilt. Our religious books are beautiful in language and art, but their gods are false and fatally contradictory. Finally, there is the horror of our alleged moral sense, which ironically leads us into endless moral morasses. Worst of all, we endure the world's fraudulence and our own bad faith without being aware of how comically absurd we appear. As Mark Twain put it in a letter of 1907:

> There is one thing that always puzzles me: as inheritors of the mentality of our reptile ancestors we have improved the inheritance by a thousand grades; but in the matter of the morals which they left us we have gone backward as many grades. That evolution is strange, and to me unaccountable and unnatural. Necessarily we started equipped with their perfect and blemishless morals; now we are wholly destitute; we have no real morals, but only artificial ones – morals created and preserved by the forced suppression of natural and hellish instincts. Yet we are dull enough to be vain of them. Certainly we are a sufficiently comical invention, we humans. (MTL 2: 804–5)[7]

The comedy of this psychological description turns on mortal vanity, which rejoices only in the artificial and remains, for the most part, ignorant of the true forces hidden beneath the surface. Here lies the key to Twain's gradually developed perception that religion and theology were a form of false consciousness, an "opiate of the masses," as it were.[8] In such a view, human behavior is intrinsically comic, because it is motivated by false and artificial ideals it believes are sacred truths. No wonder then that Huck thinks he is going to hell when he is actually performing a "heavenly" deed.

But what of the "natural" and "hellish" instincts? To watch these instincts at play we must go back to 1876, the year both "The Carnival of Crime in Connecticut" and *The Adventures of Tom Sawyer* were published. The former story offers us a Poesque demonstration of how to kill our conscience (described as an ugly fungus-covered dwarf) with pretended repentance so that it grows fat and then vulnerable to the narrator, who then murders it with relish. Then, in a truly grotesque parody of a "born again" conversion, the narrator, who is "born anew," rushes out to kill his enemies remorselessly and sell the corpses to doctors. The "born again" man is a "born again" killer, and the horror is the truth that, in this story, the natural *is* the hellish. But this truth can be revealed only when the artificial constructs of repentance and guilt are destroyed in order to "liberate" the real self. Mrs. Fairbanks, an authentic representative of Victorian culture and religious values and Twain's so-called surrogate mother, read the story and observed that only a person with a conscience could write it.[9] Just so; but one doubts whether she ever really understood the conceptual threat to her world the tale literally glories in.

On the other hand, we have the Edenic, hymnal fairy tale of *Tom Sawyer,* another version of the natural in the world of youth clinging to and playing out its instincts and need for adventure in a society sometimes angrily, sometimes lovingly, but always insistently asserting its authority over that play. Its authority, however, rests firmly on the foundation of a Presbyterian theology that the church, the schools, and the respectable families of St. Petersburg indoctrinate in stifling sermons and in family and school discipline. The rewards for conformity are ambiguous; we remember the boy who went mad from learning a thousand biblical quotations (what better prize than a Bible?) and we note that Tom, the rebel-conformist (he and Huck actually "get religion" at one point), manages to play out his instincts without subverting the world that allows him to do so – within limits. The satanic in its midst, Injun Joe, is destroyed by Tom's heroic actions. A more difficult task is for Tom and Huck to evade, ignore, or engage when absolutely necessary the pieties, apparent or real, of the town in order to protect whatever is still "natural" and innocent in them.[10] The adult narrator knows the boys are living in a world of human "insects," an image he uses several times not only to indicate our puniness in the scheme of things, but also our corrupt moral nature. There is a controlled skepticism as well as nostalgia in the narrator's style that uneasily laces together vernacular and florid varieties of Victorian rhetoric. He lives in the two worlds of fantasy and reality every bit as much as his heroes. Yet there is no resisting the civilizing forces that overwhelm their lives. The boys enjoy Edenic moments of escape on the river, but return they must. If Tom and Becky confront the horrors of the underworld in the cave, they also achieve "salvation" and triumph. Such are the promised rewards of conformity: providence provides. This will not always be so, of course, for the state of grace that is youth cannot endure. But the novel provides an Adamic victory or at least its *illusion* in the narrator's genial condescension toward his human "insects." Tom coaxes Huck back into the civilized world through the seductive image of being respectable robbers, a lovely but implicitly dangerous oxymoron that defines, in part, Tom and his culture. The "artificial" is making its headway, although Tom and Huck are not entirely aware of this process. In his narrative, Huck will struggle against himself, but he will always flaunt some vanity (he often calls himself "brash") because of his mimetic attachments to Tom's flamboyant style and "learning." Indeed, both boys, like most of Twain's characters (always excepting Joan of Arc), become vulnerable to either Twain's forgiving humor or his Swiftian contempt to the degree that each character flaunts his or her artificial behavior in the face of a reality that contradicts it. The Sunday School false piety of Senator Dilworthy in *The Gilded Age* receives the satire of contempt, while Colonel Sellers, who lives on providential economic illusions, is treated with comic compassion.

The essence of *Tom Sawyer,* therefore, remains profoundly Adamic despite some of its darker subterranean flashes. There is always a measure of Tom's and Huck's essential naturalness, however much they mimic in their games the uglier patterns and pretensions of the townspeople. But they are capable of their own small and often comic boasts because they have already internalized the civilized mores and false theology of Aunt Polly or the Widow Douglas. They can no longer distinguish between the artificial and the real in themselves or in others until an adventurous crisis reveals their good "hearts." Thus, in Tom and Huck we still respond to the possibilities of the natural without the fear of the hellish. Twain was never wiser in refusing to allow Tom and Huck to grow up and become adult liars; and we know that he projected a disastrous old age for them but fortunately left that destiny unwritten. *Tom Sawyer* thus gives us a comedy of psychological relief, a momentary "pardon" or exemption from having to face a disillusioned future and the *insane* behavior of humankind (as Twain came frequently to describe it). The Adamic mood is fixed and uncontaminated by any false illusions of the future.

A number of enduring themes emerge from "Carnival" and *Tom Sawyer,* some of them adumbrated in *The Innocents Abroad* (1869), *Roughing It* (1872), *The Gilded Age* (1873), and continued into *Life on the Mississippi* (1883), as well as many trenchant short pieces:[11] a probing and then full penetration into the underside of civilized behavior and the psychological, moral, political, and theological artificialities or shams that both help to create and endorse that behavior as nothing less than providential history.

Discovering and then unmasking the lies in that drama through a comic epistemology was less difficult and its consequences less anguishing to Twain than the despair, anger, and philosophic pessimism that overtook him at the end of the nineteenth century when he viewed the ruins he had helped expose. What price salvation then? In effect, he answered the question "what is man?" long before he wrote his gospel of mechanistic determinism. In his descendentalist vision, man had fallen to a position below the animals; moreover, he possessed an arrogance and a seemingly bottomless credulity. Twain's responses to this condition made him recoil with visceral intensity. Thus, the notion of special providences made him "nauseous" (NB 190); the doctrines of the Fall as in Genesis and atonement in the New Testament struck him as "insane," "rotten," "irrational." God, as He is portrayed in *Letters from the Earth* (1962), is a figure of contradiction who creates codes of law that make His human creations deny their innate characters or be punished for eternity.

Significantly, the atonement scheme was a theological "sarcasm," but dangerous because it promised the most to a humanity in need of illusions. In 1896 Twain wrote that God as Christ "is in the attitude of One whose anger against Adam has grown so uncontrollable . . . that nothing but a sacrifice can appease it, and so without noticing how illogical the act is . . . God condemns Himself to death – commits suicide, and in this ingenious way wipes off that old score" (NB 290).[12]

The revelation here exposes the irrational nature of God's anger toward Adam, for which there is no objective reason. It is simply there existentially and serves to victimize humanity perpetually. The real horror for Twain, however, is that man's monumental vanity allows him to believe that he is God's delight.

But Twain could predictably become an advocate of religious conformity. In 1878 he wrote to his brother Orion that "every man must *learn* his trade – not pick it up. God requires that he learn it by slow and painful processes." He goes on to criticize a burlesque of hell Orion had been writing, and discusses in passing an evolving version of what was to be *Extract from Captain Stormfield's Visit to Heaven* (1907).[13] Finally, he declares that you "can't write up hell so it will stand printing. Neither Howells nor I believe in hell or the divinity of the Savior but no matter, the Savior is none the less a sacred Personage, and a man should have no desire or disposition to refer to him lightly, profanely or otherwise than with the profoundest reverence" (MTL 1: 323). This reverential attitude, colored by Twain's own literary experience and fame plus his very real desire to save Orion from embarrassment, reveals a deference to religious convention that would seem to contradict his frank admission that he no longer believes in hell or the "divinity of the Savior." It was one thing to disbelieve, but quite another to attack the character of Jesus.

Twain knew better than most people how quickly religious moods passed, even if the guilt that prompted them lingered. In 1860, he ridiculed Orion for his readiness to believe. "You have paid the preacher! Well, that is good, also. What a man wants with religion in these breadless times, surpasses my comprehension" (MTL 1: 45). Yet at other moments he experienced a longing for faith that conflicted with his secular comic reflex. In 1867, after his trip to Palestine, he wrote in his notebook:

> Oh for the ignorance & confidingness that could enable a man to kneel at the Sepulchre & look at the rift in the rock, & the socket of the cross & the tomb of Adam & feel & know & never question that they were genuine.[14]

Despite his loss of simple faith, and the fruitless search for some alternative religious or philosophical belief, Twain could still pay lip service to Christianity. When he courted and then married Livy, for example, he tried to accommodate himself to the tolerant religious atmosphere of Nook Farm. Still, in 1887, long after he had given up any pretense to orthodox belief, he wrote, "I cannot see how a man of any large degree of humorous perception can ever be religious – except he purposely shut the eyes of his mind & keep them shut by force."[15] This line strangely echoes in style and tone his comment to Orion in 1860 but with the vitally significant difference of singling out the man of humorous perception. For many great comic artists, faith and humor were not incompatible. But not for Mark Twain. His was a deistic God of immutable law utterly indifferent to human prayer or concerns and therefore wholly unable to provide consolation for suffering and evil. This doctrine satisfied Twain's intellectual understanding of the problem, while his emotional and artistic energies were engaged in the destruction of the biblical God. He told Livy that reading the Bible made him feel like a "hypocrite"; it "contradicts my reason," he complained.[16] In 1903, he dreamed of replacing Christianity with a "New Religion . . . having for its base God and Man as they are, and not as the elaborately masked and disguised artificialities they are represented to be in most philosophies and *all* religions" (NB 376, my emphasis).

Whether the religious sentiment was "inborn" or whether it had evolved through aeons as the most spiritually effective human "adaptation" was debated endlessly. But skeptic and believer alike would have agreed with Emerson's generalization in his essay "The Comic" (1843) that "the religious sentiment is the most real and earnest thing in nature, being a mere rapture, and excluding, when it appears, all other considerations the vitiating this is the greatest lie. *Therefore, the oldest gibe of literature is the ridicule of false religion.*"[17] This is the "joke of jokes."

If, as Emerson declared, the "Comic be the contrast in the intellect between the idea and the false performance" and a "perception of the Comic seems to be a balance-wheel in our metaphysical structure," then laughter at the "joke of jokes" was evidence of freedom from those "perverse tendencies and gloomy insanities in which fine intellects sometimes lose themselves."[18] Given Emerson's perception of duality in man and nature, and his ambition to reconcile all contradictions, it is somewhat surprising that he did not fully recognize the dangerous and subversive power of the comic.

By contrast, Twain valued humor as "the great Regulator" of the human condition. "No god or religion," he insisted, "can survive ridicule. No church, no nobility, no royalty or other fraud, can face ridicule in a fair field and live" (NB 198). Here surely is the artistic and reformist motive at large in virtually all his major writings, and many of his minor works as well.[19] Of course, the hope could not be realized. A Robert Burns might "break the back of the Presbyterian Church" with his satire, but the "grotesqueness" or "funniness" of papal infallibility in particular (and all organized religions as a whole, we need hardly add) will not ever be perceived by a people without "humor-perception."[20] For the young Satan in "The Chronicle of Young Satan," mankind lives a life of "continuous and uninterrupted self-deception" and has nothing but a "bastard perception of humor" that can only "blind it to the high-grade comicalities which exist in the world" (MSM 164). Fallen mankind is so dominated by convention and its need for "self-approval" that it cannot see itself in the mirror of comic reflection. "Against the assault of Laughter," the old theological shams, the old artificialities of morality, remain intact. "Everything human is pathetic," Twain wrote in *Following the Equator.* "The secret source of Humor itself is not joy but sorrow. There is no humor in heaven" (WMT 20: 101). God does not laugh. In 1902 Twain observed, "We grant God the possession of all the qualities of mind except the one that keeps the others healthy; that watches over their dignity; that focuses their vision true – humor" (MSM 26). Is the "joke of jokes" the ironic truth that God Himself is an *agelast* – Rabelais's term for a nonlaugher – and therefore devoid of compassion and all the "healthy" qualities we assume He possesses? In such late works as "Three Thousand Years Among the Microbes" and *The Mysterious Stranger* stories, Mark Twain gravitated to ridiculous-sublime images of God as a drunken Polish tramp, or of a solipsistically created universe of endless space and time imagined by a "vagrant" self. However grotesque or nihilistic, such concepts seemed theologically more emotionally acceptable to him than those of a malicious God and His "revealed" false religions.

The conceptual seed of this idea was probably planted in Twain's mind when he met with Charles Kingsley in England in 1873. Kingsley had responded to a query as to whether God laughed. In a long letter of response, Kingsley argued that God *must* have humor as part of Christ's "human nature"; otherwise, the Deity could not be perfect or complete. Clearly Mark Twain either read the letter or discussed the problem with Kingsley. In a notebook entry of 1877 Twain briefly wrote, "The Deity filled with humor. Kingsley. God's laughter," and much later a quotation from Ps. 2:4: "He that sitteth on the circle of the Heavens shall laugh" (NB&J 2: 37, 127).[21] Kingsley worried over the apparent contradiction of a suffering savior who might weep but not laugh – who lacked the healthiest of attributes. But Kingsley argued that if Christ were a man, he *had* to possess humor. Only a year after his notation, Twain answered Kingsley with his own "syllogism":

> God made man *in his own image*. Christ, a man, was the *son of God*. – & possessed humor, of course.　　　　　　　　　　　　　　(NB&J 2: 127)

Twain is moved to sarcasm when contemplating the biblical relationship between God and man and the absurdity of a Christ who can laugh. This, for Twain, is the joke of jokes, but one that Christians lacked the sense of humor or courage to recognize.

By the 1870s Twain was committed to an Enlightenment mode of attack on institutional religion. The artistic task was to distinguish – as Voltaire and Tom Paine had – between the "true" and "false" theology, and thus to liberate a spiritually enslaved humanity. By this time as well, Twain's readings in Darwin and the "Higher Criticism" of biblical scholarship had supplied him with the intellectual weapons to broaden his attack. Finally, Twain found an ally in Robert G. Ingersoll, the most popular proponent of "Free Thought." Together, they attacked the stifling theological orthodoxies of Victorian America.[22] Nevertheless, in the 1880s he still could write, "I would not interfere with anyone's religion, either to strengthen it or weaken it. . . . It may easily be a great comfort to him – hence it is a valuable possession to him" (WIM 57). He understood quite clearly, even painfully, that religion helped most people to cope with those eternal dilemmas of faith, doubt, unjust suffering, and death itself. Years later, in 1904, as his wife lay dying, Twain suffered the anguish of having robbed her of the consolation of faith, and so became the ironic victim of his own iconoclasm.

Yet despite his sympathetic understanding of the need for religious faith, he could confidentally predict that "Christianity will doubtless still survive in the earth ten centuries hence – stuffed and in a museum" (NB 346). Nevertheless, this belief did not prevent him from admiring authentic Christians like his close friend Joseph Twichell. But clergymen like Twichell could not block the historical, evolutionary fate of Christianity, although self-deception, he knew, was as entrenched as original sin itself. Thus, his "exegesis" of Matt. 7:13:

> "Straight is the gate and narrow is the way, and *few there be*, etc." This is the utterance of the same authority which commands man to "multiply and replenish the earth." What: meekly and obediently proceed to beget children, with the distinct understanding that *nearly all* of them must become fuel for the fires of hell? The person who would obey such a command, under such an understanding, would be simply a monster – no gentle term would describe him. How easily men are self-duped. Many *think* they believe they are begetting fuel for hell, but down in their hearts they believe nothing of the kind.
>
> (WIM 58–9)

Twain seems to have imagined himself free from such false consciousness, although his sense of guilt reminded him of his own moral weaknesses. At the same time, he submitted to a form of behavioral and historical determinism – marked by immutable laws and pristine logic – which provided the only kind of consolation a man of reason (and humor) could ask for. Yet all the evidence of his later years, even after *Adventures of Huckleberry Finn* with its splendid comic triumph over a fallen providential world and the violent, hypocritical culture of civilization, testifies to a man in a kind of controlled spiritual and moral rage. The Adamic stances and affirmation of the possibility of genuine moral progress, as we know, turned into a satanic perspective on a corrupt civilization kept alive by the virtually universal assent to a "silent colossal National Lie."[23] Quite literally, Satan/Mark Twain stepped into the pulpit and began to deliver his sermons with a "pen warmed-up in hell." Where, then, was the consolation, the acceptance of reality his "philosophies" and readings in science should have given him? It is true that in 1889 Twain could still affirm that his was a "worthy calling." But the very determinism he delighted in and which would become his "gospel" of *What Is Man?* (1906), and the cold confession of Hank Morgan that all was "training," formed a philosophical obstacle to his project for humorous reform. As he wrote to Howells in 1907:

> I suspect that to you there is still dignity in human life, & that Man is not a joke – a poor joke – the poorest that was ever contrived – an April-fool joke, played by a malicious Creator with nothing better to waste his time upon. Since I wrote my Bible [*What Is Man?*] (last year) which Mrs. Clemens loathes

... and will not listen to ..., Man is not to me the respect-worthy person he was before; & so I have lost my pride in him & can't write gaily nor praisefully about him anymore. And I don't intend to try.[24]

Philip Traum defines the final indignity of humanity:

Man is made of dirt – I saw him made. I am not made of dirt. Man is a museum of disgusting diseases, a home of impurities; he comes today and is gone to-morrow, he begins as dirt and departs as stench; I am of the aristocracy of the imperishable. And man has *the Moral sense*.[25]   (MSM 55)

Such satanic pessimism and virulent contempt for the human condition simply negates consolation. In his last years, with personal and economic traumas intensifying his already growing despair about the "human condition," Mark Twain embraced the liberating grace of death – the best gift of Adam to humanity – even as he raged inconsolably against the barbarities of U.S. and Belgian imperialism.[26] The Republic itself had lost its soul, soiled by a money-sick, "religion-sick" society.

A possible answer as to why none of Twain's philosophies – including the inherently absurd radical solipsism of "44" (his last mysterious stranger) – gave spiritual comfort comes from another source: William James's 1884 address, "The Dilemma of Determinism." For James, our "regret" for a murder, for example, should lead logically to a "larger regret" for the "whole frame of things of which murder is one member." It follows that "the only deterministic escape from pessimism is everywhere to abandon the judgment of regret."[27]

However, the one thing that Twain could *not* give up were his judgments of regret, as well as the guilt from which he was never freed. From this perspective, it becomes almost fruitless to try to "reconcile" Twain's conflicting or contradictory images of "salvation." Each was an attempt to come to terms with life without the support of a traditional religious faith. Yet the most "terrible" of theological ironies that afflicted him was the primal struggle between the flesh and the spirit. In "No. 44, The Mysterious Stranger," we see a pattern of images registering the primal conflict between fleshly bondage and spiritual freedom. Thus, Emil Schwarz, August's dream self, cries out, "Oh, free me from *them;* these bonds of flesh . . . this loathsome sack of corruption in which my spirit is imprisoned" (MSM 369). There is no abstract philosophizing here; only an existential cry that echoes St. Paul's passion to be free from "the body of death" (Rom. 7:24). Only there is no savior for the humorist. In a terrible theological irony, the flesh is death and corruption, but the spirit is an ontological negation, its reality contingent only upon the dreamer.

But what Mark Twain did have at the "centre" of his moral and comic vision of reality was his passion for artistic creation, which could transmogrify his relentless regrets into a profound countertheology. To this we now turn.

THE FORMATION OF A COUNTERTHEOLOGY

What influence (if any) did Hannibal's Presbyterian ethos have on young Sam Clemens? We know that he went to Sunday School and heard hellfire sermons, some of which frightened him at night into a state of tortured repentance, dissipating by the morning. How real these experiences were we shall never know definitively, but they ring with truth. Twain speaks also of his being haunted and "harried" by his "trained Presbyterian conscience" (WMT 31: 411), and all the biographical evidence seems to support the truth of his statement. Indeed, Twain makes frequent references to his Presbyterian background, many of which, however, are satiric. He never ceased to attack the Presbyterian dogma of ungraced infants burning in hell and the irrational doctrine of election and damnation.[28] Clearly, the more "liberal" theology of Hartford appealed to him, though he never quite shook off the literalism of frontier Christianity. Was his later determinism really a secular version of Calvinistic predestination? Possibly.[29] Twain insisted that he never believed in predestination but, rather, in a scientific theory of mechanistic causality most likely derived from his early readings in eighteenth-century thought and reinforced by his familiarity with nineteenth-century concepts of determinism.

That the young Clemens became fascinated with the stories in Genesis and Exodus, and certainly learned many of Jesus' parables and other New Testament stories and doctrines, is abundantly clear. From his mother, he learned to sympathize with the case of Satan – a momentous lesson, as things turned out. Meanwhile, at Sunday School he became familiar with the workings of a benevolent providence, the desperate salvational need to develop a Christian conscience, and, finally, the equally desperate need to reform when you have "fallen" from grace. He also learned to believe, and to quickly disbelieve (like Huck Finn), in the efficacy of prayer. Dixon Wecter writes that "Presbyterianism and the Moral Sense it fostered – with its morbid preoccupations about sin, the last judgment and eternal punishment" left their "traces" through "all the years of his adult 'emancipation.'"[30] "Wildcat" religions and revivals, the Campbellites and Millerites with their millennialist and apocalyptic fervor also figured in his early experiences. In one autobiographical note he recalls a "Campbellite revival. All converted but me. All sinners again in a week."[31] This last statement fore-shadows one of Twain's great themes: the illusion of reform.

That Twain never shook off his "deference for the fundamental Protestant culture of Hannibal, Missouri," as Henry Nash Smith remarks,[32] is true enough, but the crucial significance of that truth rests in the way it became an existential part of his "philosophic centre" and informed in remarkably complex and trenchant artistic patterns his work as a whole. In the 1890s and early 1900s the "centre" broke into powerful fragments: scattered preoccupation with theories of personality and dreams, the poison of the "moral sense," physical disease and national political corruption, and the Fall – always the Fall – but with the irony of giving Satan the primary voice of protest and consolation.

Twain's later spiritual gravitation to a postlapsarian and despairing fascination with Satan had its roots in what Kierkegaard called a "misrelationship" between the awareness of the "eternal" and the "concrete." For Kierkegaard despair is the ultimate form anxiety takes when the individual, spiritually unable to make a "leap of faith," denies the God-idea of eternality within and "outside" of him- or herself and thus lives wholly on the temporal plane of existence, or uses the empirical laws of nature as an intellectual tool for knowledge that can have no bearing on the subjective truths of "immediate" existence.[33] Kierkegaard would have regarded 44's synthesis of historical determinism and solipsism not only as a "misrelationship," but as an archetypal form of nonrelationship, a "leap backward," as it were, to a symbol of negation or isolation. As a "vagrant" thought, the self has no relationship to anything outside of itself; it is a fantastic, un-humored, unanchored entity without any relationship to the awareness or *possibility* of God's eternality and His relationship to humanity's "concrete" responsible life. All it can do is fashion new or "better" dreams for itself, which then must be replaced by different dreams in an unending and non-teleological cycle of psychic entrapment. For all of 44's joy in creativity, his "vision" remains inherently despairing and philosophically absurd.

By contrast, Captain Stormfield's heaven properly reduces the planet earth to the status of a "wart" in the cosmos and provides final justice, for example, for unacknowledged geniuses like the Tennessee poet Billings. The story presents a rare instance in Twain's work of a harmonious cosmic relationship between the world and its false, earthly concepts of God and religion. Once Stormfield's illusions are replaced by the "facts" of the supernatural, he is able to accept the "new" heaven of personal fulfillment while learning the value of an authentic humility and awe of biblical figures such as Moses and Esau. The story is therefore a comic theological wish fulfillment for the reconciliation between humanity and its final destiny, between time and eternity, even between Twain and the Bible.

It is in his early "Reflections on the Sabbath" (1866) that we can see Twain seriocomically defining what was to be his stance as a counter-theologian. He asserts that the Omnipotent could have made the world in three days as easily as six and this "would have doubled the Sundays. Still, it is not our place to criticize the wisdom of the Creator" (WIM 39). Providence provides money to the corrupt but not to the "better" man. Twain explains that he had been attending Dr. Wadsworth's church and thus follows a "religious train of mind." As a good Presbyterian he abandons the gallery, which is full of sinners, and sits among the elect: "I was a brevet. I was sprinkled in infancy, and look upon that as conferring the rank of Brevet Presbyterian." Thanks to this honor, he will enjoy a "substantial punishment of fire and brimstone instead of this heterodox hell of remorse of conscience of these blamed wildcat religions." Ironically, it will be the remorse of conscience, and not really the punishment of fire and brimstone, that will torment him throughout life. Finally, Twain turns to Dr. Wadsworth's sermon, which is laced with unconscious but "first rate jokes":

> Several people there on Sunday suddenly laughed and as suddenly stopped again, when he gravely gave the Sunday School books a blast and spoke of "the good little boys in them who always went to Heaven, and the bad little boys who infallibly got drowned on Sunday," and then swept a savage frown around the house and blighted every smile in the congregation.
>
> (WIM 40–41)

At the outset of his career, then, Twain was already exploiting the phenomenon of false consciousness. Perhaps the most significant moment in the passage is the destruction of humor by a single frown from the pulpit, Twain's foreshadowing and image of the biblical God's "blight" on humanity's spirit.

As a brevet Presbyterian he will always be engaged in theological issues and the influence of the pulpit on human behavior. In 1907 he concluded that the "human race is a race of cowards; and I am not only marching in that procession but carrying a banner."[34] A few years earlier, Joe Twichell had admonished him for being "too orthodox on the Doctrine of Total Human Depravity."[35]

Our brevet Presbyterian, our preacher with a sense of humor, will infuse nearly all his works with three broad but remarkably flexible thematic subjects: providence, reform, and the lies of a fallen civilization. These themes will often be woven inextricably together, creating scenes that emerge as "deep-structures" or epistemes. They point to an ideological or theological formation controlling human experience and revealing its inherent comic – or tragic – ironies. The paradigm surfaces in *Huckleberry Finn* at its most significant moment – the "height of [American] humor," as James M. Cox has so aptly described it[36] – Huck's struggle with his conscience over freeing or reenslaving Jim. Huck complains that providence is "slapping [me] in the face and letting me know my wickedness is being watched all the time from up there in heaven." The situation forces him either to lie or to tell the truth, either of which will torment him. He finds he "cannot pray a lie," and so decides to save Jim and "*go* to hell." Whatever else the decision portends for him, it provides him with emotional and moral relief and frees him from the responsibility of any future need to reform.[37] This is only one of many strategies in Twain's works for dealing with the burdensome need to reform, a need finally lifted in the dream and fantasy worlds of *The Mysterious Stranger* stories. The paradox for Huckleberry Finn is that he is a creature of false consciousness, which he is able to transcend through his "sound heart." The scene captures the essence of Twain's countertheology: providence creates the conditions in which humanity's penchant for lying and its futile dream of moral regeneration are unconcealed; the result is a pointed satirical rebuke to those who can grasp the irony of the situation but are unable to perceive its profounder moral implications.

Another vital aspect of Twain's theological imagination is his subversion of the historical process, either as a series of cultural barbarities or as an anarchic parody of providential history. The former can be illustrated in the opening chapters of *Life on the Mississippi* describing the historical age of the river, and the latter in "The Secret History of Eddypus" (ca. 1901), an overt attack on Mary Baker Eddy and Christian Science and the historian as liar. As a young boy, he had learned "that in Biblical times, if a man committed a sin, the extermination of the whole surrounding nation – cattle and all – was likely to happen. I knew that Providence was not particular about the rest, so that He got somebody connected with the one He was after" (MTE 261). It is this perception of providence as a radically unjust, sadistic principle that he later translated, with a few exceptions, such as *The Prince and the Pauper*, into his novels and travel books. Of course, the idea of historical providence begins not only with some Darwinian "Adam-clam," but theologically in the Garden of Eden. His relationship to the Garden of Eden was not only a metaphorical one, but also an intensely personal relationship, as reflected in an 1887 letter to an old friend:

My Dear Mrs. Boardman,

You have spirited me back to a vanished world & the companionship of phantoms. But how dear they are, & how beautiful they seem! – so graced and spiritualized in the far stretch of time, whose mellowing perspectives hide all their faults & leave visible in them & remembrable only those things which made them lovely then & holy now. But I thank you for carrying me back to that old day, for in thinking of it, dreaming over it I have seemed like some banished Adam who is revisiting his half-forgotten Paradise & wondering how the arid outside world would could ever have seemed green & fair to him.[38]

Twain's description of himself as a "banished Adam" actually points to a nearly lifelong preoccupation with the myth.

It was in the Garden of Eden that the First Contradiction was made manifest to this "son of Adam," as he called himself in a little squib he wrote for Orion's *Hannibal Journal* in May 1853. He was then seventeen years old, but this comic metaphorical identification became an existential truth for him over the years. And it is not surprising that the fatalistic book of regret William James alluded to in his essay "Determinism," Fitzgerald's *Rubáiyát*, contained a stanza about the Fall that he believed to be "the most far-reaching and grand thought ever expressed in so short a space and in so few words." They were the words of stanza 81:

> Oh Thou, who Man of baser Earth didst make,
> And ev'n with Paradise devise the Snake:
> For all the Sin wherewith the Face of Man
> Is Blacken'd – Man's forgiveness give – and take![39]

Such forgiveness, however, was not forthcoming, nor, given the nature of either the biblical or deistic God, could it ever be. Unable to free himself from his "judgments of regret," Twain gave up trying to make sense of history and the dread consequences of the Expulsion. For example, in the 1890s, a decade of some of his most brilliant and significant storytelling, he wrote that God's creation and its history were marked by "sin or error," making it "the fantastic record of a maniac" (WIM 85). It is Satan's task, ironically, to provide consolation to Adam and Eve (in the Adamic diaries) and to expose (in *Letters from the Earth*) the irrationality of God's plan and the false consciousness it imposes on a gullible humanity.

Finally, we turn to the "providential tradition" in the development of the novel form itself, a complex and fascinating phenomenon.[40] In this tradition, the ideas of plot and structure are intrinsically related to the idea of providence. Thus, all a novel's episodes, as in history, are believed to be the workings of a God-inspired design. There are no real accidents, but only purpose and meaning, however concealed within the narrative. The novelist writes in *imitatio Dei;* all plots are ultimately God's plots. In Mark Twain's canon, providence appears in countless reversals of roles, twinning, and other structural and thematic patterns.

But as a countertheologian, Twain must unmask what is concealed and measure the idea of providence against the empirical experiences of life. Providence is then exposed as a sadistic law, if it exists at all, or as another form of false consciousness deluding the believer. The comic effects of such revelations may vary from Adamic or good-natured humor to a satanic contempt.

The comic providential reversals in *The Prince and the Pauper* (1882), for example, are not essentially political or social: they are *moral* and therefore reflect the possibility of creating a just world. In this novel, Tom Canty and Edward IV are rewarded, as a result of their new roles, with the knowledge that the *quality* of mercy humanizes social and political forms. They survive the cruelties of their society in order to reform it and make it consonant with the will of a benevolent deity their culture believes in. The apparent simplicity of the plot reflects the innate moral simplicity of the boys' nature: all the action is geared to their spiritual learning infused with the comedy of their moral triumph.

Huck Finn's world is, of course, much more complex, though it still contains those ubiquitous conditions of cruelty, slavery, hypocrisy, and self-deception. But Huck is able to transform his confrontations with evil only through his ingenuity and capacity to adjust to or escape from the forces that threaten him. Thus, the tragic content of the book is transformed through Huck's "innocence" into forms of comedy or satire. In chapter 3, for instance, he is taught the "two providences" of the Widow Douglas and Miss Watson. He chooses the widow's optimistic interpretation of providence, although he cannot imagine why God should be concerned with someone so "low-down and ornery" as he. Indeed, the novel is structured by a very ambivalent attitude toward this concept, one invoked both by Huck and by the duke and king, as well as the two sisters, always with ironic results.

Again, in the world of *Huckleberry Finn,* the possibilities of reform are also questioned. Huck releases himself from the burden of reforming, while pap's attempt to change ends in a farcical debacle that mocks the judge's pious hope of converting him. The king and the duke are obviously incapable of reform, as perhaps is their whole society, although at the revival meeting they know that the best method for squeezing money from the believers is to preach reform. Despite Jim's manumission, the "success" of

Tom's and Huck's adventures, and the vigilante justice that so cruelly punishes the con men, we are left in doubt if providential retribution has been truly realized. We recognize that the "escape" from civilization is at best only a temporary respite. Mark Twain's treatment of providence from *A Connecticut Yankee* to "The Man That Corrupted Hadleyburg" and *The Mysterious Stranger* stories becomes nihilistic. Predictably, by the 1860s, Twain had already developed antiprovidential narratives such as "The Advice for Good Little Boys" (1865) and "The Story of Mamie Grant, the Child-Missionary" (1868). Later, in "The Second Advent" (1881), he illustrated the disasters that would occur if people actually received the gifts of "special providences." As John S. Tuckey points out, the people of Black Jack, Arkansas, learn to pray only "*Lord, Thy Will, not mine be done.*" And so in "The Man That Corrupted Hadleyburg" (1899) "the townspeople affirm the new prayer of 'Lead Us into Temptation.'"[41] The point is obvious and subversive, and is to be encountered in many other works. Actually acting on the theological laws of Christianity – or Hinduism as Twain shows in *Following the Equator* – can only lead to the grotesque or comic-absurd.[42]

In the works of Mark Twain, providence functions not only as a theological principle, but also as a way of creating narrative irony. We find some of the best examples of this technique in the highly ambivalent endings of *Huckleberry Finn* and *A Connecticut Yankee* and in the crushing, final poetic justice of *Pudd'nhead Wilson*.[43] In the unfinished "The Great Dark" and *The Mysterious Stranger* complex, providence exists only as it is *willed* or structured, often nightmarishly, by the "vagrant" self or the Superintendent of Dreams. If it were possible to interfere with the secular or religious providence of determinism and hope to improve life, only more horrors would ensue. Thus, Theodor in "The Chronicle of Young Satan" says that "Satan had shown me other people's lives and I saw that in nearly all cases there would be little or no advantage of altering them" (MSM 147). The theme is powerfully dramatized throughout the story.

From *The Innocents Abroad* to "The Man That Corrupted Hadleyburg" with its wonderful charge contrived by the satanic "ruined gambler," Howard L. Stephenson, "*You are far from being a bad man: go, and reform*" (WMT 29: 34), we have nothing less than an "epic" of reform. The single redemptive individual and sublime reformer for Mark Twain, Joan of Arc, one of the noblest instruments of providence, achieves a mighty historical reform, only to be destroyed by the "Twelve Lies" of her opposition. Therefore, a providential God ordains that she must suffer the agony of martyrdom.[44] The narrator tells us that laughter, too, has died in a culture that could destroy her "Adamic" innocence, thus affirming the theological relationship between that innocence and humor.

It is paradoxical that Mark Twain's determinism failed to quell his "judgment of regrets," and at the same time undermined his role as a satiric moralist, which traditionally was to chasten human folly with ridicule. But if human character is the creation of circumstances and "outside" influences, then authentic reform will never be realized. There is little doubt that Twain recognized this problem, which is reflected in the final attempt to achieve reform by violent means (as Hank Morgan is compelled to do) or by at last retreating from the "real" world into solipsism.

The third dominant strand in Mark Twain's countertheology is the lie from which there is no escape. Even to the casual reader, Mark Twain's preoccupation with lies and lying is immediately apparent, for lying, in Mark Twain's moral vision, is a theological equivalent of original sin. Furthermore, a lie is not a mere untruth, but extends to all levels of institutions and culture – ultimately to the whole structure of Christian civilization. He uses the word in the most profound sense of the term, implying that the very ideals upon which that civilization is based are false. Lies persist because of man's moral sense, which dominates the conscience – "man's moral medicine chest . . . created by the Creator" (WIM 61) – and which produces all the "blacknesses and rottennesses of [human] character." Twain characterizes human nature as a body of "trunk lies" whose branches include generosity, compassion, heroism, integrity, and other apparent virtues. The one branch lie that is perhaps the most damning of all, Twain writes, is that

> I am I, and you are you; that we are units, individuals . . . instead of being the tail-end of a tape-worm eternity of ancestors extending in linked procession back – and back – and back – to our source in the monkeys, with this so-called individuality of ours a decayed and rancid mush of inherited instincts and teachings derived, atom by atom, stench by stench, from the entire line of that sorry column. (WIM 61)

Human selfishness, moreover, follows us from the cradle to the grave. Man comes into the world, "does his little dirt, commends himself to God, and then goes out into the darkness, to return no more, and send no messages back – selfish even in death" (WIM 64). The lie of individuality is central to Twain's indictment, because in a Christian civilization each individual is assumed to be imbued with free will (except in some Protestant doctrines), is subject to rewards and punishment and the striving for moral perfection.

Without the reality of a true selfhood we become nothing more than that "rancid mush of inherited instincts."

So much for the emancipating theories of Darwinism in Twain's rather crude but emotionally authentic interpretation. Ironically, evolution demonstrates what the Bible had already claimed and that Philip Traum had observed: man is dirt, inside and out. It is startling that this description of human nature was written in 1884–5, or just at the time Twain was completing *Adventures of Huckleberry Finn,* in which Huck describes pap as looking like "Adam . . . all mud" (HF 33). Huck is, after all, the master "innocent" observer *and* liar who can manipulate his lies in order to survive, to help others, to escape punishment and simply to play wonderful tricks, some of which backfire, as in his attempt to make Jim think he merely dreamed they were both thrown into the river. The lies of fiction itself, especially the romantic fiction beloved by Tom Sawyer, become in some ways pernicious, as they falsify the nature of reality. Twain's explanation in *Life on the Mississippi* that the Civil War was caused by the South's love of Scott's romances of aristocratic honor is one of his most extreme indictments of fictional lying and its influence on history.

From "The Jumping Frog of Calaveras County" (1865) to the "appalling" truths of "No. 44," Twain's writings expose what is concealed, warped, "sugar-coated," or denied by civilization's authorities: by the churches, guidebooks, historians, novelists, poets, playwrights, senators, and tobacco-spitting country sages. Inheriting a tradition of tall-tale telling, Mark Twain learned to "transcend" artistically the purely local or Southwestern modes of comic lying and to create more complex narratives embodying the tall tales of civilization and theology. With the "myth" or lie of providence and the illusion of reform erupting out of the very heart of man's trunk lies, Twain had forged an extraordinary countertheology that could well please the Prince of Lies, "Satan" himself. The only salvational hope, one that could refute this theology, lay in mankind's imagining a true God (and religion) that conformed to the truth of reality and provided compassion, humor, and justice to His creatures.

In "Aix-les-Bains the Paradise of the Rheumatics" (1891), Twain broke through to imagining that this true God was a grand possibility. In a few illuminating pages, he reveals his Protestant and historiographical method of organizing history and human behavior according to the "changes in the Deity – or in men's conception of the Deity" (WMT 29: 97), all of which are symbolically concretized in the rocks, Roman ruins, Catholic churches, and telegraph offices in and around this famous resort. He notes the evolution of mankind's God-idea from a tsarlike biblical deity controlling a "handful of Jews," to one "dreaming his eternities away on His Great White Throne" (WMT 29: 97). Evolution produces a changed deity, one of "a dignity and sublimity proportioned to the majesty of His office and the magnitude of His empire, a Deity who will in time be freed from a hundred fretting chains and will in time be freed from the rest by the several ecclesiastical bodies who have these matters in charge" (WMT 29: 98), but which still leave Him – ominously – "embarrassed" by the Presbyterian dogma of infant damnation. Twain, however, could not maintain this brief burst of optimism. In 1906, he predicted that Christianity, whose God was "the worst . . . that the ingenuity of man has begotten from his insane imagination," would one day "make room for another God and a stupider religion."[45] History demonstrated that in the "matter of religions we progress backwards."

In a world defined by lies, it became necessary for Twain to dream an optimistic end for humanity. This dream is dreamed by Simon Wheeler, detective, and is of a heaven open to all – "niggers and Injuns and Presbyterians and Irish equally."[46] But once again there is a contradiction, for Mark Twain, our comic evangelist, nevertheless came to hate those he had tried to reform. He wrote to Henry H. Rogers in 1899 (when he was working on "Concerning the Jews") that, being "without prejudice," he hoped that "both Christians *and* the Jews will be damned." His "leaning," he tells Rogers, was toward the Jew, for Judaism, unlike Christianity, has not "deluged the world with blood and tears" and so the satirist has had "hard luck with *them*," but of course, "he dasn't" say so.[47]

As Kierkegaard well knew, in the tragicomic striving for salvation, "everything resolves itself into a contradiction."[48] As Protestant evangelist, freethinker, and literary comedian, Mark Twain embodied contradictions that gave his best work a comic complexity and depth that, as Kipling knew, made him a "relation" of Cervantes. No matter what "influences" Twain absorbed in a lifetime of reading and travel, he remained, as Howells told him in 1899, a "creature of the Presbyterian God who did make you" (MTHL 2: 707).

But Mark Twain should have the last word and signature. In "Dr. Jacques Loeb's Incredible Discovery," written in 1905, Mark Twain berates the scientists who only believe by consensus and all those people ultimately afraid of new ideas and discoveries. Twain ends his piece with an "Extract from Adam's Diary," which tells us of the Consensus that decided the world could not be created out of nothing or in six days (WMT 29: 308–9). Here the countertheologian would have warmed the heart of any Presbyterian fundamentalist with or without a sense of humor:

Then the Consensus got up and looked out the window, and there was the whole outfit spinning and sparkling in space! You never saw such a disappointed lot.

his

Adam—i—

mark

NOTES

1   Jacques Barzun, "William James, Author," *American Scholar* 52 (Winter 1983): 48.

2   *Mark Twain's Letters*, 2 vols., ed. A. B. Paine (New York: Harper Bros., 1917), vol. 1, p. 527. Hereafter cited parenthetically in the text as MTL. Actually, Twain may never have mailed it.

3   *Mark Twain's Letters: 1853–1866*, vol. 1, ed. Edgar Marques Branch et al. (Berkeley: University of California Press, 1988), pp. 222–3. Hereafter cited in the text as *Letters*. Also see Paul S. Carter, Jr., "The Moralist in Disguise," *University of Colorado Studies in Language and Literature* 6 (January 1951): 65–78.

4   Mark Twain, *What Is Man? and Other Philosophical Writings*, ed. Paul Baender (Berkeley: University of California Press, 1973), p. 53. Hereafter cited parenthetically in the text as WIM. The best study of the way fiction began to displace or challenge nineteenth-century traditional religious literature and sermons is David S. Reynolds, *Faith in Fiction: The Emergence of Religious Literature in America* (Cambridge, Mass.: Harvard University Press, 1981).

5   Kenneth R. Andrews, *Nook Farm: Mark Twain's Hartford Circle* (Cambridge, Mass.: Harvard University Press, 1950), for the best general discussion of his relationship with clergymen.

6   *Mark Twain's Notebook*, prepared by A. B. Paine (New York: Harper's, 1935), p. 398. Hereafter cited parenthetically in the text as NB.

7   Twain was responding to a book sent to him by J. Howard Moore, *The Universal Kinship*, with an accompanying letter praising Twain for his "concern for the general welfare of your fellow man."

8   I have appropriated the term "false consciousness" from Marxist thought, which I feel accurately defines Mark Twain's view of religion, though of course he never uses that phrase. The term is defined by Engels in a letter to Franz Mehring in 1893 as an ideological process that does not allow the individual to understand "the true motive forces impelling him." For the whole letter, see *Marx, Engels: On Literature and Art* (Moscow: Progress Publishers, 1976), 63–7. Also, H. B. Acton remarks that "ideological thinking [in Marx and Engels] is contrasted with realistic thinking," in *What Marx Really Said* (New York: Shocken Books, 1967), p. 79. But see Twain's letter to Charles Warren Stoddard in which he asserts that all religion is based on "false premises, false history, false everything!" Cited in John Frederick May, *The Darkening Sky* (South Bend, Ind.: University of Notre Dame Press, 1969), p. 152.

9   *Mark Twain's Letters to Mrs. Fairbanks*, ed. Dixon Wecter (San Marino, Calif.: Huntington Library, 1949), p. 198.

10 For important studies on "innocence" in Twain's work, see Albert E. Stone, *The Innocent Eye: Childhood in the Imagination of Mark Twain* (New Haven, Conn.: Yale University Press, 1961), and William C. Spengemann, *Mark Twain and the Backwoods Angel* (Kent, Ohio: Kent State University Press, 1966).

11 In *The Innocents Abroad* and *Roughing It*, especially, the "myths" of travel as experienced by a putative "innocent" sinner or greenhorn enable him to explore the corroding foundations of the "Holy" Land, a spiritual and physical wasteland to which Christ will not return (Dewey Ganzel, *Mark Twain Abroad: The Cruise of "The Quaker City"* [Chicago: University of Chicago Press, 1968], p. 252) or to a frontier democracy characterized by con men, Mormons, "savage Indians," religious hypocrites, the search for great wealth, cowardly juries, desperadoes, and the rest. Both works contain the dialectic between disillusionment and affirmation, concealing or revealing the motives and values of that society. But in Hawaii, he experiences a sublime religious moment while gazing at the great volcano. It was a response he was capable of all his life. For another significant example of his "religious" attitude toward nature, see Allison Ensor, "A Clergyman Recalls Hearing Mark Twain," *Mark Twain Journal* 15 (Winter 1970): 6.

12 Twain's virtually lifelong preoccupation with Adam is abundantly evident in his works. See Allison Ensor, *Mark Twain and the Bible* (Lexington: University of Kentucky Press, 1969), a fine account of Twain's references and attitudes to biblical characters. Also see my article, "The Humor of the Absurd: Mark Twain's Adamic Diaries," *Criticism* 14 (Winter 1972): 49–64. Though we never hear or "see" God in these diaries, it is clear that His prohibition is one Adam and Eve cannot comprehend. The Fall is inevitable and patently unjust. Either God is cruelly "toying" with them or feels some inexplicable anger against them. In "Adam's Diary," however, Adam "causes" the Fall because of his first "moldy" chestnut, or joke about Niagara Falls running upward. The comic is both the cause of and consolation for the Fall. Of course, Adam/Mark Twain accepts the guilt for this.

13 See Dixon Wecter, ed., Introduction to Samuel L. Clemens, *Report From Paradise* (New York: Harper Bros., 1952), pp. ix–xxv, for an excellent discussion of the text and its meaning. Also see William M. Gibson, *The Art of Mark Twain* (New York: Oxford University Press, 1976), chap. 1, for a good study of this important story.

14 Ganzel, *Mark Twain Abroad*, p. 250. Twain's "faith" or lack of it was, of course, tested in his courting of Livy. See James D. Wilson, "Religious and Esthetic Vision in Mark Twain's Early Career," *Canadian Review of American Studies* 17 (Summer 1986): 155–72. I agree with Wilson that Twain did make an earnest attempt to "convert," but in the end it was his wife who became "cold" to God. See *The Love Letters of Mark Twain*, ed. Dixon Wecter (New York: Harper Bros., 1949), p. 168.

15 Mark Twain, *Notebooks and Journals*, vol. 3, ed. Robert Pack Browning et al. (Berkeley: University of California Press, 1979), p. 389. Hereafter cited parenthetically in the text as NB&J.

16 For his deistic concept of God, see *Mark Twain's Notebooks*, pp. 301–2, 362–3. For his letter, see *Writings of Mark Twain*, ed. A. B. Paine (New York: Harper

Bros., 1929), 37 vols., vol. 31, p. 411. Hereafter cited parenthetically as WMT.

17 Ralph Waldo Emerson, *Letters and Social Aims* (Cambridge, Mass.: Riverside Press, 1904), vol. 8, pp. 124, 164, my emphasis.

18 Ibid., pp. 157–74, passim.

19 I explore in some detail Twain's comic and theological strategies of reform in my article "Wandering Between Two Gods: Theological Realism in Mark Twain's *A Connecticut Yankee*," *Studies in the Literary Imagination* 16 (Fall 1983): 57–82. See also David Ketterer, "Epoch-Eclipse and Apocalypse: Special 'Effects' in *A Connecticut Yankee*," *PMLA* 88 (1973): 1104–14.

20 In *Mysterious Stranger Manuscripts*, ed. William M. Gibson (Berkeley, University of California Press, 1969), pp. 166–7. Hereafter cited parenthetically in the text as MSM.

21 Indispensable is Howard G. Baetzhold's *Mark Twain and John Bull: The British Connection* (Bloomington: Indiana University Press, 1970), pp. 200, 230, for all details on Twain's meeting with Kingsley as well as the important influence of Carlyle's "clothes philosophy" on Twain's thought. See *Letters and Memoirs of Charles Kingsley*, 2 vols., ed. Fanny Kingsley (New York: J. F. Taylor, 1898), vol. 2, pp. 73–4.

22 The definitive article thus far on this subject is Thomas D. Schwartz, "Mark Twain and Robert G. Ingersoll: The Freethought Connection," *American Literature* 48 (1976): 183–93. Also see Alexander E. Jones, "Mark Twain and Free Masonry," *American Literature* 26 (1954): 363–73. The tension between free thought and religious devotion is embodied in "Those Extraordinary Twins" (1894). Luigi, the freethinker, and Angelo, the pious believer, take turns controlling their grotesque body, made, as one character – without irony – says, "in the image of God."

23 Mark Twain, "My First Lie, and How I Got Out of It" (WMT 23: 169).

24 Henry N. Smith and William M. Gibson, eds., *Mark Twain–Howells Letters*, 2 vols. (Berkeley: University of California Press, 1969), vol. 2, p. 698. Hereafter cited parenthetically in the text as MTHL.

25 See my "Mark Twain's Masks of Satan: The Final Phase," *American Literature* 45 (May 1973): Sec. 4: 217–27, for a discussion of this problem, which ultimately derives from Twain's absorption of the Adamic myth and mankind's "dirt" origins. Indeed, Twain called a part of himself a "mud-image" (as opposed to his creative "self") in a letter to Howells after Susy's death. See *Mark Twain–Howells Letters*, ed. Smith and Gibson, vol. 2, pp. 664–65. But also consult John S. Tuckey, "Mark Twain's Later Dialogue: The 'Me' and the Machine," *American Literature* 40 (January 1970): 532–42.

26 William M. Gibson, "Mark Twain and Howells: Anti-Imperialists," *New England Quarterly* 20 (1947): 435–70. Also see Hunt Hawkins, "The Congo-Reform Movement: A Fury of Generous Indignation," *New England Quarterly* 51 (1978): 147–74. We learn that in 1906 Twain tried to dissuade one reformer from trying to tell the "truth" about Belgian atrocities because men are "humbugs and hypocrites who think they love the truth but actually fear it" (p. 171). He could have been talking about many of his own readers. See Roger B. Salomon, *Twain and the Image of History* (New Haven, Conn.: Yale University

Press, 1961), for the best account of Twain's loss of faith in progress. Twain's "The War Prayer" (1905) epitomizes his emotional stance toward Christianity at this time. False consciousness is savaged as we watch the minister indict the way God is used to justify the destruction of other human beings in war.

27 William James, *Essays on Faith and Morals*, selected by Ralph Barton Perry (New York: World Publishing, 1962), 8–10, 162–3. See Alan Gribben, *Mark Twain's Library: A Reconstruction* (Boston: G. K. Hall, 1980), vol. 1, p. 351, for Twain's reading and knowledge of William James.

28 Robert Regan, "The Reprobate Elect in *The Innocents Abroad*," in *On Mark Twain: The Best from American Literature*, ed. Louis J. Budd and Edwin H. Cady (Durham, N.C.: Duke University Press, 1987), pp. 223–40, expertly shows how this work is structured by the theme of "saints" and "sinners" and the kind of "theological" humor that springs from this pattern.

29 B. F. Skinner, whose behavioral determinism is similar if not identical to Twain's, claims that his own Calvinistic background very likely influenced his later psychological deterministic theories. This proves nothing about Mark Twain, but is at least suggestive. See B. F. Skinner, "Origins of a Behaviorist," *Psychology Today* (September 1983): 22–35, and Sherwood Cummings, *Mark Twain and Science: The Adventure of a Mind* (Baton Rouge: Louisiana State University Press, 1988).

30 Dixon Wecter, *Sam Clemens of Hannibal* (Boston: Houghton Mifflin, 1952), p. 88. Howard Mumford Jones also sketches in some of Twain's intellectual contradictions, but places less emphasis on Presbyterianism as a source of determinism and ultimate pessimism than on his "naive" eighteenth-century rationalism in conflict with a "romantic" subjectivism. In Twain "the spirits of Voltaire and Rousseau fought for control." See Jones, "The Pessimism of Mark Twain," *Belief and Disbelief in American Literature* (Chicago: University of Chicago Press, 1969), pp. 94–115.

31 Wecter, *Sam Clemens of Hannibal*, p. 88.

32 Henry Nash Smith, in *How True Are Dreams? The Theme of Fantasy in Mark Twain's Later Work* (Elmira, N.Y.: Quarry Farm Papers, Publication of Elmira College Center for Mark Twain Studies, 1989), p. 8. Also see Jeffrey R. Holland, "Soul Butter and Hog Wash," in *"Soul Butter and Hog Wash," and Other Essays on the American West*, ed. Thomas G. Alexander (Provo, Utah: Brigham Young University Press, 1978), p. 14.

33 A good general overview of Kierkegaard's ideas is in Patrick Gardiner, *Kierkegaard* (New York: Oxford University Press, 1988). See Gardiner's brief but clear analysis of "despair" and "anxiety," pp. 45–7, 106–9, passim. I have also consulted Kierkegaard's *Concluding Unscientific Postscript*, trans. David F. Swenson (Princeton, N.J.: Princeton University Press, 1941). In two of my studies, "Mark Twain in the Pulpit: The Theological Comedy of *Huckleberry Finn*," in *One Hundred Years of Huckleberry Finn: The Boy, His Book, and American Culture*, ed. Robert Sattelmeyer and J. Donald Crowley (Columbia: University of Missouri Press, 1985), pp. 371–85, and "Mark Twain and the Myth of the Daring Jest," in *The Mythologizing of Mark Twain*, ed. Sara Saussure Davis and Philip D. Beidler (Tuscaloosa: University of Alabama Press, 1984), pp. 136–57, I have used Kierkegaard's rich philosophical discussion of

the idea of the humorist, the nature of humor itself and its relationship to God, and the "existential spheres" of life. Ultimately, the humorist's "God-idea" stands against the system, like Hegel's or any systematized inauthentic life and evokes the contradictions in them. This is Twain's strategy, too. I am indebted to Marie Collins Swabey's *Comic Laughter: A Philosophical Essay* (New Haven, Conn.: Yale University Press, 1961), which introduced me to the vast relevance of Kierkegaard to the question of theological humor.

34 *Mark Twain in Eruption,* ed. Bernard DeVoto (New York: Harper & Row, 1968), epigraph. Hereafter cited parenthetically in the text as MTE.

35 Andrews, *Nook Farm,* p. 253.

36 James M. Cox, "The Height of Humor," in *The Comic Imagination in America,* ed. Louis D. Rubin, Jr. (New Brunswick, N.J.: Rutgers University Press, 1973), pp. 139–48.

37 Samuel Clemens, *Adventures of Huckleberry Finn,* ed. Walter Blair and Victor Fischer (Berkeley: University of California Press, 1980), pp. 156–7, 271. Hereafter cited parenthetically in the text as HF. For a good study of Huck's famous decision, see Norris W. Yates, "The 'Counter-Conversion' of *Huckleberry Finn,*" *American Literature* 32 (1960): 1–10, and Gregg Canfield, " 'I Wouldn't Be as Ignorant as You for Wages': Huck Talks Back to His Conscience," *Studies in American Fiction* 20 (Autumn 1992): 169–75.

38 I discuss the theological implications of this letter (in the Berg Collection, New York Public Library) in my study, "The Theology of Mark Twain: Banished Adam and the Bible," *Mississippi Quarterly* 29 (Spring 1976): 167–89, as well as Twain's marginalia in W. E. H. Lecky's *History of European Morals* (1869), concerning the different interpretations of the Fall in history.

39 See *Mark Twain's Rubaiyat,* introduction by Alan Gribben, textual notes by Kevin B. Mac Donnell (Austin, Tex.: Jenkins Publishing; Karpeles Manuscript Library, 1983), p. 10.

40 Consult Robert Lee Cody, "Providence in the Novels of Mark Twain" (Ph.D. diss., University of Florida, 1978); Edgar M. Branch, "The Two Providences: Thematic Form in *Huckleberry Finn,*" *College English* 11 (1950): 188–95. My own study, "Mark Twain in the Pulpit," pp. 371–85, explores the concept of providence in *Huckleberry Finn.* I have found three studies of the providential tradition most illuminating, although the subject is English fiction: J. Paul Hunter, *The Reluctant Pilgrim* (Baltimore: Johns Hopkins University Press, 1966); Leopold Damrosch, Jr., *God's Plot and Man's Stories: Studies in the Fictional Imagination from Milton to Fielding* (Chicago: University of Chicago Press, 1985); Thomas Vargish, *The Providential Aesthetic in Victorian Fiction* (Charlottesville: University of Virginia Press, 1985). Vargish writes that "in America, Hawthorne, Melville and Twain show ambivalence or hostility [to providence], often veiled because the alliance between the representation of poetic justice and the action of Providence was established in the minds of American as of English readers" (p. 28 n. 31).

41 *Mark Twain's Fables of Man,* ed. John S. Tuckey (Berkeley: University of California Press, 1972).

42 *Following the Equator* is filled with various comments and images concerning Christianity, Hinduism, and religion in general, especially Mark Twain's dream

of God as a cosmic man. Here is another comic image of false consciousness: "The Hindu has a childish and unreasoning aversion to be turned into an ass. It is hard to tell why. One could properly expect an ass to have an aversion to being turned into a Hindu" (WMT 21: 179). It is important that at this time (1897) Twain faced the fact that religions die hard: "Apparently one of the most uncertain things in the world is the funeral of a religion" (WMT 21: 161). For a good study of the idea of "The Absurd" in Twain's late works, see Richard Boyd Hauck, A Cheerful Nihilism (Bloomington: Indiana University Press, 1971).

43 For a theological analysis of this novel, see my article, "Blackness and the Adamic Myth in Mark Twain's Pudd'nhead Wilson," Texas Studies in Literature and Language 15 (1973–4): 167–76. A more recent collection of essays on the novel is Susan Gillman and Forrest G. Robinson, eds., Mark Twain's "Pudd'nhead Wilson": Race, Conflict, and Culture (Durham, N.C.: Duke University Press, 1990).

44 See William Searle, The Saint and the Skeptics: Joan of Arc in the Works of Mark Twain, Anatole France, and Bernard Shaw (Detroit: Wayne State University Press, 1976), and James D. Wilson, "In Quest of Redemptive Vision: Mark Twain's Joan of Arc," Texas Studies in Literature and Language 20 (Summer 1978): 181–98.

45 In Mark Twain: Selected Writings of an American Skeptic, ed. Victor Doyno (Buffalo: Prometheus Books, 1983), pp. 446–48. This was written in 1906. Years before, in 1884, Twain wrote Howells of a story he wanted to write that demonstrated "the religious folly you are born in you will die in, no matter what apparently reasonabler religious folly may seem to have taken its place" (Mark Twain–Howells Letters, ed. Smith and Gibson, vol. 2, p. 461). Twenty-two years later, Twain's point seemed to have been proved.

46 Mark Twain, Simon Wheeler, Detective, ed. Franklin R. Rogers (New York: New York Public Library, 1963), pp. 140–2. This detective story was begun in 1877 and developed as both a play and a story over the years, but was never published. Still, the dream scene reflects a deep conviction of Twain's. Captain Stormfield's Visit to Heaven embodies the same idea of the "bar-keepers" of this world entering heaven. This is Twain's image of theological egalitarianism, and is a vital aspect of his countertheology, which ridicules the doctrine of election and the selfishly cruel elect (as in "Letter from a Recording Angel," 1887). Still, it remains a dream. See my article, "Mark Twain and the Myth of the Daring Jest," for an analysis of Twain's "fantasy," "The Late Reverend Sam Jones's Reception into Heaven," which dramatizes the final irony that his calling earns him a place in heaven, but a place from which humorists are banned. With Sam Jones, a revivalist preacher, Twain steals his way into heaven, driving out the likes of the Borgias. On heaven or on earth, Twain felt that he belonged in the company of preachers.

47 In Samuel Clemens, Correspondence with Henry Huttleston Rogers, 1893–1909, ed. Lewis Leary (Berkeley: University of California Press, 1969), p. 354.

48 Kierkegaard, Concluding Unscientific Postscript, p. 84.

FURTHER READING

GENERAL WORKS

Cox, James. *Mark Twain: The Fate of Humor.* Princeton, N.J.: Princeton University Press, 1966.

DeVoto, Bernard. *Mark Twain's America.* Boston: Little, Brown, 1932.

Gibson, William M. *The Art of Mark Twain.* New York: Oxford University Press, 1976.

Gillman, Susan. *Dark Twins: Imposture and Identity in Mark Twain's America.* Chicago: University of Chicago Press, 1989.

Robinson, Forrest G. *In Bad Faith: The Dynamics of Deception in Mark Twain's America.* Cambridge, Mass.: Harvard University Press, 1986.

Sewell, David R. *Mark Twain's Languages: Discourse, Dialogue, and Linguistic Variety.* Berkeley: University of California Press, 1987.

Smith, Henry Nash. *Mark Twain: The Development of a Writer.* Cambridge, Mass.: Harvard University Press, 1962.

CRITICAL STUDIES

Blair, Walter. *Mark Twain and Huck Finn.* Berkeley: University of California Press, 1960.

Bridgman, Richard. *Traveling in Mark Twain.* Berkeley: University of California Press, 1987.

Fishkin, Shelley Fisher. *Was Huck Black? Mark Twain and African-American Voices.* New York: Oxford University Press, 1993.

Gillman, Susan, and Robinson, Forrest G., eds. *Mark Twain's "Pudd'nhead Wilson": Race, Conflict, and Culture.* Durham, N.C.: Duke University Press, 1990.

Harris, Susan K. *Mark Twain's Escape from Time: A Study of Patterns and Images.* Columbia: University of Missouri Press, 1982.

Leonard, James S., Tenney, Thomas A., and Davis, Thadious M., eds. *Satire or Evasion? Black Perspectives on Huckleberry Finn.* Durham, N.C.: Duke University Press, 1992.

Macnaughton, William R. *Mark Twain's Last Years as a Writer.* Columbia: University of Missouri Press, 1979.

Salomon, Roger B. *Twain and the Image of History.* New Haven, Conn.: Yale University Press, 1961.

Sattelmeyer, Robert, and Crowley, J. Donald, eds. *One Hundred Years of Huckleberry Finn: The Boy, His Book, and American Culture.* Columbia: University of Missouri Press, 1985.

Schmitz, Neil. *Of Huck and Alice: Humorous Writing in American Literature.* Minneapolis: University of Minnesota Press, 1983.

BIOGRAPHICAL

Andrews, Kenneth R. *Nook Farm: Mark Twain's Hartford Circle.* Cambridge, Mass.: Harvard University Press, 1950.

Budd, Louis J. *Our Mark Twain: The Making of His Public Personality.* Philadelphia: University of Pennsylvania Press, 1983.

Emerson, Everett. *The Authentic Mark Twain: A Literary Biography of Samuel L. Clemens.* Philadelphia: University of Pennsylvania Press, 1976.

Kaplan, Justin. *Mr. Clemens and Mark Twain.* New York: Simon & Schuster, 1966.

Hill, Hamlin. *Mark Twain: God's Fool.* New York: Harper & Row, 1973.

Neider, Charles, ed. *The Autobiography of Mark Twain.* New York: Harper Bros., 1959.

Webster, Samuel Charles, ed. *Mark Twain, Business Man.* Boston: Little, Brown, 1946.

Wecter, Dixon. *Sam Clemens of Hannibal.* Boston: Houghton Mifflin, 1952.

Cambridge Companions to Literature

Printed in the United Kingdom
by Lightning Source UK Ltd.
9676900002B/292-300